D1345126

C015777192

AD 69

procul hinc, procul este, severi

Ovid *Amores* 2.1.3

AD 69

Emperors, Armies
& Anarchy

Nic Fields

Pen & Sword
MILITARY

First published in Great Britain in 2014 by
Pen & Sword Military
an imprint of
Pen & Sword Books Ltd
47 Church Street
Barnsley
South Yorkshire
S70 2AS

ISBN 978 1 78159 188 8

Typeset in Ehrhardt by
Mac Style, Bridlington, East Yorkshire
Printed and bound in the UK by CPI Group (UK) Ltd, Croydon,
CRO 4YY

Pen & Sword Books Ltd incorporates the imprints of Pen & Sword
Archaeology, Atlas, Aviation, Battleground, Discovery, Family History,
History, Maritime, Military, Naval, Politics, Railways, Select, Transport,
True Crime, and Fiction, Frontline Books, Leo Cooper, Praetorian Press,
Seaforth Publishing and Wharncliffe.

For a complete list of Pen & Sword titles please contact
PEN & SWORD BOOKS LIMITED
47 Church Street, Barnsley, South Yorkshire, S70 2AS, England
E-mail: enquiries@pen-and-sword.co.uk
Website: www.pen-and-sword.co.uk

Contents

List of Plates

1. Silver *sestertius*, the obverse of which bears a laureate bust of a rather heavy, not to say bloated, Nero (Bologna, Museo Civico Archeologico di Bologna). Actor-Emperor, the First Beast, the Antichrist, psychotic post-adolescent, take your pick, the wicked (and doomed) Nero has been called them all. In AD 54 the fifth and last emperor of Augustus' dynasty succeeded his stepfather (and cousin), Claudius, supplanting Claudius' legitimate son Britannicus, who was conveniently done away with the following year. He had killed too many senators to please the ancient historians, who mostly had senatorial sympathies, and he had killed too many Christians, and led too outrageous a private life, to win the favour of Christian posterity. In the popular psyche, he gave Rome fiddlers, fear and fire. Nero's principate was one of the most unfortunate Rome had known. (© *Esther Carré*)
2. **Marble portrait bust of Galba (Stockholm, Antiques Museum, Royal Palace).** For a brief time the commander-in-chief of the army, he ended up its pathetic victim, the sword of a common soldier having inflicted an inglorious and pointless end upon him. His life was finally cut off in classical tragic style by the conventional divine vengeance for the conventional Greek sin of arrogance. He believed he was the right man to restore the law and order that had fallen by the wayside under Nero. As Tacitus rightly said, Galba would have made a good emperor if only he had not been one. (© *Wolfgang Sauber*)
3. **Marble portrait bust of Otho (Houston, Museum of Natural Science).** He was by turn husband, lover, debauchee, governor, general, and emperor; he mingled with courtiers, actors, whores, soldiers and royalty, with natives of Italy and Iberia, and was at home with them all. During his brief principate he did not display those faults for which he had been despised earlier in life but acted in accordance with the dignity of the office. Otho, much like Othello, killed himself with a dagger. Loyal soldiers carried his body off and buried it, some of them, overcome by grief for their beloved emperor, stabbed themselves to death on his grave. His suicide was considered an honourable and noble answer to continuing civil war, and was celebrated as such. Otho's peace was to be short lived, however. (© *Ed Uthman*)
4. **Portrait bust of Vitellius – plaster-cast copy (Bologna, Museo Civico Archeologico di Bologna, inv. 99) of the 'Vitellio Grimani' (Venezia, Museo Archeologico, inv. 20).** Here we see the fat neck, the huge jowls of the man – fat, florid, at ease – who was known as the greatest gourmand of his day, apparently

once attending a banquet in his honour in which 2,000 exotic fish and 7,000 game birds were happily consumed. Even in plaster, the hog-like Vitellius looks hungry. This portrait echoes Suetonius' statement, reputedly made by Galba, when the emperor appointed Vitellius legate governor of Germania Inferior: 'A glutton was the sort of rival whom he feared least' (*Vitellius* 7.1). What little did he know. (© *Esther Carré*)

5. **Marble portrait bust of Vespasianus (Thessalonika, Museum of Archaeology, inv. 1055).** Vespasianus was a plain, blunt man who had kept a local Italian accent. Like the elderly Tiberius before him, he was a proven soldier with experience of the provinces both east and west. Yet he had none of Tiberius' touchiness or patrician pride, and even his portrait busts, like this one, show a plain 'Italian' style of realism, not the classicizing ideal look of Augustus or Nero. In truth, he has the type of face you would not expect to see again this century. Who would have believed that he was to have so high a destiny? Yet is not it said, 'men never look like what they are'. (© *Nic Fields*)

6. **Stylized terracotta bust of Marcus Antonius Primus (Toulouse, musée des Augustines, inv. 49195), made by the artist Marc Arcis between 1674 and 1677.** This is an appropriate homage to a Gaul from Tolosa, ancient Toulouse, and his *nomen* Antonius suggests the enfranchisement, during Marcus Antonius' Gallic period in 43 BC, of a Tolosan family supporting his warring faction against Octavianus. Whatever else might be said about him (and there was a great deal to be said) his personal fortitude was never seriously at issue. Indeed, he was brave even to excess, and in the name of Vespasianus, Antonius Primus desired the short, sharp, conclusive campaign against the Vitellians, not the long, drawn-out agony of attrition for attrition's sake. He was a man bristling with pugnacity, the most martial of the Flavian generals. (© *Esther Carré*)

7. **One of the low-cut reliefs (Mainz, Mittelrheinisches Landesmuseum) decorating the column bases from the *principia* of Mainz-*Mogontiacum*. This one shows two legionaries in action, one behind the other.** The front legionary is hunkering down behind his cylindrical *scutum*, his *gladius* held horizontally and close. Such a posture does not minimize the risk of being wounded by a projectile penetrating his shield. That would be achieved by bearing his shield away from himself. He is, however, ready to perform that most effective of Roman battle drills, the punch-jab. The legionary behind has his *pilum* resting on his right shoulder, and he seems to be holding his *scutum* high as if he is protecting his comrade in front. Curiously, though the two of them wear the Imperial Gallic (aka Weissenau) type helmet, a pattern common in our period of study, they lack body armour. (© *Nic Fields*)

8. **Another of the low-cut reliefs (Mainz, Mittelrheinisches Landesmuseum) decorating the column bases from the *principia* of Mainz-*Mogontiacum*. This one shows a legionary in full marching order and the junior officer known as an *optio* (others suggest he is a *signifer*).** To help run his century, a

centurio was assisted by a second-in-command, an *optio*, so named because under the Republic *centuriones* 'adopted' (viz. *adoptandum*, Varro *de lingua Latina* 5.91, Festus 201.23) their own *optiones*. Here we clearly see the 'badge of office' of an *optio*, a stout staff (*hastile*), which was extremely useful in forcing any wavering men back into line. In battle, the *optio* traditionally took up station at the rear of his century. (© *Nic Fields*)

9. **Yet another of the low-cut reliefs (Mainz, Mittelrheinisches Landesmuseum) decorating the column bases from the *principia* of Mainz-*Mogontiacum*. This one shows an auxiliary infantryman with a flat oval shield, *clipeus*, and a Coolus type helmet.** With its wider cheek pieces and neck guard and the addition of a brow-guard, the Coolus helmet started to replace the old Montefortino pattern that had been commonly worn by legionaries of Caesar's legions. This helmet pattern, inspired as before by Celtic influence, is so named for the find made near the village of Coole in the Marne basin. As well as a *lancea* in his right hand, he carries two spares in his left behind his shield. This fighting man was in no way inferior to a legionary, despite his non-citizen status, and certainly not lightly equipped either. Note the detail of his open-style footwear, *caligae*. Juvenal (*Satire* 3.248, 16.24–5 Green) warns civilians about encountering a soldier on the street with his hobnailed *caligae*, and advises against provoking them as they might well kick their shins in retaliation. (© *Nic Fields*)

10. **Full-size manikin of an auxiliary trooper (Cirencester, Corinium Museum).** A characteristic feature of Roman cavalry helmets is the extension of the cheek-pieces to cover the ears, commonly shaped as simulated ears. The model is also wearing a Gallic-type mail shirt with shoulder-cape fastened with S-shaped breast hooks. He carries the typical flat oval shield, *clipeus*, of the *auxilia*. Made of plywood, covered in rawhide and edged in bronze, it was only slightly lighter than a cylindrical *scutum*, its greater height compensating for the latter's greater width. His *spatha* – the longer, slimmer sword type based on the La Tène sword and commonly used by Roman cavalrymen – is carried in the unorthodox position on the right swinging from a wide baldric. (© *Nic Fields*)

11. **Soldiers of the Praetorian Guard, bas-relief (Paris, musée du Louvre) from the Arch of Claudius erected in AD 51 in honour of the successful invasion of Britannia in AD 43.** The heads of the front row of figures are restored. Above is a large *aquila*-standard. The praetorians themselves are depicted in richly decorated equipment, perhaps on guard or on parade, though the Attic style helmets with thick crests housed in long crest-boxes are almost certainly an artistic convention. The central figure, with the gorgon-head on his breastplate, is probably a *tribunus*, an equestrian officer commanding one of the *cohortes praetoriae*. However, in parade uniforms or not, the events of AD 69 suggest that these men were more than just 'carpet soldiers', those creatures of monarchs more useful at court ceremonies rather than in combat conditions. (© *Nic Fields*)

civil war battle of Second Cremona was the critical engagement that decided the outcome of the year of four emperors. Early on the morning of the 25 October AD 69 the Vitellian legions were famously and bloodily defeated at the fourth milestone east from Cremona, thus setting in train the end of not just ten months of Vitellius' principate but a year-and-a-half of civil war with all its attendant horrors. In this photograph we are standing at the position of *XIII Gemina* looking towards the Vitellian centre, which would have been in the location of what is now the Cascina Malongola seen in the middle distance. The Via Postumia is just to the left. (© *Esther Carré*)

16. **What is now the Casa de' Marozzi was then the probable site of Marcus Antonius Primus' battlefield headquarters at Second Cremona.** We are looking at the brick farm building from the nearby railway line, which links modern Cremona with Mantova (ancient Mantua) and Bologna (ancient Bononia). The Via Postumia runs just behind us and the initial Vitellian positions are way off to our left. The initial Flavian battleline, from centre to left, would have run from the Via Postumia to the line of poplars in the distance, *XIII Gemina, VIII Augusta, III Gallica* and praetorians. (© *Esther Carré*)

17. **The point of contact, Second Cremona, looking south-south-west from just above Cassinetto.** The large farm buildings in the left middle distance belong to the Casa de' Marozzi, beyond which is the Via Postumia. Today, the nature of the battleground is patchy; in places it is heavily cultivated, frequently dissected by ditches, partially covered with copses. The terrain is scattered with solidly built farm buildings and has few roads. The Flavian battleline from its right flank to its centre (*III Gallica* and praetorians, *VIII Augusta, XIII Gemina*) would have stood on the left. The Vitellian battleline from its left flank to its centre (*vexillationes XXII Primigenia, I Germanica* and *XVI Gallica, vexillationes II Augusta, VIIII Hispana, XX Valeria Victrix, XV Primigenia* and *legio V Alaudae*) would have stood on the right. The point of contact between the two sides would have been roughly along the strip of stubble. (© *Nic Fields*)

18. **The site of the Vitellian camp, just outside Cremona, looking towards the modern sports stadium, with Via Brescia to the left and Via Mantova to the right.** The camp itself had been built at no great distance from the walls and suburbs of Cremona on the northeast, between the converging road from Brixia and the Via Postumia, and near their junction. When the main (southern) gate of the camp was finally forced, the surviving Vitellians threw themselves down from the ramparts and took shelter in nearby Cremona. Despite a show of surrender, the inhabitants of this affluent town fell victim to indiscriminate rape and slaughter. (© *Nic Fields*)

19. **Embossed bronze facing of a *scorpio* shield (Cremona, Museo Civico San Lorenzo) once belonging to *legio IIII Macedonica*, unearthed in 1887 some fifty metres outside the Porta Venezia, Cremona.** The find-spot lies between the walls of the Roman town and the site of the Vitellian camp, and nicely explains and collaborates eighteen hundred years later the brief

narrative of Tacitus, who tells us that in the wild stampede for safety the 'entire space between the [Vitellian] camp and the walls of Cremona were filled with slain' (*Historiae* 3.29.2). Thus, in the panic to escape, an artillery piece or two was abandoned. Anyway, originally this artefact was believed to have been the bronze facing of a wooden strongbox belonging to the said legion, the aperture through which the bolt was shot the keyhole. (© *Nic Fields*)

20. **The Roman soldier may have been adorned with various pieces of killing hardware, but each also carried one of these, a mess tin, *patera* (Cremona, Museo Civico San Lorenzo).** These three were found in Via Armando Diaz, just within the old town walls of Cremona, and date to the mid-first century AD. It is possible these particular *paterae* were lost during the sack of the town by the Flavians in October AD 69. A *patera* consists of a ladle-shaped dish with a flat bottom, sloping sides, and a long, flat handle with a hole punched in the end. A *patera*, including the handle, was spun and formed from a single sheet of bronze. Much like a modern mess tin, the Roman version not only gave the soldier something that served both as a cooking pot and eating/drinking container, but like its modern counterpart it had many other uses too. (© *Esther Carré*)

21. **Grave stele of Quintus Sertorius Festus (Verona, Museo Lapidario Maffeiano, inv. 28161), dated** *c.* AD 42–69. It was discovered in 1789 at Cisolina, province of Verona. The inscription (*CIL* v 3374 = *ILS* 2339) informs us that he was a *signifer* and then the *aquilifer* in *legio XI Claudia pia fidelis*, finally earning his honourable discharge from the same legion as a *curator* of veterans. He wears a corselet of *squamae* over an arming doublet with a single-layer kilt and upper arm defences of *pteruges*, which may have been of either leather or stiffened linen. The scales of the corselet shown in the stele do seem rather large, and would have been smaller in fact, the sculptural representation having been so cut for ease of execution. This was the Danube legion that missed the day at Second Cremona. (© *Esther Carré*)

22. **Grave stele of Lucius Sertorius Firmus (Verona, Museo Lapidario Maffeiano, inv. 28160), dated** *c.* AD 42–69. As for the stele of Sertorius Festus, they were in fact brothers; this was also discovered in 1789 at Cisolina, province of Verona. The inscription (*CIL* v 3747) informs us that he was a *centurio* in *legio XI Claudia pia fidelis*. He is depicted in ceremonial dress. He wears *lorica plumata*, a mail shirt overlaid with tiny scales 'ribbed' for extra strength, complete with scallops and *pteruges*. Over this composite armour is a leather harness bearing his military decorations, six (possibly seven) *phalerae* and two *torques*. On his head rests a *corona* (*civica* or *aurea*), an award for a single act of bravery and generally reserved for the rank of centurion and above. The decorations would have been worn in battle, but not so the crown. He wears a pair of finely embossed greaves, which were peculiar to the centurionate, as was the twisted-vine stick (*vitis*), that over ready badge of rank, as legionaries knew all too well. (© *Esther Carré*)

23. From the fort at Croy Hill on the Antonine Wall, we have two fragments of a sculptured relief carved on a slab of red sandstone (Edinburgh, National Museums of Scotland). Associated with these two fragments is an inscription (*RIB* 2158), which is even more fragmentary than the relief but bears the line I • O • M • DOLICENO…. (in Latin epigraphy Iuppiter Optimus Maximus was abbreviated to IOM). Now heavily restored, the relief depicts Iuppiter Optimus Maximus Dolichenus, who stands on the shoulders of a bull, dressed in a Phrygian cap, a Roman-style muscle cuirass and senior officer's half boots, and armed with a sword supported by a baldric passing over his right shoulder. In his hands he holds his weapons *par excellence*, a three-pronged thunderbolt and a double-headed axe, *bipennis*. Opposite him, on the right, his consort Iuno Dolichena is depicted similarly mounted upon a corresponding animal. This was a mystery stellar cult directly associated with the creation of weapons with iron, which naturally attracted devotees from the Roman military. (© *Nic Fields*)

24. Silver *denarius* (*RIC* I Vitellius: 53) issued by the imperial mint at Lugdunum (Lyon). The obverse bears a laureate bust of Vitellius with an orb at the point, with the legend A(vlvs) VITELLIVS IMP(erator) GERMAN(icvs). The reverse depicts clasped hands, with the slogan FIDES EXERCITVVM, 'Loyalty of the Army'. Whereas some coin inscriptions glorify legions or even the whole army, others such as this example disseminate the military themes of imperial propaganda, particularly when the emperor is not very confident of it. (© *Nic Fields*)

25. From Brussels and woven around 1530–50, this Flemish tapestry (Marsala, Museo delgi Arazzi, Tapestry 5) is decorated with a scene depicting the unchaining of Josephus on the orders of Vespasianus. When Iotapata fell Josephus fled to a nearby cave with a small band of followers. Here he was discovered after all but one of his men had dispatched each other in a suicide pact rather than surrender to the Romans. Dragged grovelling before Vespasianus, the future Flavian chronicler claimed to be a herald of things yet concealed by the future and so 'prophesied' Vespasianus' elevation to the throne of the world. (© *Nic Fields*)

Caricature credits

Chapter 1: Caricature of Nero by the author, based upon a rough sketch of the head of Nero and signed TVLLIVS ROMANVS MILES (Tullius Romanus, soldier), which was found in the basement of the Domus Tiberiana on the Palatine Hill, Rome.

Chapters 2–4 and 8: Caricatures of Galba, Otho, Vitellius and Vespasianus by Pedro Llorente, based upon various busts of the aforementioned emperors.

Maps and Graphics

1. Location of the legions, early September AD 69

(* = depleted by the dispatch of *vexillationes* to Italy)

Iberia
1. *I Adiutrix*   ?
2. *VI Victrix*   León-*Castra Legionis?*
3. *X Gemina*   Rosinos de Vidriales[1]

Britannia
4. *II Augusta   Gloucester-*Glevum*
5. *VIIII Hispana   Lincoln-*Lindum*
6. **XX Valeria Victrix*   Wroxeter-*Viriconium*
7. *XIIII Gemina Martia Victrix*   in transit but returning to the province

Germania Inferior
8. *XV Primigenia   Xanten-*Vetera*
9. *XVI Gallica   Neuss-*Novaesium*
10. *I Germania   Bonn-*Bonna*

Germania Superior
11. *IIII Macedonica   Mainz-*Mogontiacum*
12. *XXII Primigenia   Mainz-*Mogontiacum*

Pannonia
13. *VII Galbiana*   Petronell-*Carnuntum*
14. *XIII Gemina*   Ptuj-*Poetovio*

Dalmatia
15. *XI Claudia pia fidelis*   Knin-*Burnum*

Moesia
16. *VII Claudia pia fidelis*   Koštolac-*Viminacium*
17. *III Gallica*   Gigen-*Oescus*
18. *VIII Augusta*   Svištov-*Novae*

Italy

19. *I Italica*	from Lyon-*Lugdunum* (Gallia Lugdunensis)
20. *V Alaudae*	from Xanten-*Vetera* (Germania Inferior)
21. *XXI Rapax*	from Windisch-*Vindonissa* (Germania Superior)

plus *vexillationes* of *I Germania*, *II Augusta*, *IIII Macedonica*, *VIIII Hispana*, *XV Primigenia*, *XVI Gallica*, *XX Valeria Victrix*, *XXII Primigenia*

Rome

Praetorian Guard (sixteen *cohortes*)
urban cohorts (four *cohortes*)
e classicis legio (perhaps sailors recruited from *classis Misenensis*)

Syria

22. *IIII Scythica*	Kûrus-*Cyrrhus* (near Beroea/Aleppo)
23. *VI Ferrata*	Rafaniat-*Raphaneae* (near Emesa/Homs)
24. *XII Fulminata*	Rafaniat-*Raphaneae*

Iudaea

25. *V Macedonica*	Caesarea-*Caesarea Maritima*
26. *X Frentensis*	Caesarea-*Caesarea Maritima*
27. *XV Apollinaris*	Beit She'an-*Scythopolis*[2]

Egypt

28. *III Cyrenaica*	Sidi Gaber-*Nikopolis* (near Alexandria)
29. *XXII Deiotariana*	Sidi Gaber-*Nikopolis*

Africa

30. *I Macriana liberatrix*	Haïdra-*Ammaedara*
31. *III Augusta liberatrix*	Haïdra-*Ammaedara*

2. Organization of a Neronian legion

Legio

The chief tactical unit of the Roman army, the *legio* was divided into ten *cohortes*, all of which, during the Iulio-Claudian era, were officially 480 strong. Attached to a *legio* was a body of mounted legionaries, known as the *equites legionis* and 120 strong.

Cohortes I – X

The primary tactical unit of the Roman army, the *cohors* was subdivided into six *centuriae* of eighty men. Each *centuria* was led by a *centurio* who was assisted by an *optio*, *signifer*, and *tesserarius*.

Centuria

The *centuria* was the smallest unit of the Roman army. An administrative arrangement that served no tactical purpose, a *centuria* was divided into ten *contubernia*, 'tentfuls'. Each *contubernium* consisted of eight men, *contubernales*, who messed and slept together, sharing a leather tent on campaign and a pair of rooms in a barrack block. In the period from Augustus to Nero, a *legio* had sixty *centuriae*.

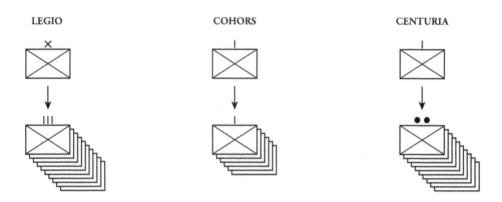

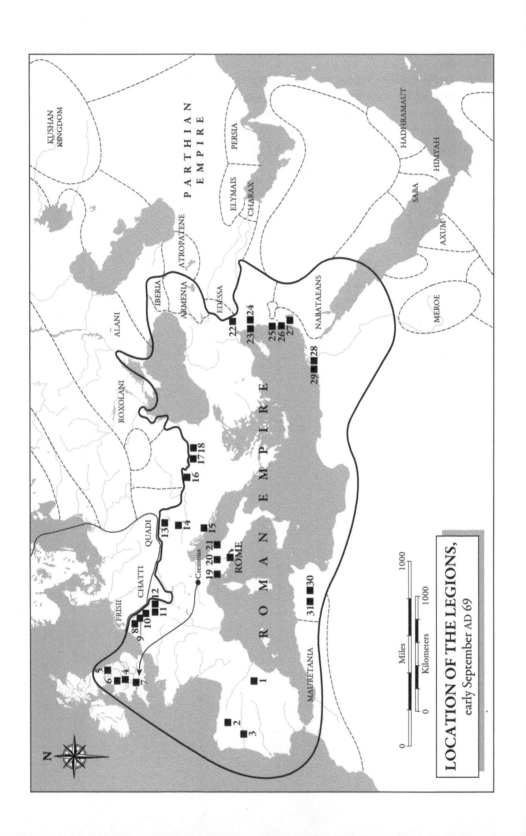

LOCATION OF THE LEGIONS,
early September AD 69

KUSHAN KINGDOM

PARTHIAN EMPIRE

PERSIA

ELYMAIS

CHARAX

HADHRAMAUT

HIMYAH

SABA

AXUM

MEROE

ALANI

IBERIA

ARMENIA

ATROPATENE

EDESSA

NABATAEANS

ROXOLANI

R O M A N   E M P I R E

QUADI

CHATTI

FRISII

Cremona

ROME

MAURETANIA

N

Miles

Kilometers

0   1000

0   1000

1

2

3

4

5

6

7

8

9

10

11

12

13

14

15

16

17

18

19

20

21

22

23

24

25

26

27

28

29

30

31

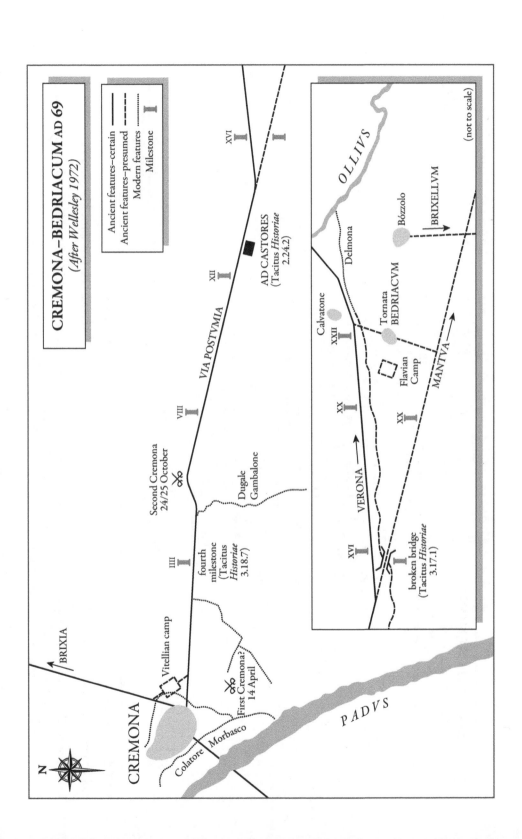

CREMONA–BEDRIACUM AD 69
(After Wellesley 1972)

Ancient features—certain
Ancient features—presumed
Modern features
Milestone

N

BRIXIA

CREMONA

Vitellian camp

Colatore Morbasco

First Cremona?
14 April

PADVS

fourth
milestone
(Tacitus
Historiae
3.18.7)

IIII

Dugale
Gambalone

Second Cremona
24/25 October

VIII

VIA POSTVMIA

XII

AD CASTORES
(Tacitus Historiae 2.24.2)

XVI

OLLIVS

Calvatone

XXII

Delmona

Bózzolo

BRIXELLVM

Tornata
BEDRIACVM

Flavian
Camp

MANTVA

XX

XX

VERONA

XVI

broken bridge
(Tacitus Historiae 3.17.1)

(not to scale)

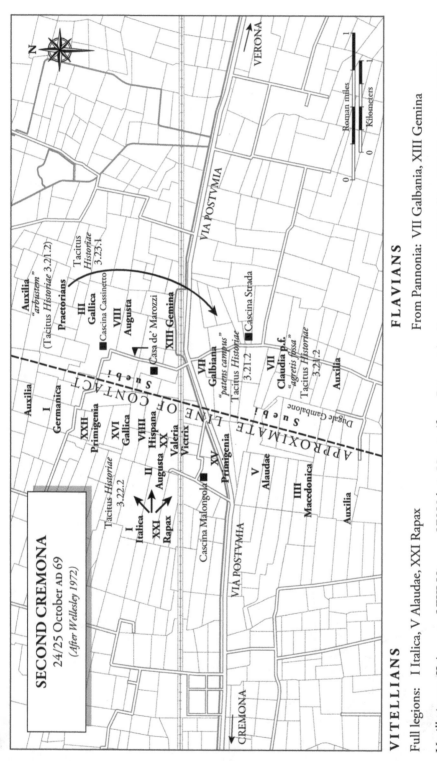

VITELLIANS

Full legions: I Italica, V Alaudae, XXI Rapax

Vexillationes: II Augusta, VIIII Hispana, XX Valeria Victrix (from Britannia), I Germanica, IIII Macedonica, XV Primigenia, XVI Gallica, XXII Primigenia (from Germania)

FLAVIANS

From Pannonia: VII Galbania, XIII Gemina

From Moesia: III Gallica, VII Claudia p.f., VIII Augusta

HQ of Antonius Primus

Prologue: Imperial Illusions

In the harrowing year of four emperors, Otho, whose principate is a byword for its unpeaceful brevity, struck gold coins that proudly displayed the sugary words PAX ORBIS TERRARVM – 'Peace of the World' – on their reverse side.[1] Nothing, of course, was said of the blacker side of the picture, since one rightly expects the message on coinage, like other political propaganda, to concentrate on heartening uplift. Still, what is remarkable about Otho's coinage is the total dissociation of its inscription from what was really going on at the time of its issue. The truth was otherwise. To the contrary, there was no peace, and we can only assume that the message of the new emperor in Rome, who was not long for this world, to the populations of his vast and heterogeneous empire was a pious hope, unless of course it was wishful thinking or just a downright lie.

So much for numismatics.

If there was one message that was being rapidly and painfully learnt, by those who did not surmise it already, it was the hard fact that in this long year of violent fluctuations of fortune and favour the provinces were not merely conquered territories but were places with Roman governors who could supplant Roman emperors chosen at home. Galba had come and gone. In three months the same fate would befall Otho, and in twelve months it would happen to Vitellius too. It is as if these three evanescing emperors had lived in an atmosphere of conventions created by themselves. In truth, they had found themselves drawn willy-nilly into the increasingly confused and violent politics of the game of thrones. The inevitable futility of this cycle of violence and intrigue was best summed up in Tacitus' epigrammatic remark on the murder of Galba: 'a crime which is always avenged by the murdered man's successor'.[2] If we only look backward, to this very singular year, it seems as though upon that sizeable stage upon which the historical drama of a nation is being played out, a group of provincial actors, availing themselves of a vacant corner, were playing out a vulgar quick-change vaudeville act. Thus it is, where there can be no agreement between two societal camps, the issue is settled in the old violent way, by civil war, a civil war fated to rob fathers of their sons and sons of their fathers.

So gentle readers: I invite you to read this book without illusions. This book will concern itself with a gruesome time in Roman history, a time with a great deal of unpleasant violence. What is more, most (if not all) of the Roman characters in it are unsympathetic and unlikeable – there are no imperishable heroes, nor are good and evil to be found in sharp, unreal contrast. Patriotic fools, pious followers, petty cheats, perfect knaves, every civil war, especially in its first stages, invariably raises on its crest all these human varieties. It is said a ruler is always in peril, no matter what, but it is a well-known fact that Chinese emperors were tea enthusiasts, some even having the leisure to contemplate the sacred art of tea and compose in beautiful calligraphy their celestial musings. Tea or no tea, this was not a luxury enjoyed by their Roman counterparts. You will see how this figures soon enough.

Historians generally like to encourage us to remember Rome as a glorious font of western civilization. I find it difficult to agree with this proposal. Rather than be dazzled by its so-called glory, Rome is better seen as 'that immense monument of human arrogance'.[3] So from here on, abandon any notions about the glory that was Rome or the noble legacy it ostensibly left us. If you hold misapprehensions on that score, let them be dispelled right here and now. Of course some would say the world was greatly different then. How tangled truth becomes. Rome was an empire, which it must be understood, was painted in colours far too warm and rich by the glowing imagination of dewy-eyed western romantics. Like Gibbon (but without his extraordinary talent) we identify this sort of sentiment as Eurocentric cultural imperialism.[4]

We Europeans have always had a tendency to exaggerate the achievements of some cultures and to denigrate others.[5] This is shameless, unbridled and prideful propaganda. We are as guilty, are we not? People only remember and see things that suit their preconceptions and fit their stereotypes. Their view is therefore incomplete and unbalanced. Behind this insidious European attitude lies the vested interests of those who seek to dominate and exploit other peoples (popular belief to the contrary notwithstanding, not everybody thinks like we think, or wants what we want). Obviously this attitude needs to be changed. No one culture is as good (or bad, for that matter) as any other. Perhaps our current version of Rome needs some serious quality control. We certainly need to make room for those dripping crosses of the Via Appia. This sort of talk may go against the grain with the academic purist perched on his or her podium in the Alice-in-Wonderland world of academe, but I write purely from a pragmatic, realistic angle. No apology is made if this flies in the face of conventional wisdom. With that said, I have lots to tell you.

So, let me set the stage. Nero is dead and four men, candidates of the provincial armies rather than of the Senate and people of Rome, seize the empire and then defend their theft with civil war. As in chess, the attacker must destroy his victim. The battle is always fought with the same single objective: the elimination of the enemy king. A dramatist or a novelist could not have written this one, which is one way of looking at it.

The story has been told before (Henderson, Greenhalgh, Wellesley, Morgan), the whole long catalogue of horrors, horror upon horror, and the reader has perhaps had enough of that kind of narrative. But it is essential to tell it as it relates to and includes the rôle of the provincial armies. My aim in this book is to inspire readers to reflect on the nature of our own societies. A parable for our own times: the cannibalism of high politics, the evil of war, the arrogance of power, the loneliness of leadership, and the comfort of comradeship. I give you the story of the year AD 69. Thus, a single year is the scene – sufficiently large and varied – of this narrative. It is all there: courage and cowardice (moral and physical), charity and selfishness, humility and hubris, sloth and industry, petty jealousies, greed, envy, self-seeking and aggrandisement, love and hate, the old sermon topics. Indeed, traits, good and bad, which lurk within us all to one degree or another. Lest we forget the most important thing of all – history would have no value if it taught us nothing, and Clio, its Muse, has never been a peacenik. Judge for yourselves, but I warn you, there be dragons.

Introduction: The Curse of Remus

'The young men went off to war with enthusiasm – because they had never been to war.'[1] How true. At the outbreak of war, eager would-be heroes have an unpleasant habit of daily flowing into recruiting centres, mere lads brimming with ebullience swallowed by the army. Intelligent lemmings? Why must every generation have its war? Satisfactory answers seldom consider the fact that war is folly, its only victors the arms dealer and the undertaker. As they say, some die in war, and some make profits out of it. As Thucydides rightly says, young men rush off to war with an enthusiasm born of the ignorance of the horror of war. For politicians (and many historians) war may be about the conquest of territory or the struggle to recover a sense of national pride, but for soldiers warfare is more brutal, more bloody, more personal, than this. 'What's the problem with war?' asks the old soldier. 'It's too violent,' he answers.

Of course, wars are not the creation of soldiers: wars are the result of calculated strategy or just simply failed statecraft. They say, 'this time it will be different', as people usually do when they set out to repeat the mistakes of their predecessors. Contrary to popular belief, people do not learn by experience. Instead, they sluggishly respond to a particular stimulus in a predictable way, and this repeatedly. Again, again, and again, generation after generation, the dismal message reappears like writing on the wall. Nothing changes. The basilisk may die, but another egg hatches.

The politicos inform us that the foe is bad, but we are too. It is a very sad state of affairs when you consider what a highly selective memory these war hawks possess, for a war does not begin in a vacuum. It is an end result of a series of happenings that occur or begin when two cultures find they have real or imagined differences and they react in accordance with preestablished behavioural patterns, unfailingly mobilizing a deep-seated animosity between 'us' and 'them'. Armed force is a blunt instrument in high politics, liable to do more damage than good unless aimed with extreme precision, just about an impossible task to accomplish. At best, it buys time and space for the politicians to repair the political mistakes that had led to violence in the first place. And how many of our most recent foreign wars have been started by lies and motivated, as ever, by those age-old motives, this cause or that greed? Still, as Europe is no longer bled regularly by war and we Britons pride ourselves on the fact that we live in an enlightened epoch, few people have any real experience of warfare at all, let alone any firsthand experience of people trying to kill them.

Certainly no one in government knows what modern warfare is really like – it is techno-industrial mass murder involving indiscriminate and impersonal weapon systems – and so warmonger politicians can commit the nation to the gore of war without knowledge of what they are committing the nation to. The politicians make it noble to do your duty for the expired idea of 'Queen and Country'. For on entering the world of politics, it seems they have shaken the dust of the real world off their feet as completely as if they have never belonged to it at all. And so, while their cannon fodder line up in strictest discipline, these magnificent servants of the people sit so high in their saddles they will never stoop low enough to see the grass their horses are eating. The *Te Deum* of the high and the mighty are often the *De Profundis* for the private citizens.[2]

Having prepared the political setting, the politicians are prepared to express their schemes in blood and iron if necessary. So words past to deeds as the political climate deteriorates, each side looking for an excuse to publicly rebuff the other, each side attempting to shift the responsibility onto the other. With that, diplomacy begins its ponderous, grimly inevitable march to war. However, regardless of these schemes, the primary burdens and hardships of war fall not on the shoulders of the politicians at home, but on the backs of the soldiers in the field. While soldiers can parrot these schemes when asked (invariably by the top brass or the mass media), they do not pretend to know what the overall 'big picture' is. The army exists to fight; its job is not to get mixed up in politics.

Thus, the main priority of the ordinary soldier, as with most soldiers in most wars, is not to worry about the politics that got them there in the first place, or to change the course of events, but to fight as best they can, support their comrades in a firefight, and to return home to their families safe and sound. Nonetheless, if it is not for soldiers to think about politics, they do know how to fight and how to die. This is more than can be said of the politicians who sent them to war, hidebound personages who have never been in a soldier's skin and who do not understand the life and conditions of existence of an army. Politics is a form of peaceful contention, and war is organized violence. All participants survive a political defeat (unless the victor is a tyrant, at war with his own people), whereas many participants do not survive a military defeat – or a victory either. War kills, our soldiers sacrificed to the betise of generals and the bullheadedness of politicians. That said, long gone are the days when the poor pariah, unshod and unclothed, became a soldier from starvation and cruel need. In truth, less than 2 per cent of the eligible male population have direct experience of military life; in a nation of millions the British Armed Forces are Lilliputian and in more recent years usually over the seas and far away in distant lands.[3] Most Britons, it seems, have little real contact with the military, while war is something in which other people are involved. The puzzled reader may ask what a population that has had no direct experience with war since the Jacobite Rebellion of 1745 has to do with ancient Rome. Let me explain.

The nature of societies that raise armies, the economic resources available to the state, and the nature and aims of the wars that the state wishes to, or fears it must, wage, are all mutually dependent. In terms of the three elements that make our kind of total war possible today – the ability to mobilize the entire male population for war, the resources that makes that degree of mobilization possible, and the technology – only the technology was obviously missing in ancient Rome. Thus, for the last two centuries of its existence, the Republic kept an average of 10 per cent of its entire citizen population under arms, or half or more of its military-age males.[4] This was an unprecedented accomplishment, made possible in a pre-industrial world only by mass plunder of the Mediterranean world – directly, by tribute, and through the exploitation of slave labour – and a very high degree of social cohesion.

When some fifty thousand of its soldiers lay dead on the field of Cannae,[5] its army having just been sucked to death by a stunningly simple stratagem, Rome never even thought of yielding to Hannibal. New armies sprang up as if from the very earth, furnished by the seemingly bottomless well of patriotic citizen soldiers. Polybios says that when the eight legions were mobilized for the fateful Cannae campaign, this had never before been done.[6] But if Polybios is right in stating there were eight Roman legions (plus an equal number of Latin-Italian legions) at Cannae, Rome had already mobilized a total of ten legions, since there were already two in Iberia, and by 211 BC, only five years after the holocaust of Cannae, there were twenty-five Roman legions in the field, which, taking the Latin-Italian legions and the men serving at sea into consideration, represented something like 250,000 men under arms.[7] As Kineas, the trusted diplomat of Pyrrhos, was said to have predicted, the many-headed monster could regenerate and struggle on.[8] This inexhaustible supply of manpower is an obvious reason as to why Rome quickly recovered after Cannae and went on to defeat Hannibal. The Roman military system was precisely that, a system. By an ironic but saving paradox, Rome did not need brilliant generals and rarely produced them; it just needed to replicate and reproduce its legions, which it did on an almost industrial basis.

By contrast, under the Principate a mere 300,000 long-service professionals, more or less equally divided between legions and auxiliary units, served along the raw edges of the empire.[9] No longer could the Mediterranean world be plundered to support a total mobilization war effort, and it was precisely the aim of the Principate to de-politicize – and hence demilitarize – the citizenry, what Juvenal scathingly called *panem et circenses*, 'bread and the games'.[10] Yet for all that, expansion continued into the Principate, as did the republican ideology of imperialism. 'He who desires peace, let him prepare for war', must be the most memorable phase in Vegetius.[11] A clear-cut distinction between war and peace – to which we are accustomed – did not exist for the Romans even under the emperors. Their provincial armies did not exist for the practice of the arts of peace.[12] They existed solely for triumphant travail in war and for this reason, by and large, the emperors had a propensity for endless imperial violence.

If war has always been barbaric, that is to say, it is about killing people you do not like in the most efficient manner, then the Romans were a lot more efficient at killing people than the so-called barbarians they faced, a classic case of new school (viz. imperialistic total warfare) versus old school (viz. machismo tribal warfare). The conquest of Gaul, for instance, looked quite different from the Gaulish side. As the Gauls had found out to their cost, Rome did not play well with others and their very existence was sometimes the only trigger necessary. (In the frank language of a predator, Iulius Caesar boasted of having killed one million Gauls.)[13] The lesson was clear. Cool and pitiless, without fear, the Romans were a violent, savage race who would stop at nothing to enslave any weaker than themselves, existing becoming a privilege instead of a right. No compromise was possible, except perhaps as a short-term tactic. As a race they were passionately unpretentious, enormously addicted to pattern, with a faculty beyond all other people of ignoring their neighbours, their surroundings, or in the last resort, themselves. Because the Romans were the worst kind of liberty takers, violence was acceptable, the unwilling cajoled and the openly hostile duly crushed, harshness and hatred for 'the Other' was actively encouraged, moderation and magnanimity was for the weak.

The Roman people hated almost everyone. It was in their nature. They expected (and usually got) an apparently 'good' war, a 'just' war, easily won, fought far away, and in which their hard-nosed professional army would make mincemeat of the raggle-taggle tribesmen of a backwoods barbarian kingdom. Peace was not an option, of course, only the solid currency of a real meat-grinding war. This patriotic, authoritarian, mine-is-mine-and-thine-is-mine, dog-eat-dog mentality of the Roman people reflected their firm belief in racial superiority and national destiny. The acceptance of a divinely ordained mission and the pervasive influence of a crude Darwinian theory of the survival of the fittest, permeated Roman society inducing a mood dominated by popular militarism, that is to say, the widespread acceptance that the practice of war, the controlled use of collective violence, was a natural and legitimate activity. Barbarians were killable because they did not share the destiny of Romulus' city. Never one to sit with folded arms, Rome was an aggressively militant warrior nation.

A people who lived for war (and were real good at it) would always be seeking new opportunities for conquests and for plunder. The goal of Rome was domination over other peoples, depriving them of their national birthright, violent seizure of alien territory. After 71 BC its battles were fought on foreign fields; even the upheavals of the triumvirate wars were largely played out on a stage far removed from native shores.[14] The people of Italy were thus spared the horrors visited upon the inhabitants of Gaul, Iberia, Greece, Africa and elsewhere. Thus, while the Other was subjected to the inherent brutality and bloodthirstiness of the Romans, society at home became more orderly and peaceful; war was simply the means by which the far-flung empire was extended and held secure. Despite all their pretensions the Romans were not really civilized. Rome was a barbaric world, inhabited by a people who had yet to overcome a barbarous past. It played by one rule: kill as many as you can, and eventually, there will be nothing left but brave corpses and live cowards. Everything is so much easier when it is black and white.

Not only do men make wars, but wars make men. So it follows that not only do societies make wars, wars make societies. And as with the men wars create, war societies are patriarchal, brutal, often psychopathic. Still, we must be doubly cautious when we study the past. One of the greatest possible errors in historical study is to ascribe the standards of one period or race upon another, yet this is precisely what we all are tempted to do, me included. We look at the other from a cultural framework of vastly different attitudes, assumptions, values, and political, social, and spiritual organization. Even those of us who are students of a particular period and its peoples can be at fault in this regard. I have called the Romans savages, and many of their practices, as we know, are utterly appalling to the civilized sensibility. Yet if we care to scratch beneath the veneer of our own acculturation we will find that *nous sommes tous sauvages*. We are capable of just as much cruelty, cynicism and covetousness as they were then. We too are as capable as the Romans of committing atrocities, of massacring women and children, of slaughtering entire communities of civilians. It seems that we are not so different, after all.

In any case, to continue. Tranquillity for Italy, peaceful conditions in the provinces, the security of the empire: these are listed by Caesar as the basic requirements for a statesman.[15] The maintenance of security, this is, and always has been, the cold logic of all empires, and the prime means of attaining this is of course the army. On the other hand, however, the instrument of war is the army too. The successful empire, ultimately and obviously by definition, is a war-fighting organism. Confucius, that wonderfully profound thinker who was the key shaper of China's tradition of the dominance of the brush over the blade,[16] recognized that soldiers were essential to the state. Their role was to protect it from external aggression (the prime rôle of any army) and to guarantee internal law and order. If they perform this rôle properly, the state is secure and at peace, and they themselves may stay quietly in the background, a deterrent rather an active force. If they fail in this duty, tragedy follows.

As both Caesar and Confucius fully appreciated, an army is always a copy of the society it serves – with this difference, that it gives social relationships a concentrated character, carrying both their positive and negative features to an extreme. When they function properly armies are institutions for organizing and channelling violence in the pursuit of some concept of the national interest. They help to focus the emotions of patriotism, self-sacrifice, and solidarity, which states need for their coherence and sometimes for their survival. Violence is not easy to control, and armies have to cope with violence within their own ranks as well as atrocities against the enemy and the civilian population. Violence and atrocities are especially prevalent, and especially horrific, in the worse of all human conflicts, civil war. The Romans were, withal, among the most pugnacious people in the ancient world, enjoying war for its own sake, and often enough going to look for it overseas, when they could not have it closer to home. In AD 69, however, war was at home.[17]

Nero's sudden demise tore away the mantle of Augustan peace cast over the empire. History was repeating itself. Once again, Rome tobogganed faster and faster with closed eyes towards a military catastrophe. Once again, the ostensible guardians of order were to become the chief agents of violence. Once again, traditional military discipline collapsed and where, as the horrified Tacitus explains, 'once they had emulated each other in valour and obedience, so now there was a rivalry in insubordination and insolence'.[18] Over the course of a single convoluted year, Rome would witness a level of strife and anarchy unparalleled since the time of the triumvirate, when the proscriptions of Marcus Antonius and Octavianus brought the great city to a state of chaos and bloodletting. And out of this chaos came civil war, anarchy, usurpation, and the death of the usurper, and so forth. It is possible to view the year AD 69 in a fratricidal context, with the idea of broken brotherhood being used as a metaphor to illustrate the larger breakdown in Roman society at the time. Romans killing Romans in a fratricidal war.

The legendary history of Rome begins with Romulus fortifying the Palatine hill, 'the scene of his own upbringing'.[19] It was also rather bloody. The story is well known: Romulus and his twin brother, Remus, quarrelled over which hill to build on,[20] and the latter was brutally cut down as he contemptuously leapt over his brother's rising walls (a vivid and compelling image still).[21] Thus making an almost biblical scenario of the kind of brotherly love, in which the winner takes all.[22]

In this way Romulus became the first king of Rome, and as mythology is usually inseparable from ritual, the traditional account of the death of Remus could be masking a ritual murder. There is never a single, orthodox version of a myth. So whichever version you choose to follow, Remus was killed and Romulus became the sole ruler of a city that he chose to name after himself. This ancestral curse, the legacy of semi-divine twins who fell foul of one another, had yet to be exorcised. Violence feeds on violence, and a civil war creates strong passions and tends to produce similar shocking events – kinsman slain by kinsman, son by father, father by son, even men who had been comrades in arms found themselves killing one another. The climax of Second Cremona, the battle that decided the issue between Vitellius and Vespasianus, was to be no exception. A signal atrocity occurred in its final, shocking phase, namely the killing of a father by his son.[23] Tacitus avows of a parallel anecdote from the same battle, whereby 'a cavalry trooper declared he had slain his brother in the late battle, and claimed a reward from the generals'.[24] In war you would think it is easier to kill men who are complete strangers, faceless victims. However, as the French poet of the air, Antoine de Saint-Exupéry, then a correspondent for L'Intransigeant, said at the start of the Spanish Civil War: 'A civil war is not a war, but a disease. The enemy is within. One fights almost against oneself. And this is undoubtedly why this war takes this terrible form. There are more executions than battles.'[25] Once unleashed, anger and hatred are such powerful motivations in a civil war.

As is common with human perversities, civil war violence is both shocking and fascinating for us. Ignatieff highlights this particular puzzlement: 'The transformation of brothers into enemies has puzzled the human imagination at least since Genesis. For Genesis begins the story of mankind not with a murder between strangers, but between brothers. It is precisely because the difference between them is so slight that the roots of the crime remain so mysterious.'[26] According to that story, Cain kills Abel out of jealousy after Yahweh slights his offering.[27] Shakespeare made good use of the concept of royal patricide in *Hamlet*. Like the stories of the Bible and Rome, the dramatist focuses on the idea of jealousy, ambition and power as the corrupting forces that lead a sacred and pure relationship between brothers to become fraught with danger and death.

Admittedly the stuff of fable demands that every hero must possess a flaw, but fratricide was an unusual twist to the type of folklore that is quite frequent for founding heroes in many societies worldwide, who invariably start their outstanding careers as foundlings. Abandoned at birth and miraculously saved from a watery death (reminiscent of the biblical Moses), the divinely begotten twins (reminiscent of the Greek heroes Castor and Pollux) were believed to have been suckled by a she-wolf and raised by the wife of a simple shepherd (reminiscent of the Trojan prince Paris or the Persian king Cyrus).[28] Naturally, as heroes the twins had to overcome these inauspicious origins before they could do anything else. In traditional mythology, the hero leaves the security of the social world behind. So in adolescence the twins made their livelihood in the backwoods by the primitive and borderland occupations of herding, hunting and raiding. 'From this they acquired strength in body and spirit.'[29] Paradoxically (of course), in a pastoral community the wolf was a terrible and common threat, with none of the lordliness attributed, alongside violence, to the lion. What is more, of all people the shepherd was considered to be an outsider and uncivilized.[30]

This abbreviated account of Rome's foundation seems a simple and comprehensible enough tale. Simplicity is probably its main virtue as the reality is rather more mundane as the myth is much later than this, but the foundation date itself is as good a one as any, is indeed better than most, and is in fact the one we are going to stick to throughout. Archaeological testimony affords positive proof that urban growth (by consolidating scattered hamlet and village communities) in Latium was certainly being stimulated in the eighth century BC through contacts between merchant-navigators from the Greek and Phoenician worlds and the native peoples of Etruria to the north. There was also a corresponding stratification (indicated by costly grave goods) within social structures that had not shown profound differences in status up to that point.

As with most founding heroes, an original core of history gathered about it a rather thick coating of legend, which then got distorted into myth and added extensively to the apocryphal side of Romulus' life. A society without myth has never been known, and the French anthropologist Claude Lévi-Strauss proposes that 'the aim of myth is to furnish a logical model for solving a contradiction',[31] such as life and death or the workings of fate. In this respect, it is important to realize that with their founding father the Romans produced more than a variation on an unoriginal theme.

Though early inscriptions demonstrate that the Romans were always Latin speaking, the hilltop site up the river Tiber was something of a frontier settlement open to both Greek and Etruscan influences. Other inscriptions, especially from Etruria, reveal a world in which men of substance moved easily from community to community (probably for better rewards and opportunities) with their families and followers. This is a world where loyalty to family, the basic economic unit of an agrarian people, and clan, the basic tactical unit of a tribal people, is greater than any other identification with a civic community.[32] At least four clan names occurring in the consular *fasti* of the early fifth century BC are of Etruscan origin (Aquillii, Herminii, Larcii, Volumnii). This possibility receives support from the ancient tradition that in 504 BC Attius Clausus, afterwards known as Appius Claudius, brought his entire clan, his treasure and his beasts to Rome from the Sabine lands. For the raider, family and belongings are an encumbrance that must be left at home, so this was no raid after loot but a migration with the whole purpose of settling down in what must have appeared a lotus land of opportunity. And sure enough, once in Rome our Sabine chieftain was not only granted land and citizenship (as were his large number of followers), but he was accepted into the patrician caste too.[33]

The hallmark of the times is movement, and in this fluid period all sorts of individuals and groups from a variety of cultural, genetic and economic backgrounds were welded together, including Latins, Sabines and Etruscans, pastoralists, hunting-stockbreeders and agriculturists. Romulus the name-giver, outcast and fratricide, was supposed to have declared his foundation to be an asylum centre for all comers, a new Noah's ark. And so it seems that the first Romans were a motley bunch, like their chief himself, a cosmopolitan bad-mash of landless refugees from the social and physical margins, seekers of that sacred second chance. Most of them were male and unmated. They were not Romans, but they were to become Romans one day. When Rome began to be Rome, a notable theme of the stories of its early years is its willingness to accept outsiders into the Tiber community, something that was certainly rare amongst the Greeks for instance, and even the infamous theft of the Sabine women issued not just a reconciliation between hostile neighbours but a willing union of two peoples.[34] Its composition was thus both varied and changing in these earliest of times, having gained and lost different elements of population, and intermarried constantly, some unfortunate brides, perhaps, being won by the spear.[35]

Lévi-Strauss tells us that typical for the clear-cut structure of myth is the 'binarism', the juxtapose of two principles, such as clever and dumb, big and small, high and low, arrogant and modest, and, of course, good and evil.[36] The Roman foundation myth does possess Lévi-Strauss' binarism, namely a deposed king and his usurper brother, a virgin daughter and a rapist god, and their twin progeny, one fated to kill the other. Yet it is a very complex one. It was also quite different from Greek ones in the way in which it does not point up positive elements like good order or natural advantages. Far from it. It focused instead on things that were agreed to be bad – usurpation, abandonment, wilderness, exile, rootlessness, brutality, homicide, and rape. The son of his father, Romulus unscrupulously added to the resources of his new foundation by reaving his neighbours. All this embarrassed the straight-laced Livy, attracted the scorn of early Christian writers, and has never stopped puzzling scholars. That the Romans said all this about their beginnings, and quite openly too, tells us much about their world view in the late Republic and early Principate. It also contributes to our understanding of the problems of kingship and succession leading to dynastic intrigues and frequent recourse to murder to remove rivals, raising moral questions no less for us today in our demythologized world than they did for the Roman people back then.

Myths follow simple and recurring patterns. That is the beauty of them. We should not be fooled by the fact that they are sometimes heavily clad with long and sophisticated tales – such as the Greek *Iliad* or the Indian *Mahabharata*, for instance. At their mythical core, that is to say, the explanation of the world they are set in, are straightforward cause and effect links, often clearly personalized. Thus, the Greeks won the Trojan war because of the trick with the wooden horse. A myth is an event that – in some sense – happened once, but that also happens all the time. Yet an uneasy attitude to myth entered the occidental mind with Plato and Aristotle. Even so, myths are not fairytales or macabre tales, seeming fantastical, comical, ludicrous, or even ridiculous, but on closer examination they are often commonsensical, plausible, and convincing. On that basis, therefore, some would argue that the slaying of Remus by his twin brother is an allegory for the merger of the two Tiber communities, the Palatine and the Esquiline.[37] This may be true,[38] but I would like to suggest that there is more to it than just this. Of course we may measure the meaning of myth-symbols as we wish, the great beauty of mythology being you can do anything. Perhaps Romulus, in his grave, had both swelled and altered: he had died a human-sized father of a modest settlement only to rise again as a titanic hero in an imperial foundation myth.[39] The Romans had transformed Romulus into the timeless, mythical hero who kills his twin brother and builds a city destined to rule the world. Now, a little speculation.

By steering away from the epic towards the every day, we can suppose that the historical Romulus – as opposed to the mythical one – was a prodigiously talented and fortunate warrior aristocrat who fought for no cause other than his own gain and personal aggrandisement, using means that in later periods would have branded him a land pirate, an armed robber, a mobster chief. When he is not butchering enemies on the battlefield, he is attacking their settlements without any kind of provocation, solely for the sake of enriching himself and his followers. The wealth of an agrarian people invariably lies in the number of head of cattle they own, which limits the amount of land that can be worked by them. He rounds up their cattle. He also seizes those people either for ransoming or to be sold off as slaves. He had a robust candid greed for gain, and we would think this shameful. An occupation that still continues with the plundering of resources, without any consideration for the needs of the indigenous inhabitants, yet few, if any, modern heads of state would dare acknowledge that a wish to seize another nation's oil revenues might be a motive for a war.

We may now continue on this hypothetical and speculative road – for we have none other to follow – by suggesting that Romulus (insofar as he was real) was perhaps a plain-speaking man of action who had made his own way, striding off into the badlands to seek a domain for himself. He gathered a considered following, loyal and disaffected men, large enough in those days to constitute a formidable private army, becoming a never-defeated warrior who rose, ducking and weaving and battling, from a status of a vagabond bandit boss to that of an unassailable warlord of an advantageously situated Latium settlement. He was an extremely dangerous enemy, a skilful chief, intelligent, popular with his men and ready to risk everything in the pursuit of his goal. Thus, in his bid for local authority, Romulus proved particularly successful, better at what he did than anyone else around him.

Nothing like this can, of course, be pressed, but if we take him for the moment as a historical fact, what does it really mean? Well, our story has a likely *dramatis persona*, endowed with considerable physical and mental strength, who overcomes a series of obstacles in pursuit of a cherished goal (in this case the foundation of a safe haven). What the Romans explained by ascribing divine ancestry to him, we would put down variously to the brightness of his wonderful luck or the result of a kind of law of nature. Either way, Romulus was blessed with all the attributes he needed to achieve the fulfilment of his every ambition, one who makes his own destiny.

This is of course highly speculative, but having chosen to downplay the supernatural element in order to emphasize the human element, it is hard not to admire our 'veritable' version of Romulus. We ought to be repelled by the casual violence and moral indifference, by his nature to leap at once to thoughts of action and bloodshed, by his arrogance and his choler, but instead we are fascinated by a man who takes such an intelligent and disarming grip on life. Romulus shone out above the ruck of men because he was better than the rest, better at being human. Like the Nietzschean 'superior man', *Übermensch*, he was above received opinion or conventional morality. He saw through the anxieties and temptations of his raw, new age. He was focused on one aim: to be distinguished from the common crowd – 'the sand of humanity' as Nietzsche so caustically put it – by his deeds and his example.[40] Rome was the foundation of a violent man for violent men: that is how it was remembered, and in this case it is probably a just remembering.

Chapter 1

The Twisted Emperor

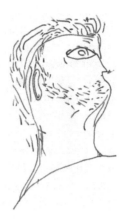

Every human quality has its perversion, and the dividing line between genius and madness is notoriously slender. But can we go so far as to say that the emperor Nero was a paragon of nefariousness? Most ancient and modern assessments of Nero are unfailingly hostile, a grinding tyrant of the first order. Indeed, he has gone down in the records as one of the worst Roman emperors, the elder Pliny writing of him as 'the destroyer of the human race', while even the prophetess Sibyl uttered divine revelations about his matricide.[1] When, in the aftermath of the murder of Thomas Beckett on 29 December 1170, William, archbishop of Sens, wrote to Pope Alexander to complain about Henry II, he refers to the actions of the Plantagenet monarch as exhibiting 'all the wickedness of Nero, the perfidiousness of Julian [the Apostate], and even the sacrilegious treachery of Judas'.[2] The modern biographers are just as severe too: Warmington has him 'frivolous and inept', Grant 'paranoid and cruel'.[3] Even his own father was said to have told a well wisher that 'any child born to himself and Agrippina was bound to be a detestable nature and become a public danger'.[4] He was quite right.

Every epoch has had its say about Nero. With the advent of the seventeenth century, the busy quill of Shakespeare brought him once more onto the stage with a take on the expression 'Nero fiddles while Rome burned'.[5] Two centuries on from Shakespeare there was to be a revival of the much earlier Nero bashing. To the essayist Thomas de Quincey (1785–1859), Nero was 'the first in that long line of monsters who ... under the title of Caesars dishonoured humanity'.[6] To the churchman and historian Charles Merivale (1808–93), Nero was 'the despot released from all fear of God and overwhelmed at the same time with the fear of man ... who has no equal in history, to whom no analogy may be found save in the pathological annals of the scaffold'. Merivale also labelled him 'vulgar, timid and sanguinary ... the last and most detestable of the Caesarian family'.[7]

The crescendo of this denunciation, in the world of popular culture at least, was probably reached when Hollywood saw Nero as nothing more than a bloated psychopath and so a fitting character for one of its 'sword and sandals' blockbusters. Many, if not most, readers will have seen that most enjoyable film epic *Quo Vadis*,[8] a 1951 Hollywood adaptation of the 1895 best seller by Polish writer Henryk Sienkiewicz.[9] A cinematic masterpiece, *Quo Vadis* is huge, magnificent to look upon, and graced by fine acting. The sets are eye-filling, Rome burns on a vast scale, crowds surge in panic, the legions have never marched better (with the correct wild-beast skins on the standard bearers for once), Christians are martyred – with, it is said, Elizabeth Taylor among them as an uncredited extra – and so far as history comes into it, the images are all that could be wished. The motion picture perpetuates almost every cliché in the Neronian repertoire. Nero (brilliantly portrayed by Peter Ustinov) is given sole credit for the burning of Rome, and sings excruciatingly. He strangles his wife Poppaea Sabina (Patricia Laffan), when in fact he kicked her to death in a fit of pique when she was gravid with his second child (and not at the time of the fire either). In fact, he was not even in Rome when the inferno started let alone fiddling while it burnt (he was in Antium,[10] his birthplace, and anyway he played the lyre), and certainly did not commit suicide until four years later.

Cinematic licence, of course. Nonetheless, the persecution of the Christians as scapegoats for the fire is truly Tacitean, and the film does not spare them. As Tacitus' own account makes clear, it was the background of popular hatred that allowed the despotic Nero to seize upon the unpopular Christians, at the time still a small and exceptional minority in Rome, as scapegoats to absolve himself of suspicions that he had ordered the great fire of 18/19 July AD 64,[11] burning, crucifying, and throwing them to the dogs.[12] The modern historian's main concern is accuracy, while the producer of film is concerned with entertainment. The unspoken premise of the first proposition is that to be accurate is to be dull, while that of the second is that to be entertaining it is necessary to distort.

Still, entertaining his readership was precisely the aim of the ancient historian, including one of the most respected and allegedly sober of all the Roman historians, Tacitus, who was writing for an audience whose only other narrative genre, apart from historical prose, was epic poetry.[13] Ancient history and modern Hollywood have not been kind to Nero, gaily painting him in the blackest of colours. It is quite fashionable nowadays to try and rehabilitate the monstrous. So it remains to ask – and this is no unimportant question, although easier to ask than answer – by softening the colours as much as possible, with regards to Nero is a more sympathetic position tenable? In truth, I do not believe so. Nero was a monster of iniquity.

And so our story begins with Nero. Actor-Emperor, the First Beast, the Antichrist, psychotic post-adolescent, take your pick, the wicked (and doomed) Nero has been called them all, and rightly so. Born plain Lucius Domitius Ahenobarbus, when in AD 50 he was adopted by Claudius he took the name Nero Claudius Drusus Germanicus Caesar, though his new stepbrother Britannicus continued to call him, to his great annoyance, Ahenobarbus. Nero came of age the following year, was named *princeps iuventutis*, next year became the city prefect, *praefectus urbi*, and the year after entered the Senate and married Claudia Octavia, Claudius' daughter by Messalina and Britannicus' sister (she was, technically, Nero's sister too after his adoption by Claudius). If Claudius died, Nero's succession was guaranteed.[14] In AD 54, just sixteen years of age and with no administrative or military experience, Nero became emperor,[15] the fifth (and last) of the ill-assorted, ill-starred Iulio-Claudian dynasty, thereby supplanting Britannicus, who was ingeniously poisoned at Nero's table the following year.[16] As emperor, he went on to murder his own mother, and then his two wives.

It had been his mother in fact who had orchestrated his smooth accession.[17] A powerful and ambitious personality, Agrippina minor had already gained much courtly experience as a sister and as a wife of two emperors, and so it was she eased herself into the rôle of controlling much of her son's – and so the state's – business. Tacitus' critical assessment of Agrippina's influence (in this case upon her husband Claudius) is memorable:

> Then came a revolution in the state, and everything was under the control of a woman, who did not, like Messalina, insult Rome by loose manners. It was a stringent, and, so to say, masculine despotism; there was sternness and generally arrogance in public, no sort of immodesty at home, unless it conduced to power.[18]

To be sure, Tacitus portrayed her as being power-mad, self-indulgent, intolerably arrogant, dominating or manipulating her son, advancing her own creatures in office, pursuing implacably all enemies and rivals, engaging in unlimited intrigue and wire-pulling. Such charges may not be without some foundation. Use her power she did, to the hilt. She listened to senatorial debates from behind a curtain and, when an embassy arrived from Armenia, she almost mounted the imperial dais to take up station beside the emperor.[19] Such outrageous parity is hinted at in the coinage of Nero's early years, which show mother and son nose-to-nose, on an equal footing.[20] Her influence, however, was not to last. Finally, when mother-son relations reached breaking point, Nero had her done away with.

Nero was obsessed with violence, and not only within the family circle. It was rumoured that he would roam the streets of Rome with a band of armed rowdies, pretending he was an ordinary young hoodlum. They would keep honest citizens awake at night by their scandalous goings on, which included singing ribald songs, molesting and beating up all who happen to be awake in the streets, and challenging the watchmen to tussles and running fights. Suetonius tells us that 'as soon as night fell he would snatch a cap or wig and make a round of the taverns, or prowl the streets in search of mischief – and not always innocent mischief either, because one of his games was to attack men on their way home from dinner, stab them if they offered resistance, and then drop their bodies down the sewers'.[21] On one such occasion a senator whose wife Nero had assaulted struck the emperor. Nero decided not to pursue him. He was in disguise, after all, and the senator could not have known that he had hit the ruler of the world. But Nero learnt otherwise when the senator came to the palace on his own initiative, to offer a trembling apology. Nero was appalled and the honest but luckless senator was obliged to commit suicide.[22] Apparently citizens began to emulate their emperor. At night, like some macabre Venetian carnival, the alleyways and byways of the capital were thronged with figures disguised as Nero, causing havoc with their gangs of cronies.[23]

Nero was no stranger to sexual violence too. After killing his second wife in a fit of rage – it was said he kicked the pregnant Poppaea to death when she criticized him for coming home late – he castrated and married a young freedman because he bore an uncanny resemblance to her.[24] He was a persistent peril to men and women, a perverted sexual predator. In just this way are monsters born. First, the emperor plays harmless games: splashes senators in the baths, serves wooden food to his dinner guests, plays practical jokes on close friends; and no matter what he says or does, everyone laughs and flatters him, finds witty his most inane remarks. That is a human failing, but it is a failing none the less. The emperor is playing the tease, the joker, the cat who suddenly lifts its paw and lets the mouse run, demonstrating his power not by exercising it but by refraining from doing so. But it is not an easy matter to flatter the omnipotent. And so the small jokes begin to pall. There must be something more amusing, more exciting – more and more and more. One day he finds it amusing to rape another man's wife, as the husband watches, or the husband as the wife looks on, or to torture them both, or to kill them. When the killing begins, the emperor is no longer a man but a monster, a monster that is above the law, answerable to no one. And then – what else? Well, any senators will lose friends or kinsmen to the capricious cruelty of the mad, bad emperor, depending of course on whether the mad, bad emperor was in a good mood that day or not. And so forth. With the immense power wielded by the emperor almost any crime is possible.

Initially there was no real reason to suspect things would turn out that way. Right after his accession Nero acquired the best support Rome could offer, counting among his advisors the soldier Sextus Afranius Burrus and the philosopher Lucius Annaeus Seneca. His hard-headed mother adored him and lavished attention upon him. Yet, for all that, he was pathologically vain, weak-willed and insecure – qualities that do not make for good Roman emperors – and the follies and crimes of Nero were owing to his own feeble fibre and the mollycoddling of his mother. He is remembered most for his perverse mind and his persecution of the Christians, and this was reason enough for later Christian writers to portray him as a bad emperor in every respect.[25] In the eyes of the Catholic Church, Nero is the first Antichrist,[26] beating into second place Martin Luther, the leader of the Protestant Reformation. In this way, a violent realignment of imperial power brought about the ruination of the house of Augustus, employing Nero as an instrument of evil, the author of its doom. The more pragmatic critic would argue that one ancestor was taking his genetic revenge, Nero (as was that earlier freak Caius Caligula too) being the great-grandson of the man who should have been king, Marcus Antonius.[27] Let the reader judge.

Monarchy is by its very principle bound up with the personal. This in itself justifies an interest in the personality of that emperor whom the moving forces of history brought face to face with the end of a dynasty. Nero inherited from his ancestors not only a giant empire, but also a standing army, a redoubtable weapon ready to hand. And they did not bequeath him one quality that would have made him capable of governing an empire or even a province or a town. He did possess other qualities, however.

Nero fancied himself an artist of some accomplishment. He wrote poetry and performed music and greatly admired Greek culture. To some extent his building programme reflected 'a Greek form of liberality'.[28] After the enormous conflagration of AD 64, which had reduced a large part of Rome to ashes, the construction of the Golden House, the *domus aurea*,[29] which was not in itself 'Greek', was an adventure in architecture and very un-Roman, a stupefying palace to end all palaces. It also cost a great fortune and stood on land once occupied by housing. Little wonder then stories such as Nero fiddled with noteworthy insouciance while Rome burned came into being.[30] Similarly, his five-yearly festival, the *quinquennial Neronia*, was highly controversial as its format was entirely based on Greek games such as the Olympian, Pythian and Isthmian Games, festivals of music, poetry, gymnastics and horsemanship as opposed to the standard fare of blood sports much favoured by the Romans.[31] His 'Greekness', which was a big part of his mental makeup, of course attracted a lot of criticism. The pro-Greek exhibitionistic emperor even went so far as to receive senators in a skimpy, flowered tunic and muslin scarf, and shocked one of our authors, the Greek-speaking Cassius Dio, by using bath-salts. I suppose there is nothing quite like the converted. If this commitment to all things Greek seemed both eccentric and contemptible to a Roman senator, the Greeks welcomed an emperor who shared their values and freely identified with them.

Roman and Greek had never got on very well, not surprisingly since one was the conqueror and the other the conquered. In one of those historical might-have-beens, the question is asked if, on 2 September 31 BC, those Olympian lovers Marcus Antonius and Cleopatra had won the sea battle off Actium, matters might have turned out differently. For Cleopatra was a Greek and Marcus Antonius was pro-Greek, behaving as he did like a magnificent Hellenistic monarch with cosmopolitan Alexandria as his capital, and had they been victorious, they might well have inaugurated, under Roman overlordship, a régime aiming at marriage between the two cultures. But Octavianus (the future Augustus),[32] who had made himself master of the known world by vanquishing them, believed that the Romans should maintain political supremacy over the Greeks – the supremacy that his admirer Virgil openly admired, but there again Virgil was a very proper Roman poet.[33]

When Virgil wrote of Actium, he described the battle not as part of a Roman civil war (which it was) but as a struggle between Octavianus' Italians and their un-Roman oriental foe personified by the effete Marcus Antonius enslaved by his painted Egyptian paramour, Cleopatra. And so it was that the vanquished at Actium were quickly identified with a foreign enemy.[34] This was the crudest form of propaganda, which usually employed the standard attacks such as accusing women of sexual promiscuity and men of effeminacy or physical defects.[35] They were invariably baseless. Octavianus himself had to combat accusations of impotence and passive homosexuality, primarily of course from Marcus Antonius.[36] Yet sexual invective is a powerful tool. Even so, Octavianus, before he assumed the very respectable title of Augustus, had been no plaster saint. He had divorced his wife Scribonia, to marry Livia while she was still pregnant by her divorced husband, and (we hear) he had even before that had a remarkable career as a libertine, a rake, and a seducer of essentially defenceless women.[37] Ever busy is the god of lust, and even the immortals (they say) are powerless in his lascivious grasp.

Greece provided Rome with a back-catalogue of potent warlike heroes from Achilles to Alexander and military ideas such as the Spartan model of training and discipline. But 'Greek love' as espoused in, say, Plato's *Symposium*, was hardly calculated to reinforce the Roman code of masculinity. The notion that the good life involved ascending a ladder of love that proceeded in an unbroken progression from the buggering of boys to rumination of the divine did not sit well with an ideology of stoically stomaching cold baths and route marches. Even so, the idea that the Romans were better than the Greeks was common but untrue: the relationship between the two was simply that of winner and loser. When all is said and done, the Roman tendency to look down on the Greeks was perhaps little more than a natural resentment of Greece's continuing superiority in those things that were important: the seven liberal arts – grammar, rhetoric, dialectic (or logic), arithmetic, geometry, astronomy (or cosmology), and music (or harmony).

The Romans may have considered the Greeks of the distant past, well before the Romans fought and beat them, as good men. However, their descendants were degenerate and debauched. 'I cannot, citizens, stomach a Greek Rome. Yet what faction of these dregs is truly Greek? For years now eastern Orontes has discharged into the Tiber its lingo and manners, its flutes, its outlandish harps with their transverse strings, its native tambourines, and the whores pimped out round the racecourse'.[38] This is powerful stuff, but it does not do for us to forget that Juvenal was a vehement and bitter satirist, a saturnine judge of contemporary society, and as such enjoyed soaring to the dizzy heights of caustic invective. He needs checking against other evidence.

Juvenal's fierce dislike for the 'hungry Greeklings',[39] amongst other clever foreigners, had good literary antecedents. The elder Cato and the elder Pliny, self-appointed guardians of good old-fashioned Roman values, utterly detested them and thought Greek culture, in public at least, was an abomination: in particular they were prejudiced against Greek doctors, whom they regarded as quacks and snake oil sellers.[40] Nevertheless, in actual fact the Greeks, powerful and unconquerable as a cultural force, were very well integrated into Roman society. 'Conquered Greece took her uncultivated conqueror captive,' as Horace had very nimbly said.[41] This paradox, of course, is what Juvenal finds particularly nettlesome, yet even those at the very pinnacle of Roman society held similar, if not so rancid, xenophobic attitudes. In an official communiqué to the younger Pliny, then serving as the legate governor of Bithynia-Pontus, Trajan observes that 'those silly Greeklings all love a gymnasium'.[42] Pliny himself sneers at the 'Greekling managers' of Domitianus' gymnasia, and complains that physical training is no longer the province of old soldiers loaded with military decorations, but *Graeculi*.[43] To the militaristic Romans, Greek athletics was not a good training for war. As Pliny's friend Tacitus would explain, you could give Greeks the benefit of Roman military organization, arms and equipment, as well as the privileges of Roman citizenship, but they remained Greeks: indolent and undisciplined.[44] Such views say much about the Roman aristocratic mentality.

Yet despisers are often despised in turn. During his principate Nero himself would enter the dramatic competitions at the public games – he usually won. He was so pleased with his success that he entered the Greek competitions as well. He won those too, thus greatly irritating the Greeks. Rumour has it that a trip to Greece in AD 67 won him a haul of 1,808 first-place prizes in the various games,[45] even for a ten-horse chariot race in which he fell off and did not complete the course.[46] Back home in Rome he decorated his bedroom with some of his trophies, and gave a public exhibition of all them. And making an exhibition was the name of Nero's game.

The emperor's passion for the lyre and poetry was also shared by such eminent figures as Caius Calpurnius Piso, who sung tragic parts, or Publius Clodius Thrasea Paetus (*cos.* AD 56), who composed verse.[47] The major difference, however, was that both men appeared in private performances, a trend of the times. But for the emperor to race chariots, start Greek games and appear in person on stage, for a proper Roman this was indeed a Rake's Progress.[48] Dynastic murders might be accepted as inevitable, but improper and un-Roman behaviour, especially in public, obviously outraged the sensibilities of traditionally minded senators.[49]

Nero was capable of murderous cruelty when angered. As briefly touched upon earlier, within five years of becoming emperor he murdered his own mother (it even gets a mention in Chaucer's *Canterbury Tales* and Shakespeare's *Hamlet*),[50] no angel herself. Nero wanted a detachment from the Praetorian Guard to go and kill Agrippina, but their prefect, Afranius Burrus, declined to vouch for their obedience, explaining 'that the praetorians were attached to the whole family of the Caesars',[51] and so he ordered a century of marines from the naval base at Misenum to do the dirty deed. This event followed hard on what was seen as an earlier botched attempt to have her drowned at sea, having persuaded her to travel home from a dinner party on a special collapsing galley of the Misenum fleet. That may have been a genuine boating accident. Whatever else one may say, the marines did the job.[52] Officially it was alleged that she had plotted to kill him, a case of eat or be eaten. Nobody believed the official version. He later hurried to his death, amongst others, his political adviser and onetime personal teacher Seneca, who had the favour of being allowed to open his veins, along with Seneca's brothers, Gallio and Mela, and his nephew, the poet Lucan,[53] and the novelist Titus Petronius (*cos.* AD 61), to be identified as Nero's 'arbiter of elegance',[54] and Thrasea Paetus. He has his first wife, Octavia, cruelly murdered in particularly revolting circumstances. His personal greed and vanity were only matched by the fervour of his bloodlust. The homicidal Nero was a danger to those around him.

Nero was cruel – not with the active cruelty of Augustus in the pursuit of historic aims, but with the cowardly cruelty of the playground bully. Murdering one's mother certainly created problems for Nero, and was not approved of. Without doubt the horrible tale of matricide as told by Tacitus is amazing,[55] but what was Nero's true motive? Nero had fallen head over heels in love with Poppaea Sabina, the scandalous and ambitious wife of one his boozing buddies, a scoundrel who shall loom large later in our story. Tacitus hints darkly that Poppaea bullied and badgered her lover into the deed because Agrippina would not have allowed her precious son to divorce Octavia and marry her, but this is rather thin logic. First, Nero was no longer under the ambrosial influence of his domineering mother, that addiction had been kicked back in AD 57, when Agrippina was expelled from court to finish up living near the naval base down in Misenum. Second, there are clear signs that the relationship between Poppaea and Nero has been backdated so as to provide the matricide motive. If Poppaea's pressure was the immediate cause of Agrippina's death, why did the love struck Nero allow three years to elapse between that murder and his divorce of Octavia? Besides, there are signs that Agrippina, a terribly dangerous woman with iron nerves even at the best of times, lioness hearted and snake minded at all times, was going to strike first. It seems the Roman world (any more than its coinage) was not big enough for the both of them. Whatever, the killing of his mother damaged Nero's popular image, which was never really to recover. Indeed, Josephus puts it well when he says 'he got rid of Britannicus in a way most people knew nothing about but he openly murdered his mother'.[56]

A good argument can be made to the effect that subsequent misfortunes, including the advent of the Flavian dynasty, might have been avoided if instead of Nero an emperor of clear head and strong character had stood at the helm of Rome. Nero possessed neither of these attributes. Or did he? But this is to speculate and to digress.

In his inauguration speech to the Senate, written by that noted stylist and orator Seneca,[57] Nero speaks of honouring the traditional rôle of the Senate as Augustus had done and repudiated the abuses of his predecessor, Claudius. To this effect Nero makes three promises. First, he will not be the judge of all matters, and especially will not judge matters behind closed doors, an obvious backward reference to Claudius. Second, there will be a clear definition between the imperial household and state affairs, again an attack on Claudius, the prevailing mood being his freedman had become executives in their own right, and had attained, in senatorial eyes, unwarranted wealth and dangerous powers.[58] Third, he insists that the duties of the emperor and those of the Senate remain separate and distinct, whereby the latter will attend to the affairs of Italy and the senatorial provinces, while the former will take charge of the army and the imperial provinces.[59] While the previous emperor had made the same claim initially, Nero actually honours his promise, Tacitus even going so far to say that Nero 'was true to his word and several arrangements were made on the Senate's authority'.[60] This explains why the emperor left the Senate to deal with such matters as the riots that swept Puteoli (Pozzuoli), or the number of gladiators allowed by a festival to be held in Syracuse, or the slaves who murdered their masters.[61]

Nero may have choked with the enthusiasm of his 'own' inaugural speech, but the first five years of his reign, if we excuse the death of Britannicus, were traditionally held to be outstanding, as a golden period that promised much. Even the conqueror and colonizer Trajan, always considered as one of the 'good' emperors, is reported to have said that the *quinquennium Neronis* was a time of good government, a time of sanity when the emperor was taking sound advice.[62] When he did turn his attention to affairs of state, he was capable of being effective, as his plans for construction in Rome demonstrate ('What worse than Nero, what better than Nero's baths?' asked Martial),[63] but he seldom paid attention. He preferred his social life and his poetry and his lyre.[64] He was an egotistic entertainer who wanted everyone to love him as much as he loved himself. None of this narcissistic behaviour naturally won the favour of the army. The Roman Empire was a military autocracy, but the Roman emperor was not a warrior and sometimes not even very military. After all, had he not ordered the death of his own top general – but you will hear of that when the time comes. Nero, unlike Augustus or Claudius before him, clearly had no intention of seeking a military reputation for himself.[65] Properly speaking, Nero was little more than a hedonist, not a soldier. His energies were most happily deployed in his pleasures.

Not that Nero's burlesque farce of a reign was without military success (viz. as well as the suppression of the rebellion of Boudica, there were the campaigns of Cnaeus Domitius Corbulo against the Parthians, and a planned expedition to the Caucasus), but his personal neglect of the army was a critical error. Having only inspected the Praetorian Guard at its morning exercise in Rome, the emperor had no idea of a campaigning soldier, let alone ever seen a man killed in battle. Judged by the standards of the ancient world, greatness tended to be equated with scale of conquest, large numbers of the enemy slain or enslaved being an added bonus – *vide* Alexander and Pompey, both bore the soubriquet 'the Great'. If the evidence from a single wall painting (Trojan Hector's final farewell to his beloved wife Andromache) from the *domus aurea* is anything to go by, Nero even decked some of his guardsmen in Hellenistic-style panoply.[66] In a milieu where the appeal of the muscular often eclipsed the martial, Nero even went as far to raise a new legion, *I Italica*,[67] which consisted of specially selected Italian-born recruits all at least six Roman feet tall.[68]

Destined for the Caucasus expedition,[69] which never happened, true to form Nero gave his new legion the grandiose title of The Phalanx of Alexander the Great.[70] Roman soldiers were not supposed to look impressive, but they did need to be tough enough to withstand maltreatment, resist diseases and recover from wounds quickly. Physical durability was far more important than brawn. Whether or not these Neronian phalangites of imposing stature would stand up to the physical and emotional pressures of battle is for us to find out later. And when Nero himself left Rome, it was not to review his soldiers in the field but to compete in Greek games. Nero – thespian, charioteer and socialite – was beginning to reveal his inadequacies as a soldier. The playboy emperor was becoming an acute embarrassment to those that mattered.

Scarcely beyond his teens, it seems his ambition to outshine everyone else caused him to become reckless, unbalanced his mind, and eventually would make him the victim of a military coup that swept away Rome's first imperial dynasty. Nero, like Iago, delighted in the wickedness of which he was a witness and in the crimes of which he was the instigator. His lavish expeditions and building programmes were bankrupting the treasury. But his careful paranoia kept him in office longer than the equally dreadful Caius Caligula had managed. In AD 62 Burrus died (in somewhat questionable circumstances) and Seneca retired from public affairs,[71] and it was these two gentlemen that were generally seen as the ultimate source of good influence upon the emperor during the initial years of his reign.[72] Though they could not improve their emperor's irresponsible, reckless character, they stayed firmly, for five years, at the summit.

The removal of the only remaining restraints on him meant Nero was able to appoint to a position of power the man who was to become his evil genius, Caius Ofonius Tigellinus, a libertine Sicilian who bred horses for racing.[73] This devious and unsavoury person was to endorse the outrageous and paranoid behaviour, which had previously been checked by Seneca and Burrus. It also gave him *carte blanche* to divorce Octavia, which was done on the spurious grounds that she was barren, and to marry Poppaea.[74] According to Cassius Dio, Burrus had always strongly opposed the idea of divorce, saying, 'Well, then, give her back her dowry,'[75] which obviously meant the Principate. Anyway, the divorce stirred the barefoot rabble to riot in favour of Octavia and against Poppaea.[76] This indeed was an important moment, a turning point even, the first popular opposition to Nero. Eventually, he had Octavia permanently removed.

A born victim and a born political tool, and that is how Octavia is represented by Tacitus. Her rôle is passive, in every sense of the word; but it is also political. Her existence was not only inconvenient for Poppaea, it could have been a dangerous political focus for anyone seeking to replace Nero. Poppaea apparently instigated one of Octavia's servants to accuse her of adultery with a slave and Nero had her banished to Campania.[77] This was the despicable deed that sparked those pro-Octavia riots. Poppaea was not to be beaten though, and Octavia was then accused of adultery with Anicetus, commander of the fleet at Misenum and 'perpetrator of the matricide'.[78] Anicetus confessed to the act after having been secretly bribed, and was then banished to Sardinia, 'where he endured exile without poverty, and died a natural death'.[79] Poor Octavia was not to enjoy the same fate, and her terrible end is recorded with full drama and pathos by Tacitus.[80]

As the Principate descended into tyranny and chaos, the next event of significance was the fire of AD 64, with its terrible rumours of imperial incendiarism, while the following year's big feature was the conspiracy aiming to replace Nero with Calpurnius Piso, he of the lyrical voice and a great noble unconnected with the imperial family.[81] After this plot, which was hopelessly bungled, Nero was more than ready to entertain the idea that all and sundry were out for his head. And so Nero roped in a number of high-profile suspects. Among them were those great men of Stoic principles, Thrasea Paetus and Seneca. Since his retirement, Nero's former tutor and political advisor had been busy turning himself into a full-blown philosopher, the Roman Sokrates. When he received the customary invitation to take his own life, Seneca grabbed the chance for glamorous martyrdom. Opening his veins, he stepped into a warm bath to hasten the flow of blood, and died (as he himself made sure to proclaim) in the cause of Liberty.[82]

Seneca was indeed a fountain of wisdom, and Nero was fortunate to drink of his depths. But let us pause for a brief moment and consider a much darker, paradoxical side to Seneca, namely that he combined immense wealth with preaching Stoic philosophy, in which worldly goods were not to be valued. Seneca certainly valued his earthly riches. When news reached Rome from Britannia of the Boudican rebellion, Roman financiers who had invested heavily in the young province, including a certain Seneca, chose the time to call in their loans made to some of the chieftains there. Seneca, at the time the virtual co-regent at Rome, was recalling all at once a large personal loan of forty million *sestertii* at a high rate of interest.[83] Stoic philosopher, moralist, man of letters, statesman, and dramatist, yes the brilliant Seneca was all this and much more besides. For instance, he was mightily greedy too. His wealth was notorious, once being asked by what philosophical principles he had, within four years of imperial favour, amassed 300 million *sestertii*.[84] Though Tacitus clearly brushes aside the charge, if indeed true it was a damning and unanswerable question. Seneca it seems had the brisk style of a swindler who would stop at nothing.

But back to Seneca's young tyrant. By the late sixties, the psychotic post-adolescent Nero had managed to alienate just about everyone around him. Worryingly, the emperor knew something awful was afoot, but he was not sure what. And so the curve of imperial respectability continued sharply downward, with the final straw coming when he even managed to make the army disgusted with him. This is made clear by the words of Subrius Flavus, one of Nero's praetorian tribunes who had got himself involved in the Piso conspiracy. When quizzed by Nero why he had forgotten his military oath, Flavus blurted out, 'Because I detested you! I was loyal as any of your soldiers as long as you deserved affection. I began detesting you when you murdered your mother and wife and became a charioteer, actor, and incendiary.'[85] The man was certainly brave, for it is a startling list.

Everything was going against Nero. Acts of ill fortune seldom come singly: his qualified friends were becoming opponents; his opponents, enemies; his enemies were taking arms. Paradoxically it may seem, it was Seneca, in his rôle as tragedian, who promoted the scriptural sentiment that to kill an infamous tyrant at any time without trial was more than acceptable. And so Hercules, in his role as the heroic exterminator of all tyranny, says: 'There can be slain / No sacrifice to Jove more acceptable / Than an unjust and wicked king.'[86]

As a man, let alone as a 'wicked king', Nero was not worth a hair on Corbulo's cropped head, yet the enforced suicide of that distinguished senatorial general was an indication of the sort of gratitude that prominent men could expect of a suspicious and unbalanced tyrant.[87] Before Nero and his court left Italy for the emperor's arty expedition to Greece, a spate of executions marked the unearthing of a senatorial conspiracy – whether real or imagined is impossible to say. One of the alleged ringleaders was Corbulo's son-in-law Lucius Annius Vinicianus, who had recently served in Armenia as *legatus legionis* of *V Macedonica*. Corbulo was summoned to join the emperor in Greece where he was permitted the luxury of forestalling execution by perpetrating *felo-de-se*.

Cnaeus Domitius Corbulo (*cos.* AD 39) was the conqueror of the desert heights of the Armenian badlands, a country populated by tough individualists. The place had always been a cockpit between the great warring powers of east and west even before the days of Dareios and Alexander. A neutral zone or the battleground between two empires? Take your pick. At the time Armenia was debatable land, being as it was the bone of contention between Rome and Parthia. Anyway, Corbulo is the only senatorial general of our period to be mentioned in Frontinus' *Strategemata*, and not just once but in five separate anecdotes.[88] It is from one of these five little gems we gather that he was a commander, like commanders from time immemorial, who realized that if he could keep his soldiers' hands and minds busy, hardship and boredom were more easily endured (digging was a way of life to his men, and this chore, occupying them with physical toil, preserved their discipline).[89]

A striking-looking man, muscular of body, eloquent of speech, and a coldly competent martinet with a brutal stubble extending to both face and scalp, Corbulo not only looked every inch the part, he was military to the very bottom of his soul too.[90] His first-class physical condition, his logical thinking on all subjects and his extreme professional competence were obvious but perhaps not appealing. Such qualities are not as common as we seem to think, at least not in the same person, and men who are in complete control of themselves are seldom popular with those who are not. A part of the enmity that unfailingly ensues is caused by that petty jealousy that stodgy, unimaginative men always feel for the brilliantly successful. As is often the case, petty jealousy soon turns to considerable envy.

Any emperor could not afford to be outshone by a senator, most especially in the field of military endeavour, which remained of cardinal importance to the Roman aristocracy. The beady-eyed Nero became envious of Corbulo and he was obliged to fall on his honoured sword, which he did with great aplomb, his last words being 'I have it coming!'[91] With that the rugged old campaigner disappears from history with a laconic final flourish (AD 67) – for us moderns the terrible simplicity of his valedictory is like something out of Shakespeare.

So perished a man who had served the empire and the emperor faithfully, and whose military talent and integrity entitled him to the name of a genuine Roman. The cropped-haired, square-jawed, weather-beaten, lean warrior did not deserve such a cruel fate – at least not from those flabby hands. It goes without saying that military yes-men are easy to come by, but real leaders are rare, and Corbulo can be described as a real leader in every respect. Yet Nero, exhibiting the folly of a weak man trying to appear strong, had no interest in military genius, he wanted obedience, not brilliance.

It was too late. It was now early summer AD 68 and Nero was only an emperor in name. His allusions would vanish all too soon. When he tried to have some generals arrested, it only prompted others to form a conspiracy to topple him,[92] and with this final crisis the debit side of Nero's reputation proved, in terms of *auctoritas*, to exceed the credit side. When Nero learned of the plot, which involved the Praetorian Guard too, he tried to flee. At the moment of imperial crisis the emperor only thought about dodging the blow, not dealing it.

It was a sad sight. One by one, his supporters faded away into the night, until at last Nero was hemmed in and well-nigh alone. A man made for musical contests, but not for a civil war, the performing emperor was about to play his last scene. Hiding out in the suburban villa of the imperial freedman Phaon, to which he had fled from Rome, Nero was obliged to put an end to his life. He tried, but was unable to keep his hand steady. So instead he forced his freedman and secretary, Epaphroditos, to deal 'him the finishing stroke'.[93] The story of Suetonius is that Nero's dying words were: 'What an artist dies with me!'[94] We do not really know if he muttered this through his tears, but the fine rhetoric is certainly in character, and the image of a performing Nero delivering this valedictory line is not easy to forget. He, however, was not deified.

So Nero was dead. Some would sum up his death in three words: no great loss. Yet human nature can sometimes be rather perverse when it comes to characters evil and nefarious. In this respect, it is pertinent to note those posthumous imposters, the so-called 'false Neros', who were to proliferate and win many followers (and a degree of temporary notoriety) in the decades to come, one of whom even got Parthian support.[95] What is more, some top people were said to have been influenced in backing Nerva for emperor by his friendship with Nero thirty years before.[96] Was this simply loyalty to the last of the dynasty? Or did Nero have qualities to which the senatorial tradition represented in our sources has turned a blind eye? Certainly Tacitus would like us to believe that Nero's death was heartily welcomed by senators and others of the Roman nobility, but unlike Suetonius and Cassius Dio he does add that those who were upset by the news were merely the 'degraded populace, frequenters of the arena and the theatre, the most worthless of the slaves, and those who were supported by the infamous excesses of Nero'.[97] Yet to those in the empire who felt themselves culturally Greek, Nero's death was evidently mourned because he 'restored the liberties of Hellas with a wisdom and moderation quiet alien to his character', and 'held our liberties in his hand and respected them'.[98]

Still, Nero was the author of his doom, a narcissistic and wicked man, and a lover of power, especially over the weak and defenceless. For future dynasties, with the handwriting on the wall, the message was clear: a reigning emperor who neglected the traditional institutions of Rome, Senate and army, did so at his peril.

The Delphic oracle is reputed to have once told Nero 'to beware the seventy-third year',[99] a prediction that eventually turned out to be remarkably accurate. Every prophecy is open to interpretation and if it turns out that its meaning was other than what one thought, it is not the fault of the immortal gods but of us mortals who have sadly misinterpreted their signs. Barely thirty years of age, the lyre-playing emperor thus looked forward to another forty-three years of enjoying the splendour of his position and performing to his captive audience. But already Galba, aged seventy-three, was marching on Rome. Such are the devious designs of the gods.

Chapter 2

The Septuagenarian Emperor

With the death of Nero by his own shaky hand, the ill-sorted, ill-starred Iulio-Claudian dynasty had come to an ignominious end. This was 9 June, AD 68.[1] The following year was probably one of Rome's worst. In the maelstrom of the actual events, the owl of Minerva made her flight too late, and Rome became the place where will was law and reason put in exile. 'In elective monarchies', as Gibbon remarked upon darkly, 'the vacancy of the throne is a moment big with danger and mischief.'[2] The modern writer is unable to improve on this sombre and straightforward statement of fact. Machiavelli, that great Renaissance figure much vilified by posterity, had plausibly argued before Gibbon, without too much exaggeration, that the faulty constitutional arrangements responsible for this situation were what eventually brought Rome down some four hundred years later. But that is another story, for our story concerns the dramatic events of AD 69 when the jealousies and squabbles of ambitious and unscrupulous governors of the empire brought chaos out of order. Rome was up for the taking and there were a number of candidates who reckoned themselves well placed to seize power. He whose grasp was the most brutal could now rise to untold heights: an imperial candidate, ruling emperor, a revered god.

The first serious candidate, Servius Sulpicius Galba, had lived through all five emperors of the Iulio-Claudian dynasty, and nobody, apart from himself perhaps, would ever have thought that he would become the sixth emperor of Rome. The patrician Sulpicii Galbae had been prominent in senatorial politics for more than two centuries and Galba's claim to the purple of the Caesars was at least in part based on belonging to this great and illustrious clan whose name resounded in Roman history.[3] He himself cut a good public image, having been a praetor (AD 20), a consul (AD 33), and a close colleague of the reforming Claudius, who had selected him as proconsul of Africa Proconsularis (AD 45). There he had served ruthlessly for two years, the province at the time suffering from the licentiousness of the Roman soldiers and by the incursions of neighbouring tribes.[4] On his return to Rome he was honoured with the *ornamenta triumphalia*, and with the dignity of three priesthoods, including that of the *Augustales*.[5]

Galba was now legate governor (*legatus Augusti pro praetore*) of Hispania Tarraconensis, the largest of the three Iberian provinces, and had been for the last eight years. Nero had just returned from his artistic tour of Greece, when in March AD 68 news reached him that Caius Iulius Vindex, governor of one of the Gauls (probably of Gallia Lugdunensis, a province without a legionary garrison, possibly of Gallia Belgica),[6] and himself an Aquitani chieftain,[7] had raised the flag of rebellion. Vindex did not command regular troops, and there is little doubt that the basis of his support was the Gaulish aristocracy.[8] Plutarch puts an absurd figure of 100,000 men under arms, but if we take perhaps his figure for their apparent grievous losses – 20,000 – as the total for the rebel forces we are plausibly in the right ballpark.[9]

But why the insurrection in the first place?

Cassius Dio says that while Nero was fiddling and prancing to his doom in Greece 'the inhabitants of Britannia and of Gaul, oppressed by the taxes, were becoming more vexed and inflamed and angry that ever'.[10] Vindex convoked a meeting over this pressing matter, and the speech delivered by him contains a number of points worth considering: Nero had plundered the Roman world, had destroyed the flower of the Senate, had raped and murdered his mother, and was incapable of maintaining the standards of an emperor.[11] Vindex's speech ends with a clarion call to free the world from tyranny.[12] None of these points is to be despised. Yet these complaints would have been quite irrelevant to your average Gaulish noble. In fact, they come across as more like a Roman senator's view of things Neronian. The Roman senator was living in the apple's core, to use a suitable metaphor, and the canker in that core did not show on the skin or impair the wholesomeness of the flesh. Your Roman senator, therefore, would be more concerned about the central canker than about the still unblemished and fragrant outer part. Perhaps we should be generous to Cassius Dio and argue that Vindex was trying to persuade the nobility of Rome to join him, an instance of resisting tyranny in the old Roman tradition.

Though the aim of the revolt was to replace Nero by a man free of his lusts (and so of his monetary needs) and acceptable to the Senate, to some extent it was a native revolt too. Vindex succeeded in persuading large numbers of Gauls, both in his own and in neighbouring provinces, to follow him in rebellion under their own tribal leaders.[13] Indeed, Vindex's rebellion was not an isolated affair; seven years previously there had already been trouble in Britannia with the Boudican rebellion, and currently at the other end of the empire the Jews were confidently taking on the Roman legions in Iudaea. In both cases Roman taxation and Roman conscription had played their part to spark insurrection against Rome. Thus, for example, the

Great Edict of Tiberius Iulius Alexander, the prefect of Egypt, in the name of Galba, goes out of its way to alleviate such provincial problems.[14] So Vindex was taking a chance and was playing on the severe discontent felt by provincials. Yet he needed wider support, and therefore wrote to other provincial governors. Galba down in Hispania Tarraconensis went over.[15] He was an excellent ally for Vindex, of impeccable republican aristocratic pedigree and despite his advanced years he was highly acceptable to the Senate, as would be Nerva thirty years hence. As the old saying goes, good blood tells and never fails to recognize itself.

Indeed, Galba began his association with the ruling Iulio-Claudian family with an affectionate pinch on the cheek from Augustus when he was a nipper, and thereafter he was a personal acquaintance of the emperors from Tiberius to Nero, having been on friendly terms with them all, except – latterly – Nero. Agrippina minor, the daughter of the great Germanicus and the mother of Nero, was apparently infatuated with him,[16] and he enjoyed an especially close relationship with Livia, the wife of Augustus. She had marked him out for preferment when he was still a youngster, and he had amply justified the trust she had placed in him. Suetonius tells us she made Galba her principal heir, leaving him a legacy of half a million *aurei*, but then her son Tiberius, wise with pecuniary wisdom, nullified her bequest on a technicality. The sum had been written in figures, not in words, and he ruled that 5,000 was all the testatrix had intended.[17] As Tiberius never paid a single one of Livia's legacies, this did not make much difference at the time, but when Caius Caligula paid Livia's legacies in full, it was bad luck for Galba that the emperor was unaware of his predecessor's fraud. Galba did not press for the whole 500,000, and perhaps it was as well for him that he did not, for if he had done so Caligula would have remembered the incident when he ran short of funds. Nonetheless, Galba was not only senatorial, but also extremely wealthy and very well connected.

Unfortunately for Vindex all this did not do him much good. Legions from the Rhine army led by the legate governor of Germania Superior,[18] Verginius Rufus (*cos.* AD 63),[19] marched down from the Rhine frontier to confront Vindex in the name of Nero, or so said Cassius Dio,[20] and promptly invested the main rebel base at Vesontio (Besançon), the tribal capital of the Sequani. A hurried conference was held between the two leaders, but Verginius Rufus' soldiers, apparently without orders, marched out and in short order chopped into mincemeat Vindex's inexperienced troops, a classic case of raw beginners up against front-liners.[21] That English realist Thomas Hobbes sums it all up very tidily, 'covenants, without the sword, are but words'.[22] One very good epitaph for Vindex who, like a good Roman, fell on his sword.

So much for Vindex.

An ambiguous character, Verginius Rufus mourned the death of Vindex, but the victorious legionaries hailed him *imperator*, and then begged him as their own general to assume the supreme power. Verginius Rufus, plausibly realizing what a poisoned chalice it could be, sensibly declined the offer of the top job in the empire. When they subsequently destroyed the images of Nero, Verginius Rufus stood before them to persuade them to await the decision of the Senate. This was certainly a strange request, for the Senate, that advisory council which formerly guided the decisions of the state, had already become a subordinate and somewhat pitiable body under the Iulio-Claudian emperors, though not yet the toothless tiger of later times.

Cassius Dio continues, making it quite clear that Verginius Rufus had revolted from Nero and did not throw his lot in with Galba. True, Verginius Rufus had marched against Vindex in the name of Nero, so his loyalty was not initially impugned. Only after that mysterious conference do we see signs of military revolt,[23] but we have no reason to doubt Verginius Rufus' initial intentions, viz. to crush Vindex. Nonetheless, Verginius Rufus would not and probably could not face Galba in battle, but was he really keen to be emperor? Tacitus implies that a defect of birth, namely he was the son of 'a mere *eques*', prevented him from becoming emperor.[24] He was certainly slow to declare for Galba,[25] but he fell into line once the Senate had put its weight behind the new emperor, he having no ground to stand on anymore. Indeed, the *legatus legionis* of *I Germania* stationed in Germania Inferior, Fabius Valens – we shall meet this unscrupulous gentleman again later as one of the chief Vitellians – led his own legion in taking an oath of allegiance to Galba and organized a *coup d'etat* against Fonteius Capito, the popular and easygoing governor of the province. The legate had the governor put to death on the plea that he was intending to revolt, but not, as many thought, because he had refused to take up arms at the solicitation of Fabius Valens.

It was this development that finally decided Verginius Rufus to throw his lot in with Galba, realizing that he would not get anywhere in the pursuit of the purple, and perhaps thinking that this was the sort of honour that you took with you to a quick grave. Incidentally, Fabius Valens had endeavoured to persuade Verginius Rufus to seize the empire, and when he refused to do so, Fabius Valens sought to blacken his good name.[26] Nonetheless, this was the act that gave Verginius Rufus his finest hour, his *gloria*, or so says the younger Pliny.[27] It is this author who relates a marvellous anecdote concerning Verginius Rufus' ambiguity. Verginius Rufus lived on to AD 97, aged eighty-three,[28] and his tomb, seen by Pliny, bore the following boastful epitaph:

Here lies Rufus, who once defeated Vindex and set free the imperial power.
Not for himself, but for his country.[29]

In the same letter Pliny records the conversation between Verginius Rufus and the senatorial writer Marcus Cluvius Rufus when the latter begged Verginius Rufus' forgiveness in advance for any inaccuracies written in his histories. Verginius Rufus simply replied, 'Don't you realize, Cluvius, that I did what I did so that the rest of you should be at liberty to write as you please?'[30] This is marvellously equivocal stuff.

Meanwhile, in Iberia, the soldiers of *legio VI Victrix* declared their own man emperor in the legionary camp.[31] The elderly but soldierlike Galba accepted, and eventually, once Nero had passed forever from the stage of world history, the Senate (and the Praetorian Guard) confirmed the soldiers' declaration.

Returning to Nero. Initially, there had been no panic. On hearing the news of Galba's march on Rome, Nero made moves to create his own loyal legion from sailors of the Misenum fleet.[32] Even when more bad news followed, namely the defection of the legions of Germania Superior, Nero still had other possibilities, for the legions under Fonteius Capito in Germania Inferior remained loyal and the Praetorian Guard still stood by him. Galba was declared *hostis*, a public enemy, by the Senate.

Even so, his principate was already dead but stubbornly evading its own funeral. The Praetorian Guard, under those abominable wretches Caius Ofonius Tigellinus and Caius Nymphidius Sabinus, were soon to be implicated in a plot to proclaim Galba emperor with senatorial support,[33] Nymphidius Sabinus promising the praetorians lavish rewards for their cooperation and at the same time putting men loyal to him in positions of importance.[34] It is essential for us to realize that Sabinus' tampering with the loyalty of the praetorians was aided by the fact he had convinced them that Nero had fled the capital, a lie given substance by Nero's retirement to his private gardens in Rome.[35] Tacitus implies that the prefect had tricked the praetorians, which he brings up in a speech he puts into the mouth of a member of Galba's coterie: 'Even with Nero, it was he that deserted you, not you that deserted him.'[36] Once the loyalty of the Praetorian Guard was lost all was up for Nero.

By the time Galba reached Rome, apparently marching all the way from Iberia 'wearing a large sword at his side ... old and weak of sinew as he was',[37] Nero had breathed his last and the public enemy of yesterday was the emperor of today. For the moment, he refused the imperial titles,[38] but it is clear that the Principate was his goal. To this end, he organized an inner cabinet or *concilium* of advisors in order to make it known that any decisions were not made by him alone but only after consultation with a group. The arrangement was meant to recall the healthy working relationship between the first emperor and the Senate, a return to the old ways, imitating Augustus, who was content to be first citizen. For though Augustus had reduced the Senate to a subservient rôle from which it never emerged again, its members were the leading men of the state next to the emperor himself and still retained an importance that could not be ignored.

Even more revealing of Galba's imperial ambitions were slogans such as LIBERTAS RESTITVTA ('Liberty Restored'),[39] ROMA RENASCENS ('Rome Reborn'),[40] and SALVS GEN(eneris) HVMANI ('Salvation of Mankind'),[41] preserved on the coins he issued as emperor, and it is relevant to note that Vindex, before he went down, had urged Galba to 'make himself the liberator (*adsertor*) and leader (*dux*) of mankind'.[42] These crisp catchwords were not specious claims to restore the long defunct Republic his ancestors had patriotically supported, for Galba was more than an ineffectual representative of a bygone *antiquus rigor*, but an imperial constitutionalist eager to promote an anti-Neronian stance and to publicize the virtues of an Augustan-style principate. After all, Augustus was the most active promoter of the 'winds of change' myth, having created for himself the rôle of liberator whereby he set free 'the Republic when it was oppressed by the tyranny of a faction'.[43] Back then the peril was the despotism of Marcus Antonius, whereas now it was that of his ancestor, Nero. Galba was to reinforce his chosen identity as 'liberator of the Republic' on one coin in particular. The obverse depicts the personification of Liberty, while the reverse displays a *pilleus*, the pileus worn by a freed slave, with two daggers on either side and the legend R(es) P(vblica) RESTITVTA ('The Restored Republic').[44] But the 'winds of change' were to blow over.

It is important for us to understand that when a government had no mass media of communications and postage stamps (or even the Internet) to advertise its achievements and intentions, it would obviously advertise them through the designs and inscriptions stamped on coinage instead. The only announcements the Roman emperors could be sure that very many people would see were those on two small pieces of space that each coin provided. When was the last time any of us looked at the official propaganda on our own coinage? What is more, how can we possibly imagine what must it be like to be the emperor of Rome, to know that one's face on coins is known to all the world? Which nicely brings us to another usurper and his particular brand of coinage.

Out in Africa there was a potential rival, Lucius Clodius Macer. Like Galba, Clodius Macer was an experienced governor who had renounced his allegiance to Nero, and having only one legion to hand, *III Augusta*, had also raised a second locally, the short-lived *legio I Macriana*,[45] which he designated *liberatrix* on the reverse of his coinage.[46] He likewise awarded this honorific title to *III Augusta* to mark its rôle in the ending of Nero's tyranny,[47] and these coin issues were meant to encourage the allegiance of the two African legions to his cause. It is remarkable that he employed on some of these coins the formulaic abbreviation SC, *senatus consulto*,[48] an abbreviation that seems to have fallen out of use sometime after 40 BC. It was perhaps a way to demonstrate that his revolt was against Nero, not the Senate, which is probably why Clodius Macer chose to restrict himself to the title *propraetor Africae*, propraetor of Africa.[49]

Beyond his base of power in Numidia, the permanent home of *III Augusta*, Clodius Macer had very little support,[50] but he had improved his lot by seizing Sicily, thereby not only 'holding back the grain supplies in Africa',[51] but those in the island too. Tacitus disparages Clodius Macer as a 'pretty tyrant',[52] but acknowledges his real potential for 'fomenting sedition'.[53] His next move was to lead his two legions out of Numidia and seized Carthage, the great maritime capital of the original *provincia Africa*, which still possessed a notable naval base. We surmise the intention was to pirate the north African coast so as to further disrupt the vital flow of grain to Rome. But it was the road to nowhere. Elsewhere another had become emperor, and he sent his agents to treat with Clodius Macer, but the latter refused to accept the decision of the Senate. On Galba's order Trebonius Garutianus, his newly appointed procurator to the province, had Clodius Macer murdered in the early autumn of AD 68,[54] thereby ending the African crisis.

Before we leave the intriguing topic of Clodius Macer, we should briefly touch upon one other shadowy character who was in all likelihood intimately involved in his insurrection, Calvia Crispinilla, Nero's sinister wardrobe mistress. Possibly of African origin, Calvia Crispinilla was, as Tacitus says, 'Nero's tutor in vice'.[55] She took advantage of her position with Nero to commit theft on a grand scale. When the emperor married Sporus in AD 67, she was 'entrusted with the care of the boy and with the oversight of the wardrobe'.[56] However, the following year, according to Tacitus, her political stock in Nero's court slumped dramatically, and subsequently she prodded Clodius Macer into rebellion.[57] When Clodius Macer was put to death by the command of Galba, there was a public outcry that she also should pay for her crimes with her life, but she received the emperor's protection. Calvia Crispinilla afterwards married a man of consular rank,[58] and 'lived unharmed through the reigns of Galba, Otho, and Vitellius', eventually to become 'powerful as a rich and childless women, circumstances which have as great weight in good as in evil times'.[59] These were evil times indeed, and it has been suggested that this lady of rank survived because she also helped to engineer Clodius Macer's assassination.[60] True or not, it is no far-fetched theory. Calvia Crispinilla was clearly a dab-hand when it came to the most perfidious intrigues and made cunning use of circumstances. Not so Galba.

Galba, according to Tacitus, 'by common consent possessed the markings of a ruler – had he never ruled'.[61] Tacitus' verdict is ultimate and damning, and Galba's principate was to be firm, flat-footed, and fleeting. Even though not a bad administrator, the septuagenarian emperor was lecherous, cruel, and possessed a temper incurably soured, a temper that had ended by alienating everyone in his entourage. Not only that, he was striking in his hardness, an old man with a unhealthy fancy for old-fashioned discipline.[62] When asked to honour a promised bonus, admittedly made in his name but without his authority, for the soldiers of the Praetorian Guard and of the Rhine legions, Galba took the line of high principle and notoriously declared, 'I choose my soldiers, I do not buy them.'[63] Generous of phrase but stingy of money, this was hardly going to improve morale. No one likes a smart aleck, especially not a penny-pinching one, but the rather startling notion that an emperor could rip off his soldiers was quite laughable. Not only was this a *faux pas* of the highest order, it being critical for any emperor, novice or experienced, to gain and to retain the loyalty (either through earning their genuine devotion, or through successful bribery) of his soldiers. And before too much time had passed, Galba had occasion to recall that remark in bitter, bloody circumstances.

Proven fighter he no doubt was, reasoned diplomat he certainly was not, and it was the soldiers on the Rhine that were to be the initiators that began the actual train of events that was to unseat Galba only six months into his principate. To them Galba was alien, hostile, hateful. A general who was known for executing first and asking questions later, it was he who had brutally suppressed the Rhine legions back in AD 40, which had mutinied against their commander-in-chief Caius Caligula.[64]

Galba was living in a fool's paradise. When Homer said that Zeus (to employ the Greek term) first makes mad those whom he designs to destroy, he summed up in superstitious form a profound historical observation.[65]

From the start, almost from the day he became emperor, Galba radiates an aura of misfortune. It never diminishes. It almost seems as if the gods poisoned their gift to him. You can believe this or not, but Galba certainly misused his golden opportunity. Understanding this fundamental truth helps to illustrate how important it was for an emperor to gain and then retain the loyalty of the army. An allegiance once changed can change again, and since nothing is free, to each his price. A Roman soldier received a regular income that he was used to being paid at fairly wide intervals (225 *denarii* per annum for an ordinary ranker usually paid in three instalments) as well as donatives in lieu of looting. Almost as remarkable as Galba's legacy as emperor for seven months is the good life he enjoyed before he claimed the purple. He was among the wealthiest men in the empire, and it is said that he never went anywhere, not even on a casual afternoon jaunt, with less than ten thousand *aurei* in a second carriage.[66]

Moreover, aside from the jealousies such a victory as gaining the throne of the world aroused, there was the problem of the vanquished. Having secured the support of the Senate and, initially, that of the Praetorian Guard too, Galba needed to pursue a policy of reconciliation so as to defuse the obvious fear in the minds of those who had backed the wrong horse. Iulius Caesar, for instance, attempted to act magnanimously towards former enemies and welcomed them into his fold. In any civil war, and this one was no different in this respect from the one Caesar had fought and won, since no one can know the future, it is quite easy to pick the wrong side. Toleration should have been the order of the day, but Galba systematically eliminated those individuals who had opposed him – only lip service appears to have been paid to niceties like evidence – and then went on to offer 'jobs for the boys' on a lavish scale. This made his principate seem more corrupt than it really was, and even those worthy of office were made to feel left out and finally alienated.[67]

As for 'jobs for the boys' the list was grand indeed, which is certainly not the case with those listed, men described by Tacitus as detestable. Take for instance, Titus Vinius Rufrinus (*cos.* AD 69), born in AD 21, who fell from grace under Caius Caligula but enjoyed honours under Claudius, praetor, legionary legate, proconsul of Gallia Narbonensis, a man who 'applied his powers to vice or virtue' with equal vigour.[68] Then there was Cornelius Laco, a freedman, or Icelus, another freedman and very close to Galba, in fact so close Suetonius hints at a homosexual relationship between the two.[69] Icelus was seen as a social upstart, specially so when Galba made him an *eques* and awarded him the name Martianus,[70] which was contrary to the Tiberian law that laid down no freedman could be elevated to equestrian rank without first having three previous generations of free birth. And finally the antihero of our story, one of the future Flavian chieftains, the smooth opportunist Marcus Antonius Primus (b. *c.* AD 20),[71] thrown out of the Senate by Nero for fraud (AD 61),[72] made his way to Iberia and joined Galba, who finally restored his senatorial rank and gave him command of the newly minted *legio VII Galbiana* (later officially *Gemina*).[73]

With the benefit of hindsight we can all now see, Galba would have been more prudent to have collected about him the eminent men of Nero's reign. However, as we know well, he chose to estrange them. Thus, the plot to remove Galba hatched by Nymphidius Sabinus. Between the death of Nero and the arrival of Galba in Rome Nymphidius Sabinus had been a very busy man, for he had orchestrated the early retirement of his colleague Ofonius Tigellinus and so when the new emperor reached his capital the Praetorian Guard was commanded by one man.[74] Understandably, Nymphidius Sabinus was outraged when Galba promoted to praetorian prefect the freedman Cornelius Laco as a replacement for Ofonius Tigellinus.[75] Moreover, he had expected a better reward for bringing the praetorians over to Galba. The plot failed horribly and Nymphidius Sabinus was killed by his own men. On top of this Galba had other pressing problems, namely the lack of coin in the imperial coffers.[76] Which brings us around to Galba's avarice. This was a further cause of resentment (and would be the prime cause of his imperial exit). Galba, for example, penalized those Gaulish and Iberian towns that had opposed him, the punishment taking the form of massive taxation and removal of their gold and the like.[77] More serious of course was his failure to honour the rewards promised by the now dead Nymphidius Sabinus to the Praetorian Guard.

In retrospect – although this was not evident at the time – this can be seen as the beginning of the end of Galba, since no emperor can long survive without control over the Praetorian Guard. But of course all this is wisdom after the event. A good way to illustrate the several troubles at Galba's feet is by looking at the relationship between him and that rather queer unit inaugurated by Nero in the last days of his reign, viz. *legio I Adiutrix*.[78] Raised by taking sailors from *classis Misenensis*, it was stationed in nearby Neapolis (Naples). However, Nero had failed to complete the formalities of turning these onetime leghorns into pukka legionaries, that is to say, the award of Roman citizenship, citizen status being a prerequisite for service in the legions.[79] It is clear that Nero had promised them citizenship, and they wanted Galba to honour that promise. When the new emperor stood before the tiro legion he simply sent it packing, which incited a riot. Galba called out his cavalry, which proceeded to cut the rioters down. Once order was finally restored, Galba then revived the old custom of decimation, executing by lot a proportion of the legion's soldiers, which only made matters worse because it guaranteed to kill innocent men.[80] As the saying goes, they that sow the wind shall reap the whirlwind. It was no surprise, then, that *I Adiutrix* was one of the first legions to declare for the next contestant seeking to be raised to the throne of the world.[81]

Nearly six months after having taken up the reins of abusive power, Galba was still at large. Yet on the Kalends of January AD 69 his end was literally in sight. The legions of the Rhine mutinied, refusing to take their annual oath of allegiance to Galba as commander-in-chief and proclaiming their own emperor instead.[82] This was a serious warning. After this Galba's principate galloped from crisis to collapse.

There is a commonsense proverb recited by Homer, 'better to flee from death than feel its grip'.[83] Yet those who say that one always senses the approach of death are probably wrong. Death is not something the victim realizes. It comes like the night. When the twilight falls, it is there already tugging at your elbow, following you like your shadow, and you cannot avoid it. For death knows neither clemency nor forbearance nor justice; it is death. And so it was for Galba a fortnight later. He never saw death coming until it was upon him, a dirty, brutish fellow who drove a sword deep into his throat. The more general account is that upon realizing what was happening he presented his throat to his assassins and told them to do their duty.[84] In broad daylight and in the Forum, Galba was untidily butchered like some sacrificial pig by his own praetorians,[85] seduced by a certain Otho who thereby took by force the Principate he had hoped for by adoption.[86] Otho had wanted the throne, he took the throne, and that was that.

Chapter 3

The Hundred Days' Emperor

I t was a cheap and ugly death that had overtaken Galba, the emperor, to be cruelly murdered by one of his own soldiers. Perhaps he would have avoided that if he had adopted Otho instead of Piso Licinianus. If he had done that, he may have lived a little longer to enjoy the power he had usurped.

On the other hand, perhaps not.

Military revolts almost always did fail, mainly for two reasons. First, all the Iulio-Claudians bar Nero had worked hard to build links with the soldiers independent of the chain of command. Soldiers received gifts on imperial accessions and anniversaries, gifts paid in good coin that often celebrated the military achievements of the Augustan family. A ruler who depended on military support could not afford to be indifferent, and sensible emperors made sure that they and those who featured in their dynastic plans visited camps and met the men. Take for instance the military revolt of Lucius Arruntius Camillus Scribonianus. When he tried to get the soldiers to march against Claudius the eagles could not be anointed with perfumed oils and dressed with floral garlands, and the standards resisted all efforts to remove them from their turf altars. The soldiers took it as an omen and backed down.[1] For soldiers to go against an emperor, who was virtually a living god to them, was no easy matter by a long chalk.

The second obstacle was the fragmentation of the Roman élite, the only body from which any plausible successor could emerge. Empire wide at any one time there were some twenty-five senators commanding legions, and about as many governing provinces. Then from the *ordo equester* there were a clutch of governors of the smaller provinces, the commanders of the main fleets, the prefect of Egypt in Alexandria along with two *praefecti legionum*, and a few dozen procurators here and there. In Rome there were the rest of the senators, five hundred or so, and the commanders of the Praetorian Guards and of the *cohortes urbanae*. Staging a *coup d'état* meant forging some sort of consensus among all these. It did work out for Otho in Rome, but only at first and not elsewhere.

Marcus Salvius Otho was one of Nero's closest friends and confidants, and as a member of the emperor's inner circle this made him a powerful figure.[2] But influence cannot be counted on to last for long, and Otho's imperial favour wavered when the emperor took too strong a liking to his wife, the gorgeous but notorious Poppaea Sabina who was said to bathe in the milk of 500 donkeys, and the jilted husband was 'banished' to the remote Atlantic province of Lusitania to serve as its governor.[3] This he did for ten years 'with considerable moderation and restraint'.[4] Out of revenge (and in hopes of great personal gains) Otho assisted Galba to become emperor.

When the elderly Galba, whose two sons had both died at a young age,[5] adopted as his son and successor Lucius Calpurnius Piso Frugi Licinianus, a long-named but a little-known scion of old Roman nobility – he was a descendant of those republican warlords Pompey and Crassus – a firm friend was turned into a mortal enemy. Although the Iulio-Claudians had used adoption, the idea that a successor might be selected on the basis of merit and not on the basis of his familial relationship to the emperor was a novel one.[6] The thirty-one-year-old Piso Licinianus was highly acceptable to the Senate, enjoying as he did the considerable advantage of having been one of Nero's victims, not, like Otho, one of his favourites. However, he was entirely unknown to the army and extremely inconvenient for others in the Galban camp. The scene was now set for the horrors of AD 69.

Friendship in these dark days is ironic at best, treacherous more commonly. The coal of resentment was perhaps burning brightly now, and so Otho decided to deal with Galba the biblical way: 'No man, no problem.' If Galba believed in omens, as he obviously did in prophecies, then the clearest sign of his impending downfall came on 15 January, the day of his death. While he was making a sacrifice on an altar before the temple of Apollo on the Palatine, the *haruspex* Umbricius,[7] on examining the entrails of the victim, warned the emperor that danger was lurking and his liquidators were close by. Otho, by contrast, who was standing just behind Galba, interpreted this warning as a favourable omen. He felt sure of success when one of his freedmen came and informed him that the architect and the contractors were waiting for him. 'It had been arranged thus to indicate that the soldiers were assembling, and that the preparations of the conspiracy were complete.'[8]

Having turned to the praetorians, who happily proclaimed him emperor, Otho then had them remove Galba, along with the detested Piso Licinianus, who, for a brief five days, had been officially Servius Sulpicius Galba Caesar, son of Augustus. One cannot help but wonder, with the twilight of eternity closing down over his principate, if Galba recalled his own triumphant elevation and formal recognition all those months ago. Perhaps he felt a sudden cold certainty that this was how it had been meant to end, in a short and meaningless spate of violence, a fulfilment of a prophecy of the first emperor. For Augustus had once beckoned the young Galba to him, quizzed him on personal matters and finally conjured up a one-line horoscope in Greek: 'You too will taste a little of my power, child.'[9] And a little taste it was indeed. The Senate, in indecent haste, recognized Otho on the same day.

Otho's claim to power depended partly on his association with Nero. In age and appearance, style and taste – even taste in women, we are told – he was closest to the man whom he had helped Galba to topple.[10] In supplanting Galba, Otho revived causes that had been Nero's. Otho was even billed as the 'New Nero' and 'Otho Nero',[11] a desperate attempt to find popular support for his principate, which did initially work. The legions of the Danube took the oath of fidelity to Otho, as did those in Syria, Iudaea, Egypt and Roman North Africa.[12] Fortune did not favour the new emperor, however, because, as Tacitus points out, law and order were in the hands of the soldiers who now named their own officers and demanded reforms, such as an end to the paying of bribes to centurions so as to escape menial tasks.[13] Still, Otho's biggest problem was the fact that his forces were scattered and he was immediately faced with Vitellius' powerful provincial army (the seven Rhine legions having given him the imperial salutation), which was now marching rapidly on Rome. Though he had been the prime beneficiary of the toppling of his predecessor, he realized that it could be repeated to his cost. Otho therefore proposed a system of joint rule and was even willing to marry Vitellius' daughter, or so said Suetonius.[14] All this to no avail as we shall see, and besides, the Rhine tide could not be turned. Otho had no diplomatic cards left to play. For the emperor there was no other solution than to face his rival's army.

On 14 March Otho left Rome and made camp at Bedriacum (now the village of Tornato), just north of the Po. On 14 April the decisive confrontation took place, in a neighbourhood dotted with vineyards somewhere between Bedriacum and Cremona.[15] Badly outnumbered by that of Vitellius, Otho's army was overcome, the restlessness of the praetorians being a factor in the result too. Vitellius' generals had delivered on his behalf in open battle the knockout blow, and he travelled to Rome at his convenience. Deserted, Otho, having put his affairs in order and burnt all letters containing disparaging remarks about Vitellius, had taken his own life.[16] He had been emperor for a little more than three months, dying 'in the ninety-fifth day of his reign'.[17]

Modern commentators, amateur and professional alike, have found one major problem with Otho's campaign in the alluvial wetlands of the Po basin, namely its timetable. Galba fell on 15 January, but Otho did not quit Rome and head north until 14 March, the battle being fought one month later on the 14 April. Why did Otho start the campaign to save his principate so late? Was this a strategic blunder on the emperor's part? Those who argue so are indulging in the second guessing that is so simple long after the event. Moreover, not only are they making too much of the luxury of hindsight, but they are also failing to consider three significant facts.

First, the Vitellian forces were certainly not expected to be in northern Italy by mid April, the month the main Alpine passes were thawing. Unfortunately for Otho, the winter of AD 68/9 turned out to be an unusually mild one.

Second, the Othonians themselves were expecting to engage the Vitellian forces outside Italy and, as Tacitus says, 'within the limits of Gaul'.[18] Events would soon show how badly mistaken they were.

Third, Otho needed time to muster his army, particularly the four legions from Dalmatia and Pannonia.

This last point is more important than many a modern commentator will readily admit, but for myself, I shall make no bones about it. All Otho's planning was frustrated by the Vitellian generals who led the invasion forces, Aulus Caecina Alienus, legate of *legio IIII Macedonica*, and Fabius Valens, legate of *legio I Germania*. Despite their faults, which seem to be many, they were both very able men who wasted no time in traversing the trouble-free Alpine passes much earlier than expected.[19] Caecina Alienus even found the time en route to pick a quarrel with the Helvetii, many of whom, ill-armed and ill-trained, were either slaughtered or sold into slavery.[20] But why did the Othonian legions seem slow to mobilize and march to join the emperor in Italy?

According to Tacitus the four legions of Dalmatia and Pannonia, 'from each of which a *vexillatio* of 2,000 were sent on in advance', exhibited 'a tardiness of movement proportionate to their strength and solidity'.[21] However, he does not provide us with any details on the progress of these Danube *vexillationes* marching to northern Italy. We do know that the *vexillatio* of *legio XIII Gemina* took part in a skirmish action prior to First Cremona, and that the whole legion fought at the battle itself,[22] and the *vexillatio* of *legio XIIII Gemina Martia Victrix* actually made the battle but not its main body, which was 'a few days away'.[23] But what of the other three legions from Dalmatia and Pannonia, especially the one commanded by Marcus Antonius Primus? Of this matter concerning this particular *legatus legionis* more will be said later. The one legion from Dalmatia (*XI Claudia pia fidelis*) arrived far too late to participate in First Cremona, while the three legions from Moesia (*III Gallica, VII Claudia pia fidelis, VIII Augusta*) got no further than the town of Aquileia at the head of the Adriatic.[24]

Otho wasted no time in vain regrets for what might have been, and it is now time for us to consider the background to the council of war called by the emperor, the issue at stake being to either fight immediately or hold back and delay. Tacitus only offers one side of the argument, that is to say, the case for delaying.[25] Plutarch, on the other hand, presents both sides of the argument, the high moral of the Othonian army after the initial skirmish with the Vitellians having prompted many senior officers to push for an immediate decision there and then, and besides, they saw no sense in waiting for the Vitellian army to be reinforced.[26]

Among Otho's generals was Caius Suetonius Paulinus, onetime legate governor of Britannia and nemesis of Boudica. It was he who had defeated, along with Publius Marius Celsus, Caecina Alienus during a brush at a location Tacitus calls *ad Castores*.[27] This was a small wayside shrine on the Via Postumia rather less than thirteen Roman miles east of Cremona, which was dedicated to Castor and Pollux of heavenly origin,[28] Leda's twin boys, eternally fixed in the ephemeral stardust. However, victory gained, Suetonius Paulinus would not allow his men to follow up their advantage and was consequently accused of treachery. As Tacitus reports, 'it was very commonly said on both sides, that Caecina and his whole army might have been destroyed, had not Suetonius Paulinus given the signal of recall'.[29] Worse still, in the eyes of his accusers, now that Fabius Valens had joined his forces with those of Caecina Alienus, Suetonius Paulinus was very much in favour of further caution, arguing that the Vitellian generals, unlike themselves, would have no more troops to hand. Moreover, he reasoned, it was preferable to wait for the summer, by which time the Vitellians would be tightening their belts for want of supplies.[30]

Notwithstanding, Otho overruled the very experienced Suetonius Paulinus and made the decision to fight post-haste, with no reason being given. This may seem astonishing. But we must remember, it is far easier to recognize disaster the day after, than the day before. To know and understand the motives of another person is practically impossible even when those concerned live in daily contact with each other, and to evaluate correctly the motives behind the decision made by the emperor on this occasion is well nigh impossible. Both Tacitus and Plutarch speculate upon why the scales were tipped in favour of immediate action, the latter authority reckoning the high moral of the praetorians, champing at the bit and thirsting for victory, prompted Otho to stake all on the lottery of battle.[31] More telling, perhaps, is the fact that there was a move afoot, initiated by the senior officers of both sides, to seek a peaceful settlement, and certainly some of these trimming gentlemen were quite prepared to jettison one or both emperors, and even contemplated offering the throne once more to Verginius Rufus.[32]

At the time Otho made his fateful decision one does not need to be possessed of an overly vivid imagination to appreciate that the emperor was probably rather anxious about the loyalty of his soldiers, not to mention some of his senior officers, and a sustained defensive stand along the Po could possibly see his army gradually melt away. All these thoughts must have run through the emperor's head as he made up his mind. Besides, if Plutarch is to be believed, with the enthusiasm of the praetorians at fever pitch, these stalwart Othonians would have been in no mood for a long, uneventful defensive campaign. And, like a good general, Otho decided quickly enough that the best defence is attack.

Let a general assemble his men for action and lead them on to the battlefield. He may not be prepared outwardly to admit it, but in the pit of his stomach he will probably know exactly how they may be expected to perform. He knows how well or badly they have been drilled in the use of their weapons, and how quickly they can change formation as the action demands. He knows how fast they have marched to the field. He knows if and when they were last rewarded or worse, perhaps they have been existing on promises. At his back he can hear their muttered grumbles, he can smell their fear. And being human himself he is caught up in the general feeling within his army, be it one of outright determination or abject terror. His outward calmness will have a limited effect, but will it be enough?

When his men advance into mêlée, the chips are well and truly down. The enemy, who until now are a mere faceless mass, are about to become individuals. It is kill or be killed. So we are faced with the simple truth of it, the fact that until each general puts his force to the test he has only a slight idea as to the final outcome. Sleeting missiles and cold steel are only partial battle winners. The key to victory is morale.

There does not seem to be much point in delving minutely into the meaning of the word 'morale', most people nowadays having a very good appreciation of what it means but, just for the record, let me quickly say that, in military terms, it is the state of mind of a single soldier in particular or of a unit in general, with special reference to his or its enthusiasm, expertise, training, faith in the immediate command element, physical state, fatigue and a host of other relevant factors. Morale, a movable factor, varies as the battle ebbs and flows, as casualties mount, as the enemy breaks and runs, as the unit standard bearer is cut down and his beloved standard is carried away in triumph by his killer. What it really boils down to is the question of whether soldiers will carry out the mission assigned to them, no matter how fraught with difficulties it may be, or whether, as a result of unwillingness – in this particular event, are they willing to fight and die for Otho's cause or are they pressed men with little stomach for the job? – their experience, especially in regard to the battle losses they may already have suffered, or their lack of confidence or training, causes them to be incapable of obeying orders and to shrink from the perils involved in achieving the objective they have been assigned.

While, of course, it is abundantly apparent that the better the training, the greater the length of service, and the more genuine their enthusiasm for the cause for which they are fighting, the more likely it is that soldiers will obey orders that are likely to put them in the greatest danger, this yardstick of obedience and behaviour does not always hold good and, while still within the framework of the possible, the unpredictable could and did happen. Which brings us nicely back to First Cremona.

We are pretty sure that the Vitellian army included *V Alaudae* and *XXI Rapax*, and strong *vexillationes* from all the other five Rhine legions. There was also *I Italica*, which had been picked up en route at Lugdunum, the provincial capital of Gallia Lugdunensis. The Othonian army included *I Adiutrix* and *XIII Gemina*, as well as a *vexillatio* from *XIIII Gemina Martia Victrix*,[33] the praetorians, and a force of gladiators from Rome. On the day, Otho himself remained behind with a sizeable force of praetorians at Brixellum (Brescello). Tacitus rightly sees this as a grave mistake on Otho's part, not only because it meant the absence of those detailed to protect the emperor, 'but the spirit of those who remained was broken, for the men suspected their generals, and Otho, who alone had the confidence of the soldiers, while he himself trusted in none but them, had left the generals' authority on a doubtful footing'.[34]

Leaving a strong detachment to guard their camp at Bedriacum, thereby reducing their numbers yet again, the Othonians marched towards Cremona along the Via Postumia. A short distance from that town they unexpectedly encountered the Vitellians, the Othonians evidently tired after their long march. It was now that the men of *I Adiutrix*, the leading Othonian legion, got it into their heads that their Vitellian opponents had decided to desert to their side. The cheers and greetings of the Othonians were answered by fierce yells and abuse from the Vitellians. This inauspicious incident was doubly unfortunate for the Othonians. It convinced the Vitellians that they had no fight in them, and the bizarre behaviour of the greenhorn *I Adiutrix* created the uneasy feeling amongst its fellow formations that it meant to forsake them.

One does not have to be a student of military matters to be aware that, in warfare, terrain features, whether they be woods, rivers or hills, exercise a powerful influence on the conduct of operations and that the possession of a certain piece of real estate, elevated ground for example, can be of inestimable value to a military force, operating greatly to the detriment of an enemy army. So, without further ado, we should turn to the real physical setting of these events, a flat landscape crossed by two linear features, the river Po and the Via Postumia, though visibility and movement were restricted by the water ditches, poplar trees, fields of millet and barley and vineyards. Thus, like the two opposing armies in chess, one the mirror image of the other, the Vitellians and the Othonians glared at one another across a maze of vineyards and watercourses, which made up the small deadly space between them. All that remained now was them to rush together and get to grips in the massive vulgar brawl provided by hand-to-hand combat.

Some of the heaviest fighting was where *I Adiutrix*, recently raised from the Misenum marines and eager to gain its first triumph, and the veteran *XXI Rapax* clashed head to head. Despite their initial *faux pas*, the former marines acquitted themselves extremely well, even managing to overrun the front ranks of their opponents and capture their eagle. The eagle, *aquila*, was the totem animal of the legions, so to lose it was the ultimate disgrace for a legion, and *XXI Rapax* gathered itself and charged the attackers in turn, which showed that the resolution of this legion was still unbroken and betokened the discipline of veteran soldiery. The fighting was obviously vicious, the legate of *I Adiutrix*, Orfidius Benignus, fell fighting as the Vitellians strove to retrieve their sacred eagle. This they failed to do, but they did harvest a number of standards and flags.

Much earlier we asked the question if the tall, fit and superbly disciplined men of *legio I Italica* could fight. In the centre of the battlefield Nero's handpicked legionaries came face to face with the Otho's praetorians who, as we know, had been itching for battle. The two sides, equally determined, slogged it out hand-to-hand, throwing against each other the weight of their armoured bodies and bossed shields.[35] Before contact, the usual discharge of *pila* had been discarded, and *gladii* and axes were used to puncture metal and man. We will have more to say about Roman fighting techniques in a little while.

At the other end of the Othonian battle line, however, *XIII Gemina* and the *vexillatio* from *XIIII Gemina Martia Victrix* were roundly defeated by *V Alaudae*.

Tacitus' details are rather vague at this point, but it appears that *XIII Gemina* turned on its heels and fled at the sight of the charging *V Alaudae*. This left the heavily outnumbered *vexillatio* of *XIIII Gemina Martia Victrix* in the lurch, and consequently it 'was surrounded by a superior force',[36] and presumably either annihilated or the survivors given quarter.

While these events were unfolding *I Adiutrix* met its own fate. Reeling from the loss of its legate, and presumably many of those around him, the legion eventually gave way when the Batavi, flushed with their thumping victory over the gladiators, took them in the flank. Earlier in the day Otho had ordered Flavius Sabinus to stage a diversionary attack from the south bank of the Po, and consequently he had loaded his gladiators onto boats supplied by the *classis Ravennas*. Having landed on the other side and ventured a ways from the riverbank, they were suddenly pounced upon by the Batavi under Alfenus Varus. Most of them made it back to the river only to be cut down by other Batavi positioned there to block their escape. So, with the right and left now gone, we can safely speculate that the praetorians in the centre threw in the towel and called it a day. The surviving Othonians fled back to their distant camp at Bedriacum, and the next day, with some reluctance it should be said, took the oath of allegiance to Vitellius.[37] These are the bare bones of First Cremona.

We mentioned earlier Roman fighting techniques. The combatants at First Cremona were trained swordsmen, and this had been so for legionaries since the days of Marius.[38] As recruits they had been taught to attack with the *gladius* by thrusting and not by slashing. When the term 'martial art' is mentioned, most of the world usually assumes it to be synonymous with 'Asian fighting art'. This is no surprise since the medium of film is notorious for misrepresenting Roman fighting techniques. The *gladius* stars in most films about ancient Rome and the legionary's craft with this fearsomely effective weapon is often reduced to the Hollywood myth that he merely crudely bludgeoned his opponent or hacked and slashed savagely.

Yet Roman swordsmanship was not the hewing, blade-on-blade, ring of steel affair so common on the silver screen today. 'A slash-cut, whatever its force, seldom kills' Vegetius said,[39] but it makes for great artistic drama. As he rightly emphasized, a thrust with the sword has penetrating power, whereas the slash, which often is difficult to aim and control, may strike a bone or the opponent's shield and so will do comparatively little damage. On the one hand, the thrust is delivered with the strength of the entire body, while the slash is executed solely by the elevation of the right arm and carries the weight of the weapon. On the other hand, a slashing blow can be performed more quickly than a thrust, and with the last technique there is always the danger of getting the blade stuck. No thrust can be made with effect or security where the sword does not at once free itself from the object to which it is applied. Otherwise it must be turned in the hand and give a contusion rather than a stab wound, for which reason those wounds are most severe that are made nearest the point. Even so, to raise the arm to make a slashing blow exposes the entire right side of the body, and a legionary knew it was unnecessary to thrust his blade in deeply to slay his opponent because such action wasted precious time in recovering the weapon.

The swordplay itself had a typical scenario that pitted the training and discipline of a Roman legionary against the courage and individualism of a 'barbarian' tribesman. Thus, legionaries were accustomed to facing and fighting an enemy who followed a rough and ready tactical doctrine – a headlong rush towards the opposition – which made the best of a war-band culture. Protected by armour, welded by a comprehensive system of military training and institutionalized discipline into an efficient fighting machine, the legionaries, as long as their line absorbed and contained the sheer ferocity and raw energy of the Celtic, Germanic, Dacian – take your pick – attack, could expect to thrash the living daylights out of any of them. Ferociously brave they undoubtedly were, but they lacked the key protocols of forbearance and discipline.[40]

Roman battle drills are a phenomenon easily described. Having thrown the *pilum* and charged into contact, the standard drill for the legionary was to punch the enemy in the face with the shield-boss and then jab him in the belly with the razor-sharp point of the *gladius*. The use of the thrust also meant the legionary kept most of his torso well covered, and thus protected, by the *scutum*. We catch a glimpse of this sort of thing at the battle of Mancetter (AD 61), for in his version of events of that day Tacitus has the Roman commander Suetonius Paulinus delivering a pre-battle speech in which he instructs his legionaries to knock over the Britons by punching them with their shields and then to jab them with their swords. In other words, he is reminding them that they have three offensive weapons, *pilum*, *scutum*, and *gladius*: 'Just keep in close order. Throw your javelins (*pila*), and then carry on: use your shield-bosses (*umbonis*) to fell them, swords (*gladii*) to kill them. Do not think of plunder. When you have won, you will have everything.'[41]

Essentially, this is how it probably worked. Having drawn his *gladius* the legionary now adopted a very slight crouch, with the left foot forward, holding the *scutum* horizontally in front with the left hand and using it to cover the upper legs, the torso, and lower face.[42] By keeping the *scutum* close to his body, the legionary not only gained optimum protection but also increased the range of the punch. His body would have been slightly turned in profile to his opponent to present as small as target as possible, with his elbows tucked close to the torso so as not to expose the vulnerable underarm. His feet were roughly a shoulder width apart. In this balanced position he could put all his body weight, which rested on the back leg, behind a punch with his *scutum*. The footwork was simple and direct as walking, for the legionary instantly stepped forward with his right foot, the weight of the body now helping to deliver a jab with the *gladius* held in the right hand with its edges up and down, perpendicular to the ground. It is important to note here that although the right shoulder would deliver some of the power behind the thrust, the real power of the thrust came from the rotation of the legionary's hips as he stepped forward.

A panel from the Adamklissi Tropaeum Traiani shows a legionary punching his opponent's face with the boss of his *scutum*, in this way unbalancing him, and jabbing him in the belly with his *gladius*.[43] Here the *gladius* is being used primarily in an upward thrust directed from below the *scutum*, the legionary getting in under the opponent's attack and penetrating his lower stomach or groin, the soft, fleshy parts below the rib-cage. Penetration wounds to these exposed areas were almost always fatal, leading in a few days, if not hours, to an agonizing death from shock, peritonitis, or other infections, as the contents of the intestines spilled out into the abdominal cavity and the victim shrank from blood and fluid loss. The belly wound was what Homer described as 'the worst the god of battle deals to wretched men'.[44] And there it is, punch-jab, the fighting technique that made the legionary a formidable fighter.

'It is not the "free creations of the mind" of generals of genius that have revolutionized war', Engels once wrote, 'but the inventions of better weapons and changes in the human material, the soldiers; at the very most the part played by generals of genius is limited to adapting methods of fighting to the new weapons and combatants.'[45] This was certainly so with the Roman legionary and his *gladius*.

Nowadays it is fashionable to allege that the Principate army was the finest one in the world. I am willing to concede that it was powerful by the standards of the time. The question of military effectiveness can be approached from a variety of angles, and if one starts with the obvious criterion of battlefield performance, the Principate army emerges with considerable credit. But people who argue along these lines fail to grasp the fact that the Principate army, for all its rigorous training and emphasis on swordsmanship, was a serious force *only* against semi-barbaric peoples, small neighbours and disintegrating third-world states. To understand this point better, let us take a look at Tacitus' description of First Cremona, and we will quote him in full, for he deserves it:

2.42 At this moment, the enemy [i.e. the Vitellians] advanced with unbroken ranks. In fighting qualities and numbers he had the advantage. As for the Othonians, scattered, outnumbered and weary as they were, they went into action gallantly. Indeed, as the battle was fought over a wide area thickly planted with a maze of vines and vine-props, it presented a variety of aspects. The two sides made contact at long and short range, in loose or compact formation. On the high road [Via Postumia], Vitellians and Othonians fought hand-to-hand, throwing the weight of their bodies and shield-bosses (*umbonis*) against each other. The usual discharge of *pila* was scrapped, and swords (*gladii*) and axes (*securis*) used to pierce helmets and armour. Knowing each other [i.e. the Othonian praetorians and *legio I Italica*][46] and watched by their comrades, they fought the fight that was to settle the whole campaign.

2.43 As it turned out, two legions made contact in open country between the Padus (Po) and the road [Via Postumia]. They were Vitellian *legio XXI Rapax*, long known and famous, and on the Othonian side *legio I Adiutrix*, which had never fought before, but was in high spirits and avid of distinction in its first action. *Legio I Adiutrix* overran the front ranks of *legio XXI Rapax*, and carried off their eagle (*aquila*). Smarting under this humiliation, the latter got their own back by charging *legio I Adiutrix*, who lost their legate (*legatus legionis*), Orfidius Benignus, and a great number of standards (*signa*) and flags (*vexilla*). In another part of the field, *legio V [Alaudae]* punished *legio XIII [Gemina]*, while the *vexillatio* from *legio XIIII [Gemina Martia Victrix]* was outnumbered and rolled up. Long after the Othonian commanders had fled, Aulus Caecina Alienus and Fabius Valens [i.e. the Vitellian generals] were still bringing up reinforcements to strengthen their men. Then, at the eleventh hour, came the Batavi [*cohortes*], after routing the force of gladiators.[47] These had crossed the Padus in their ships only to be done to death in the very water by the *cohortes* confronting them. As a sequel to this success, the Batavi now delivered their onslaught on the Othonian flank.[48]

When Roman armies were pitted against each other we might expect sophisticated tactics skilfully applied. But Tacitus' brief but dramatic account tells us this was far from the case. First Cremona was a straightforward pounding match between lines of grim legionaries, with no opportunity for elaborate tactics, and victory going to the side that did not break, one based on dogged perseverance rather than tactical brilliance. Roman tactics were basically aggressive, with the doctrine of the offensive dominant, relying more on raw, crude strength than on surprise.[49] Such spirit of aggression was effective, but could be costly. As Appian said of Romans fighting Romans in another context, 'they spoke a single language, shared a single technique of fighting, and their training and endurance were similar'.[50] Moreover, we must not forget what a grudge fight is like, for that is what we are witnessing here at this frantic civil war battle fought on ground 'thickly planted with a maze of vines and vine-props'.[51] The fighting had been hectic, bitter even. As Colonel Ardant du Picq, the French military theorist, noted: 'Sword to sword combat was the most deadly. It presented the most sudden changes, because it was the one in which the individual had the greatest and most immediate influence. Other methods of combat were simpler.'[52]

All battles essentially have the same end. You win them or you lose them. Otho lost this one. The dissipation of the praetorians was ruinous, so was his own absence from the field of battle. It is a truism that a soldier's primary *raison d'être* was to wage war, to kill without being killed, and as Ardant du Picq sagely remarks, 'man does not go to war in order to fight, but to win'.[53] Fighting, like soldering, differs little from time to time or place to place. It is something that cannot be properly understood by those who have not been there. Even among soldiers themselves, there exists a gulf between men who have 'seen the elephant' and those who have not. This gulf is well illustrated by an incident in the immediate aftermath of First Cremona, as told by Suetonius. Suetonius Laetus, our biographer's father, was a military tribune in *XIII Gemina* and he told his son what happened when a soldier brought the news to Otho of the defeat of his army: 'When the garrison [of praetorians at Brixellum] called him a liar and a cowardly deserter, the man fell on his sword at Otho's feet.

At this sight, my father reported, Otho cried out that he would never again risk the lives of such gallant men, who had deserved so well'.[54] It was not to be so.

'In other matters, as Cato says, mistakes can be corrected afterwards; errors in war do admit of amendment, because the penalty follows immediately.'[55] The decision to fight was wrong but understandable. Otho was roundly defeated, and his suicide quickly followed. Whatever else he may have been, the emperor was not a coward in any sense of the term, and in Plutarch's opinion Otho's self-destruction to prevent a bloodbath and to spare the state was the most honourable deed ever performed by him.[56] Thus ended the hundred days' rule of the usurper Marcus Salvius Otho, inaugurated by an act of homicidal betrayal, terminated with a deed of patriotic self-sacrifice.

There is an old saying I have learnt to trust: never judge a book by its cover. To be sure, Otho was best remembered for his bosom association, for better or worse, with the late Nero. Yet he remains an enigma – part profligate Neronian wastrel and part conscientious military commander willing to give his life for the good of the state. Having liked the soft life too much, none of his contemporaries thought he would have ever made a man of war. But, 'utterly unlike what common report had pictured him', he had donned an iron cuirass and, unkempt and ill-shaven, led his men out of Rome in person and on foot for the war with the Vitellians.[57] Our literary sources are at a loss to explain the paradox too, Tacitus possibly encapsulates this Othonian paradox best when he reasons philosophically: 'By two daring acts, one most atrocious, the other singularly noble, he earned in the eyes of prosperity about an equal share of infamy and of glory.'[58]

Perhaps, like that other great survivor Petronius, Otho saw it was safer to appear a *roué* in Nero's perverted court,[59] and Tacitus does warn us of the dangers of complacent responses to a man's outward appearance when he says that the 'soul of Otho was not effeminate (*mollis*) like his person'.[60] Indeed, his gifts were not of valour alone, but generalship and statecraft. Otho proved to be an organized and efficient general, who appealed more to the professional soldier than to the private civilian. He seems to have been a capable governor too, with administrative talents that recalled those of his brilliant father.[61] Nonetheless, his violent overthrow of Galba, the lingering doubts that it raised about his character, and his unsuccessful offensive against Vitellius are all vivid reminders of the turbulence that plagued the Roman world between the principate of Nero and that of Vespasianus. Regrettably, the scenario would play itself out one more time before relative peace and stability returned to the empire.

But our story has got ahead of itself. Let us reverse three or so months and address how the Vitellian march on Rome came to be conceived and put into action. For this we must return to the Rhine frontier.

Chapter 4

The Epicurean Emperor

On becoming emperor, Galba had appointed Aulus Vitellius (*cos.* AD 48) to the governorship of Germania Inferior, a post recently vacated by the liquidation of its previous incumbent during a nasty little military *putsch*. Here we can postulate that another grave error on Galba's part was the recall from the Rhine of that careful commander, Verginius Rufus, the only man it seems who could restrain the fractious provincial army there.[1] We have no evidence to suggest that Vitellius was a Galba man, but he arrived in the province armed with an imperial mandate to sort out the troubles with the legions stationed there.[2] When Vitellius heard that the next-door legions had refused to pledge allegiance to Galba, the soldiers of *IIII Macedonica* and *XXII Primigenia*, even going so far as 'to break into pieces the images of Galba',[3] he sent a somewhat cryptic dispatch to his *legati legionum* telling them either to move against their dissident neighbours or to find themselves a new emperor.[4] Almost surely Vitellius was testing the waters by putting himself up for bid.[5]

We now find matters moving apace. The sequence of events went like this:

Although on the Kalends of January the legions of Germania Inferior had taken, albeit rather reluctantly, the oath of allegiance to Galba, two days later at Bonn-*Bonna*, Fabius Valens of *I Germanica*, 'the most energetic of the legates',[6] led his soldiers in taking an oath of loyalty to Vitellius, and the other three legions (*V Alaudae, XV Primigenia, XVI Gallica*) quickly followed suit. Forthwith, the three legions (*IIII Macedonica, XXI Rapax, XXII Primigenia*) in Germania Superior, along with the legate governor Hordeonius Flaccus, followed their example on the same day, partially out of ferocious hatred for Galba, who had been an insufferable martinet of the old republican type when legate governor of the same province thirty years before,[7] and partially out of genuine fondness for the good-humoured, unpretentious, easygoing Vitellius.[8] What is more, these Rhine soldiers had lost commanders who were anti-Galban but popular with the men, and genuinely felt they had lost out in the game of thrones, for Galba was certainly not their emperor but one who had been 'made in Iberia'.[9]

For a modern soldier this sort of attitude is hard to understand because first and foremost among the military virtues is loyalty, above all to one's salt. Correspondingly, the most despised military sin – beyond even cowardice – is betrayal of the oath of service. But before we condemn the Rhine rank and file we should look at the role of their senior officers in all this discontent. Take for instance the new legate of *legio IIII Macedonica*, Aulus Caecina Alienus. At the time of Nero's death he had been a quaestor in Baetica and was one of the foremost in joining the party of Galba. Despite his youth, he was rewarded by Galba with the command of a legion in Germania Superior. However, shortly afterwards he was caught misappropriating public funds, a weakness not to the liking of the new emperor, and orders were issued to have the embezzler prosecuted. Caecina Alienus, in revenge, induced his soldiers to switch their allegience to Vitellius.[10] Caecina Alienus had a strong motive for swapping his own allegiance at speed and, as we shall discover, he would do so again. It is difficult to avoid using adjectives such as wily, unscrupulous, ruthless and opportunistic to describe a man who merited his reputation for choosing the winning side in a conflict. As we shall find out in due course, Caecina Alienus will not disappoint us in this respect, turning out to be a man for all treasons.

And what about his future rival in the Vitellian triumvirate, Fabius Valens? As we recollect, he had already played a prominent if somewhat dubious part in the game of thrones, having pressed Verginius Rufus to take the plunge and assume the purple, and had removed Fonteius Capito from the stage for his apparent refusal to take up arms. His character is certainly drawn in the blackest colours by Tacitus, and among the various profligate commanders in that year of military anarchy, Fabius Valens seems to have been the most notorious for his avarice, venality and ruthlessness. He certainly built up a robust reputation for being an expert looter for his own personal benefit, and he certainly did not discourage his soldiers from following his example. And so, on the arrival of Vitellius in Germania Inferior as the successor of Fonteius Capito, Fabius Valens was one of the first to urge him to seize the chance to become master of the world.

Anyway, whether for personal motives or else, neither the legionary legates nor the military tribunes worked to restore the loyalty of their soldiers to the military oath,[11] and indeed some played notable parts in the affair while others just stood by and watched from the sidelines, not lifting a finger to dampen down the growing disorderliness as discipline slid towards ruin. In Germania Superior, for instance, when four centurions of *legio XXII Primigenia* honourably did their duty and moved to protect the threatened portraits of Galba, Hordeonius Flaccus, a rather 'indolent and timid' man,[12] did nothing to restore the iron rigours of discipline. The four were clamped in irons by the angry soldiers and later executed on Vitellius' orders.[13] For reasons of self-interest or personal survival, therefore, centurions perhaps tended to fall in with the views of the soldiers, the majority of which were well disposed to Vitellius while scorning Galba. Tacitus comments on the failure of these four centurions to prevent the revolt of their legion against Galba: 'After this no one retained any sense of duty, any recollection of his late allegiance, but, as usually happens in mutinies, the side of the majority became the side of all.'[14] There are no secrets in an army.

The speed of this military revolt was not only greatly helped by the lack of secrecy along the Rhine, but also by the concentration of troops there. Roman commanders favoured large concentrations of soldiers and generally, prior to Domitianus, legionary fortresses were permanent camps accommodating two legions. This was a concentration of some 10,000 legionaries in a single spot, and we find two such locations on the Rhine where in AD 69 Xanten-*Vetera* was garrisoned by *V Alaudae* and *XV Primigenia* and Mainz-*Mogontiacum* by *IIII Macedonica* and *XXII Primigenia*. Meanwhile, only some twenty Roman miles downstream from Mainz-*Mogontiacum* was the fortress of *Bonn*-Bonna, garrisoned by *I Germanica*, the prime instigators of the pro-Vitellius insurrection.[15]

Vitellius found the seven legions of the Rhine alert, ready for a spring campaign. He gathered up two of them (*V Alaudae, XXI Rapax*), along with *vexillationes* from the other five, and sent them onto Rome to topple Galba.[16] As we know, there were two lines of march over the Alps, Fabius Valens with 40,000 men from Germania Inferior and Caecina Alienus with 30,000 men from Germania Superior.[17] But events in Rome had moved apace, Galba having been replaced by Otho, and Tacitus reports the overall mood of gloom and doom in the capital, brought about because 'two men, who for shamelessness, indolence, and profligacy, were the most worthless of mortals, had been selected, it would seem, by some fatality to ruin the empire'.[18]

It is said military intelligence is of little value unless it is timely, but we are in the days when a galloping horse provided the fastest speed at which news travelled. Upon learning of Galba's assassination and Otho's accession en route,[19] the Vitellians did not turn back but without hesitation decided to topple Otho instead. Big events were clearly in the air. The spark will kindle a flame. The flame had been kindled. It had already reduced to ashes Galba's principate. Still, Vitellius was not a natural soldier and he certainly had no military talent: his preferred habitat, if Tacitus is to be believed, was the banqueting hall, not the campaigning tent, the sort of man who carried in his head the best recipes and testified to them by his bulk.[20] Anyway, Vitellius stayed safely put on the Rhine while his army did his dirty work near the Po, meeting death to secure his throne. When the hapless Otho committed suicide, the hedonistic Vitellius was left as sole emperor, lord of the Roman world. Or so it seemed.

Vitellius was soon recognized by the Senate who despatched a delegation to praise him for his recent military success. It met the new emperor, who had finally taken the road to Rome, at Ticinum (Pavia) around 18 May, almost a month after having left the capital. It was here, while Vitellius was holding a dinner party, to which he had invited his potential rival Verginius Rufus, that an inter-service wrestling match between a Roman legionary and a Gaulish auxiliary attracted a large crowd of soldiers. However, the excessively partisan spirit displayed by the rival supporters spoiled the match, as Tacitus reports:

> Thus it happened that two soldiers – one belonging to *legio V Alaudae*, the other a Gaulish auxiliary – were induced by high spirits to engage in a bout of wrestling. The legionary took a fall, and the Gaul jeered at his discomfited opponent. Thereupon the spectators who had gathered round took sides, the legionaries set about the auxiliaries, and two cohorts were annihilated.[21]

The number of dead – close to a thousand men, if Tacitus is correct – in what should have been a piddling dispute was a stark reminder that civil war had seriously sapped discipline.

From Ticinum Vitellius and his court moved eastward to Cremona, reaching there about 25 May. After a sightseeing tour of the battlefield, which was still carpeted with the putrefying remains of humans and horses some forty days after the battle,[22] Vitellius finally entered Rome in the middle of July, not in civilian dress but 'mounted on a splendid charger, with military cloak and sword'.[23] Having 'captured' the capital, with serene confidence he then proclaimed himself *consul perpetuus*, consul for life. He officially adopted the cognomen Germanicus too, a title first bestowed upon him by his army.[24] Militarily he had done nothing to deserve this title, but obviously, despite what Tacitus will have us believe, it was a political move to identify him and his family more closely with the Rhine legions, his chief supporters and their candidate, and this is surely confirmed by the fact that Vitellius also conferred the title on his six-year-old son.[25] He eventually took the normal imperial titles as well, including that of 'Augustus', so far refused, but not that of 'Caesar'. Like Otho before him, Vitellius wanted to create a working relationship with the Senate.[26] He was particularly conciliatory towards those men of senatorial rank who had backed Otho, letting off many of the Othonian generals such as Suetonius Paulinus and Marius Celsus, even Otho's brother Lucius Salvius Titianus. It is clear that neither vindictiveness nor cupidity were characteristics of the new emperor. All the same, these men would never appear again in public life.

Vitellius made it a habit to attend the Senate even when the agenda were trivial. He also allowed senators to take an active part in discussing all affairs, no matter how great or small. This was something new, for a working relationship between emperor and Senate was only rarely achieved; it had been so under Augustus and initially under Nero. Vitellius made all the right moves, unlike Galba, and even went as far as recalling all exiles, an intelligent concession to the Senate. The majority of his imperial measures were obviously made in order to pander to the prejudices of the senatorial aristocracy, but one apparent blot on his record was his alleged acts of wanton cruelty.

This particular accusation rests on two supposed crimes: the assassination at his bidding of the patrician Publius Cornelius Dolabella; the poisoning of the affluent and amiable Iunius Blaesus. The details of such stories have clearly been taken up by the Flavian agitprops, for Tacitus recalls how on hearing of Dolabella quitting his place of banishment with the intention of returning to Rome, the city prefect, Flavius Sabinus, charged him with treasonable behaviour. It was rumoured Dolabella was courting Othonian sympathizers with the intention of taking over those legions still loyal to Otho's memory and therefore making a bid for the purple.[27] Vitellius summoned Dolabella to appear before his imperial presence, but he was murdered en route at a wayside hostelry.[28] It seems that Dolabella was thought too dangerous to live. As a matter of interest, the city prefect was Vespasianus' elder brother, and the man who denounced Dolabella to Flavius Sabinus was one of his most intimate friends, Marcus Plancius Varus. Afterwards, he was to do well for himself, becoming the proconsul of Bithynia-Pontus under Vespasianus.[29]

The Blaesus tale is even more twisted. Tacitus tells us that while Vitellius was severely ill during the month of October, good friends of Blaesus held a Homeric repast in his honour for he, as governor of Gallia Lugdunensis, had aided the Vitellian move south into northern Italy and had brought over to the Vitellian cause *legio I Italica*, which had been stationed at the time at Lugdunum (Lyon).[30] Vitellius, however, observing all the splendour and unrestrained gaiety of the guests while he was ill, wondered why they should be enjoying themselves while he was not. Furthermore, his brother Lucius, an arch enemy of Blaesus, accused Blaesus of plotting treason, pointing out to Vitellius his prominent and noble lineage (the Iunii and Antonii were among his ancestors) and hence he was a possible rival. Tacitus then coolly tells us that Vitellius was 'determined to destroy him by poison', and then, the deed having been done, took a delight in the fact that 'he had feasted his eyes on the spectacle of his enemy's death'.[31] However, Tacitus does imply that Blaesus had been approached by that adept double-dealer Caecina Alienus to defect, but he had refused, being a 'righteous man and a lover of peace, who coveted no sudden elevation, much less the throne'.[32] It is impossible for us now to prove or disprove the Blaesus affair, and again we may have another example of distortion by the Flavian scribblers. Afer all, Vitellius' crimes come to pass after the summer when Vespasianus had finally decided to throw his hat into the ring.

We return now to the immediate aftermath of Otho's defeat and demise. The Othonian soldiers, now deprived of their beloved emperor, turned to Verginius Rufus, 'and in threatening language, at one time besought him to accept the principate, at another, to act as envoy to Caecina and Valens'.[33] Once again the wily Verginius Rufus refused the throne, but on this particular occasion he earns the soldiers' resentment as a result. As Tacitus points out, the man who could have been emperor 'was still admired, still retained his high reputation, but they hated him with the hatred of those who are despised'.[34]

As for the man who was emperor, his most pressing problem was what to do with his own as well as the Othonian legions, the latter edgy and scarcely inferior numerically to the Vitellian forces and, it must be said, not rendered worthless as a fighting force despite defeat.[35] For on entering northern Italy Vitellius had found it full of surly soldiers, those of his own legions and those of Otho, who were viciously quarrelling with one another. To prevent further disorder, Vitellius dispersed the Othonian legions in different places. Thus, *VII Galbiana* and *XI Claudia pia fidelis*, currently marching from the Danube frontier, were ordered to return to their respective stations in Pannonia and Dalmatia. Unlucky *legio XIII Gemina*, which had played such a prominent part in First Cremona, was punished by being allotted the unenviable task of building amphitheatres at Cremona and Bononia (Bologna), where Caecina Alienus and Fabius Valens intended to host competing spectacles. In the meantime, *legio I Adiutrix* was packed off to cool down Iberia as a complement to *X Gemina* and *VI Victrix*, though the beaten legion did not forget its hostility to Vitellius.[36] Which brings to us to the most truculent formation among the Othonians, namely *legio XIIII Gemina Martia Victrix*.

It is now proper to devote a little space to a brief discussion of the rôle of *legio XIIII Gemina Martia Victrix* in the year of four emperors. Though Britannia was somewhat on the sidelines throughout this period of military anarchy, it had its own worries at the time, troops of the Roman occupation forces there took part in some of these upheavals. Thus, in the Othonian army we find *legio XIIII Gemina Martia Victrix*, which had been recalled to Italy three years previously to spearhead Nero's proposed project in the Caucasus.[37] The Caucasus expedition never took place.

Having covered itself in blood and glory during the Boudican rebellion, *legio XIIII Gemina*,[38] as it was then known, became Nero's firm favourite, who declared its members 'as his most effective troops',[39] and gained the additional titles *Martia Victrix*.[40] The Romans had a fine faculty for inventing warriorlike names, and nor were such titles merely hollow sounds or extravagantly hyperbolic. Nero's favour and titles 'had made them long faithful to Nero, and kindled their zeal for Otho'.[41] Little surprise, therefore, the current attitude of the legion constituted a problem for the new emperor, and when its discipline failed the result was ugly. Proud in a tradition of military glory that had forgotten how to recognize defeat, it saw the affair at First Cremona rather differently, refusing to acknowledge that it had been defeated on the Othonian side, saying that only a *vexillatio* had shared in the débâcle, the bulk of the unit having been in transit somewhere in Dalmatia. It was a bizarre and irrational thought: a sign of the strain the unit personnel were under, but a sign also of the way they saw the whole affair, which, as far as they were concerned, had been unnecessarily hurried and in which, but for their absence, the outcome of the battle might have been different. Recriminations flew backwards and forwards.

The corporate personality of *XIIII Gemina Martia Victrix* was tenaciously spartan, perhaps the most spartan of all legions at the time. It had all the advantages of a truly professional legion that had been together for years, where the man with the lined face and the chiselled squint of the old hand was commonplace. It was a proud fighting unit, but such overweening pride made the unit unpopular. Moreover, it seemed that its constituent members did not care whom they slaughtered. At one point they picked a quarrel with some Batavi with whom they had long bad relations, possibly since service back in Britannia.[42]

But there was worse. To Vitellius' further chagrin, the far from submissive legionaries then decided to run amok in the city of Augusta Taurinorum (Turin), part of which they torched and good riddance, behaving more like a foreign occupation army than a legion of Roman citizens. Vitellius took the only possible course and packed the hard and rapacious legion off back to Britannia, where its battle-scarred, turbulent soldiers were hardly likely to have been greeted with enthusiasm by their old comrades who, though not taking any active part in the civil war, favoured the Vitellian cause.[43] They had become in some measure independent of all authority. They felt they had the right to some slack. They felt themselves misused. Within a year the formidable but fractious legion was on the road again, this time removed from Britannia to become a part of the Rhine army, never subsequently returning to the island it had know since Claudius' invasion. These legionaries were not one of the most attractive groups to study. They had few intrinsic virtues and many vices. They were really hard cases.

Anyway, let us return to the man of the moment, Vitellius. Contrary to expectations the new emperor showed himself to be moderate. Cassius Dio, for instance, tells us that the new emperor killed few of Otho's followers, though it seems that hard-core Othonians could only be converted six feet under, for Tacitus says he executed those brave centurions most loyal to Otho, which apparently caused much alarm and resentment amongst the Danube legions.[44] It can be said with some certainty that these brutal executions proved to be a fatal error. Blunder too was his one blatant act of revenge, the one he took on the Praetorian Guard. It had taken Galba out and put Otho in charge; so he wanted to make sure it could never take him out and put somebody else in charge. Vitellius had its centurions executed and disbanded the existing cohorts.[45] It was an extreme measure – very bad politics, as well as very bad behaviour. The praetorians never forgot or forgave the contumely.

Vitellius then created sixteen (instead of twelve) new praetorian cohorts and four urban cohorts (instead of seven),[46] each a thousand strong (instead of 500),[47] recruited from the legionaries and auxiliaries of his own forces.[48] With excellent pay and prospects,[49] the vacancies were quickly filled up, thereby removing some 20,000 men from the regular army.[50] This, as can be appreciated, was viewed with serious misgivings. These fears were perhaps unfounded, for as subsequent events were to show, Vitellius bound to himself a large body (the equivalent of about four legions) of totally devoted and desperate men who could be relied on to fight to the last for their prince and their prerogatives.

But the good times were drawing quickly to an end. By early August Vitellius received word that the legions of the east had declared themselves in favour of yet another popular hopeful, the legate governor of Iudaea, and before long the Danube legions followed suit. The disbanded praetorians were soon departing Rome for a fresh start with the new pretender to the throne, and these Othonian stalwarts 'constituted the main stay of the Flavian party'.[51]

O yes, I forgot to tell you. There is a hitch. Any look at the writings of our ancient authors, even a rapid and succinct one, seems to offer the impression that Vespasianus was destined to be the eventual winner in the game of thrones, while the other three contestants, Galba, Otho and Vitellius, were only waiting to be swept away into the rubbish heap of history. To this we can give a simple but a sufficient answer: at the time, without the gift of foresight, you could not have said who will begin and who will finish. The victory of Vespasianus was not a foregone conclusion. It may have been obvious for Tacitus, for instance, but it was not so obvious then who would wax strongly enough to create a new dynasty. As was to happen so frequently in the future, as it had done so in the past, the victors felt compelled to tinker with history to put their own spin on it, to recast history to their liking. After all, no one condemns a victor.

Understandably, therefore, it is doubly difficult to compose a coherent account for the brief principates of Galba, Otho and Vitellius, emperors whom the victory of others has made into usurpers. Tacitus, master of belittling innuendoes and snide remarks, a sly wordsmith with a stylus dripping with vinegar, is the primary source for much of what is known about the bloody and bittersweet happenings of the year of four emperors. Often recognized as the greatest historian of ancient Rome, a Roman Thucydides some would say, Tacitus is known for being generally reliable if somewhat biased toward what he saw as Roman immorality, and for having a uniquely direct if not blunt writing style. Thus for Galba, the literary sources (and here we must include the relevant biographies of Suetonius and Plutarch) concentrate on either the personality of the man, thereby failing to offer a balanced account of his policies and a firm chronological base for his actions, or they focus on the final fortnight of his life at the expense of the earlier part of his principate. As a result, relying as we do upon the chronicles of his enemies, a detailed account of Galba's principate is difficult to write.

Likewise, Vitellius has not escaped the hostility of his biographers, who played up his private vices but not his public acts. Perhaps it was too easy to dance on his grave, especially as he may well have been a fat porker, gluttonous and greedy, but his depiction as indolent, cruel, extravagant, the abdominous villain of the piece sunken in monstrous and Babylonian vices is based almost entirely on the dubious, partisan Flavian reports probably generated at Vespasianus' instigation.[52] Even a 'good' emperor's regard for the truth was such that he would have said whatever he wished to have posterity to believe, knowing full well that none of those present would have dared to contradict him. But then victors in every conflict, as ever, are allowed to speak, to write, and to publish. What is more, those same victors enjoy the added privilege of writing the accounts of their achievements in a way that downgrades those whom they conquered – or blotting them out – and it is the perquisite of power to invent its own past. A victorious cabal always finds ways of legalizing itself.

Vitellius was the last loser in the game of thrones and thus the one Vespasianus had been fighting directly; the more flawed Vitellius appeared to be, the more justified Vespasianus' action became in challenging him. Sometimes our authors work overtime portraying Vitellius in the most terrible aspect permitted by their fertile imaginations. Thus, Josephus describes Vitellius' final moments:

> Out of the palace came Vitellius, drunk, and as a last fling gorged to the eyes like a glutton he was. Dragged through the crowd, insulted and tormented in every possible way, he was knifed to death in the heart of his capital, after a reign of eight months and five days: if he had happened to live longer I doubt whether the empire could have satisfied his lust.[53]

So our arch-Flavian author has the trencherman emperor gratifying himself with a spectacular *grande bouffe*, not knowing of course that this was to be his last supper this side of the grave. How the mighty fall, and sometimes do so speedily, or to borrow that marvelous lyrical phrase of the professorial Henry Kissenger, 'on a pinnacle, that was soon to turn into a precipice'.[54] For it was not all that long ago when Vitellius had entered the heart of his capital. Which brings us to Tacitus' malicious pleasure when he describes Vitellius' triumphal entry into Rome:

> In front of the eagles (*aquilae*) marched the camp prefects, tribunes and first-rank centurions (*primi ordines*), all dressed in white. The other centurions each flanked their own centuries, resplendent in their weapons and decorations. As for the soldiers, they glistened with their *phalerae* and *torques* [military decorations]. It was an awesome sight, an army worthy of an emperor other than Vitellius.[55]

Tacitus was clearly a sorcerer with words, and such a comment makes Vitellius easy to remember, but of course it is an oversimplification; one or two vivid strokes with a pen do not delineate a man. Apparently at Brixellum (Brescello), Vitellius was shown his rival's tomb, which looked like any private person's (said Philostratos) and seemed one modest enough (thought Tacitus) to deserve survival.[56] It bore the simplest of inscriptions (seen by Plutarch): 'To the memory of Marcus Otho.'[57] According to Suetonius, Vitellius gazed at it for a moment, and then curtly remarked: 'A little grave for a little man!'[58] Similarly Suetonius' acid accusation that on his battlefield tour 'Vitellius cheered his companions with the brazen remark: "Only one thing smells sweeter to me than a dead enemy, and that is a dead fellow citizen." Nonetheless, he took a good swig of neat wine to counteract the stink and generously passed the flagon around.'[59] This may sound unlikely. Indeed it does sound unlikely. But the victor, in a victorious mood, may have been luxuriating in his new victory. Yet five months later poor Vitellius himself would be stinking up the streets of Rome, the victim of a Flavian lynch mob, perhaps an object lesson to emperors who coin deathless dictums.

Yet is easy to build up a case on the other side, and certainly there is space for compromise. For whatever moderating tendencies this short-lived emperor did show were overshadowed by his clear lack of military expertise. It was this deficiency that forced Vitellius to rely in critical situations on lieutenants who had their own selfish interests at heart, with betrayal, mendacity and manipulation being their common currency. For both Caecina Alienus and Fabius Valens each had his own axe to grind, regardless of the common aim, and Tacitus introduces them to us as a pair 'distinguished above all for boundless ambition and singular daring'.[60] And if that was not enough, each nourished the secret jealousy of rival contenders for Vitellius' ear and favour; the first thought the second was interested only in feathering his own nest, while the second regarded the first as a conceited poser.

With friends like that, the unwarlike Vitellius did not need enemies, but unfortunately for him, he had them and they were tenacious and dedicated. As a result he was no match for his businesslike Flavian opponents, and his humiliating demise was perfectly in keeping with the overall fiasco of his fleeting principate.

Reconstructing the historical Vitellius is not easy. Tacitus enjoyed belittling Vitellius' gluttony and slovenliness, in truth a picture of an emperor that, while not a caricature, is the likeness of a cannibalic, repast-seeking buffoon – evidently some methods of modern journalism are not new. Dehumanization enabled desensitization. But behind the Tacitean spite we can perhaps detect an amiable figure, whose easy manner and spherical form belied a surprising strength of character and flexibility of mind. And if he really did utter those gloating words at Cremona, it would be wise for us to understand that the general opinion of men who face each other in combat is one of hatred mixed with fear and occasionally a bit of grudging mutual respect. It is only after the passage of time, seasoned in a calm world and long peace, that combatants begin to remember their erstwhile enemies with something akin to respect or at least tolerance. All in all, Vitellius was poorly served by his lieutenants in the greatest moment of his career.

To conclude this chapter on Vitellius' brief principate, let us talk about food. Vitellius, the emperor-to-be, was said to have spent his boyhood and adolescence with Tiberius' pervert *sphintriae* on the island of Capri; he had been popular with Caius Caligula because he liked racing chariots, and with Claudius because he enjoyed playing dice, while Nero appreciated all these Vitellian talents and others besides.[61] But Vitellius is best remembered for his love of food.

When we imagine ancient Roman cooking and eating habits, we picture too readily the pagan gorging orgies of imperial times, with their casts of thousands. Or we think of the poisoning of Claudius with his favourite food, which his successor Nero later openly called 'the food of the gods'.[62] Likewise, we tend to think of the brutality done not only to one another but also to the innocent edibles. We take as the rule rather than as the exception, the over indulgences satirized by Juvenal, sneered at by Tacitus, the extravagance inveighed against by the fastidious Seneca, or Trimalchio's outrage to good taste and digestion vivified by Petronius and magnified by Fellini. Rarely, if ever, does the silver screen offer us another view of the togaed people at table than a version of this decadent and indecent gormandizing.

This view certainly reveals how kitchens have dwindled to mere stage-sets they often seem to be today, when people treat them as a combination of living room and dining room. When is the frugal Roman diet, washed down not with Falernum wine, the Châteauneuf-du-Pape of its day, but cabbage water, recommended by the elder Cato brought to our attention, or the simple and healthful meals the younger Pliny and Martial enjoyed with their intimate friends? In fact, if we take a look at the actual recipes and procedures, and especially the menus of real dinner parties that have survived from Roman times, we receive the impression of a simple diet. Moreover, we witness a culinary art that made use of natural foods, cooked to retain the best flavours, delicately seasoned and naturally coloured.

A prosperous Roman citizen could choose from an enormous variety of foodstuffs from the lands and seas of the empire, prepared with many exotic, imported herbs and spices. There were, however, some obvious omissions, namely the tomato, the potato, coffee and sugar.[63] Honey and reduced wines took the place of the latter. Other differences were matters of preference, not geography. Instead of butter, Romans cooked with olive oil. Milk was obtained from the goat rather than the cow. Unlike people of the Near East and northern Europe, the Romans did not brew beer. Wine, like the Greeks before them, was their staple drink, their primary food colouring, and often their preservative. As that rather vulgar man Trimalchio said in the *Satyricon*, 'wine is life!'[64]

A great deal of what we know about Roman cuisine comes from the gastronomic discoveries of Marcus Gavinus Apicius, a voluptuary of extraordinary wealth who flourished during the principate of Tiberius.[65] Under the emperors, Romans habitually took three meals a day. The *ientaculum* (breakfast) was eaten immediately after sunrise. This was a very light meal consisting of a little bread and fruit. The *prandium* (midday meal) was a collation of some fish, eggs, cold meats, vegetables, and bread. It was thought vulgar to consume a large lunch. Seneca, for instance, once boasted that he required only a little bread and some figs to sustain himself at lunchtime.[66] These modest habits, however, were soon forgotten at *cena* (dinner), which began at the ninth hour of the Roman day (around four o'clock) and continued into the evening, or even into the night. Readers of Petronius' *Satyricon* will recall that it was midnight before Encolpius and Ascyltos could escape from the *triclinium* (dining room) of the glutton Trimalchio. The *cena* itself had consisted of eight courses, the menu having included dormice sprinkled with honey and poppy seeds, roast whole female wild boar with dried dates suckled by piglets made of marzipan and stuffed with live thrushes, and boiled whole pig stuffed with sausages and blood puddings. These comestibles had been washed down with the *non plus ultra* of Roman wines, Falernum.[67]

The social anthropologist Desmond Morris has divided the development of modern man's eating habits between practices of two primal groups: the hunters and the gatherers. The first eat nothing all day, but in the evening they enjoy whatever they had hunted. The second search all day for nuts and berries and the like and eat them as they find them. Of the two extremes, the Romans, unsurprisingly, tended towards the hunter rather than the gatherer. They often skipped breakfast and lunch; only the major meal, dinner, *cena*, was important.[68]

On the whole, the *cena* had three parts: the *gustatio* (hors d'oeuvres), the *fercula* ('dishes that are carried', i.e. from the kitchen), and the *mensae secundae* (dessert courses). The *fercula* were at least three in number and could increase to five, seven, or more courses according to the purse of the host, with one main item, the *caput cenae*. Included in the *fercula* were fish and shellfish dishes, poultry, feathered game, joints of meat, and stuffed animals cooked whole. Of course, the variety and size of Roman dinners were nearly infinite. Then, as now, people ate and drank in moderation or to excess in a manner consistent with their mood, their desires, their prosperity, and their luck. The social-satirist Martial once invited his friend Toranius to a 'cheerless, solitary dinner party'.[69] Thinking that such details may be of interest to a portion of my readers, I will give the precise menu, which was as follows:

Gustatio
Honeyed wine (Martial calls this *mulsum*)
Cappadocian lettuce ('cheap')
Leeks ('smelly')
Chopped tuna fish in sliced eggs

Fercula
Fresh boiled broccoli
Sausage on white polenta pudding
Pale beans and streaky bacon
Served with wine that *'tu facies bonum bibendo'*

Mensae secundae
Homegrown grapes ('withered', i.e. raisins)
Syrian pears
Roasted Neapolitan chestnuts
Picenian olives ('fresh from the trees')
Hot chickpeas
Warm lupins

According to Suetonius the emperor Augustus gave frequent dinner parties, usually arriving late and leaving early, letting his guests start and finish without him. 'The *fercula* usually consisted of three courses', continues Suetonius, 'though in expansive moods Augustus might serve as many as six.'[70] The emperor was not noted for his extravagance. Moreover, his eating habits were somewhat frugal, preferring, as Suetonius says, 'the food of the common people *(vulgaris)*, especially the coarser sort of bread, small fishes, fresh hand-pressed cheese, and green figs of the second crop; and would not wait for *cena*, if he felt hungry, but ate anywhere'.[71] He was also 'a habitually abstemious drinker ... Raetian was his favourite, but he seldom touched wine between meals; instead, he would moisten his throat with a morsel of bread dunked in cold water; or a slice of cucumber or the heart of a young lettuce; or a sour apple either fresh or dried.'[72]

Which brings us nicely back to that most unwarlike of emperors Vitellius, and the culinary dish he dedicated to that most warlike of goddesses Minerva, and named Shield of Minerva the Protectress of the City. According to the testimony of Suetonius, the recipe 'called for pike livers, pheasant brains, peacock brains, flamingo tongues, and lamprey milt; and the ingredients, collected in every corner of the empire right from the Parthian frontier to the Pillars of Hercules, were brought to Rome by naval captains and triremes'.[73] It is assumed that the dish was prepared after the fashion of one of the two extravagant dishes Apicius describes as *patinae*, a sort of stuffed omelette or tart like a quiche.[74] As Suetonius implies, Vitellius, as ruler of the world, could get hold of whatever delicacies he desired for his table, but everything had its price: 'By Hercules, emperor Vitellius once assembled a *patina* that cost him one million *sestertii*.'[75] The Shield of Minerva must have been the mother of all *patinae*. It is hardly surprising, therefore, to find that this colossal smorgasbord of a dish being roundly denounced by that Flavian hatchet man Licinius Mucianus in a speech that attacked Vitellius' memory for 'his great swamp-like dishes'.[76] We are left with the rather lifelike image of Vitellius tucking in with gusto, that is to say, consuming his Shield of Minerva with the urgent pleasure of a predator at a kill.

Cassius Dio adds another detail of interest, that in his day certain cakes and dishes were named after Vitellius.[77] This we know independently, for Apicius supplies recipes for Vitellian peas, Vitellian beans and Vitellian suckling pig.[78] Human beings want to be a lot of things, and Roman emperors were in a far better position than most other people to make their ambitions come true. Whereas most of them, if not all, wanted to be remembered as divine, Vitellius was the true emperor of all gastronomes, a picture charmingly illustrated by Suetonius' little sketch of his attempt to disappear from the Roman scene before the arrival of the Flavian army: 'Stowing himself furtively into a sedan chair, and accompanied by only two companions, his pastry-cook and chef, he hurried to his father's house on the Aventine. He had planned to escape from there into Campania.'[79] Black comedy, maybe, but an epicurean resignation would not end his troubles; the Flavian jackals were getting ready to pick his bones.

Chapter 5

The Emperor Maker

As Cicero once observed, 'no war can rightly be undertaken save for vengeance or defence'.[1] Certainly, too, the pose of avenging a fallen ally is one of the favourite justifications for war. Suetonius refers to a 'copy of a letter (possibly forged) in which Otho begged him [Vespasianus] most earnestly to avenge his death and come to the aid of the empire'.[2] This convenient voice from beyond the grave was a shrewd device. Dramatic descriptions of Otho's heroic self-sacrifice could stir up the soldiers' emotions and galvanize them to support Vespasianus in his role as self-proclaimed avenger. Residual loyalty to Otho amongst the Othonian legions endured, and Vespasianus would have been foolish to ignore such a valuable manpower resource. Indeed, it was his *eminence grise*, Licinius Mucianus, who pinpointed the fact that the defeated Othonians were 'fired to valour by anger, by hatred, by the desire of vengeance'.[3] After all, his bid for power was incontrovertibly illegal. History may have forgiven him for the deed, but it was an act of rebellion all the same.

Vespasianus had supported Galba, whom the Senate had confirmed as emperor, and likewise Otho. According to Tacitus, Vespasianus had despatched his son Titus, now twenty-seven years old and *legatus legonis* of *XV Apollinaris*,[4] to Rome with the purpose of demonstrating Flavian loyalty to Galba. It also allowed Titus to stand for the praetorship. Rumour, the harbinger of truth, began to circulate in the Galban camp that the ageing Galba intended to adopt Titus.[5] Rumour may have crossed the empire quicker than the fastest courier, but Titus only got as far as Corinth when he heard the disturbing news of Galba's demise. Titus sent his friend Herod Agrippa II of Iudaea on to Rome while he hurried back to his father. Stopping off at Cyprus en route, Titus paid a quick visit to Aphrodite (Roman Venus) at her renowned temple at Paphos (Palaepaphos) and there he apparently consulted the oracle of the goddess as to his pending voyage and future fate. The omens proved to be favourable, and in a private interview the high priest Sostratos assured Titus of his great destiny. Having heard the prospects of his own fortunes with regards to the throne of the world, Titus left with 'his spirits raised'.[6] Is it possible that in this context we are witnessing the beginnings of Flavian aspirations?[7] All the same, back in Iudaea the legions had taken the oath of allegiance to Otho, as had the prefect of Egypt, Tiberius Iulius Alexander.[8] Rome was thus assured of its grain supply.

However, continuance of civil war and the rapid exits of the two emperors made Vespasianus realize he himself could perhaps make a play for the purple. Though all our sources show him as rather hesitant over taking the imperial plunge, there are signs that the senior men in the eastern command contemplated a bid for the empire.[9] In fact, the legate governor of Syria, Caius Licinius Mucianus (*cos.* AD 67), though he thoroughly despised Vespasianus, 'had but lately resolved on concerted action', but 'the others had done so long before'. Their motives were mixed, the 'worthiest among them were moved by patriotism; many were wrought upon by the attractions of plunder; some by their private embarrassments'.[10] It is important to stress the existence of the support of a small clique of military men in Vespasianus' bid for the right to sit on the throne of the world. These senior men in the eastern command clearly wanted to unseat Vitellius and to clear the throne for their own candidate, and the prime mover in this was Licinius Mucianus, who, though no fan of Vespasianus, was a close friend of his elder son Titus, whose amiable and easy-going character was congenial to the childless senator. More to the point, perhaps, while possessing the gifts and competence of an excellent maker of rulers, Licinius Mucianus lacked the will to be one himself. Besides, love him or hate him, Vespasianus was a no-nonsense professional soldier with two grownup sons, his efficiency proved by the ongoing Jewish war, three factors that would ease his path to power.[11]

As for the eastern legions, though Vespasianus had only three (*V Macedonica, X Fretensis, XV Apollinaris*) under his direct command,[12] when the five (*IIII Scythica, VI Ferrata, XII Fulminata* [from Syria], *III Cyrenaica, XXII Deiotariana* [from Egypt])[13] under the control of his political backers, the legate governor of Syria and the prefect of Egypt, hailed him emperor, the fifty-nine-year professional soldier accepted the position of pretender to the purple.[14] In one sense he was being offered a position that looked like a compliment, but could so easily be a death sentence, if he failed to play his cards right. But Vespasianus, to pun a line from Homer, was not going to allow fickle fate to wrap him in 'death's purple'.[15]

'A safe general is better than a bold one' wrote Euripides,[16] and in the month of August Vespasianus had met with his advisors and backers at Berytus (Beirut) in Syria, and like shady gangsters plotting a crime they perfected their strategy for stealing the empire.[17] The aim of a general in war is to impose his will on his opponent or to prevent one's opponent imposing his will on oneself. The means whereby this might be achieved vary according to the circumstances at the time, and the Flavian strategy for whipping the Vitellians had not been an exception to this rule. Licinius Mucianus was to march on Italy via Asia Minor and Thrace with an expeditionary force consisting of *VI Ferrata* from Syria (the longest-serving legion in the province, having been there since 30 BC), together with 13,000 assorted legionaries drawn from the remaining formations (viz. 2,000 each from *IIII Scythica, V Macedonica, X Fretensis, XV Apollinaris, III Cyrenaica* and *XXII Deiotariana*, with a thousand from *XII Fulminata*, which had been badly cut up back in AD 66).[18]

Leaving his son Titus to deal with the Jewish problem, Vespasianus, the emperor-to-be, was to starve Rome into submission from Egypt and Africa by cutting off the capital's vital grain supplies. In the meantime, the legions of Pannonia would block the Iulian Alps until they, together with those of Moesia, were to be taken over by Licinius Mucianus. As for the five Rhine legions, already depleted by the *vexillationes* dispatched to Italy, they would be paralysed by a mock revolt staged by the Batavi at the mouth of the Rhine. Even the bravest, meanest troops cannot fight when they are dying of starvation. Almost without a blow, Italy would fall, a fat moist decadent warm fruit, into the lap of Vespasianus.[19]

In the event, all fell out otherwise.

Others were ready to strike hard and strike fast. The legions of the Danube may have been remote from the Flavian nerve centre in Berytus, but they were a lot nearer to Italy. Moreover, some of them were eager to avenge their old commander-in-chief Otho, and were like winter wolves eager to supplant the legions of the Rhine. We can imagine the Danube soldiers now saying, to the last man: 'Enough of Vitellius! What good is the new emperor if he is not ours? And if there is an opportunity for self-enrichment from bounty and from pillaging – well, that's just gravy.'[20] Anyway, they had a natural and gifted commander in the restless Marcus Antonius Primus, the rough, tough fighting legate of the recently formed *legio VII Galbiana*. We have already met the name of this legion, which had escorted Galba to Rome and was currently stationed in Pannonia and later to be renamed *Gemina*, in the events of the first months of the civil war.[21] Its current name, as well as that of its steely combative commander, was to dominate coming events.

Antonius Primus had repeatedly written to Otho offering his services. The new emperor neglected the offer, being, according to Tacitus, very suspicious of one who had been a close associate of Galba.[22] Moreover, it was equally clear that the Danube legions were too far from Italy to be of any immediate help. So when the claims of Vespasianus were canvassed along the Danube frontier, the impetuous Antonius Primus played a leading role in the nascent pro-Flavian movement there and was readily supported by his legionary colleagues, namely from the *legati legionum* downwards.[23] As for the legate governors of the three Danube provinces, they were the men with most to lose (not to mention their lives too) if they backed the wrong candidate, men such as Marcus Aponius Saturninus legate governor of Moesia, heavy in years and rich to boot. So, though *III Gallica* under its *legatus legionis* Titus Aurelius Fulfinius, had promptly opted for the Flavian cause, Aponius Saturninus hesitated and actually reported the matter in a missive to Vitellius 'before he too attached himself to the party of Vespasianus'.[24]

But that was not the end of it, for Aponius Saturninus also sent a senior centurion to rub out Tettius Iulianus, the *legatus legionis* of *VII Claudia pia fidelis*. This was the Othonian paladin who had been decorated by Otho for his part in the successful repulse of the February invasion of the Rhoxolani, a Sarmatian tribe of horse warriors.[25] Though the excuse for the attempt on his life was because Tettius Iulianus was deemed a traitor, Tacitus informs us that this dastardly deed was initiated by a personal quarrel between the two men.[26] A foolish action, and small wonder then the soldiers stationed in Aponius Saturninus' province mutinied. Tacitus, however, chose to look at it differently, for this was the occasion for his famous remark about the collapse of traditional military discipline: 'If once they had emulated each other in valour and obedience, so now there was a rivalry in insubordination and insolence.'[27] This explanation is characteristic of Tacitus and would seem to leave nothing to explain, requiring neither correction nor supplement.

Meanwhile, in next-door Dalmatia we have the equally hesitant and elderly Marcus Pompeius Silvanus. It should be remembered that one of the two legions stationed here, namely *XI Claudia pia fidelis*, had been quite slow in coming to the aid of Otho and, according to the sharp-tongued Tacitus, 'when things turned out well, became uneasy because of its failure to cooperate … Silvanus, too lazy to be a fighter, frittered away the time for action in talk'.[28] A rôle that was (probably deliberately) ambiguous. Once again, it was only after news of the victory of Antonius Primus at Second Cremona, as we shall discover in good time, that stirred *XI Claudia pia fidelis* to march under Pompeius Silvanus and join the Flavian march on Rome. However, as Tacitus implies in the same passage, the prime mover for this action was its *legatus legionis* Lucius Annius Bassus, who would reap the reward of one of the consulships of AD 70; Pompeius Silvanus would have to wait for his consulship (his second, in fact) until AD 75.

The legate governor of Pannonia, Lucius Tampius Flavianus, had troubles of his own to contend with. For not only was he a relative of Vitellius,[29] but he had been appointed to the governorship by Galba, so his loyalty was doubly in doubt. The soldiers of his two legions certainly targeted him as a potential traitor, accusing him of sluggishness over his failure to arrive in time for First Cremona. At the first signs of Flavian activity in his province, he threw up his command and promptly fled towards the apparent safety of Italy.[30] However, his officers persuaded him to return and lead his command on behalf of Vespasianus, for the Flavians needed men of consular rank so as to give their cause, which presently lacked big name followers, a certain amount of clout. Once in Italy, however, his soldiers turned against him, and it was only the prompt intervention of Antonius Primus, who ordered his arrest and got him away the same night, that saved Tampius Flavianus' precious consular hide.[31] These were the fortunes of war. Lucky for him, because he went on to become the proconsul of Africa under Vespasianus,[32] and then *curator aquarum*, superintendent of the Rome aqueducts. Soon after he received his second consulship with Pompeius Silvanus.

So, taken all around, the three legate governors were men who had achieved rank and position. Peace gave them a chance to enjoy what they had gained, and so it was no accident that they had very little desire to risk life, or even their comfort and health. They thought that by doing little or nothing, they would anger neither side, and so be able to deal with the eventual winner. Sometimes that tactic works. But if these senior men were intent on preserving the appearance of watchful neutrality, the legates, the tribunes and the centurions, men like our antihero Antonius Primus, or the reckless procurator of Pannonia Cornelius Fuscus, 'a man in the prime of life and of illustrious birth',[33] or the *legatus legonis* of *XI Claudia pia fidelis*, Annius Bassus, had other, much more dynamic ideas. These professional servants of the state were the men of the hour – and of many other hours to come.

At first they stirred the pot, sending despatches to those intransigent Othonian legions, *I Adiutrix*, now kicking its heels in Iberia, and *XIIII Gemina Matrix Victrix*, once more back in Britannia.[34] Next, they got together all the senior officers of the Danube legions, who met in conference at Ptuj-*Poetovio*, the headquarters of *legio XIII Gemina*. The mission was to hammer out a workable plan of campaign.[35] There were two options open to them: first, to sit tight and await events, or second, to march straight into Italy. Those who favoured the first option (incidentally, Tacitus does not name them) argued that Vitellius would be starved out of Italy, but Antonius Primus (obviously ignoring the desires of the Flavian bigwigs in the east) advocated immediate action with a quick strike. His trajectory began with a passionate speech noted more for its fire than its reason.[36] Notwithstanding, he carried the day, so great was the power of one man who knows what he wants over several who were not sure of themselves.

Antonius Primus was one of those men who believed that the wrong action taken decisively and in time was better than the right action taken later. This was clearly a classic case of the most being made of every opportunity, the principle of maintenance of momentum, whereby what can be taken immediately by a relatively small force may be a different story if left until later. It was a good time for a man like Antonius Primus. Everything was starting up for him.

It is possible for one man, with audacity, skill and luck to fly in the face of objective circumstances. That is the point of Machiavelli's famous chapter in *The Prince* on the goddess Fortune – she is a fickle painted whore, but if she is to be mastered, 'it is necessary to beat her and ill use her; and it is seen that she allows herself to be mastered by the adventurous rather than by those who go to work more coldly'.[37] Antonius Primus wanted to deal a blow; Vespasianus merely wanted to show his fist.[38]

There was such a lot to do, and the energetic Antonius Primus was planning to move very fast. This was no military parade he was organizing here. This was serious business, killing business. Maybe worse. But Antonius Primus was a clever operator, he got things done, he was just the man to transform the Flavian mission. And so it was that five of the six Danube legions (*III Gallica*, *VII Claudia pia fidelis*, *VIII Augusta* [from Moesia], *VII Galbiana*, *XIII Gemina* [from Pannonia], absent was *XI Claudia pia fidelis* [from Dalmatia]) that put an end to Vitellius' principate at Second Cremona; not the slow scourge of starvation. But we have run somewhat ahead of events.

Under the leadership of Antonius Primus (the governors *must* have been glad to see the last of him), a modest auxiliary force set off post-haste to make a rapid descent on Italy. He was accompanied by Arrius Varus, a brave and talented officer who had gained his reputation serving as a *praefectus cohortis* under the great Neronian general, Cnaeus Domitius Corbulo, in the war against Parthia. It was rumoured he had denounced Corbulo to Nero (true or false, this was to be the cause of his destruction under Domitianus),[39] thereby earning for him the prestigious rank of *primus pilus* of a venerable legion (in this case *III Gallica*).[40] On the death of Nero he held this rank in *VII Galbiana*, Antonius Primus' legion, and for the coming campaign he was to serve as Antonius Primus' cavalry commander. If this initial strike met with success, the six Danube legions would quickly follow.

Having occupied Aquileia unopposed, Antonius Primus took the Via Annia and pushed on to Patavium (Padova) and Ateste (Este), both towns readily opening their gates to the Flavian vanguard. It was at the later town that he gained the intelligence that the Vitellians held nearby Forum Alieni with three cohorts and *ala Gallorum Sebosiana*,[41] peacefully encamped by a makeshift bridge they had thrown over the Athesis (Adige). Coming upon them at dawn, the Flavians 'killed many before they could arm'.[42]

Hearing of this success, the two Pannonian legions, *VII Galbiana* and *XIII Gemina*, under the legate Vedius Aquila, force marched to Patavium.[43] Antonius Primus had already pushed on to Vicentia (Vicenza), birthplace of Caecina Alienus, where he picked up the Via Postumia and quickly turned southwest towards Verona, his preferred seat of war owing to its surrounding plains, which were 'suitable for the action of cavalry, in which they [the Flavians] were very strong'.[44] According to Tacitus, Caecina Alienus, who was holding a strongly fortified camp at Hostilia (Ostiglia) thirty Roman miles south of Verona, should have seized the moment to crush then and there the outnumbered Flavians, but 'by various delays betrayed to the enemy the early opportunities of the campaign'.[45] It seems that Caecina Alienus was already preparing to abandon the Vitellian cause – his colleague Fabius Valens was still back in Rome incapacitated by an illness. In the meantime, Aponius Saturninus arrived with *legio VII Claudia pia fidelis*, then under the temporary command of the senatorial tribune Vipstanus Messalla,[46] its legate Tettius Iulianus having fled into Thrace to escape the assassin sent against him by Aponius Saturninus.[47] Antonius Primus now had three legions.

On the arrival of two further legions, *III Gallica* led by Dillius Aponianus and *VIII Augusta* by Numisius Lupus, it was necessary to throw up an earthen rampart on the undefended southern side of Verona, its other three sides being conveniently surrounded by a loop of the Athesis (Adige).[48] It was at this point that the soldiers turned against the two legate governors, Tampius Flavianus and Aponius Saturninus, calling them traitors and clamouring for their immediate execution. In peril of their lives, the two were spared a nasty end at the hands of the mutineers only by the personal intervention of Antonius Primus. It is with customary innuendo that Tacitus closes his narrative of these two mutinies: 'There were those who believed that both these mutinies were set on foot by the intrigues of Antonius, in order that he might engross all the prizes of the war.'[49] Whether or not we choose to believe this was a saga of rivalry eventually vanquished, the presence of two legate governors and four other *legati legionum*, the first being of consular rank, the second of praetorian, did call into question the authority of Antonius Primus, who was, after all, only a *legatus legionis*. Yet the effect of the departure of the two *consulares* was to make Antonius Primus the undisputed leader of the Flavian army in Italy, and to impose upon its movements a unified and, as it turned out, successful strategy.

So it came to pass that during the night of 24/25 October, practically at the same spot outside Cremona where Vitellius' army had been so successful before, there was a decisive battle. The details of this most crucial of engagements will be discussed in the next chapter, suffice to say here that the Vitellians were soundly trounced and gutted militarily. To borrow three lines from Arthur Conan Doyle, 'They have marched from far away / Ere the dawning of the day, / And the morning saw them masters of Cremona'.[50] For the following four days the victorious Flavians wreaked bloody havoc on Cremona, which became a horrific example of what Roman soldiers could do to Roman civilians in time of civil war. It is easy for us to minimize the rape of Cremona – if this is not the deliberate act of an invading army, I do not know what is – but it was painfully real and surely stands as an indelible stain on Antonius Primus' military record. Still, in the greater scheme of things, if Paris – fated for later greatness – was one day going to be well worth a mass, then Cremona was a small price to pay for power.[51]

Once the surviving Vitellians had been rounded up and returned to their standards, 'the vanquished legions were scattered throughout Illyricum'.[52] Clearly the intention was to rid Italy of them, but at the same time make use of them by strengthening the weak Danube frontier. Around about the same time, a new legion was organized from the sailors of the *classis Ravennas* who had deserted Vitellius for Vespasianus at the instigation of their *praefectus*, Sextus Lucilius Bassus.[53] The élite of the marines of this fleet, 'who demanded permission to serve in the legions',[54] joined the army of Marcus Antonius. This was to be *legio II Adiutrix*.[55]

The sailors of Ravenna were soon to be joined by their comrades in the fleet at Misenum. The betrayal was down to the daring of a single man, Claudius Faventinus, 'a centurion cashiered (*per ignominiam ... dimissus*) by Galba, who forged letters in the name of Vespasianus offering a reward for treachery'. It seems their *praefectus*, Claudius Apollinaris, was 'a man neither firm in his loyalty, nor energetic in his treason'.[56] Now a soldier might be released from military service by honourable or dishonourable discharge (*missio honesta* or *missio ignominiosa*), or even for reasons of ill health (*missio causaria*),[57] so it seems our marine centurion agitator was either a bad lot or an adherent of Otho, and hence, too, of Vespasianus.

As for Claudius Apollinaris, his appointment as *praefectus classis* was all too recent, for he was the successor to Lucilius Bassus, who, until his defection, had been the prefect of both fleets.[58] An ex-praetor, Apinius Tiro, who happened to be conveniently near at Minturnae (Minturno), put himself at the head of the revolt. Worse still, Vitellius' makeshift force under Claudius Iulianus, one urban cohort and a handful of gladiators from Rome, promptly went over to the naval rebels, who now made themselves masters of the seaport of Tarracina (Terracina), which was only a three-day march from the capital.[59] Starr surely puts his finger on it when he says 'Despising Vitellius as they had favored [sic] Otho, the Italian fleets wore a thin cloak of loyalty; various incidents even suggest that the party of Vespasian had through secret emissaries prepared for their revolt at a suitable opportunity ... The course of events insistently demands the assumption that Vitellius could not rely on the Italian fleets, and that Vespasian [sic] knew this.'[60] After all, as Starr implies, Vespasianus' strategy of starving Italy into submission needed the connivance, or at least their passivity, of the two major Roman fleets.

During the intervening time Vitellius, shrugging off a reputation for idleness and displaying uncharacteristic energy, had seen fit to react to these alarming developments. He detailed his younger brother Lucius to crush the rebellion with the use of six praetorian cohorts.[61] These former Rhine soldiers were obviously loyal to their emperor, and his brother was a hard man who stood no nonsense. He quickly invested Tarracina, the rebels showing no inclination to venture beyond the town walls,[62] and set about taking the place. One ominous omission of the rebels was the garrisoning of the hill that dominated both town and bay, and as it always seems in circumstances of these sorts, Fortuna came in the guise of a local traitor who offered to put Lucius Vitellius in possession of the unoccupied height. Noiselessly taken under a half-moon, the praetorians 'descended to what was more a massacre than a conflict'.[63] The defenders were cut down as they fumbled in the dark for their weapons, though a few gladiators put up some sort of fight before they too fell. The rest of the gladiators, sailors and men of the *cohors urbana*, hastened for their ships, of which only six got away. On board one was Claudius Apollinaris, but his fellow rebel chief, Claudius Iulianus, was not so fortunate. He was dragged before Lucius Vitellius, 'and, after being ignominiously scourged, was put to death in his presence'.[64]

But what of Fabius Valens? As we know, illness had prevented him from leaving Rome in the company of Caecina Alienus and the army. By the time Fabius Valens had sufficiently recovered, Second Cremona had been fought and lost and his rival defected to the other side. Loyal to the end, Fabius Valens tried to continue the struggle on behalf of Vitellius, and departed ship from Pisa for Gallia Narbonensis in an attempt to raise a fresh army. He put in at Hercules Monoecus (Monaco), but was advised not to march inland as the procurator of the province, Valerius Paulinus, had rallied to the Flavian troops disbanded by Vitellius, particularly former praetorians of Otho, 'in which force he had once been a tribune'.[65] So Fabius Valens sailed on, but was compelled by a storm to land on the Stoechades (Iles d'Hyères, off Toulon). Here he was caught by surprise by a flotilla of four *liburnae* sent after him by Valerius Paulinus and captured.[66] The procurator sent him back to Italy, where the loyal and determined Vitellian general was beheaded at Urbinum (Urbino) on Antonius Primus' orders. His head was taken to Narnia (Narni) to be displayed on a pole before the Vitellian soldiers who were still resisting there with the hope of Fabius Valens' return with an army. The sight of his bloody head was enough to persuade them enough was enough.[67]

Before his brother Lucius had wreaked bloody havoc in Campania, of which mention has just been made, Vitellius had seen fit to occupy the Apennine passes in Umbria in an attempt to arrest the Flavian advance. Accordingly, the emperor had ordered Iulius Priscus and Alfenius Varus, the praetorian prefects,[68] with fourteen praetorian cohorts and his entire cavalry force to Mevania (Bevagna) on the Via Flaminia. 'A legion of troops drafted from the fleet followed.'[69] However, on receiving news of the defection of the fleet at Misenum, Vitellius withdrew from Mevania, leaving part of his army at Narnia under the praetorian prefects and deputed his brother Lucius with six praetorian cohorts and 500 horsemen to encounter this new danger down in Campania.[70] It seems Vitellius held hopes of holding onto his principate.

It did not happen.

Vitellius' men were having none of it and deserted in droves. They seem to have concluded that if 'he who fights and runs away, will live to fight another day' is true, then he who avoids battle all together has a still greater chance of survival. The instinct of self-preservation is a monstrously strong one, and on this particular occasion it held sway over loyalty to an emperor whose days were surely numbered. There are few desertions in a winning army, and Vitellius, whose optimism had blinded him to the realities of the situation, now had no choice but to scuttle back to Rome. The issue of the war had been decided and his principate was coming apart at the seams, but Vitellius did not know it. Although hanging on to the purple power, he himself feared to make any use of it. The growing force of Flavian opposition paralyzed Vitellius' will to the last fibre.

On the other hand, Antonius Primus was very much on the move and spoiling for another fight. In an impressive display of rapid marching, his rush down Italy echoed the approach of his Olympian namesake, Marcus Antonius, by relying on speed and decisiveness to surprise the enemy. Despite the dark depths of winter fast approaching, he took advantage of the flight of the Vitellians to cross the snows of the Apennines, for it was now the month of December.

And collapse the Vitellian cause did, as its supporters began to defect. But the new praetorian cohorts whom Vitellius had enrolled from the Rhine legions insisted on fighting it out. Vespasianus' supporters in Rome had decided to occupy the Capitol, 'a miscellaneous body of soldiery, and some senators and equestrians',[71] which the Vitellians proceeded to take by fire and sword, burning down the great temple of Iuppiter in the process.[72] They also managed to capture Vespasianus' brother, Titus Flavius Sabinus, city prefect since Otho's succession, whom Vitellius had not removed.[73] He was heavily manacled and dragged before Vitellius, whose slender authority was unable to save him. In the spirit of unsparing hatred and savage inhumanity, the city prefect was butchered and mutilated by the Vitellian soldiers.[74] His nephew Domitianus, however, had managed to disappear as soon as the Capitol fell.[75]

By 20 December Antonius Primus had reached the gates of Rome and his army fought its way in at three points, the Via Flaminia, along the left bank of the Tiber, and along the Via Salaria to the Colline Gate.[76] 'The populace stood by and watched the combatants; and, as though it had been a mimic conflict, encouraged first one party and then the other by their shouts and plaudits'.[77] As Tacitus remarks, the battle for the capital was more like a hideous public spectacle, a no holds barred fight to the death in street, shop, house, bath and tavern.

The last episode of the battle for Rome was played out in the *castra praetoria*. The praetorians were above reproach; they all fought to the last and died like veterans, 'with their wounds in front and their faces turned towards the foe'.[78] There is something about defensive fights by an overwhelmingly outnumbered small force that stirs national pride and interest. As you might imagine, popular literature is replete with examples of fights 'to the last stand'. This may have happened, but they are only the rarest of occurrences. Are we not morbidly fascinated by battles in which one army is exterminated? Thermopylai. Saltus Teutoburgiensis. Masàda. Roncevaux. The Alamo. Camerone. Little Bighorn. Khartoum. Shangani Patrol. Men outnumbered fighting to the last, playing the desperate part to the end, meeting heroic defeat and death. Just consider how many times King Leonidas' Three Hundred, Colonel Travis' tiny garrison or *Captaine* Danjou's tight little band have been annihilated in prose, poetry, and on canvas. Engels once wrote to his dear friend Marx: 'The more I mug up on war, the greater my contempt for heroism – a fatuous expression, heroism, and never heard on the lips of a proper soldier. When Napoléon was not haranguing or making proclamations but speaking coolly he never spoke of *glorieux courage indomptable* [glorious and undaunted courage] etc., but would say at most, '*il s'est bien battu*' [he fought well].[79]

Soldiers universally fight for the same reasons: to do a job, for the sake of their fellow soldiers, to kill rather than be killed. How are we to account for this? It goes like this. The 'buddy-buddy' system, a simple human chemistry cutting across race, creed, and colour and, without reason or second thought, requiring a man to lay down his life for his 'buddy'.[80] It is a love not of flesh but of spirit, whose expression is not self-assertion but self-abnegation. It is a bond of the kind only men can have. And so a commander worth his salt will foster that ephemeral quality, *esprit de corps*, the individual's confidence in himself and his unit, the collective camaraderie and commitment to one another. This is what reinforces the sense of comradeship, which is essential to the soldiers' survival in combat. This is why soldiers are willing to go on fighting for their comrades even when the war they are caught up in seems to have lost any purpose. It must have seemed that way for the Vitellian praetorians, who had made up their minds to die and so sold their lives dearly for a commander who no longer commanded. A new principate was but hours away.

The tragic year AD 69, begun with the slaying of an emperor, was going to end in the vengeful murder of another. Once inside the city a group of Flavian soldiers hunted down Vitellius and publicly humiliated him. When a tribune tried to get a laugh out of the crowd with scornful remarks, Vitellius retorted by saying, 'Yet I was your emperor.'[81] Then, in a senseless act of lynch law, they slowly tortured him to death, finally throwing his corpulent naked corpse into the Tiber.[82] An ugly death in an ugly time. It was not the way an emperor was suppose to die. He was not the first and certainly not the last individual to wind up in inside a wolf he thought he could ride. Nonetheless, this messy murder brought an end to the horrors of anarchy and civil war and ushered in an era of much needed peace. The empire's darkest year to date did not make it totter, on the contrary, it came out of experience of AD 69 alive and strong enough. It was, in fact, proof of its stability.

So far, then, the Flavian revolt had taken place in the slipstream of a former exile who had showed no fear, favour or prejudice. He was answerable to no one.

He was having a time of his life. He knew he was for now a kingmaker, a puppet master. He was also a fulfiller of prophecies. Vitellius, on the road to Rome, was holding court in Vienna (Vienne) when a rooster perched first on his shoulder, and then on his hand. This omen was construed as meaning that a Gaul would terminate his life, *gallus* being both a 'rooster' and a 'Gaul' – his origins may have been obscure to the point of shadiness, but we do know that Antonius Primus, native of Tolosa, had borne the boyhood nickname of Becco, 'rooster's beak'.[83] For a few days, Antonius Primus was virtually master of Rome, and in recognition of the fact the Senate bestowed upon him the rank and insignia of a consul. It must have been his finest hour.

Prophecy is a history-creating force, and this 'Roman holiday' is the pivot on which his life's story swings round. On the arrival of Licinius Mucianus, Antonius Primus left the Eternal City. For those of you delighting in the choreography of power, this is a telling moment. Was Antonius Primus content to withdraw from the dust and turmoil of Roman political life? Surely not. He had been a loser in one particular way, all his life by rubbing against the hair of people, instead of going with their whims; but he could not go otherwise – this would have been against the grain of himself. Like Achilles, he was a man who fitted uneasily, if at all, into a chain of command. The embodiment of ferocity, a fierce restless warrior, he could not, or would not, march in step. There are many ways to lead an army. Being a warrior is one way and not necessarily the best. In short, Antonius Primus stood on the threshold of greatness but never crossed it.

Now, Caius Licinius Mucianus was a very different kettle of political fish. He was Antonius Primus' antithesis; Athens to his Sparta, Odysseus to his Achilles. Licinius Mucianus was a political game player whose labyrinthine machinations made him the *eminence grise* of the Flavian movement. His character is drawn in a few bold strokes by the masterly hand of Tacitus. He was a compound of self-indulgence and industry, courtesy and arrogance, good and evil. When he had nothing to attend to, he wallowed in unbridled pleasures, but when business beckoned, he displayed great abilities. Still, Licinius Mucianus can hardly be accused of self-seeking. His talent for diplomacy, intrigue and organization was employed to make an emperor of another, not of himself.[84]

As a politician Antonius Primus belonged to a type by no means uncommon: men of action, organically inclined toward adventurism and careerism. The most highly developed traits in such individuals are: an insatiable craving for power, strong will, perseverance and creaseless cunning coupled with a complete disregard for principles and loyalty. Yet for all his achievements, Antonius Primus, the hero of the Flavian invasion, had to yield to a man who was the emperor's alter ego. For him, it was the last of his glory days. For those, however, who wished for promotion under the new régime they courted Licinius Mucianus and him alone. He, for his part, understood power and thus kept himself well in the public eye, constantly meeting and greeting. It was also noted that he retained inside the capital his own personal bodyguard. In short, Licinius Mucianus was a firm believer in that age old truth of never getting more popular than the boss unless, of course, you intend to sack him.[85]

Chapter 6

The Fourth Milestone

It is fitting, I think, that we begin this chapter with a warning. If it is always hard to look into the past and get a satisfactory answer to the questions of where people were and when, let alone why they were there in the first place; it is doubly difficult to do so for battle scenes. Your on-the-spot eyewitnesses are invariably preoccupied, trying not to succumb to the one of the many invitations to death that combat offers, rather than paying too much attention to the unfolding battle while at the same time taking accurate notes for future historians like you and me. If this makes any firsthand accounts of a battle of dubious reliability, it holds particularly true for accounts by contemporaries who relied on those eyewitnesses. Besides, the hero returning from war is hardly likely to confess to the prodding questions of wannabe historians that he spent the battle back with the baggage train, for instance, and inevitably an element of fabrication creeps in. More than likely, our returning hero will follow the line that a tale of a derring-do is better than a straight answer. After all, there is the universal tendency to believe a cracking good story regardless of its claims to authenticity.

So, when one has to add misinformed speculation, deliberate propaganda and pure fiction into the mix, it gives some idea of the near impossibility of the task of deducing what happened on the vineyard strewn fields outside Cremona during a moonlight autumnal night. No participant for this engagement ever had a clear overview. Combat is a very confused situation at best, and the view from the battlefield, unlike that from hindsight, is therefore wrapt in doubt and obscurity. All the combatants move in the dust, grime, and excitement of battle, making it doubly difficult to tell even from the accounts of participants and eyewitnesses exactly what did happen, and what did not. As commonly even in our own world, twenty eyewitnesses render twenty tales. In this case a wholesome amount of scepticism is the essential ingredient of consideration.

Having said all this, however, one should never write about any battle that one has not walked over and carefully studied topographically with the aid of good maps and autopsy. Here there might well be some dissent, so to please my potential critics (and why not?), I should perhaps add the phrase *from my point of view*. There again it would be a pity to spoil their fun. Leastways, I shall try and show how the battle outside Cremona came about and to give a possible picture of what the engagement was like. As should be the case with all battle reconstructions, the emphasis here is on the men who fought and the fragility of the human spirit in the maelstrom of combat. In the intensely pressurized environment of the combat zone the best laid plan can go awry, and only the actions of key battlefield leaders drive on lesser mortals to achieve the ultimate objective. It is never appropriate for us to skip over the dark drama of battle, rife with its human wretchedness, and just concentrate on the tactical events, or worse still, legends of heroism. In the traumatic reality of battle soldiers see horrible things and some of them do horrible things.

As you will have gathered by now, much of what really happened in this battle is unclear. The account that follows is based upon the few coherent facts we have, and some possibilities and a fair amount of speculation. What I have in mind with regards to the last is the sort of thing Lieutenant Colonel Alfred Higgins Burne used in his military writings. In building up a coherent account of a battle, his level-headed findings were based upon original sources plus what he called IMP, the Inherent Military Probability of an action.[1] To those readers that already know all this, I apologize – but it may still help if you know how I think. Anyway, Burne's system involved contemplating, for instance, a historical battle for which the sources were scanty or at odds and, from the facts available and a technical consideration of the military pros and cons, to decide as far as possible what actually was most likely to have taken place. Even though this system presupposes that war leaders across the centuries share the same thought patterns, it does treat them as intelligent, thinking creatures, something Colonel Burne was qualified to assess with his long experience of active service. As a general rule, such a commonsense system helps to dispatch any high-flown theories about a battle – some of them spun, it may be added, without even bothering to examine the battlefield in question – which have a tendency to be lengthy sermons on what must have been without observing whether or not it was geographically possible. So, in view of these circumstances, such yarns must be viewed with decided scepticism. Anyhow, we must now turn our attention to the second fight at Cremona, the one between the Vitellians and the Flavians, and discover what may have taken place in the vicinity of Cremona on 24/25 October AD 69.

In the evening of 24 October, as the autumnal light was fading, the Flavian army arrived in the vicinity of Cremona to do battle with the Vitellian army. When Vitellius had heard of Antonius Primus' march on Italy, he despatched Caecina Alienus with a powerful army composed of *I Italica*, *V Alaudae*, and *XXI Rapax*, together with *vexillationes*, each roughly 2,000 men strong, from eight other legions (*I Germanica*, *II Augusta*, *IIII Macedonica*, *VIIII Hispana*, *XV Primigenia*, *XVI Gallica*, *XX Valeria Victrix*, *XXII Primigenia*) and a strong force of auxiliaries, both horse and foot.[2] The first of the Flavian legions (two, to be precise) had safely made it to Verona, but though urged to attack them before the remainder of the Flavians arrived, Caecina Alienus declined to do so. Apparently, he had been plotting with Sextus Lucilius Bassus to switch sides.[3] Lucilius Bassus was a former Othonian who had been promoted by Vitellius from command of an *ala* of horse to be *praefectus* of the *classis Ravennas*, but he had failed to obtain the plum command of the new Praetorian Guard.

However, the soldiers violently refused to follow their turncoat general's treacherous example, and quickly put back the images of Vitellius and clapped

Caecina Alienus in irons.[4] They then elected to the command Fabius Fabullus, currently *legatus legionis* of *V Alaudae*. They also decided to abandon their position at Hostilia and fall back to Cremona 'in order to effect a junction with the two legions, *I Italica* and *XXI Rapax*, which, with a portion of the cavalry, Caecina had sent to occupy Cremona'.[5] This they did. During the intervening time, his rival, Fabius Valens, who had been delayed by illness, had set out from Rome, 'and Fabius was loyal to Vitellius, and not without military skill'.[6]

Though still missing their general, the Vitellians occupying Cremona appear to have decided amongst themselves to initiate events. Leaving the camp they had built just outside the town walls, the two legions, with an advance guard of cavalry, marched eastwards along the Via Postumia. Antonius Primus, who had left Verona and was now based at Bedriacum, was advancing towards Cremona with a force of 4,000 cavalry. Having reached the eighth milestone from Bedriacum, the Flavian cavalry then started to plunder the countryside. Meanwhile, Flavian scouts, which were reconnoitring ahead, spotted the Vitellian advance guard on the Via Postumia and sent one of their number back to Antonius Primus. While he deliberated, Arrius Varus, without orders it would appear, hastily advanced against the Vitellians and a brisk skirmish ensued. Such uncontrolled violence quite often will carry the day although not necessarily, and after initial success, the Flavian cavalry was thrown back and broken. Antonius Primus, keeping a cool head, 'transfixed with a spear a flying standard-bearer (*vexillarium*), and then, seizing the standard (*vexillum*), turned it towards the enemy'.[7] No more than a hundred troopers rallied around their fearless general, but a small reverse was prevented from becoming a big one. His eternal instincts – when in a jam, turn and face the enemy – may have helped to save the day, but a broken bridge across a sloughy stream with bluff banks was surely a gift of the goddess Fortuna.

To his mind attack and victory were practically synonymous terms, and he knew too that the pace of the campaign had to be fast and fluid, in contrast to the Flavian supremos' plodding, pedestrian, plans. For what is victory but the driving of the foe from the field? Luck counts, Napoléon once believed that.[8] But it is no use at all if you do not know enough to take advantage of good luck. 'In the long-run luck is given only to the efficient.'[9] In other words, luck may be just luck, as everybody knows, yet more often it is the result of ability, instinct, or knowledge. Moreover, luck often enough will save a man if his courage holds. Antonius Primus believed in luck, which may be relevant, and luck was precisely what he was supposed to process in abundance. Thus it was that wherever he met the enemy, he advanced like a fighting cock and trusted to his luck. That was Antonius Primus' way.

With that Antonius Primus pursued those that fled, and the rest of his cavalry, having rallied from fleeing or returned from plundering, joined in the chase. It was at 'the fourth milestone from Cremona',[10] as Tacitus says with unaccustomed preciseness (he is undoubtedly following Vipstanus Messalla here), the fugitive Vitellians saw the glittering standards of *I Italica* and *XXI Rapax* and must have felt help was at hand. But the Vitellian legionaries refused to open their ranks or 'attack an enemy now exhausted by so protracted a pursuit and conflict'.[11] Exhausted they may have been, but the Flavian cavalry continued their pursuit, followed hard by Vipstanus Messalla, who was at the head of an auxiliary cohort from Moesia. 'The horse and foot, thus mixed together, broke through the line of the legions.'[12] Understandably, Antonius Primus now wanted to call it a day, but as the autumnal daylight diminished the Flavian legions arrived post haste from their camp at Bedriacum and, believing that it was all up for the enemy and there were rich pickings to be gleaned, 'demanded that they should advance to Cremona ... ready to break through all discipline, unless they were led as they wished'.[13]

Mutiny once again was in the air, and Antonius Primus addressed himself to his men at large, sensibly explaining the dangers of storming an unknown town at night without prior preparation and planning. But his men were having none of it. They were only brought to their senses on hearing news that the main force of Vitellians, which had forced marched that day from Hostilia, was preparing for battle and would soon be approaching.[14] This decision to fight after such travail speaks volumes on the *esprit de corps* and combat fitness of the Vitellians.

All thoughts of storming Cremona having been forgotten, the Flavians quickly took up a position either side of the Via Postumia, with *XIII Gemina* on the road itself. Thus centrally placed, this legion was supported on its left consecutively by *VII Galbiana* and *VII Claudia pia fidelis*, the latter protected on its front by a drainage ditch (*agger fossa*), and on its right by *VIII Augusta* and *III Gallica*, and the Othonian praetorians, whose standards were close to *III Gallica*. Out on the wings were the auxiliary infantry, while ranged in the front of the Flavian battle line was a screen of Suebian horsemen led by their chieftains, Sido and Italicus.[15] As for Flavian numbers we can only speculate. Later, Tacitus reports 'forty thousand armed men burst into Cremona',[16] which sounds about right if you consider there were five Flavian legions and the Othonian praetorians, say 30,000 men, together with auxiliaries, less battle casualties, put by Josephus at 4,500.[17]

The Vitellians, though road weary and still leaderless as Fabius Valens had yet to make an appearance, set up their artillery on the Via Postumia and prepared to attack in the darkness.[18] Their centre was a powerful force of some 15,000 legionaries: the *vexillationes* from Britannia (*II Augusta, VIIII Hispana, XX Valeria Victrix*), these being 'the flower of the army of Britannia',[19] the veteran *legio V Alaudae* from Xanten-*Vetera*, which had done so well at First Cremona,[20] and the *vexillatio* of *XV Primigenia* from the same Germania Inferior garrison. On the right was the *vexillatio* from *IIII Macedonica*, the left the *vexillationes* of *XXII Primigenia, I Germanica* and *XVI Gallica* in that order. Elements from the battered *I Italica* and *XXI Rapax* 'were mingled with all the *manipuli*' (viz. the other legionary cohorts),[21] while the auxiliary horse and foot were posted at the extremities. The Vitellians then hurled themselves violently on the Flavians as if they were the external enemy of Rome. The ensuing battle was to continue through the night.

Now here is an interesting tale. Tacitus writes of an incident during the night action in which the praetorians were suffering greatly from one particularly large stone throwing *ballista* operated by the opposing *XVI Gallica*. Antonius Primus had transferred the praetorians from his right to bolster up the solely tried *VII Galbiana* exposed in the open ground (*patens campus*) they held,[22] and so now the *ballista* lay uncomfortably close to their battleline. Some of these Othonian praetorians, as recent battlefield enemies of the Vitellians, must have known the terrain only too well, and two *praetoriani* picked up a couple of shields from the enemy dead to disguise their true identity (a difference of shield patterns, perhaps a unit insignia).[23] In this way they were able to infiltrate the Vitellian lines and get close enough to the artillery piece to hack through its upright springs of sinew or hair before they were cut down.[24] Their destruction could not quickly be repaired, and the *ballista* of *XVI Gallica* would be out of action for some time.

Nowadays it is fair to pose the question: was it stupidity or inspired bravery that motivated the two *praetoriani*? It has been said that in ninety-nine times out of a hundred our courage is nothing more than an expression of common politeness or sense of duty. And in the remaining case an expression of our insanity. Nonetheless, in order for a soldier to be good in combat he must have good discipline and morale. Whereas discipline can be instilled into a soldier and changes with time, the human element, morale, remains the same, capable of just so much endurance, sacrifice, effort and no more. Thus, from Tell Megiddo to Mount Tumbledown (and beyond), this essential factor in battle endures unmodified. Of the truth of this latter assertion, we will have more to say.

But what about leadership? The tradition of the Republic had been that a senator should be prepared to serve the state in whatever capacity it demanded, and be proficient. A practical people, the Romans believed that the man chosen by the competent authority would be up to the task in hand. In the Republic that authority had been the electorate, under the Principate it would be the emperor. Rome never developed any equivalent to the officer corps of a modern western army. In other words, there was no training for the job. It was a world without experts. To the end of the empire, the man sent to command an army would have to learn the skills himself, from the leisure of reading books or the harder lesson of the battlefield.

It is interesting that handbooks on military tactics and the art of generalship continued to be written under the emperors, notably by Onasander (under Claudius), Frontinus (under Domitianus), Aelian (under Trajan), Arrian (under Hadrian) and Polyainos (under Antonius Pius). All these authors claimed to be writing with a rationale purpose, namely to elucidate military matters for the benefit of senatorial commanders, and even the emperor himself. So Frontinus, in the opening lines of the preface of the *Strategemata*, explains his intentions:

> Since I alone of those interested in military science have undertaken to reduce its rules to system, and since I seem to have fulfilled that purpose,[25] so far as pains on my part could accomplish it, I still feel under obligation, in order to complete the task I have begun, to summarise in convenient sketches the adroit operations of generals, which the Greeks embraced under the one

name ςτρατηγημάτων. For in this way commanders will be equipped with specimens of wisdom and foresight, which will serve to foster their own power of conceiving and executing like deeds. There will result the added advantage that a general will not fear the issue of his own stratagem, if he compares it with the experiments already successfully made.[26]

As under the Republic, the emperors saw no need to establish a system to train future commanders. On the contrary, it was still believed that by using handbooks and taking advice, a man of average ability could direct a Roman army.[27] Thus, a good Roman commander had the Roman virtues of thoroughness and doggedness, and he did not look upon military tactics as something that came to one instinctively. On the contrary, he would have studied every campaign recorded, and have read all the best tactical manuals, Greek and Latin alike.

Little wonder, therefore, the Romans had an organized but uncomplicated approach to tactics. The principles were simple: the use of cavalry, which was divided and placed on either wing of the main battle, for flank attacks and encirclement; the placing of a force in reserve; the deployment of a battle line that could maintain contact, readiness to counterattack, flexibility in the face of unexpected enemy manoeuvres. As the disposition of forces and the tactical placing of reserves were vital elements of generalship, the Roman commander needed to be in a position from where he could see the entire battle. The underlying rationale of this style of generalship is well expressed by Onasander when he says the general 'can aid his army far less by fighting than he can harm it if he should be killed, since the knowledge of a general is far more important than his physical strength'.[28] To have the greatest influence on the battle the general should stay close to, but behind his fighting line, directing and encouraging his men from this relatively safe position.

This was certainly what Antonius Primus did at Cremona. In bright moonlight the Flavian commander rode around urging his men on, 'striving to shame some with reproaches, stirring many with praise and encouragement, and all with by hopes and promises'.[29] In this respect, he was particularly hard on the Othonian praetorians, calling them bumpkins (pagani) and telling them, as if they did not know already, that 'defeat is death, for disgrace you have exhausted'.[30] After all, they had betrayed Galba for Otho, failed Otho against Vitellius, whom they now attacked in support of Vespasianus. That other renowned Flavian general, Quintus Petilius Cerialis, is depicted during the rebellion of Civilis doing the same thing, which occasioned no small risk.[31] He we shall meet in a due course.

To illustrate the art of Roman generalship a little more, we have some written wisdom from Lucius Flavius Arrianus, or Arrian. During his governorship of the large and important frontier province of Cappadocia, Arrian had to deal with a threatened invasion of Transcaucasan nomads, the Alani (AD 134). Arrian wrote in Greek an account of the preparatory dispositions he made for this campaign, the *Ektaxis katà Alanon*. This unique work, in which the author represents himself as the famous Athenian soldier-scholar Xenophon, sets out the commands of the legate governor as if he were actually giving them. At his disposal he had two legions, *XII Fulminata* and *XV Apollinaris*, and a number of *auxilia* units, in all some 20,000 men. Arrian himself took charge of the dispositions and recognized the need for personal, hands-on leadership:

> Xenophon (i.e. Arrian), the commander of the entire army, mostly ought command in front of the infantry standards. Let him accompany the entire formation and observe how they proceed [when] deployed. He should bring the disorderly back into formation and praise those proceeding in [good] order.[32]

To carry out his orders Arrian could look to the legionary legate (one of the *legati legionum* seems to be absent), the military tribunes, centurions and decurions. Nonetheless, it is interesting to note that the tactics advocated by Arrian are safe and simple, competent rather than brilliant.

Of all the senior officers in a legion, however, it was the centurions that were the key to an army's success in battle. Centurions were a strongly conservative group who had a vital role to play in preserving the discipline and organization of the army and providing continuity of command. Yet they owed their position of command and respect to their own bravery, ferocity and effectiveness in close combat, and when they stood on the field of battle they were directly responsible for leading their men forward. Thus, their understanding of an intended battle plan was vital for success simply because they were the ones commanding the men on the ground. Understandably, a centurion who had the courage to face battle time after time was not the kind of man a legate wanted to lose.

The *aquilifer* played an important if comparatively minor leadership role in battle too. He was, after all, the man who carried the eagle, *aquila*,[33] emblem of the legion, and so served as a rallying point during the chaos of battle, and could urge hesitant soldiers forward during a particularly dangerous moment. The Othonian general Suetonius Paulinus, in his former capacity as legate governor of Britannia, had formed his army up opposite Mona ready to assault, but his soldiers wavered at the eerie spectacle of incanting Druids and frenzied women on the shoreline, 'their limbs trembling in terror'.[34] They were spurred into action, however, when 'onward pressed their standards'.[35] Probably since the time of Marius, the *aquila* represented the continuity and identity of individual legions, and to lose it in battle was considered a mighty disgrace. When we consider the singular value the soldiers placed on their *aquila* and how its loss to the enemy would mean a permanent stain on the honour of their unit, it comes as no surprise to learn that some sacrificed themselves in its defence. At Cremona the *aquila* of Antonius Primus' own legion, *VII Galbiana*, was only saved by Lucius Atilius Verus, 'who, after making a great slaughter among the enemy, at last fell'.[36] Atilius Verus, once a centurion of *V Macedonica*,[37] was the *primus pilus* of *VII Galbiana*.[38] At battle's end, its baptism of blood would cost this rookie legion all six of its senior centurions.[39]

Let us proceed. As well as bringing the emperor into a closer relationship with his soldiers, the *imago* became of increasing significance with the rise and fall of dynasties. Thus, when the emperor's portrait was torn down from the *imagines*, it was a sign of military revolt. Just before Cremona, when Caecina Alienus succeeded in winning over his senior centurions and some few soldiers to the cause of Vespasianus while the rest were otherwise engaged with routine duties outside the camp, the turncoats signified the change by tearing down the portraits of Vitellius and taking an oath to Vespasianus. But when the rest of the soldiers returned to camp and saw Vitellius' portraits had been torn down and Vespasianus' name inscribed on the *vexillum*, they were stunned. Once they came to their senses and realized what had happened, they refused to accept the change of allegiance, set up Vitellius' portraits again and placed Caecina Alienus under arrest.[40]

Closely associated with these sacred standards, the *aquila* and the *imago*, was the *cornicen*, a junior officer who blew the *cornu*, a bronze tube bent into almost a full circle with a transverse bar to strengthen it. Another instrument was the *tuba*, a straight trumpet, played by another junior officer, the *tubicen*. Music was used for lights out, reveille and the changing of the guard,[41] but its main function was tactical. Therefore upon the battlefield itself, different calls, accompanied by visual signals such as the raising of the standards, would sound the alarm or order a recall.[42] Naturally, when the troops charged into contact and raised their war cry (*clamor*), the *cornicines* and *tubicines* blew their instruments so as to encourage their comrades and to discourage the enemy. Tacitus does not mention the musicians at Cremona, but we can be assured they were doing their duty.

Turning back to the battle. War is full of uncertainty and never more so than on the field of battle. This crucial civil war engagement was a scrambling affair fought between the hours of night and day, with victory finally going to the Flavians as the sky was growing grey and a pale pink radiance, the harbinger of the scintillant sun, was in the air. The Vitellian collapse came very quickly. It is apparent that throughout the history of warfare rain, fog, hail and snow have affected quite a number of battles. But what about the sun affecting play? Well, as aurora's early pallor penetrated the failing shades of darkness, *III Gallica*, a crack legion long stationed in Syria, must have felt the day coming behind them, rather than saw. So they turned to salute the rising sun, 'as is the custom in Syria',[43] and this created rumours of reinforcements, heartening the dog-tired Flavians and striking dismay into the equally exhausted Vitellians. Fact is often considerably duller than fiction, but this was not a fiction. This was the crisis of the battle, just as a doctor maintains that there is a crisis in a fever when the equilibrium is broken and all at once it is decided whether the patient lives or dies. The Flavians lived. The Vitellians died. For the latter, the halcyon days of April to October were well and truly over.

Normally the first dawning eases the fears and perplexities of man, and most often it is like a balm and a benediction. Most often, but not always; for the Flavians this was so, but not so for the Vitellians. 'Thus it is', as Cassius Dio rightly observes of this day, 'that the smallest things can produce great alarm in men who are already exhausted.'[44] Fear is the engine. Impelled by dread, a man seeks to withdraw from prominence, to add one pace to the distance between him and those who seek his slaughter. He backs half a step into the formation, onto the comrade at his rear. This fellow, driven by his own fear, yields as well and presses in turn upon the man at his back. Fear is contagious. Motion multiplies. Cohesion breaks down. The formation becomes a mass, then a mob. Once a body of men begin to run away, the effect other men is contagious, as in most armies. This is what happened to the Vitellians that Cremona dawn when they incontinently broke and ran.[45] This was the famous deed that decided the day. It would have been a trifle before seven o'clock by our reckoning.[46]

This is a convenient point to pause and consider briefly the history of the sun worshipping *legio III Gallica*. Part of Caesar's consular series formed in 48 BC, the legion had fought for the Caesarian cause at Munda (45 BC),[47] and again at Philippi (42 BC).[48] Staying on in the Roman Near East, the legion had fought extremely well under the *triumvir* Marcus Antonius during his fighting retreat from Parthia (36 BC),[49] as it was to do again under Cnaeus Domitius Corbulo during his campaign in Armenia (AD 62–63).[50] The legion had been part of the garrison of the Roman province of Syria as early as 4 BC,[51] if not before,[52] and had built the upper Tigris fortress at Kesserik-*Ziata* in AD 64.[53] Four years later the legion was transferred by Nero from Syria to Moesia, and as it had personal knowledge of Vespasianus, he 'counted upon as devoted to himself, and it was hoped the other legions of Illyricum would follow its example'.[54]

As we can see, *III Gallica* had been closely associated with Syria for a couple of generations, and though recruiting for it was by no means limited to its own province, by at least the time of Nero it came to consist largely of local provincials.[55] With this local recruitment, therefore, the legion had obviously acquired a tradition of worship of a Near eastern solar deity, possibly Iuppiter Optimus Maximus Dolichenus, a syncretization of Iuppiter and a warlike Baal cult (from the small town of Doliche in Commagene) directly associated with the creation of weapons with iron.[56] The other possibility of course was the god of Emesa (Homs), not far from their camp at Rafaniat-*Raphaneae*.[57]

After its brilliant showing at Second Cremona, *III Gallica* was billeted for a short time at Capua, having been sent to this pro-Vitellian city by Antonius Primus.[58] However, it was not to enjoy the corporeal pleasures of Capua for long as it was sent back to Syria,[59] which needed garrisoning as many troops were fighting in Iudaea under Titus. This transfer to its old stamping ground, where many if not most of its soldiers had their families, was seen as a reward for its sterling services to Vespasianus.[60] One of the legion's military tribunes in these years was the younger Pliny. He saw no active service, being busy as he was with administrative duties in the province on the behalf of the legate governor.[61] By the time Cassius Dio was writing it was quartered in southern Phoenicia,[62] and no doubt still recruiting locals into its ranks. We last hear of it during the period of the Tetrarchy and Constantine, holding Hafer-*Danaba*, the military station between Damascus and Palmyra. But if you are wondering if this legion was an anomaly, it was not. The men of Vitellius' Rhine legions, besieging Plancentia in northern Italy several months before Second Cremona, seemed to the praetorians of Otho's army, Italians to a man, an uncouth and foreign bunch.[63]

It requires scant imagination to conjure the state of the minds of those Vitellians that morning outside Cremona, when it was thought those Flavian sunworshippers were hailing reinforcements. This was enough to chill the guts of the most courageous of them and they promptly turned and streamed off to the rear. The hours of darkness were not normally the time for the Romans to conduct tactical operations. Little wonder, therefore, the nocturnal phase of the engagement, despite the full moon, had been a confused and bitter affair and, as Tacitus says, 'on both sides weapons and uniforms were the same, frequent challenges and replies disclosed the watchword and standards were inextricably confused as they were captured by this group or that and carried hither and thither'.[64] And this confusion was probably considerably more than Tacitus lets on, chiefly because the human eye has much more serious limitations than one normally believes. Military history abounds with examples of how friendly forces were fired upon in error just because they could not be identified as such before coming so close that, had they been unfriendly, disaster might have ensued.[65] What is more, the battle had exhibited the bruising characteristics of an old-time no holds barred fist fight, with every man for himself, dying and dealing death. This is, however, to anticipate matters a little and it is now necessary to look at what was happening elsewhere.

The Vitellian camp had been built at no great distance from the walls and suburbs of Cremona on the northeast, between the converging road from Brixia (Brescia) and the Via Postumia, and near their junction. Clearly wishing to capitalize on the desire of his men for bold and swift action, the alternatives were returning to Bedriacum or to resort to the pickaxe and the construction of a camp, Antonius Primus ordered the Vitellian camp to be invested, assigning each of his five legions to a particular section of the defences. So *III Gallica* and *VII Galbiana* took up their station close to Via Postumia, *VIII Augusta* and *VII Claudia pia fidelis* the right rampart, and *XIII Gemina* opposite the northern gate (viz. *porta decumana*). Then armed with picks (*dolabrae*) and spades, bill hooks (*falces*) and scaling ladders, the Flavians 'advanced to the rampart in a dense *testudo*'.[66] The Vitellians responded with heavy stones and long poles, thereby breaking up the 'tottering *testudo*'.[67] The Flavians retreated, reformed, and returned with a second *testudo*.

'The fiercest struggle was maintained by *III* and *VII* legions', says Tacitus, 'and Antonius in person with some chosen auxiliaries concentrated his efforts at the same point.'[68] While '*VII* [*Galbiana*] in wedge-like array endeavoured to force an entrance', *III Gallica* attacked the main (viz. *porta principalis*) or southern gate of the camp 'with axes and swords'.[69] When this was finally forced, the rest of the Flavians surged forward to exploit the vulnerability of the Vitellians. The first man in deserves to be named. 'All authors are agreed',[70] continues Tacitus, 'that Caius Volusius, a soldier of *legio III*, entered first.'[71] Overpowering all those who stood in his way, Volusius gained the top of the rampart, from where he gesticulated and shouted to his comrades below that the camp was theirs. If he survived the fight, Volusius could well see himself being awarded a *corona vallaris*, a crown made of gold and ornamented with a rampart and given (even in a civil war) to the man (usually restricted, but not always, to centurion rank and above) first over the enemy rampart or *vallum*.[72] Anyway, the battle for the camp now became a slaughter within it, and the surviving Vitellians threw themselves down from the ramparts and sought shelter behind the more solid walls of Cremona a few hundred metres away, and there was no Geneva Convention to hinder. It was a case of every man for himself – and the devil take the hindmost. The Flavians chased off afoot, harrying the foe.

The next major task for the victorious Flavians was the capture of Cremona itself. 'Difficulties of another kind presented themselves in the lofty walls of the town, its stone towers, its iron-barred gates, its garrison who stood brandishing their weapons, in its numerous population devoted to the interests of Vitellius, and the vast conflux from all parts of Italy which had assembled at the fair regularly held at that time.'[73] Tacitus might be laying it on a bit thick here. Take for instance those numerous visitors to the autumn fair, who undoubtedly were more horrified than happy to find themselves caught up in a civil war that they had probably believed would pass them by. On the other hand, the stone walls and towers of Cremona were real enough, and certainly a lot tougher to overcome than the earthen rampart and wooden towers of the Vitellian camp. So Marcus Antonius sensibly ordered the firing of the finest building outside the walls in the hope of weakening the inhabitants' will to resist. Such buildings as stood near to the walls and equalled or surpassed them in height were manned by picked soldiers with instructions to dislodge the defenders on the parapet 'hurling beams, tiles, and flaming missiles'.[74] The siege had begun in earnest.

But the town chose not to resist, the Vitellian leadership having lost heart, believing that all further resistance was futile. Accordingly the images of Vitellius, along with all traces of his name, were removed, a ceasefire called, and the one man who could possibly save their skins released from confinement. And so it was the perfidious Caecina Alienus returned to centre stage, taking on a new rôle as appeaser. Terms of capitulation were duly arranged by him, by which the unarmed Vitellians funereally marched out of Cremona but still bearing their sacred eagles and standards. Caecina Alienus now had the temerity to reemerge conspicuously attired not as a soldier but as a consul and preceded by the regulation twelve lictors. It was a crass mistake. For as he 'came forward thrusting aside the crowd, the victors were fired with indignation, and reproached him with his tyranny, his cruelty, and so hateful are such crimes, even with his treason'.[75] The Flavian soldiers (and perhaps too, the Vitellian ones) were ready to lynch him, but true to his form, Antonius Primus managed to whisk him away under escort to Vespasianus in Egypt, and for several years Caecina Alienus was to bask in Vespasianus' imperial favour.

Naturally it easy for us ensconced in the cocoon of our humdrum lives to express criticism of a political trimmer like Caecina Alienus, but in these dangerous times there were many like him who opted to forget their oath to one emperor when another appeared to offer better prospects. Had not Tacitus' own father-in-law held office under Galba and Otho at Rome, and after being called away to Liguria by his mother's tragic death promptly metamorphosed himself into a diehard Flavian? As Tacitus himself points out in the context of the Vitellian leadership, 'the higher their rank, the more readily they succumbed to fortune'.[76] In civil war oaths of fidelity are but feeble trammels.

While the leaders of both sides were busy with the surrender formalities, the Flavian soldiers, in high glee, and their camp followers made their way into Cremona, which was already burning. Old scores needed to be settled, particularly by the legionaries of *XIII Gemina*, which, if we remember, after First Cremona were adscripted to construct two amphitheatres, one at Bononia and the other here at Cremona, where the local civilians, pro-Vitellian to boot, 'had wantonly provoked and insulted them'.[77] The Flavian soldiers fell into a wild orgy of enjoying their spoils.

In any war it is the civilian caught up in the conflict that suffers the most, and the inhabitants of this affluent town were to be no exception; despite a show of surrender, they fell victim to indiscriminate looting, rape and butchery, the most frightful forms of soldier licence, the last vices of war. A holocaust of death and destruction cleaned the entire town. 'In an army which included such varieties of language and character, an army comprising Roman citizens, allies, and foreigners, there was every kind of lust, each man had a law of his own, and nothing was forbidden. For four days Cremona satisfied the plunders.'[78] It sounds as though Cremona lay in the path of the Cimmerians.

In essence the rape of Cremona was no different from the aftermath of countless other sieges throughout history.[79] It was the way a victorious army usually collected its reward, and the losers generally paid for defeat. Soldiers are seldom models of good behaviour, except in propaganda hyperbole. 'The military establishment is an all-male culture which normally tolerates behavioural excesses to a greater degree than mixed civilian society.'[80] A society made up of males only is bound to be abnormal. In the barracks, the pressure from friends and family to behave is replaced by the diametrically opposed pressure to conform to the norm of the rough, tough, swaggering, vice-loving fighter. As Kipling expressed it, 'Single men in barricks don't grow into plaster saints.'[81] Instead they hang around, grumble about their superiors, and the stupidity of the military machine in general, avoid extra duties, scourge for food, try to get drunk, think and talk incessantly about women, boast disgracefully, and engage in clownish behaviour, which sometimes degenerates into bullying and physical violence. Good men can suddenly become bad men.

The Flavians were now completely out of hand. They roamed unchecked through the town, raping and murdering, looting and destroying, and then they slept drunken on wine and lust and blood. Such was the rape of Cremona.

Soldiers are generally feared as rapists, lustful brutes who are not restrained by the normal social controls that protect women. The fear is associated especially with invading foreign armies; the particularly anguishing aspect of rape in Cremona was that it was not barbarian soldiery who sexually assaulted Roman women, but Roman soldiery. A terrible exemplification of the impact upon civilians of soldiers whose discipline and sense of responsibility to a firmly constituted authority have evaporated into thin air.

Looting is a cataclysmic, terrifying experience for its victims. Looters, who are simply soldiers released from army discipline who take advantage of the anarchy they create in an unarmed society, descend like the whirlwind and blow out only when the soldiers are satiated. The only defence for civilians is to hide themselves and their portable possessions, or to seek refuge elsewhere. Soldiers loot when they are disgruntled, or when they know they can get away with it. At Cremona it was the latter case, because they were led on 'by the madness of the leading men'.[82]

We know that war implies that things that would not be acceptable under normal conditions turn out not only to be permitted but are obligatory, even. There is, in essence, an inversion of the values of everyday life, with one difference, that of degree. Innocence is simply not a recognized concept. Soldiers are licensed rapists and looters. Licensed by the weapons they carry. Rape satisfies lust; looting satisfies greed. All wars lead to an epidemic of amorality. Genuine heroism and self-sacrificing comradeship do, of course, exist. But these are always accompanied, in all wars and in all armies, by murder, torture, cruelty to prisoners, rape, and violent looting, especially when the army is operating in a foreign land.

But the Flavian army was not in a foreign land. Like Pyrrhos, but far less honourably, the Flavians won a victory at the price of their esteem.[83]

Mao Tse-tung's famous line that 'historical experience is written in iron and blood',[84] was probably meant to be provocative, but it seems to me obviously true. For what we generally regard as civilization may bring settlement and culture, but it also brings property, compulsion, war, tyranny, religion, physical and mental enslavement. It also encourages the inhumanity of man to man – hunger, humiliation, ignorance, vice, greed, extortion, violation, trickery, torture – for justice is the tool of the strong, to be used as the strong desire. On the other hand, divine justice, like the gods, is a dream of the weak. There are no gods, no laws but those men make themselves with iron and blood.

The sack of a Roman provincial town by Roman citizen soldiers would send a thrill of horror through the empire. There was no radio, no newspaper, no television channelled popular information at the time. Again and again, rumours, distortions and plain lies circulated and many must have wondered if they would be next to experience such brutality. As Augustine would later ask, 'what fury of foreign people, what barbarian cruelty, can be compared with the harm done by civil wars?'[85] Cremona is a terrible and sanguinary drama which, properly or not, is usually looked upon as the great moment of decision. Still, although the battle had been won and a town wasted, this particular civil war was not yet over. A battle is not a war, and wars are not won by weapons, but by the will to win them. I feel most will agree with this premise.

Finally, we must return briefly to the battle outside Cremona. 'On the question as to whether one should speak of the art or the science of war, he says that, more than anything else, war resembles commerce. Combat is to war what cash payment is to commerce; however seldom it need happen in reality, everything is directed towards it and ultimately it is bound to occur and prove decisive.'[86] This was Engels on another German genius, Clausewitz and his *Vom Kriege*. Whether or not he has read his Clausewitz, a general worth his salt would know that an engagement is won and lost on many factors. Flaws in any one and defeat is usually assured. Let us analyse:

First, there are imponderables such as spirit, eagerness for victory, experience and discipline. The two armies at Second Cremona were strong in all these, except perhaps the Vitellians with regards to the last. Let it be said, the Vitellians were still formidable opponents despite Tacitus' earlier claims that their prolonged summer holiday in Rome meant they were softened by a climate considerably more deliberating than that to which they were accustomed, and the allurements of a strange metropolis they had savoured to excess.[87]

Second, there are the tangibles such as weapons, organization and tactics. Obviously at Second Cremona there was nothing to choose between the two sides in any of these.

Third, an ever-present element in battle is numerical strength. This was the dominant single material factor in this battle, as it usually is in war between similar troops. We have already supposed the Flavian army, not counting the auxiliaries, contained more or less 30,000 legionaries. As for the Vitellian legionary numbers, there were perhaps some 26,000,[88] of which 15,000 were used for a hammer-blow against the Flavian centre. And so, a classic military doctrine came into play: when discipline and morale are more or less equal, numbers will tell. Indeed, you could finally subsume all the immutable rules and fundamental principles of the art of war under the one, absolute axiom: the stronger always overcomes the weaker.

Look at it this way. Even in the Computer Age we really are still living by the law of the Stone Age: the man with the biggest club is right. It is exactly like mopping up a battlefield: all those who are hopelessly disabled or in agony you dispatch with one swift blow of your club. You move on, to new fields of battle, to new triumphs or defeats. Our weapon of choice here simply represents brute force – 'nothing to boast of, when you have it, since your strength is just an accident arising from the weakness of others'.[89] The ability to compel those weaker than yourself to obey seems to confer the right to do so, and there is no real restriction on the degree of violence employed in the process. Organized violence writes its own rules. Right or wrong, for better or worse, this is the way things seem to get done. That is history. That was the Romans.

It is wise to remember that all this carnage for the Romans was accomplished at close range, mostly in horrific hand-to-hand combat. When Rome was no longer Rome, the technology of war slumped to low levels, as did most other military organizational skills. The lethality of small arms manifested a similar decline when compared with that of the Principate army. To suggest one likely example, a smoothbore, flintlock musket used by Napoleonic infantry was only marginally accurate at fifty metres or thereabouts, and its killing power dropped off to almost zero at around a hundred metres or so – at this time infantry were considered mere cogs in a walking battery and so the frequent order being not to fire until you could see the whites of the enemy's eyes. This weapon approximately matched the Roman legionary's *pilum* in range but was far less likely to kill. Such a decline in the lethality of weapons during the long stretch between the fall of Rome and the American Civil War helps to explain to a large degree the very high numbers of battle casualties suffered by ancient armies compared with those suffered by latter armies.

In almost all respects, the conduct of war was not to return to a level of sophistication demonstrated by the Romans until the nineteenth century with the invention first of the breech loader and subsequently of the magazine rifle, of smokeless powder, of quick firing cannons. Tactics, as a practical art, declined, and the tactical flexibility as demonstrated by the triple-lined legion (viz. *triplex acies*) remained easily a thing of the Roman past until the era of Napoléon. Indeed, war as a human institution had been pushed forward to a very advanced state long before the introduction of so-called modern weaponry. A number of military historians have pointed out that Alexander the Great's army could have fought Napoléon's troops of some two millenniums later. Despite some obvious differences they were surprisingly similar in weapon power, tactics and strategy.

The Siamese twins, state and army, have never been separated since they were born around the time of Sumer – and most of the time, the state is the stronger of the twins, which is the natural order of things. Armies exist to serve the interests of the states that own them, and their legitimacy comes solely from the fact that they belong to states.

The town of Cremona was treated with frightening barbarity by its conquerors. But it was not foreigners that were the victims of the nearly incredible cruelty and the vicious, uncontrolled behaviour the Flavians. Safe in the comfort and security of our own homes, we can only guess at the unspeakable horrors visited upon the civilian residents of Cremona.

Chapter 7

Conflict with Civilis

T here is one vital point that should be stressed with regards to the professionalism of the Principate army. Current weaponry is highly complex, changes frequently and is increasingly designed to be 'idiot proof' and easy to use so that men can be trained to use it in relatively short periods of time. When weapons are so designed, there is unlikely to be much difference between what one user and another gets out of them regardless of individual skill. But this emphasis on training a recruit in the intricacies of his craft before being let loose on the world is a relatively recent phenomenon. In our period of study warfare was dominated by men who were not trained in any meaningful sense of the word, but who had learned their military skills in childhood and adolescence as a part of their total cultural environment. The all-important exception, of course, was Rome. The advent of military training – the imparting of unfamiliar military skills to individuals who were themselves generally unaccustomed to warfare – depended upon the development of relatively simple weapons that could compete effectively with traditional methods of warfare.

The Romans attached a great deal of importance to military training, and it is this that largely explains the formidable success of their army, 'for we see no other explanation of the conquest of the world by the Roman people than their drill-at-arms, camp discipline and military expertise'.[1] 'And what can I say about the training of legions?' was the rhetorical question once aired by Cicero. 'Put an equally brave, but untrained soldier in the front line and he will look like a woman.'[2] Evidently the rhythm of Roman warfare had an inner logic that was more apparent to contemporary observers than it is to us modern historians of their art. 'It would not be far from the truth to call their drills bloodless battle, their battles bloody drills,' so runs the most celebrated line of Josephus.[3] The patriot-turned-partisan presents a rather idealized view of the Roman army's efficiency, and he may have been exaggerating. But he is not far wrong when he places his failure down to the effectiveness of the arduous training given to the legions.

A legionary had to be physically and mentally stronger than his 'barbarian' adversary. 'Military exercises give the Roman soldiers not only tough bodies but determined spirits too,' a clear indication of the tactical mentality of Roman warfare, as Josephus points out.[4] Moreover, training gave Roman soldiers a psychological edge over their foe, helping them to cope better with battle wounds, to suppress fear and panic.[5] Training brought not only efficiency and effectiveness but discipline and confidence too, or in Varro's very appropriate dictionary definition: 'Army, because it is made better by means of training.'[6] The standard infantry training – route marches, field exercises, physical training, weapons training, drill – was very harsh.[7] So were the centurion instructors. But when it came to the dreaded lottery of open battle, this training was to give the legionary superiority over the 'barbarian'.

Men who have not undergone training should not be led into battle. This was said well by Arrian.[8] In fact an episode from the campaign of Quintus Petilius Cerialis against Civilis demonstrates this well enough. Well trained, and therefore well disciplined, Roman soldiers without qualms accepted an order from their commander that obviously exposed them to enemy fire because they appreciated that the sacrifice of losses would bring them a resounding victory. So, in the words of Tacitus:

... Cerialis moved with more rapidity. He sent to the Mediomatrici (Gaulish tribe) persons commissioned to conduct the legions which were there by the shortest route against the enemy; and collecting such troops as there were at Mogontiacum (Mainz) and such as he had brought with himself, he arrived in three days' march at Rigodulum (Riol). [Tullius] Valentinus, at the head of a large body of Treveri, had occupied this position, which was protected by hills, and by the river Mosella (Moselle). He had also strengthened it with ditches and breastworks of stone. These defences, however, did not deter the Roman general from ordering his infantry to the assault, and making his cavalry advance up a hill; he scorned the enemy, whose forces, hastily levied, could not, he knew, derive any advantage from their position, but what would be more than counterbalanced by the courage of his own men. There was some little delay in the ascent, while the troops were passing through the range of the enemy's missiles. As soon as they came to close fighting, the barbarians were dislodged and hurled like a falling house from their position. A detachment of the cavalry rode round where the hills were less steep, and captured the principal Belgic chiefs, and among them Valentinus, their general.[9]

The Treveri had been the allies of a certain Civilis, who had seen fit to raise an army in rebellion, which included eight cohorts of Batavi formerly of the Principate army. These veteran cohorts had been withdrawn from Britannia by Nero in preparation for his planned Caucasus expedition (AD 66). As we well know, this did not happen and events turned out otherwise for Nero. Consequently, the eight Batavi cohorts had been ordered back to Britannia, presumably by Galba. Nonetheless, by the end of AD 68 they were still marching through central Gaul, having only got as far as the territory of the Lingones.[10]

For a time before Nero's fall, the Batavian noblemen Iulius Civilis (his adopted Roman name, not his native one), along with his brother Claudius Paulus, had been placed under arrest suspected of complicity in the revolt of Vindex. Paulus was executed by the then legate governor of Germania Inferior, Fonteius Capeio, 'on a false charge of rebellion',[11] Civilis was packed off to Rome in chains, where he was heard and acquitted by Galba, then arrested again, this time by the Vitellian army. In the meantime, Galba had disbanded Nero's *Germani corporis custodes*, 'who had served previous emperors and proved loyal in many critical tests'.[12] Generally composed of Batavians, the bodyguard, under their commander, a former gladiator, Titus Claudius Spiculus, had held out for Nero to the bitter end.[13] It is highly possible that after their disbandment the erstwhile members of the *Germani corporis custodes* ended their days as the bodyguard of Civilis.[14]

Not long after his *coup d'état* of New Year AD 69 Vitellius had Civilis, 'a man of commanding influence among the Batavi', released least 'that high-spirited nation should be alienated by his execution'.[15] The eight cohorts of Batavi therefore joined the Vitellian march on Italy,[16] and took part in the decisive battle of First Cremona.[17] Initially, the Batavi had been ordered to the relief of Gallia Narbonensis, then under threat from Othonian forces, but the Vitellian legions grumbled that if these 'veteran troops victorious in so many campaigns' were detached it would be like tearing 'from a body its very strongest limbs'.[18] As Tacitus describes the Batavi, they 'had had long training in the German wars, and they had gained further renown in Britannia'.[19]

Although there were specialist units of archers and slingers,[20] it would be wrong to view these infantrymen of the *auxilia* as some species of light infantry. Weighed down with helmet, body armour, sword, dagger, spear and shield, this equipment is not that of a nimble skirmisher.[21] On the contrary, they formed the first line at Idistaviso (AD 16) and Vetera (AD 70), operated in close order using the traditional sword-fighting techniques of the Principate army at Mons Graupius (AD 83), and could even stand up to and beat legionaries as the Batavi did during the revolt of Civilis.[22] For instance, at Mon Graupius the Batavi punched the enemy with their shields and then jabbed them with their swords. Again, we see the *scutum* and *gladius* being employed in a tandem offensively:

> Agricola exhorted the four Batavi and two Tungri *cohortes* to fight hand-to-hand at sword's point. This was what they had been trained for in their long service ... Accordingly when the Batavi began to exchange blows hand to hand, to strike with the bosses (*umbonis*) of their shields, to stab in the face, and after cutting down the enemy on the level, to push their line uphill, the other *cohortes* [of Tungri], exerting themselves to emulate their charge, proceeded to slaughter the nearest enemies.[23]

The essentially similar fighting techniques of the legions and the infantryman of the *auxilia*, which is to come to close quarters and to use both *scutum* and *gladius* offensively, emphasized the degree to which the latter became an essential and very efficient part of the Principate army. That these tactics were the practice of the period is amply shown on Trajan's Column where at least three scenes of battle depict auxiliaries in action and legionaries in reserve.[24]

We come now to those veteran Batavi cohorts fighting for Vitellius. Soon after the Vitellian victory at Cremona, the Batavi showed a complete lack of discipline, for at Augusta Taurinorum (Turin) their bad relations with *legio XIIII Gemina Martia Victrix* erupted into an all-out battle.[25] Vitellius decided to send the Batavi cohorts 'back to Germania, lest they should venture on further violence'.[26] The legate governor in Germania Superior, Hordeonius Flaccus, regarded the Batavi as suspect.[27] When news of Vespasianus' bid for power reached the capital, Vitellius began levying new troops, including from the *insula Batavorum*, which was contrary to an old agreement and 'caused indignation'.[28] Civilis, who had already been canvassed by Antonius Primus to support Vespasianus,[29] took this as an excuse to rebel from Vitellius.

The timing was certainly right. With *V Alaudae*, *XXI Rapax* and *vexillationes* from the five other Rhine legions absent in Italy, Civilis, under a cloak of loyalty to Vespasianus, roused his fellow Batavi against Vitellius. The rebel alliance, besides Civilis' own people and the eight cohorts of Batavi, consisted of Germanic tribes who contributed *auxilia* to Rome, and Germanic tribes further east of the Rhine. When Vitellius was overthrown, Civilis should have placed himself at the disposal of Vespasianus – who was claimed by Civilis to be his personal friend.[30] But many of the Gallic auxiliaries in Gallia Belgica, including the Tungri, deserted Rome after Second Cremona, and Civilis ultimately made common cause with Iulius Classicus and Iulius Tutor, Treveri noblemen who concerted plans for a revolt of all Gaul. Worse still, Hordeonius Flaccus was dragged from his bed one night and murdered by his mutinous soldiers.[31] But that was not all, for two of the Rhine legions (*I Germanic*, *XV Primigenia*) felt the situation hopeless and transferred their allegiance to the rebels.[32]

According to Tacitus, the rebels were fighting for a variety of reasons, 'the Gauls for freedom, the Batavi for glory, the Germans for plunder'.[33] Whatever the true motives, Civilis' head was evidently turned, and the revolt turned into an independence movement.[34] Civilis was certainly a frightening figure to behold: he had lost an eye during his twenty-five years in the service of Rome,[35] which had been distinguished, and on the day of taking up arms against Rome he let his hair grow long and dyed it red.[36]

Once the new emperor had regained control of Italy, a powerful expeditionary force of eight legions under the consul Petilius Cerialis, the reckless but able commander whom we met at the beginning of this chapter, was sent to the Rhine. His army included former Vitellian legions as well as Flavian; even the troublesome *XIIII Gemina Martia Victrix* was summoned from Britannia again.[37] This time the 'conquerors of Britannia',[38] as Petilius Cerialis hailed the legion, were never sent back. The force thus made up must have needed a man of Petilius Cerialis' unconventional stamp to hold it together.

During the previous year Petilius Cerialis had been held hostage in Rome by Vitellius, but he had managed to escape disguised as a peasant and join Antonius Primus' march on Rome,[39] serving thereafter as one of his cavalry commanders.[40]

Petilius Cerialis may have been closely connected with the emperor (son-in-law?), and like him, may have been a Sabine too. All the same, he was a dashing general. Tacitus, who obviously had a soft spot for the man, describes his raffish and maverick character, careless of the trappings of discipline and a brilliant improviser. A man whose career is remarkable for the number of times he escaped from the brink of military disaster, or, as Tacitus would say, 'Fortuna helped him even when skill had failed'.[41] In a singular speech to the Treveri and the Lingones of northeast Gaul, the occasion being the most critical point of the great provincial revolt on the Rhine, Tacitus would attribute to him that crisp appraisal of military imperialism: 'no peace without armies, no armies without pay, no pay without taxes'.[42]

The campaign against Civilis turned out to be extremely hazardous, Petilius Cerialis coming very near to defeat several times, saved again by his genius for improvisation, shrewd diplomacy, and of course his uncommon luck; it would seem that Fortuna was a mistress whose favours he refused to share with anybody else.[43] He was finally triumphant over Civilis' rebels, though at first almost done for, gaining a complete victory in a battle at Augusta Treverorum (Trier).[44] His next assignment for the new Flavian dynasty was Britannia.

Command in the far province was time and time again felt to require the appointment of some of Rome's greatest generals, and of course Petilius Cerialis was no exception. Yet had someone suggested to him when he was a legate in Britannia that he would return to the province as its legate governor, Petilius Cerialis probably would have been greatly amused.[45] Anyway, Fortuna graced him once more with her divine favour. He would take Agricola to Britannia as one of his *legati legionum*,[46] to command *XX Valeria Victrix*.[47] As is well known, it would be his second stretch there.[48] Tacitus proudly broadcasts, 'when Britannia with the rest of the world was recovered by Vespasianus, generals became great, armies excellent, and the enemy's hopes languished'.[49] For our distinguished historian, hardly surprisingly, the greatest of these 'great generals' would be his own father-in-law, the legate governor fated to direct a major assault on the northern half of the island. Nonetheless, prior to that Petilius Cerialis would successfully govern Britannia between AD 71 and 73/4. He was the founder of York-*Eboracum* as a base for his old legion, *VIIII Hispana*, which was moved there from its old camp at Lincoln-*Lindum*.

This is hardly the place to deal at any length with the events of Petilius Cerialis' governorship of Britannia. Let us rather return to Civilis' rebellion. With the defeat of the Treveri at Rigodulum, their territory was occupied and the short-lived *imperio Galliarum* collapsed. Next fought was that 'near-run thing' at Augusta Treverorum,[50] followed by another pitched battle at Vetera.[51] Civilis narrowly missed a piece of good fortune, which might at least have protracted the campaign. Petilius Cerialis nearly fell into his hands. He had gone to inspect the winter camps then being erected at Bonn-*Bonna* and Neuss-*Novaesium*, and was returning to the seat of war. The discipline of his escort had been corrupted by the lax and libertine habits of their general. They were surprised by a night attack, and suffered significantly after the Germans 'cut the ropes of the tents, and slaughtered the soldiers as they lay buried beneath their own dwellings'.[52] Petilius Cerialis narrowly escaped captured, he being elsewhere in the arms of a local beauty, but the praetorian trireme he was travelling in was rowed off in triumph.

Petilius Cerialis then 'mercilessly ravaged *insula Batavorum*, but, with a policy familiar to commanders, left untouched the estates and houses of Civilis'.[53] Emissaries were sent by him to make private offers of peace to the Batavi, and a pardon to Civilis, who found that he had no alternative but to lay down his arms. Such lenient terms for insurrectionists certainly indicates that Vespasianus had an initial hand in the insurrection, no matter the course it finally took. Civilis himself sought and obtained an interview with Petilius Cerialis, and the 'bridge over the river Nabalia was cut down, and the two generals advanced to the broken extremities'.[54] Tacitus' *Historiae* breaks off suddenly just after the commencement of Civilis' speech to Petilius Cerialis. His fate is unknown. That the Batavi were treated favourably by Rome seems evident from a passage in a later work of Tacitus.[55]

After Civilis' rebellion four Rhine legions (*I Germanica, IIII Macedonia, XV Primigenia, XVI Gallica*) were disbanded by Vespasianus for having seriously disgraced themselves.[56] Of the other Rhine legions, *V Alaudae* was moved to Moesia (it had been posted there immediately after Second Cremona), *XXI Rapax* (conspicuous by its courage at Augusta Treverorum) and *XXII Primigenia* (conspicuous in holding Mainz-*Mogontiacum*) were left on the Rhine but moved to different bases. By the end of AD 70, *XXI Rapax* was at the rebuilt fortress at Bonn-*Bonna*. Also in Germania Inferior, *VI Victrix* was at the rebuilt Neuss-*Novaesium*, *X Gemina* at Nijmegen-*Noviomagus*, where a new stone fortress was built on the site of the old Augustan camp, and *XXII Primigenia* at Xanten-*Vetera*, the two-legion fortress there, reconstructed in stone under Nero but heavily damaged during the recent siege and battle there, being replaced by a new one-legion fortress. In Germania Superior, Mainz-*Mogontiacum* now became the home of those former Othonian legions, *I Adiutrix* and *XIIII Gemina Martia Victrix*, the latter unit making a return visit after a twenty-seven-year absence, while the Flavian legions, *XI Claudia pia fidelis* and *VIII Augusta*, were respectively at Windisch-*Vindonissa* and the rebuilt Strasbourg-*Argentoratum*.

Chapter 8

The Victorious Emperor

Some ninety years after the sea battle off Actium, the Iulio-Claudian dynasty had come to a tragic and untimely end. In the pithy observation of Tacitus, Nero's death by his own shaky hand had 'divulged that secret of empire, that emperors could be made elsewhere than at Rome'.[1] This was no mere Tacitean figure of speech, simply because imperial authority was ultimately based on control of the military. Thus, to retain power a player in the game of thrones had to gain an unshakable control over the legions, which were dotted along the fringes of the empire. Of course, this in turn meant that the soldiers themselves could impose their own choice. Indeed, it turned out that even if an emperor gained recognition in Rome, this counted for nothing in the face of opposition from the armies out in the frontier provinces. Thus, the events of AD 69 openly demonstrate the importance of provincial armies and their commanders. For it was to take a tumultuous year of ruinous civil wars and the untimely deaths of three imperial candidates before a fourth candidate could come out on top, remain there, and establish for himself a new dynasty.

Nero was the descendant of Marcus Antonius, of Augustus. Like the founding father Romulus, Vespasianus' pedigree was his own creation. Most dynasties start with ruthless buccaneers, or lucky soldiers, or dogged barbarian invaders, and the Flavian was certainly no exception. Titus Flavius Vespasianus (b. AD 9) was a senior senator of obscure Italian origin, 'baseborn' in the eyes of those that 'mattered'. Nonetheless, this represented a culmination of an important process, which brought an Italian into government, many Italians having made a name for themselves during Octavianus' bloodstained rise to power. Like the men closest to Octavianus, Vespasianus was not a member of the traditional Roman nobility; his family had run a banking business in Rieti. His paternal grandfather, Titus Flavius Petro, became the first to rise above the common herd, gaining the rank of centurion and fighting at Pharsalus for Pompey in 48 BC. Surviving the civil wars, he subsequently became a tax collector.[2] Vespasianus and his elder brother, Titus Flavius Sabinus, were the first of the family to gain entrance to the Senate. Vespasianus was a surefooted commander and a shrewd politician, though he obviously came across more as a tough old soldier than anything else (one suspects that he was born a soldier and only made a politician).

The history of Vespasianus' rise is full of lessons. As a young officer he had risen steadily through the ranks, having served in Thrace, Crete, Cyrenaica, and Germania. He had been an aedile and a praetor under Caius Caligula, and it was during his aedileship that he incurred the wrath of the emperor, who was furious that the streets were unclean. As it was one of Vespasianus' duties as aedile to keep the streets clean, the apoplectic emperor ordered some soldiers to stuff his toga with filth, which they did with gusto.[3] Luckily, he had been well liked by Claudius, being granted the trappings of a triumph for his part in the invasion of southern Britannia as the *legatus legionis* of *II Augusta* (AD 43),[4] where 'he fought thirty battles, subjugated two warlike tribes, and captured more than twenty *oppida*, besides the entire Vectis (Isle of Wright)'.[5] This was followed by a consulship (AD 51) and the proconsulship of Africa (AD 63). However, he ran foul of Nero, who packed him off to troublesome Iudaea to handle the rebellion there, which had flared up and speedily assumed monstrous proportions (AD 66).[6] In the court of the actor emperor the old soldier was wildly out of place, like a switchblade knife fight at a polite tea party. It was not his trade, all that mincing and pretending. Vespasianus had learned the necessary manners of a senator, but never that of a fawning courtier. Still, Iudaea was about as far from the imperial throne as a soldier could be sent in those days. You could also say that, next to Hades, it was the worse place to be sent. Yet Vespasianus succeeded in quelling the violence in Iudaea, and was set to invest Jerusalem when Nero played his last scene.

Apparently, Nero had entrusted Vespasianus with the command in Iudaea (three legions, and four more to hand in Syria) because he was 'an energetic commander, who could be trusted not to abuse his plenary powers... nothing, it seemed, need be feared from a man of such modest antecedents'.[7] Significantly, Vespasianus, along with his son Titus, would acquire from the bitter Jewish war a reputation for sharing the toils of the army and identifying themselves with the rank and file, that part of the knack of man management known as the 'common touch'. Soldiers know well enough what they want from their commanders: competence and fairness, personal courage, tactical skill, and a sense that their lives will not be sacrificed unnecessarily. What they do not want are commanders more concerned with promoting their own careers than caring for their soldiers' lives. These are concerns of soldiers throughout the ages.

The cultivation of the common touch, which father and son practised quite naturally, enhanced their reputations as soldiers (especially with their own men), but it was not widely imitated. In particular, Vespasianus was a man of a strong mind, with all the sentiments of a soldier: he led the column-of-march in person, selected camp sites, pursued the enemy day and night, and would even venture into the line of battle if necessary, thus committing himself to the trial of combat. Nowadays, personal courage in a commander is an admirable trait, but it need not be demonstrated because it is assumed. Not with the Romans. Combat usually found Vespasianus (like Caesar before him) at the point of the heaviest fighting, and often in the midst of it himself. His men had a general who knew how to lead them (even from the front), shared their dangers, and made them feel good about themselves and their army. What is more, in dress and appearance Vespasianus (unlike Caesar) was much the same as an ordinary ranker, not much given to the glitter and filigree of the military profession, and ate whatever rations were available, 'in short, but for his avarice, he was equal to the generals of old'.[8]

So much for leading by example. The other universally accepted fact is that as a commander, the men must come first. This is known nowadays as loyalty down the chain of command. Good commanders practise it. Bad commanders put themselves and their careers first and to hell with everyone else. Vespasianus, who obviously came across as more a soldier than a politician, built up an excellent rapport with his men, attracting them to him by his simplicity, sociability, and attentive kindness. It does not take too much of an imagination for one to envisage each night, and night succeeding night, Vespasianus making his rounds from campfire to campfire, stopping to lend a word, share a jibe, or simply let his soldiers to feed upon his presence, he who would be emperor.

Such then, was the nature of this ruler. The imperial pretence was that power came from the Roman people by voluntary grant, whereas in reality it was either inherited (as in the case of Tiberius) or seized (as in the case of Vespasianus). Likewise, the fairytale fiction that the army was the army of the Roman people was preserved. Tiberius may proclaim 'the soldiers do not belong to me, but to the state',[9] but in truth the emperor commanded what was virtually his own private army. This reminds us of the theory and practice in the now defunct Soviet Union. Henry Kissinger, politically active when that Orwellian régime was huge and still seemed powerful, majestically commented:

> No Communist state has solved the problem of regular succession. Every leader dies in office, or is replaced by coup-like procedures. Honorific retirement is rare and nonexistent for the supreme leader. No Soviet leader's reputation, except Lenin's, has survived his death. In every Communist state a leadership group seize power, grow old together, and are eventually replaced by successors whose ability to reach the pinnacle depends on their skill in masking their ambitions... they know that they will probably be denied by their successors the accolade of history, which is the incentive of most statesmen.[10]

Were it not for its sclerotic and senile leadership, gerontocrats like Leonid Ilich Brezhnev, perhaps everything would have worked out differently. But I digress.

Beside Kissinger's last point we can place a comment by the senatorial Cassius Dio, that is to say, 'no injunction can have any weight against the ingratitude or the might of one's successors'.[11]

As our portrait suggests, Vespasianus in Iudaea was the 'born soldier', but he was much more than this, as subsequent events were to prove. At first, as we remember, Vespasianus supported Galba, whom the Senate had confirmed as emperor, and then Otho. But the ensuing civil war and rapid departures of those two emperors had made Vespasianus realize that he himself could make a play for the purple. When the legions under the control of Vespasianus and his political allies declared him emperor, the Senate confirmed it. This brought an end to the civil war, and in recognition of this accomplishment Vespasianus built a new temple of Peace, the Templum Pacis, and ordered the ceremonial closure of the temple of Janus Quirinus.[12] Augustus had closed it three times,[13] Nero once,[14] but in all the centuries preceding them only two similar occasions were known.[15]

Peace, and here he was echoing Augustus, was a major theme of Vespasianus' principate, being widely broadcasted through the agency of coins bearing the legend PAX AVGVSTI, 'Peace of the Emperor'.[16] The tragic events of AD 69 hold importance as they illustrate how fragile imperial peace really was. Provinces had been wrecked, provincial towns destroyed, provincial armies wasted. Vespasianus therefore emphasized the stability of Roman power with the empire once again set on the firmest foundations both politically and militarily. Here we should take note of an essential development during the year of four emperors, for as soon as each usurper declared himself emperor, he promptly issued the money that was needed to shore up his soldiers' loyalty and at the same time the new specie served the practical purpose of spreading abroad the knowledge of his name and image. Vespasianus was less the successor of Nero than he was the heir of Augustus.

If the elevation of Vespasianus had ushered in a period of peace and stability, which was to last until AD 193, then the only public charge held against Vespasianus was his unattractive relationship with money. The emperor himself liked money, but disliked personal profligacy, and it seems he could pinch a penny as hard as any loan shark.[17] The disease of avarice was an infection that Vespasianus never cured, even as an emperor. For he not only put up existing taxes but even brought in new ones, the most infamous of them surely being that put on public urinals (urine being an important ingredient in the tanning and the laundry trades). When his son Titus objected to this, or so the story goes, his father thrust a coin under his son's nose and asked him if it stank. On replying in the negative, the emperor simply informed his son that the coin had come from the urinals. And so *pecunia non olet* – 'money doesn't stink' – would become a popular catch phrase of his principate.[18] True or not, such measures as the tax on urine (*vectigal urinae*) can be seen as part and parcel of Vespasianus' stabilizing programme, which obviously involved sorting out the dreadful state of the finances after a profligate Nero and a ferocious civil war. Naturally those paying the tax were the buyers of the urine, not those passing it.

Taken overall then, Vespasianus can be counted among the 'good' emperors. He was a conscientious, firm, and responsible leader – exactly what the empire needed. He steered clear of the grave mistakes his three predecessors had made by not just rewarding his old cronies who had helped him along the bloody, brawling path to power but also allowing a wider group of people an interest in his continued principate, that is to say, he restored and revitalized the senatorial and equestrian orders by throwing out those whom he thought unworthy and putting in 'the most eligible Italians and provincial candidates available'.[19] And besides, Vespasianus was fortunate too in the fact that all the big provincial armies had now had their go at breaking and making emperors (besides, soldiers welcome continuity because it guarantees security of pay and donatives), and generally all thoughts and aspirations were for one thing only – peace. With that, a nation once divided by civil war became united in a desire for peace.

Just to make sure, however, Vespasianus straightaway attended to the matter of his succession, declaring in the Senate that either his two sons would succeed him or no one would. He restored military discipline and reorganized the army, filled the nation's coffers that the profligacies of Nero and the horrors and violence of the recent civil war had sucked dry, began building the Flavian Amphitheatre, better known to history as the Colosseum, and taught his son Titus about governing so that the Flavian dynasty would thrive after his death. Of his impending death and the signs that foreshadowed it, the emperor apparently cracked many a joke. For instance, upon seeing a long-tailed comet, the bald Vespasianus joked that it could only presage the death of the long-haired king of Parthia.[20] His sense of humour stayed with him all the way to his deathbed, where, racked with fever, he is reported to have uttered the words, 'Dear me! I must be turning into a god'.[21] How right he was.

We may be tempted of course to laugh at this, as perhaps the sardonic Vespasianus (the man, not the god) intended us to, but we should reflect that at the base of the human brain there is a tiny pine-cone shaped gland known as the pineal. Only human beings have this gland; only human beings worship Supreme Beings and have the desire and need to do so. The psychic and spiritual centre of the human body, intuition and conscience are associated with the pineal gland. Anyway, Vespasianus was right, for he was hailed with genuine gratitude as *divus*.[22]

He was no god, but a man, Vespasianus, though men called him divine.[23] Godhead is, after all, a matter of fact, not a matter of opinion: if a man is generally worshipped as a god then he is a god. And if a god ceases to be worshipped he is nothing. After all, even though all other animals lean forward and look down toward the earth, man stands fully erect and can look directly into the heavens. As Homer once sung, without the gods man is but a zero. For those of a sceptical nature there is the argument that when men are old, concerned with their name, their legend, what their lives will mean to the future, they become vain with the names they own, their claims to have been the first man, the strongest army, the cleverest ruler. It is when he is old that Narcissus wants a graven image of himself (or so the story goes).[24]

The climax of Vespasianus' remarkable career not only makes evident that traitors who prevail are Roman patriots, but usurpers who succeed are divine emperors too. After all, if successful, the victor mythologizes his violent insurrection to sustain the social identity of the victorious cause, while the loser becomes an insurrectionist in a criminal act of violence against the legitimate state. All duels, most drunken punch-ups, and a great many wars, have derived at least part of their motivation from the notion that the winner of a fight proves conclusively that he is the 'better man'. If we pass from Vespasianus the traitor to Vespasianus the patriot, we learn that he was to be remembered as a noble and gracious ruler who had given stronger proofs of his loyal devotion to Rome and the empire than the Olympian gods themselves. Moreover, his equally patriotic son Titus was to succeed to the imperial throne automatically, having been already a 'partner in the empire'; the two held the office of consul together seven times,[25] and since AD 71 Titus had the authority of tribune (*tribunicia potestas*) and was addressed as *imperator*. Father and son had also acted together as censors.

But perhaps the most important position Titus held during his father's principate was commander of the Praetorian Guard. Vespasianus harboured no illusions about the recent troubles with praetorian prefects who had broken their oath of allegiance to the emperor,[26] and therefore he wisely appointed his son to that important post (and he alone), which had hitherto only been discharged by Roman *equites* directly answerable to the emperor (thereafter, the prefecture became the most senior post on the equestrian ladder).[27] Titus did exactly what his father wanted, ruthlessly eliminating his father's confidants at the slightest hint of disloyalty. Indeed, we hear no more of that quadruple turncoat Caecina Alienus till the very end of the principate of Vespasianus (AD 79), when he entered into a plot against the emperor.[28] He was slain, by order of Titus, in the imperial palace on the Palatine 'as he rose from a meal with his intended victim'.[29]

By the time Titus formally assumed the purple in his own name, he had enjoyed singular advantages. He had been groomed, trained and advanced under the aegis of his sensible father. Secured in power under his father when the latter gained the throne, Titus had an almost unmatched opportunity of apprenticeship in ruling the Roman world, which allowed him to obtain in that ten-year period the very experience his father had to quickly learn on the hoof. And so, his mission accomplished, Vespasianus is changed into a god.[30]

Chapter 9

The Eternal Emperors

O n his deathbed Vespasianus handed over the imperial mantle to his eldest son, Titus, who would rule until AD 81, too short a time to have turned monstrous before the eyes of his critics. Titus' younger brother, the dark Domitianus, then took the helm and retained the purple of the Caesars until AD 96. He turned out to be a 'bad' emperor, rivalling Caius Caligula and Nero in the unpopularity stakes, and his entire palace was a sea of suspicious eyes. He therefore suffered a 'bad' end by being butchered in his bath at the hands of his personal masseur, who was actually fronting a palace revolution, possibly with the secret connivance of none other than the empress, Domitia Longina. Luckily for the empire and its people no civil war followed and the next four emperors, Nerva, Trajan, Hadrian, and Antoninus Pius ruled with steadfast and stable minds – what Gibbon describes as 'the period in the history of the world, during which the condition of the human race was most happy and prosperous'.[1] The institution of monarchy, having survived beyond the suicide of the last Iulio-Claudian, had been firmly established and thus worked effectively regardless of any glitches.

In some ways this is surprising because the impression we gain from our ancient authors, obsessed as they are with the personalities of the emperors, is one of paradox. We would fully believe, on reading their histories and their biographies, that nobody could now find himself at the head of the state without giving way very soon to madness, tyranny, caprice, cruelty, waste, and of course lust. Starting right from the beginning of the Principate we have Augustus, a bloodthirsty conniving maniac, then comes Tiberius, a crabby old man who for his own gratification performs unnatural acts with small boys in his swimming pool. Up next is the cruel, capricious and cowardly Caius Caligula, a jejune crackpot, a complete and utter weirdo – probably 'certifiable' by the time he was assassinated – while his uncle Clau-Clau-Claudius, considered by many a spastic creature and thus unfit for rule, was the world's authority on pig breeding. And then we have an old acquaintance of ours, Nero, who must rank top of the listings for homicidal maniacs with a passion for lyre playing, sodomy and arson. Next Vespasianus, a nice ordinary chap, his first son Titus much the same. However, his second son, Domitianus, takes up where Nero left off, complete with an incurable bloodlust and a deep-rooted suspicion of everything and everybody. Domitianus had a far greater appetite for blood and far less compunction in shedding it than Nero.

So, if that is what the Roman emperors were really like, then it does appear a little odd that the Romans put up with them. Believe it or not, some emperors were even missed in certain quarters, Nero for example. Take for instance the spate of false-Neros who posed a potential threat to the Flavian dynasty, while each and every year people placed upon the real Nero's tomb bouquets to commemorate his imperial exit. Nowadays it is reasonable to ask why did certain emperors receive 'bad' press, and what made a 'bad' emperor bad?

We can better understand the answers to these two questions when we realize that a constant theme throughout the Principate was the positive interest in the dynamic development of monarchial rule. This basic consideration must be kept in mind, because our ancient authors tend to be touched with a bit of nostalgia for a vanished Republic. By ignoring the lessons of the last decades of the Republic, dominated as they were by the monarchic warlords, Sulla, Pompey and Caesar, there is the risk of their readers taking for granted that this sort of maudlin republicanism was the prevailing mood of the day. As commonly even in our own world, discontent with their own times drove them to idealize the past.

Republic did not turn into Principate in a day, naturally. Perhaps the Republic Cicero idolized had been dead before he ever entered politics. The world surely changed when Sulla first led Roman soldiers into Rome. The Roman historian Ronald Syme in his magisterial *Roman Revolution* views the period between the death of Caesar and Actium (44–31 BC), and indeed onwards, as one when the old nobility of Rome was overthrown in a *putsch* staged by a young upstart who had surrounded himself with similar upstarts. After 18 BC the Roman nobility came to terms with the Augustan régime and was once more willing to serve the Roman state. Syme, writing under the satanic shadow of fascism in Europe, sees the essential point Augustus did not have to justify his position, and therefore monarchy was inevitable. Let us not forget, the whole issue of who was to step into the shoes of the deified Caesar was decided on the high seas off Actium in 31 BC, and from this particular point in time everybody knew, as Cassius Dio rightly punctuates, who was at the helm of state.[2] Octavianus, triumphant and omniscient, was king in all but name.[3]

The rise of Octavianus from relative obscurity of holding no official position, through the triumvirate, to a position of the greatest authority in Rome was startling in its rapidity. Marcus Antonius, who was both a successful and a popular commander, had seemed set to assume the mantle of Caesar's *auctoritas* (a semi-technical term combining our sense of authority with respect, responsibility, and the capacity for leadership) along with the leadership of the Caesarian *factio* (the group of men who favoured Caesar and whose careers or fortunes were bound closely to his). Still, a popular man arouses jealousy, and Marcus Antonius was a very popular man. And so it was, at the moment of his greatest confidence, misfortune struck. Confidence breeds distraction and that is when one is most vulnerable.

It was to be the nineteen-year-old Octavianus, adopted in Caesar's will and thus the inheritor of his name, who was to succeed in taking over the authority, powers, respect, and legions. In fact the young Octavianus, absolutely ruthless in his search for power, presents a stark contrast with the benevolent, wise Augustus, a fact that was often ignored by the ancient authors.[4] But then again, to the victor went the spoils, and the spoils in this case were some sixty war-hardened legions and absolute power. Still, the black thirteen-year interval between the assassination of Caesar and the sea battle off Actium had fully prepared the way for monarchy; people had become used to the idea of one-man rule, which is what Octavianus was to establish.

When Octavianus returned from his campaigns in the east in the summer of 29 BC, and down to 19 BC, he carried out an elaborate, if tentative, constitutional settlement. He had been left with the massive problem of how Rome and its empire was to be run, and on the surface it looked as if his settlement was a return to the very essence of republican government. For instance, as under the Republic, the people elected the magistrates. Likewise, as under the Republic, the Senate operated as an advisory body. However, there was one distorting factor in this constitutional settlement, namely Augustus. For having created the institution of one-man rule, which, it must be said, was widely welcomed, one of the biggest headaches for Augustus was who would take over the reins of government on his demise.

As we well know, when Caesar was killed there was a long period of calamitous civil wars, in which Italy had been utterly battered by predatory armies, and so there was no real doubt in people's minds about the legitimacy of succession. There existed a firm desire for a peaceful transition, and this was of course aided by the fact that Augustus lived for so long. The extraordinary consequence of his longevity was the existence of a generation of Romans who had grown up under his rule and therefore had no experience of republican government. On his death a man had to be already past middle age (and to have survived war, anarchy and purge) to remember back behind his very long rule, and so the question 'Principate or Republic?' seemed already an academic one. How few, asks Tacitus, were alive in AD 14 who had seen the Republic.[5]

Without going too deeply into the question – and this would be very easy – there were just two options open for Augustus when it came to choosing his heir and successor. First, picking the best man available, namely chosen from outside the family, chosen for his suitability alone, but this option potentially led to civil war. Second, a dynastic solution, namely keeping it in the family. Augustus could claim that the chief ingredient of his position was the pertinent fact he was the adopted son of the divine Iulius.[6] That is to say, he was who he was and therefore his aim was to pick a successor from his own family. This was partly because he was apt to feel it safest to rely upon his family, but partly also since such nepotism genuinely seemed to provide the best hope of a stable and nonviolent handover. Augustus had hoped to produce a male heir, and with that groom and raise him to his position. It was not to be, and in the end Augustus had to adopt someone so as to mark him out as his successor. On the death of Augustus in AD 14 Tiberius, the first son of his wife Livia by her first marriage,[7] took over without threat to life or limb, which surely stands as a fitting testimony to the grim genius of Augustus.[8] There is no reason to doubt that Caesar genuinely adopted Octavianus, but we do not know what he saw in him. The future, perhaps?

So the emperors of the first half of the first century came from within a broad dynastic family, which we know as the Iulio-Claudian. What Augustus had created in essence was a dynastic principle to which Romans swore an oath of loyalty, an oath to the emperor and his family and not the empire. 'Peace under a monarchy' came to Rome, as Tacitus wryly observes.[9] There were of course Romans who disliked emperors and what they stood for, and thus a threat to their lives and position was always there skulking in the background.

The murder of Caius Caligula on 24 January AD 41 was important as it can be seen as a deliberate attempt by the senatorial aristocracy to reestablish the old Republic. However, there was not the slightest chance of the Republic recovering its vigour and the plot failed in a rather dramatic way. After the slaying of the emperor the Praetorian Guard (even though its senior officers were involved in the plot) held a soldiers' assembly and it was at this council of war that it dawned upon the praetorians that under the Republic there were no emperors and thus no need for the Praetorian Guard, the military unit at Rome that was supposed to protect the person of the emperor.[10] You cannot ask a wolf not to eat an unprotected sheep. It is his *raison d'être*. The praetorians obviously needed to maintain their privileged position, and it now became their nature to make and unmake emperors. And so it was, in this seething crucible of plot and counterplot, a new emperor was found. For in the course of looting the imperial palace, some praetorians found an old man hiding behind some curtains.[11]

It was Claudius, uncle to Caligula. Claudius was aged, terrified, and generally regarded as an idiot. He held no magistracies or powers; his only qualification seems to have been his relationship to Germanicus. The praetorians acclaimed him as emperor, perhaps seriously, perhaps only in jest. But when they paraded the old man through the streets and the crowds likewise hailed him as *imperator*,[12] the die was cast. 'Poor old Uncle Claudius', the family embarrassment, was thus called to the purple, the first of a long line of princes who owed their elevation to the favour of the praetorians. In the cutting words of Gibbon, 'while they [the Senate] deliberated, the Praetorian Guards [sic] had resolved'.[13] In the Senate there had been plenty of talk of declaring the Republic restored and dispensing with emperors all together.[14] It was all vacuous. Claudius rewarded each praetorian with an enormous cash donative of 15,000 *sestertii*,[15] no less than five years' salary. At the yearly anniversaries thereafter each praetorian received one hundred *sestertii*,[16] presumably as a nominal payment but nonetheless an important way of reinforcing the praetorians' sense of loyalty to the emperor. Bribes are dangerous goods; they have a nasty way of getting larger.

From a purely legalistic point of view, Claudius can be regarded as a usurper, not having any Iulian blood in his veins (thence Iulio-Claudian dynasty). Still, with their swords the praetorians had decided otherwise, and their decision was accepted by a jittery Senate soon after. The shockwave of these events of AD 41 stirred up a military revolt in the following year, that of Lucius Arruntius Camillus Scribonianus (*cos.* AD 32).[17] The legate governor of Dalmatia and a descendant of

Pompey, Scribonianus initially proclaimed for the Republic only to find that his soldiers would have nothing to do with such sheer and unadulterated republican nonsense. So Scribonianus then opted to raise himself to the purple, with the soldiers' aid after a promise of a payoff. His 'principate' lasted all but five days.[18] The lesson of course was that no longer would the quest for the old Republic be the main driving force behind plots and insurrections against the emperor. The Republic, with its external wars and internal dissensions, was a splendid subject for history not for restoration. From now on, most conspiracies would seek the removal of a 'bad' emperor and replace him with a 'better' candidate. The first year of Claudius' reign was a watershed in Rome's history; the Principate was here to stay. So the real question was who was to rule?

What happened next? On Claudius' death it was not his natural son, Britannicus, who donned the purple of the Caesars, but his adopted son Nero, who did have Iulian blood in his veins. There are periods in human history that represent fundamental turning points. Such periods are characterized by great social, political and cultural transformations. The gallery of heroes and villains of the year of four emperors demonstrates that anyone with riches to hand and military muscle behind them could feasibly set themselves up as a potential emperor. The first violent bid for the same high stakes came from Galba, a character noble in birth and statue. Galba came from an old and distinguished aristocratic family with plenty of experience serving the state, and so he might have been remembered by posterity as a 'good' emperor if he had not fumbled his own chances of success. He made all the wrong moves, while his narrow partisan attitudes with followers from Iberia angered outsiders. The second bid came from Otho, a candidate who could be represented as heading the side of legitimacy.[19] Otho, as well as wearing a wig imitating Nero's coiffure, found it politically advisable to honour his memory.[20] He certainly seized his chance through Galba's mistakes, but unfortunately for him the legions stationed along the Rhine frontier had other ideas, and so with Vitellius' bid came civil war. Vitellius was victorious, but the legions in the east felt that what the Rhine legions could do they could do better.

Enter Vespasianus, who turned out to be nobody's fool, and even those who had backed the wrong man in AD 69 were to be accommodated under his reign. Only a fool covets power without appreciating its delicate uses or fearing its inherent perils. Of course, one of those perils was of a military nature, and the whole crux of the year of four emperors was the role played by the various provincial armies, east and west. The Roman army was the 'kingmaker', a rôle it had played even as far back as the murky beginnings of the Principate. After all, armed and dangerous, the young Octavianus, all nineteen-years of him with no concrete experience, had marched on Rome at the head of an illegal, private army and seized one of the vacant consulships (July 43 BC),[21] and then changed sides and formed a triumvirate, or three-man rule (November 43 BC).[22] Having effectively arrived via a military coup, he then retained the loyalty of the soldiery of Rome thereafter. All of which goes to prove that ruling is not so much a matter of an iron fist as it is of a firm seat.

When a man has triumphed in violence and seized control of the state, it would be plain idiocy to regard the new chief as a likeable and upright character. Though Tacitus reckons Vespasianus, 'unlike any of his predecessors, was changed for the better by power',[23] even 'good' emperors were also utterly ruthless and implacably cruel when they had to be. They would not survive long otherwise. Under Vespasianus' principate there was still extortion, torture, and murder. Many of the Romans who saw this side of Vespasianus did not like him at all. Nonbelievers aside, Vespasianus' level-headed charm and iron will, combined with his political and organizing flair, and the fact that he was also genial and unstuffy, meant he had the capacity to make himself agreeable. Vespasianus, even as emperor, had simple tastes. When one foppish young man, reeking of perfume, came to thank him for awarding him a commission, Vespasianus turned his head away in disgust and in a stern voice said, 'I should not have minded so much if it had been garlic',[24] and cancelled the appointment.

All emperors faced opposition from the word go. Caesar had been struck down in a Senate meeting and Augustus could not escape from the fact and was clearly worried about it. Suetonius wrote that Augustus once wore a sword and breastplate under his tunic, 'with ten burly senatorial friends crowding around him',[25] when he addressed the Senate. He also reported that senators were only allowed to approach the emperor singly and after they had been searched for concealed daggers.[26] He also surrounded himself with a bodyguard of Germans, fierce warriors who dedicated themselves to defend the emperor's own person.[27] During the Catiline conspiracy Cicero, then consul, had appeared on the *campus Martius* wearing beneath his toga 'a broad and conspicuous cuirass, with a strong guard of intrepid men'.[28] They were hired thugs and brawlers, if the truth be known, and Catiline, too, had his personal guard, made up, according to Cicero, of 'all the gamblers, and adulterers, all unclean and shameless citizenry'.[29] Caesar had neglected these elementary precautions on the Ides of March.[30]

The threat was always there; Caius Caligula was murdered, Claudius may have been, Domitianus murdered too. The killing of an emperor was always a possibility, and Suetonius provides the interested reader with what almost seems an endless catalogue of conspiracies and plots, with the daggers of conspirators and plotters being sharpened against the emperor. There is little doubt that down to AD 41 opposition was motivated by thoughts of restoring the Republic. After that date, nearly all – apart from Scribonianus' revolt of AD 42 – conspiracies were geared to remove a 'bad' emperor and replace him with a more 'suitable' one (e.g. Messalina's marriage to Caius Silanus; the Piso conspiracy of AD 65).

Naturally, keeping the Praetorian Guard, the army and the Senate sweet helped no end, but alongside all this there was the so-called intellectual opposition, small but vocal, headed by men who wrote pamphlets, the critics of emperors. Such men are often labelled the 'Stoic opposition', men like Publius Clodius Thrasea Paetus under Nero or Helvidius Priscus under Vespasianus. However, this label is rather misleading. Although these men were certainly Stoics there is nothing inherent in Stoicism to suggest opposition to an emperor. After all, Seneca was a Stoic but he had supported Nero root and branch. In fact, Stoicism recommended opting out and not taking an active role in politics when faced with the personification of evil, and not vain and fruitless confrontation.

Although we would expect Tacitean praise for Thrasea Paetus' action when the Senate voted in AD 59 honours for Nero after he had murdered his mother – he walked out of the Senate – Tacitus is rather sceptical, informing his readership that Thrasea Paetus had achieved little bar endangering his own life. Such scepticism extends to others of this group. The men of the Stoic opposition, for want of a better label, were seen by Tacitus as conceited seekers after martyrdom, bringing ruin upon themselves without helping Rome, senators such as the stiff-necked Helvidius Priscus, the son of a centurion who had made it his life's work to avenge his father-in-law, Thrasea Paetus, Nero's victim. The continued campaign of opposition to the Principate was to win for himself and for his son notoriety and death.[31]

In all likelihood the opposition senators, first led by Thrasea Paetus and then by Helvidius Priscus, considered their fellow senators as a gutless crew, who, their privileges safe, had allowed Nero to plunder Rome, ruin its finances, and vulgarize debauchery. However, Tacitus was sceptical because his own father-in-law, Agricola, like many other senators of his day, had had to cooperate with Domitianus, difficult as the task had been. What is more, Agricola had been highly successful under this 'bad' emperor, and thus Tacitus could hardly praise senators like Thrasea Paetus or Helvidius Priscus, for it would suggest that his own actions were no more than craven. And there is the rub. Tacitus writes of men like his father-in-law who could still lead a life of integrity even under the likes of Domitianus.[32] So, Tacitus cleverly scotches any attempt to brand him and his ilk as moral cowards for thriving under a repressive régime. He equally rejects the unrealistic refusal of the opposition senators like Helvidius Priscus to look at the facts. Instead, Tacitus recognizes the fact that the Republic had been consigned to the dustbin of history, and any talk of its restoration was pure sentimentalism.[33] The Principate, as a practical necessity, was here to stay, and while all hoped for a good emperor, all must take him as he came. Hence the aristocratic apologia for its existence, a moral justification of the need for an emperor and the preparedness to serve under one, good, bad or indifferent.[34]

So the terrible year of four emperors saw Galba, Otho and Vitellius successively toppled and their lives terminated. Which brings us to the rôle played by that one special unit outside the army, the Praetorian Guard. Nero was abandoned by the praetorians because they thought he had abandoned them, so they switched their allegiance, a bribe facilitating this decision, to Galba. He was discarded by them once he failed to pay the promised donative, their allegiance now being offered to Otho. He, some would say a mere puppet in the hands of the praetorians,[35] took his own life after being defeated by Vitellius. He disbanded what he saw as an Othonian guard and replaced it with his own guard. Vitellius desperately tried to hang on to the throne, but when a new pretender, Vespasianus, appeared, the end came for him too. Vespasianus, the final victor in the game of thrones, disbanded the Vitellian guard, reinstated the Othonian one, but under the sole command of his son Titus.

It seems that no emperor could disregard the power of the praetorians. A telling example of this phenomenon perhaps, is seen in the events befalling Otho one night soon after his accession. A group of drunken praetorians, afraid that a senatorial plot was being hatched to destroy Otho, forcefully broke into the palace, where Otho was holding a banquet. The emperor's guests, senators and their wives in the main, fled for their lives, while the emperor in tears stood on a dining couch desperately beseeching the soldiers to be patient and trust him. The next morning Rome resembled a captured city. Few citizens walked the streets and the soldiers that did were sullen. After they were addressed by their two prefects, Licinius Proculus and Plotius Firmus, and promised a douceur of 5,000 *sestertii* each, Otho entered the *castra praetoria*. Only two men were punished.[36] Common soldiers are in one respect like children: they forget the sorrows of yesterday in the delights of today, and give glad song in the same voices that a few hours previously were loudest in grumbling and petty complaint. So it was, we can well imagine, with Otho's praetorians.

One question needs to be raised, and that is, what about the common soldier? More than a passing interest to us, despite their aristocratic flavour, is the fact that our ancient sources do highlight the fascinating aspect of society within the Principate army. Thus, we witness soldiers forming a distinct subculture with their own codes of honour, their own web of loyalties, and their own taboos, rituals, peculiar habits, and slang too. Even in times of military anarchy it would be wrong of us to miscalculate the staying power of and inner dynamics of established institutions. In a year of bloody confusion and planned caprice, men would sacrifice themselves for a cause already lost just as other men would fall for a cause already won.

The difference between an army and a mob is tradition and discipline. Discipline cannot be enforced on a mob, even if it is armed, and so men have to be reminded they are soldiers. What is more, there can be no better basis for success in battle than the iron rigours of discipline. Ceremonies are one of the most powerful tools for doing that. Men fight for pride, not for money, and no army that does not give them pride will last very long. Bits of bright cloth and shiny metal, and men will die for them. It was no less so for the Romans with their *aquilae* and *coronae*. The old military game.[37]

The establishment of the Principate by Augustus had banished war to the social and geographical periphery. Wars were now fought by skilled professional soldiers, and these normally took place on distant frontiers, even occasionally beyond the fringes of the empire. 'The legions, the provinces, the fleets, all things were linked together'.[38] So Tacitus portrayed the peaceful empire and its armed forces. But with the death of Nero, the last of Augustus' bloodline, the empire was plunged into a civil war as vicious as any of those that had dogged the final decades of the ailing Republic. This situation had never arisen before, since in all previous successions the new emperor had some familial connection to his predecessor. Ironically the Iulio-Claudians, who began the whole process, were hoist on their own petard, destroyed by the army that they had done so much to create. Danger and opportunity are often the same thing, and naturally, when ambitious and unscrupulous men fall into a bloody power struggle to decide who has the right to wear the purple of the Caesars, the wider issue is one of immediate survival and long durance. How could a new man become the ruler of Rome – which meant the ruler of the world – and safely establish his own dynasty? An extremely difficult challenge indeed, especially as the world in which he lived was one in which self-interest governed all. He could easily sit upon his throne only to have it wash out from under him.

But a word or two of caution. It was Bertolt Brecht who sagely pronounced: 'Unhappy is the Land that needs a hero.'[39] Yet the fashion still persists for a historical approach that focuses on individuals as agents of historical change, regardless of the unavoidable truth that the most critical leaps in history are wars and revolutions. It was Carlyle who once unreservedly proclaimed: 'Universal History, the history of what man has accomplished in this world, is at bottom the History of the Great Men who have worked here'.[40] Yet it is a widely held misconception, and one that is actively promoted by certain commentators to this day, that history unfolds as a result of the free will or conscious desires of the 'great man', potentates, politicians, or philosophers. Nothing could be further from the truth. People make history, but do not do it entirely in accord with their free will and conscious intentions. So in the great crises of human history, both ancient and modern, men and women are not merely puppets of blind historical forces. At the risk of incurring the ire of supporters of Great Man History, those historians who are still unsympathetic to the idea of ordinary men and women making history, I believe that conditions produce the 'hero', not the other way round, but conditions rather tend to pick the right man anyhow. And so a man is 'chosen' to lead. He passes. But people endure. History has an uncanny knack for discovering such 'great men'. Such was the case with Vespasianus, as it was with Augustus before him.

War, civil or otherwise, is the product of human choice. It is neither a play of fate nor an outcome of uncontrolled circumstances. Thus, a century of internal peace and stability was shattered as provincial armies were assembled and pitted against each other by four emperors in quick succession. It had been demonstrated clearly in this year of four emperors not only that emperors could be made outside Rome but also that men of comparatively obscure origins could hope for the throne of the world.

If history teaches us anything, therefore, it is simply this: every revolution carries the seed of its own destruction, and that empires rise and one day fall. There is no escaping this. Even the daddy of them all, the Roman Empire, had to live its time and then die. Indeed, the belief that world empires are fated to fall could easily suggest that they deserved to fall; even their very rise was evil. During the principate of Trajan the Stoic preacher Dio Chrysostom wrote that the rise and fall of the Assyrian, Median, Persian, and Macedonian empires were simply examples of the wretched consequences of greed.[41] He does not mention the last world empire, now expanded to its fullest extent, but perhaps he felt he did not need to, the implications for Rome being clear enough.

History is such a wheel that no man can stand upon it for long. And it always, at the end, comes round to the same place again. As I write, even our own mighty, culturally monolithic, but economically unstable behemoth of the 'McWorld' is beginning to crumble around its edges. The empire totters. It has now only to fall. Why do people behave as they do? Why are they driven to take what belongs to others, and to inflict harm in the process? Baruch Spinoza once wrote: 'I have striven not to laugh at human actions, not to weep at them, nor to hate them, but to understand them.'[42] That is sound advice.

1. Silver *sestertius*, the obverse of which bears a laureate bust of a rather heavy, not to say bloated, Nero (Bologna, Museo Civico Archeologico di Bologna).

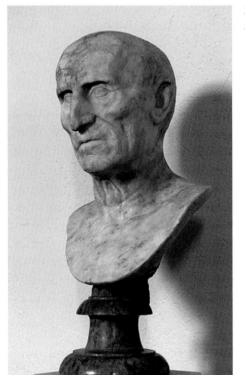

2. Marble portrait bust of Galba (Stockholm, Antiques Museum, Royal Palace).

3. Marble portrait bust of Otho (Houston, Museum of Natural Science).

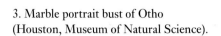

4. Portrait bust of Vitellius – plaster-cast copy (Bologna, Museo Civico Archeologico di Bologna, inv. 99) of the 'Vitellio Grimani' (Venezia, Museo Archeologico, inv. 20).

5. Marble portrait bust of Vespasianus (Thessalonika, Museum of Archaeology, inv. 1055).

6. Stylized terracotta bust of Marcus Antonius Primus (Toulouse, musée des Augustines, inv. 49195), made by the artist Marc Arcis between 1674 and 1677.

7. One of the low-cut reliefs (Mainz, Mittelrheinisches Landesmuseum) decorating the column bases from the *principia* of Mainz-*Mogontiacum*. This one shows two legionaries in action, one behind the other.

8. Another of the low-cut reliefs (Mainz, Mittelrheinisches Landesmuseum) decorating the column bases from the *principia* of Mainz-*Mogontiacum*. This one shows a legionary in full marching order and the junior officer known as an *optio* (others suggest he is a *signifer*).

9. Yet another of the low-cut reliefs (Mainz, Mittelrheinisches Landesmuseum) decorating the column bases from the *principia* of Mainz-*Mogontiacum*. This one shows an auxiliary infantryman with a flat oval shield, *clipeus*, and a Coolus type helmet.

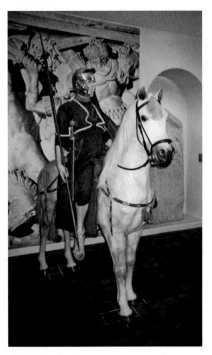

10. Full-size manikin of an auxiliary trooper (Cirencester, Corinium Museum).

11. Soldiers of the Praetorian Guard, bas-relief (Paris, musée du Louvre) from the Arch of Claudius erected in AD 51 in honour of the successful invasion of Britannia in AD 43.

12. At the twentieth milestone on the Via Postumia.

13. (*Above*) Viewing the battleground of First Cremona.

14. (*Right*) Via Postumia, the still functioning Roman road that traverses the battle site of Second Cremona.

15. The battleground of Second Cremona, where a head-on collision between total legionary forces on each side took place, recalling Pharsalus, Mutina, Philippi and other fearful names of civil strife.

16. What is now the Casa de' Marozzi was then the probable site of Marcus Antonius Primus' battlefield headquarters at Second Cremona.

17. The point of contact, Second Cremona, looking south–south–west from just above Cassinetto.

18. The site of the Vitellian camp, just outside Cremona, looking towards the modern sports stadium, with Via Brescia to the left and Via Mantova to the right.

19. Embossed bronze facing of a scorpio shield (Cremona, Museo Civico San Lorenzo) once belonging to *legio IIII Macedonica*, unearthed in 1887 some fifty metres outside the Porta Venezia, Cremona.

20. The Roman soldier may have been adorned with various pieces of killing hardware, but each also carried one of these, a mess tin, *patera* (Cremona, Museo Civico San Lorenzo).

21. Grave stele of Quintus Sertorius Festus (Verona, Museo Lapidario Maffeiano, inv. 28161), dated c. AD 42–69.

22. Grave stele of Lucius Sertorius Firmus (Verona, Museo Lapidario Maffeiano, inv. 28160), dated c. AD 42–69.

23. From the fort at Croy Hill on the Antonine Wall, we have two fragments of a sculptured relief carved on a slab of red sandstone (Edinburgh, National Museums of Scotland).

24. Silver *denarius* (*RIC* I Vitellius: 53) issued by the imperial mint at Lugdunum (Lyon). The obverse bears a laureate bust of Vitellius with an orb at the point, with the legend A(vlvs) VITELLIVS IMP(erator) GERMAN(icvs). The reverse depicts clasped hands, with the slogan FIDES EXERCITVVM, 'Loyalty of the Army'.

25. From Brussels and woven around 1530–50, this Flemish tapestry (Marsala, Museo delgi Arazzi, Tapestry 5) is decorated with a scene depicting the unchaining of Josephus on the orders of Vespasianus.

Winners and Losers

In Tacitus' judgement, Antonius Primus was a man 'brave in action, ready of speech, clever at bringing others into odium, powerful in times of civil war and rebellion, greedy, extravagant, in peace a bad citizen, in war an ally not to be despised'.[1] To Tacitus' keen observations on the fibre of Antonius Primus it could be added that he loved to take part in events rather than to brood over them, despising those who preferred the assurance of comfort to the risks of adventure. He loved war. It nourished and energized him. It triggered those complex mechanisms of intellect and instinct that made his tactical decisions nearly flawless. In war as in no other milieu, Antonius Primus flourished.[2] He had been an inspirational leader who had enjoyed the battles, winning his actions through decisiveness, daring, improvisation and pugnacious skill. The year AD 69 was in truth for Antonius Primus a goodly time, and nothing else in his life could (or would) compare with it.

This is what happened to Antonius Primus. Exiled for a second time, he settled in his home town of Tolosa (Toulouse) to enjoy his remaining years in tranquillity (*tutos respicit annos*, as Martial remarks).[3] He was only about fifty, but, like an old man whose glory days are over and done, he found himself discarded and forgotten by those he had served so well once the crisis was over. He was a warrior without a war, a hero without a plot. Unless they are members of the pantheon of dead but death-defeating heroes, the saviours who (like Jesus Christ, Arthur and Charlemagne) one day will come again, routine heroes normally must see to their own fame as no one else will. However, Antonius Primus, the antihero of this particular story, was fortunate to have known the brilliant epigrammatist, Marcus Valerius Martialis, whom we know as Martial (d. *c.* AD 102/103),[4] who accordingly burnished his legend for posterity by lavishing three memorable epigrams on him. Herewith a choice example:

> This portrait I deck with violets and roses,
> do you ask whose face it is, Caedicianus?
> It's Marcus Antonius Primus in his prime:
> in this the old man sees his younger self.
> If art could show his mind and character?
> No picture in the world would show lovelier.[5]

Ergo, Antonius Primus did not have to toot his own horn. There again, literary praise can be a double-edged weapon, particularly so if is promoted by Martial, a court poet and social pornographer, whose epigrams are satirical, presenting a vivid picture of sexual perverts (of *all* persuasions), legacy hunters, spendthrifts, domineering spouses, would-be poets, incompetent doctors, body odour, the vain, the bald, the ugly, the rich and the poor. Anyhow, it had all started when Antonius Primus had written to Martial from his native Tolosa, requesting an author's copy of his published works, then the vogue in the capital.[6] He was later congratulated with a pleasing epigram on reaching the grand old age of seventy-five years,[7] was sent also a very flattering set of verses (quoted above) inspired by the portrait he had presented the poet, and fulsome thanks for the gift of a very fine toga, 'a toga not such as Fabricius, but as Apicius would have been glad to wear'.[8] Antonius Primus can look back with such joy at his tranquil life, 'he feels he has lived it twice over'.[9] To some poetry may owe less than prose, holding aloof from it as profane and frivolous. True, it can be dull, it can be doggerel, it can lack smoothness and regularity, it can have the sound of a hammer striking a wooden anvil. But also poetry, especially in the shape of the short, sharp epigram, can be unencumbered by fiction or allegory, and rich in images, metaphorical, and subtle.

Let us now turn our attention to a career inscription, one that charts the sudden rise during these turbulent times of a certain Lucius Antonius Naso.[10]

Early in January AD 69, as part of his drive on tightening discipline within the city garrison, Galba had seen fit to cashier four tribunes, two of the praetorian cohorts, and one each of the urban cohorts and the *vigiles urbani*. One of the sacked praetorian tribunes was Lucius Antonius Naso. The inscription, found at Baalbek (ancient Heliopolis) in Lebanon,[11] tells us that he had already had an honourable military career. Decorated by Nero[12] 'with a *corona vallaris*,[13] a *corona aurea*,[14] two *vexilla*,[15] and two *hastae purae*',[16] he had served as a centurion in two legions, *III Cyrenaica* (in Egypt) and *XIII Gemina* (in Pannonia). While a centurion in the latter unit, he was appointed *praefectus civitatis Colaphianorum*, a local community near to the legion's headquarters at Ptuj-*Poetovio*.[17] Still serving with *XIII Gemina*, he rose to become its top soldier, *primus pilus*, and it was probably on leaving the legion at this rank (usually held for one year) that he received his military decorations.[18] At the time of the emperor's death he was *tribunus cohortis XV urbana*, which was based at Puteoli, and then before the end of AD 68 successively tribune of *cohors XI urbana* and of *cohors IX praetoria*, both at Rome.

Before joining *cohors XV urbana*, Antonius Naso held the post of tribune with *cohors IIII vigilum*,[19] and before that was a military tribune with *legio I Italicae*. So he had moved rapidly from *tribunus militum legionis* to *tribunus cohortis vigilum* to *tribunus cohortis urbanae*. Having done the rounds of the paramilitary tribunates in the capital, by January AD 69 he was in the Praetorian Guard as *tribunus cohortis IX praetoriae*. Still to come were the posts of *primus pilus* of *legio XIIII Gemina Martia Victrix*,[20] *tribunus* of *cohors I praetoria* and *procurator provinciae* of Bithynia-Pontus.[21] As late as AD 77/8, another inscribed stone, from Bursa (ancient Prusa in that province), records his road-building activities in the locality.[22] All in all, it does seem rather odd that Galba would have sacked a man of this calibre, unless of course his loyalty was suspect.

The case of Antonius Naso is particularly instructive on a number of accounts. First, he was almost certainly from Heliopolis, for not only was his career inscription found there but he was enrolled in the tribe (Fabia) of that place.[23] Second, he began his military career in an eastern legion (*III Cyrenaica*). Third, he almost certainly read and spoke Greek too,[24] which would have stood him in good stead in Bithynia-Pontus. Fourth, a man of the Praetorian Guard was well placed to catch the eye of the emperor, for better or for worse. The sacking by Galba meant his promising career lay in ruins, whereas he probably owed his comeback very largely to the usurpation of Otho and the rewards that followed soon after. Antonius Naso, albeit for a short while, knew the bitter experience of what it was like to be deprived of office (and influence). It was no easy task to steer a safe course through the long year of AD 69. If we disregard fine shades, it is easy to distinguish those who did as the winners, and those who did not were the losers.

Nobody lives long enough to be anything but an amateur, this was wonderfully well said by the great Charlie Chaplin. This statement certainly applies to historians, for studying any kind of history is a continuous, never-ending process of learning and discovery – which is what makes being a historian such a fascinating and rewarding line of work. In any event, it has been my aim not to pontificate, or so I believe. If so, *mea culpa*. To study the affairs of antiquity is to become acutely aware that even the simplest of facts are prone to most varying interpretations, and as a result I stress that the principles I have set out – and the ideas I have derived therefrom – do not form a body of immutable law. If, however, what I have written does prove of interest and utility, my satisfaction will be lively and truly sincere.

FINIS

Appendix 1

Provinciae Imperii Romani

In the history of the world there have been few rulers, if any, who had greater power and ruled over a vaster area than the Roman emperors. In the first two centuries AD the Roman world encompassed an enormous area centring on the Mediterranean but extending, significantly in places, into continental Europe, Asia and Africa. From the Tamis in the north to the Tigris in the east was 4,654 kilometres; the empire was large, with some fifty-odd provinces by the turn of the second century it covered nearly five million square kilometres with a population conventionally estimated at about fifty-five million.

When the Romans used the term, Orient, *Oriens*, they were speaking about a different region from the area we think of as the Orient today. The Romans considered what we now call the Near East and Middle East to be the Orient, as well as the mysterious lands of India and China much farther east. Their Orient therefore consisted of the Parthian empire, as well as the eastern provinces of Syria, Mesopotamia, Phoenicia, Iudaea and, sometimes, Egypt, an important source of grain, which was shipped in bulk to Rome.

Roman literary sources leave the reader in no doubt about the importance of north African agriculture, which included intensive olive and wine production, and the area was famous for the size of its estates, whether in private or imperial ownership. From Libya west to the Atlantic coast, a band of mountainous land separates the Sahara desert from the fertile Mediterranean coastal strip. The coastal zone is characterized by numerous cities, which participated in the flourishing maritime activity of the time, whilst to the south a complex system of forts, roads and boundary ditches marked the edges of the empire, and watched over semi-nomadic peoples who entered and left the empire according to their seasonal needs for fields or grazing.

The Iberian peninsula was divided into three separate provinces: Lusitania in the west, Hispania Baetica in the south, and Hispania Tarraconensis to the east and north. Trajan was the first Roman emperor of provincial origin, born in Italica near modern Seville. Hadrian, his successor, was also of the same origin. From our period of study we have the man who was probably the most powerful citizen in the empire for seven years from AD 55, Lucius Annaeus Seneca, born in Corduba (today's Córdoba). Writers such as Strabo and the elder Pliny celebrated the fertility of Hispania Baetica, and provincial families like those of Seneca, Trajan and Hadrian drew their wealth from the lucrative agricultural produce of this southern end of the Iberian peninsula. Notable exports were fish sauce (*garum*) and olive oil from the littoral region of Hispania Baetica, and metals such as gold (northwest), copper and silver (southwest).

Roman Gaul occupies the portion of Europe that now forms France and parts of Belgium and Germany. Gaul was divided into three provinces known as the Three Gauls: Gallia Aquitania in the west, Gallia Lugdunensis to the north and east, and Gallia Belgica in the northeast. There was also a further Gallic province in the south, Gallia Narbonensis, which had come under permanent Roman control in the second century BC. It had much in common with Italy, as Provence does today, and there the vine and the olive could be cultivated along with other crops by means of Mediterranean 'dry farming' techniques. In our period of study Roman Gaul was a peaceful land with plenty of sun and warmth and water and splendid soil. It was, *tout ensemble*, an important agricultural region, producing grain and wine, and with perhaps thrice the population of Italy it supplied valuable manpower for the army.

Pannonia and Dalmatia are names that describe roughly the same area in what is known today as the northern Balkan peninsula and encompasses the modern countries of Croatia, Slovenia, Bosnia, Herzegovina, Serbia, and Montenegro, all of which painfully emerged from the bitter breakup of Tito's Yugoslavia. This area, known to the Greeks as Illyria, was home to tough mountain peoples during pre-Roman times. After the area was conquered by Rome and became the Roman province of Illyricum (in AD 10 divided into Pannonia and Dalmatia) these same hardy barbarians – if such they were – enlisted in the Roman army and became some of the best soldiers in the legions.[1] This region thus became one of the prime recruiting areas for the Roman legions. From the late second century onwards many able commanders came from Pannonia, but its importance for our particular story, however, arises from its possessing a legionary garrison nearer to Italy than any other.

One final, but very important, point, despite the vastness of the empire, the actual management was a small, close-knit senatorial family, and every governor and general knew or had heard of every other governor and general. These men had to maintain discipline among the soldiers under their command, keep order in their province, and defend it against external attack. They had, therefore, to be men of education and status, for they must, in the name of the emperor, give commands and inspire respect. In the context of Roman society, even under the emperors, this meant that the commanders were invariably drawn from the aristocracy.

The Roman aristocracy, which made up a mere 2 per cent of the citizen population, was divided into two orders, the senatorial order (*ordo senatorius*) and the equestrian order (*ordo equester*). The minimum property qualification required for membership of the *ordo equester* was 400,000 *sestertii*, compared to one million for membership of the *ordo senatorius*. To put this figure into some perspective, one million *sestertii* was enough cash (with some change to spare) to pay the legionaries of two full-strength legions their annual pay. Most governors and generals of our period were senators, which is not surprising since traditionally the senatorial order commanded the armies of Rome and Augustus desired to provide them with opportunities to win fame and distinction in the traditional republican way. Indeed the senatorial order, with its long experience of government and military life, was initially the only body capable of providing enough men to govern the provinces and command the armies of the Principate. However, these men were no longer the proconsuls or *pro*praetors as of old, but representatives of the emperor himself, who was technically governor of all the provinces just as he was titular commander of every legion. They were answerable to him alone.

Appendix 2

Principate Army – Origins

The professionalization of the Roman army after Marius' reforms led directly to the use and abuse of consular power by individual generals seeking to usurp the power of the Senate. Consequently the last five decades of the Republic were characterized by two important features: the jostling for power and status by a number of dynamic political players, and the calamitous civil wars generated by their personal, be it selfish or altruistic, ambitions. It was the last of these republican warlords who was to emerge victorious as the first Roman emperor under the new name of Augustus. Officially he was addressed as *princeps*,[1] that is the first citizen of the state, and his reign was the beginning of the Principate.

The army of the Principate established by Augustus drew heavily on the nomenclature and traditions of the dead Republic. But it was new. He decided to meet all the military needs of the empire from a standing, professional army, so that there was no general need to raise any levies through conscription (*dilectus*), which in actual fact he did on only two occasions, namely following the military crises in Pannonia (AD 6) and Germania (AD 9). Military service was now a lifetime's occupation and career, and pay and service conditions were established that took account of the categories of soldier in the army: the praetorians (*cohortes praetoriae*), the citizen soldiers of the legions (*legiones*), and the non-citizens of the auxiliaries (*auxilia*). Enlistment was not for the duration of a particular conflict, but for twenty-five years (sixteen for the praetorians), and men were sometimes retained even longer. At the end of service there was a fixed reward, on the implementation of which the soldier could rely.[2] The loyalty of the new army was to the emperor, as commander-in-chief, and neither to the Senate nor the Roman people.

Cassius Dio, writing of the events of 29 BC, reports two speeches made before Augustus by his counsellors, Marcus Vipsanius Agrippa and Caius Maecenas, in which the best way of securing the continuation of the Roman state and defence of its empire was discussed. Agrippa apparently advocated the retention of the traditional system (by which men would be conscripted to serve short periods, and then released into civilian life). Maecenas, on the other hand, argued for 'a standing army (*stratiōtas athanatous* in Cassius Dio's Greek) to be recruited from the citizen body [i.e. *legiones*], the allies [i.e. *auxilia*] and the subject nations',[3] and despite Agrippa's contention that such an army could form a threat to the security of the empire, carried the day.

Dialogues were a convention of ancient historiography, and these speeches need not be judged the true record of a real debate between the two. In part at least they reflect the political situation of Cassius Dio's own time and were aimed at a contemporary emperor, perhaps that psychopathic fratricide and builder of the eponymous baths in Rome, Caracalla (r. AD 211–217). Nevertheless, in 13 BC, after he had returned from Gaul, Augustus ordained that terms of service in the legions should in future be fixed at sixteen years, to be followed by a four or five-year period 'under the flag', *sub vexillo*,[4] to be rewarded by a fixed cash gratuity, though this could be commuted to a plot of land, measuring 200 *iugera* (*c.* 50 ha), in a veteran-colony in the provinces.

However, the scheme did not work, for in AD 5 discontent was rife and in the following year major army reforms were carried out by the emperor. The fundamental problem was that veterans were discontent with *sub vexillo*, which apparently entitled them to lighter duties after their sixteen-year stint.[5] But no government, ancient or modern, is noted for keeping its promises. So some alterations were made to the conditions of service. The number of years that the new recruit had to serve under arms was raised to twenty years, with a further period (not specified, but probably at least five years) in reserve. The cash gratuity was now fixed at 12,000 *sestertii* (3,000 *denarii*) for an ordinary ranker, a lump sum the equivalent of more than thirteen years' pay.[6]

Seemingly as part of this same package, but recorded by Cassius Dio under the following year (AD 6),[7] Augustus masterminded the creation of a military treasury (*aerarium militare*). Its function was to arrange the payment of bounties to soldiers. Augustus opened the account with a large gift of money from his own funds, some 170 million *sestertii* according to his own testimony,[8] but in the longer term the treasury's revenues were to come from two new taxes imposed from this time onwards on Roman citizens: a 5 per cent tax on inheritances and a 1 per cent tax on auction sales in Rome. The introduction of these taxes caused uproar, but taxation was preferable to displacement, acrimony and ruin, which had been the consequences of land settlement programmes of the civil war years. Augustus thus shifted a part of the cost of the empire's defence from his own purse to the citizenry at large. But the wages of serving soldiers (225 *denarii* per annum for an ordinary ranker) continued to be paid by the imperial purse; Augustus could brook no interference, or divided loyalties there. The management of the army, particularly its pay and benefits, were from the start one of what Tacitus calls 'the secrets of ruling'.[9] Power was protected and preserved by two things, soldiers and money. And so the security and survival of the emperor and *his* empire was now the sole responsibility of the emperor and *his* soldiers.

The legions had been the source of Augustus' power. However, serious mutinies broke out in Pannonia and Germania in AD 14 partly because the legionaries were worried about their conditions of service after the death of Augustus, so closely had he become associated with their emoluments. But there was obviously significant discontent with low rates of pay, especially in contrast to the praetorians, long service, and unsuitable land allocations. Here Tacitus takes up the story:

Finally Percennius had acquired a team of helpers ready for mutiny. Then he made something like a public speech. 'Why', he asked, 'obey, like slaves, a few commanders of centuries, fewer still of cohorts? You will never be brave enough to demand better conditions if you are not prepared to petition – or even threaten – an emperor who is new and still faltering [i.e. Tiberius]. Inactivity has done quite enough harm in all these years. Old men, mutilated by wounds, are serving their thirtieth year or fortieth year. And even after your official discharge your service is not finished; for you stay on with the eagle as a reserve (*sub vexillo*), still under canvas – the same drudgery under another name! And if you manage to survive all these hazards, even then you are dragged off to a remote country and "settled" in some waterlogged swamp or uncultivated mountainside. Truly the army is harsh, unrewarding profession! Body and soul are reckoned at ten *asses* a day – and with this you have to find clothes, weapons, tents, and bribes for brutal centurions if you want to avoid chores.'[10]

Percennius, a common soldier, was the ringleader of the mutineers in Pannonia, then garrisoned by three legions (*VIII Augusta, VIIII Hispana, XV Apollinaris*) based in a camp near Emona (Ljubljana). Once the mutiny was crushed, he was to be hunted down and executed for his troubles.

These mutinies clearly showed the danger of having too many legions (there were four involved in the Germania mutiny) in the same camp. Also, living in tents, even during the summer months, on the Rhine and Danube frontiers must have been miserable to say the least. The bleakness of life under canvas is the subject of a telling passage of Tertullian: 'No soldier comes with frolics to battle nor does he go to the front from his bedroom but from tents that are light and small, where there is every kind of hardship, inconvenience, and discomfort.'[11]

As mentioned above, in the time of Augustus the annual rate of pay for a legionary was 900 *sestertii* (225 *denarii*), Percennius' piddling 'ten asses a day'.[12] But Percennius' complaint was all in vain, the basic rate remaining so until Domitianus, who increased the pay by one-third, that is, to 1,200 *sestertii* (300 *denarii*) a year.[13] Wages were paid in three annual instalments,[14] the first payment being made on the occasion of the annual new year parade when the troops renewed their oath to the emperor. Official deductions were made for food and fodder (for the mule belonging to the mess-group, *contubernium*). In addition, each soldier had to pay for his own clothing, equipment and weapons,[15] but these items were purchased back by the army from the soldier or his heir when he retired or died. These were the official charges. As we know, Tacitus records that one of the complaints of the mutineers was that they had to pay sweeteners to venal centurions in order to gain exemption from fatigues. Another complaint was that time-expired soldiers were being fobbed off with grants of land in lieu of the gratuity of 12,000 *sestertii*, and these plots tended to be either waterlogged or rock-strewn.

Principate Army – Organization

A great body of information on the unit size and organization of the Principate army has been amassed by the patient work of several generations of scholars. The literary sources are often obscure or contradictory on the details of unit structures, but we are fortunate in that much information has been derived from epigraphic, numismatic and papyrological record as well as that of archaeology. Here contemporary evidence, if not overabundant, is explicit and reliable. As a result a fairly coherent picture of the army's structure has emerged and what follows, then, is the briefest of sketches of the army as it existed in Neronian times.

As an instrument of war the Principate army presented a powerful picture, and there is certainly little about it that a modern infantry soldier would fail to recognize. The professional standing force of a modern size, conscription, military training, institutionalized discipline, weapons factories, administrative and combat staffs, military maps, roads, logistics systems, military hospitals, intelligence services, communications, strategy and tactics, efficient killing technologies, siege machines, rank structures, scheduled promotions, permanent records, personnel files, uniforms, regular pay, and even military pension schemes – to name but a few – had already become part of every day, military life.

Legion

Men had a thousand reasons for joining the army, but mainly they were escaping from poor local conditions or looking for what they hoped would provide a regular source of food and income. Unsurprisingly, therefore, the army seems to have been most attractive as a definite career to the poorest citizens. For such men, long underfed and ill-clothed, the legions offered a roof over their head, food in their bellies, and a regular income in coin. Basic military pay was not the road to riches, but there was always the chance of bounties and donatives, and the certainty of a discharge bonus, a rich contrast to civilian unemployment. Army pay certainly did not depend on the weather, taxation, rent, interest payments or fluctuating prices. Overall, a soldier's life was more secure than that of an itinerant labourer (an unpaid labourer would starve; an unpaid soldier still ate), and he enjoyed a superior status too.

Of course, we must remember the harsher side of such a career. The rewards of army life may have been greater, but so were the risks. A soldier ran the risk of being killed or crippled by battle or disease, but also on an everyday basis was subject to the army's brutal discipline. And then there was maltreatment, which did not include the routine harshness or the standard Spartan quality of military life. The dividing line between discipline and maltreatment was crossed when officers treated their men with unnecessary severity, when they paid no attention to their welfare, and when they expected fear rather than respect from their men. Such officers firmly believed that you got more out of men by using brutality, than by treating them with patience tempered by firmness. Most of us are familiar with the martinet centurion Give-me-Another,[1] nicknamed because of his habit of beating a soldier's back until his gnarled *vitis* – the twisted vine-stick that was his badge of rank – snapped and then shouting for a second and a third.[2]

Such a bully and a beast was common in the army, the general assumption being that soldiers had to be treated roughly so as to toughen them up for fighting, yet to many people in the empire who struggled to survive at subsistence level, the well-fed soldier with his ordered existence in his well-built and clean camp must have seemed comfortably off. Soldiers also shared a comradeship with their fellow soldiers, which was often warm and comforting. And so the legions became permanent units with their own numbers and titles and many were to remain in existence for centuries to come.

Most prominent in the life of the empire was the army, the organization of which began, and almost ended, with the legion. Yet from Augustus onwards the emperor commanded no more than twenty-five legions in total (twenty-eight before the Varian disaster of AD 9), which seems paltry considering the extent of the empire. Legions were probably in the order of 5,000 men strong (all ranks) and composed of Roman citizens, though sickness and death could quickly pare away at this figure. Legionaries were mostly volunteers, drawn initially from Italy (especially the north), but increasingly from the provinces. As the first century progressed, many recruits in the west were coming from the Iberian provinces, Gallia Narbonensis, and Noricum, and in the east from the Greek cities of Macedonia and Asia. Thus, by the end of the century the number of Italians serving in the legions was small. Statistics based on nomenclature and the origins of individuals show that of all the legionaries serving in the period from Augustus to Caius Caligula, some 65 per cent were Italians, while in the period from Claudius to Nero this figure was 48.7 per cent, dropping even further to 21.4 per cent in the period from Vespasianus to Trajan. Thereafter, the contribution of Italians to the manpower of the legions (but not of the Praetorian Guard naturally) was negligible.[3] It must be emphasized, however, that these statistics represent *all* legionaries in the empire. In reality, there was a dichotomy in recruitment patterns between the western and eastern provinces, with legions in the west drawing upon Gaul, Iberia, and northern Italy, while those stationed in the east very quickly harnessed the local resources of manpower.

Ordinarily a legion consisted of ten cohorts (*cohortes*), with six centuries (*centuriae*) of eighty men in each cohort, apart from the first cohort (*cohors prima*), which from AD 70 or thereabouts was double strength, that is five centuries of 160 men. Commanded by a centurion (*centurio*) and his second in command (*optio*),[4] a standard-size century (*centuria*) was divided into ten eight-man subunits (*contubernia*), each *contubernium*, mess-group, sharing a tent on campaign and pair of rooms in a barrack block, eating, sleeping and fighting together. Much like small units in today's regular armies, this state of affairs tended to foster a tight bond between 'messmates'.[5] There would have been a strong *esprit de corps* among men built upon the deep concern each had for everyone. In the pressure cooker environment of small combat units where soldiers are forced into close contact with one another, they worked together, they fought together, they shared discomfort and death and victory. This was man-to-man friendship, a gutsy bond. A spirit of military brotherhood would explain why many soldiers (*milites*) preferred to serve their entire military career in the ranks despite the opportunities for secondment to specialized tasks and for promotion. Nonetheless, a soldier (*miles*) who performed a special function was excused fatigues, which made him an *immunis*, although he did not receive any extra pay.[6]

Finally, there was a small force of 120 horsemen (*equites legionis*) recruited from among the legionaries themselves. These *equites* acted as messengers, escorts and scouts, and were allocated to specific centuries rather than belonging to a formation of their own. Thus, the inscription on a tombstone from Chester-*Deva* describes an *eques* of *legio II Adiutrix pia fidelis* as belonging to the *centuria* of Petronius Fidus.[7] Citizen cavalry had probably disappeared after Marius' reforms, and certainly was not in evidence in Caesar's legions. However, apart from a distinct reference to 120 cavalry of the legion in Josephus,[8] the *equites* seem to have been revived as part of the Augustan reforms.

Detachments

When territory was added to the empire, a garrison had to be put together to serve in its defence. New legions were sometimes raised, but normally these green units were not themselves intended for service in the new province. So when an invasion and permanent occupation of Britannia became a hard possibility under Caius Caligula, two new legions, *XV Primigenia* and *XXII Primigenia*, were formed in advance. Their intended rôle was as replacements for experienced legions earmarked to join the invasion force: *XV Primigenia* to release *legio XX* from Neuss-*Novaesium*, and *XXII Primigenia* to release *XIIII Gemina* from Mainz-*Mogontiacum*. The invasion force that eventually sailed for southern Britannia in the summer of AD 43 consisted of *XX* and *XIIII Gemina*, along with *II Augusta*, which had been at Strasbourg-*Argentoratum*, this camp was now left vacant, and *VIIII Hispana* from Sisak-*Siscia* in Pannonia,[9] which may have accompanied the outgoing legate governor, Aulus Plautius, on his journey to take up his new post as the expeditionary commander. It must be said, however, that only *II Augusta* and *XX* are actually attested as taking part in the invasion itself,[10] though all four legions are recorded very early in Britannia.[11]

Nevertheless, transfers of legions to different parts of the empire could leave long stretches of frontier virtually undefended, and wholesale transfers became unpopular as legions acquired local links. An extreme case must be that of *II Augusta*. Part of the invasion army of AD 43, its *legatus legionis* at the time was in fact the future emperor Vespasianus, this legion was to be stationed in the province for the whole time Britannia was part of the empire.[12] An inscription from near Alexandria, dated AD 194, is of particular interest to us as it records the names of forty-six veterans of *legio II Traiana fortis* who had just received their honourable discharge and had begun their military service in AD 168. Of the forty-one whose origins are mentioned, thirty-two came from Egypt itself and twenty-four of these state the camp as their place of birth, or more precisely *origo castris*, 'of the camp'.[13] It is likely that most of them were illegitimate sons born to soldiers from local women living in the nearby *canabae legonis*, that is, the extramural civilian settlement associated with the garrison. So it seems that many recruits were the sons of serving soldiers or veterans, and in time these soldiers' sons became a fertile source of recruits, particularly so as soldiers' sons did not have to make a major adjustment from a civilian to a military world. With bastard sons following their soldier fathers into the army, the custom developed of sending not an entire legion to deal with emergencies, but detachments drawn from the various legions of a province. As we have seen, in the year AD 69 legionary detachments played a major rôle in the formation of the Vitellian and Flavian armies.

Detachments from legions operating independently or with other detachments were known as *vexillationes*, named from the square flag, *vexillum*, which identified them. Until the creation of field armies in the late empire, these *vexillationes* were the method of providing temporary reinforcements to frontier armies for major campaigns. And so it was that Cnaeus Domitius Corbulo received a *vexillatio* from *legio X Fretensis*, then stationed at the Euphrates crossing at Zeugma, during his operations in Armenia. Later he was to take three *vexillationes* of a thousand men (i.e. two cohorts) from each of his three Syrian legions (*III Gallica*, *VI Ferrata*, *X Fretensis*) to the succour of Caesennius Paetus, whose army was retreating post-haste out of Armenia.[14] Likewise, despite the disaster to *legio VIIII Hispana* during the Boudican rebellion,[15] no new legion was despatched to Britannia, but a *vexillatio* of 2,000 legionaries gathered from the Rhine legions.[16]

Auxiliaries

Under Augustus the rather heterogeneous collection of auxiliary units, *auxilia*, serving Rome was completely reorganized and given regular status within the new standing army. Trained to the same standards of discipline as the legions, the men were long-service professionals like the legionaries and served in units that were equally permanent. Recruited from a wide range of warlike peoples who lived just within or on the periphery of Roman control, with Gauls, Thracians and Germans in heavy preponderance, the *auxilia* were freeborn non-citizens (*peregrini*) who, at least from the time of Claudius, received full Roman citizenship on honourable discharge after completion of their twenty-five years under arms.

Tacitus tells us that the Batavi, on the lower Rhine, paid no taxes at all, but 'reserved for battle, they are like weapons and armour, only to be used in war'.[17] The Batavi made capital stuff for a soldier, and from Tacitus we hear of eight *cohortes* and one *ala*, nearly 5,000 warriors from the tiny region of Batavia serving Rome at any one time.[18] He also remarks of a *cohors Sugambrorum* under Tiberius, as 'savage as the enemy in its chanting and clashing of arms',[19] although fighting far from its Germanic homeland in Thrace. Further information concerning these tribal levies comes from Tacitus' account of the ruinous civil war. In April AD 69, when Vitellius marched triumphantly into Rome as its new emperor, his army also included thirty-four *cohortes* 'grouped according to nationality and type of equipment'.[20]

Take the members of *cohors II Tungrorum* for instance, who had been originally raised from among the Tungri who inhabited the northeastern fringes of the Arduenna Silva (Ardennes Forest) in Gallia Belgica. Under the Iulio-Claudian emperors it was quite common for such units to be stationed in or near the province where they were first raised. However, the events of the AD 69, with the mutiny of a large proportion of the *auxilia* serving on the Rhine, would lead to a change in this policy. After that date, though the Roman high command did not abandon local recruiting, it did stop the practice of keeping units with so continuous an ethnic identity close to their homelands.

As expected, by the late first century, units were being kept up to strength by supplements from the province where they were now serving or areas adjacent to it. Such units retained their ethnic identities and names, even if they enlisted new recruits from where they were stationed. The epitaph of Sextus Valerius Genialis tells us that he was a trooper in *ala I Thracum*, and his three-part name indicated he was a Roman citizen. But it adds that he was a 'Frisian tribesman'.[21] So, Genialis came from the lower Rhine, served in a Thracian cavalry unit stationed in Britannia and styled himself a Roman. So after the military anarchy of AD 69, auxiliary cohorts were plausibly made up of a great diversity of individuals of all kinds of nationalities. Nonetheless, despite such conflicting backgrounds and cultures, the Roman military system forged these foreign cohorts into cohesive, aggressive fighting units.

Auxiliary cohorts were either 480 strong (*quingenaria*, 'five hundred strong') or, from around AD 70, 800 strong (*milliaria*, 'one-thousand strong'). Known as *cohortes peditata*, these infantry units had six centuries with eighty soldiers to each if they were *quingenaria*, or if *milliaria* had ten centuries of eighty soldiers each. As in the legions, a centurion and an *optio* commanded a century, which was likewise divided in to ten *contubernia*.

Now to turn to matters concerning mounted *auxilia*. Cavalry units known as *alae* ('wings', it originally denoted the Latin-Italian allies, the *socii*, posted on the flanks of a consular army of the Republic) are thought to have consisted of sixteen *turmae*,[22] each with thirty troopers commanded by a *decurio* and his second-in-command the *duplicarius*,[23] if they were *quingenaria* (512 total), or if *milliaria* twenty-four *turmae*

(768 total). The later units were rare; Britannia, to cite a single example, had only one in its garrison. Drawn from peoples nurtured in the saddle – Gauls, Germans, Iberians and Thracians were preferred – every horseman of the *alae* was well mounted, knew how to ride, and was strong enough and skilful enough to make lethal use of his long straight sword, the *spatha*. The *alae* provided a fighting arm in which the Romans were not so adept.

Additionally there were mixed foot/horse units, the *cohortes equitatae*. Their organization is less clear, but usually assumed, following Hyginus,[24] to have six centuries of eighty men and four *turmae* of thirty troopers if *cohors equitata quingenaria* (608 total), or ten centuries of eighty men and eight *turmae* of thirty troopers if *cohors equitata milliaria* (1,056 total). An inscription, dated to the reign of Tiberius, mentions a *praefectus cohortis Ubiorum peditum et equitum*, 'prefect of a cohort of Ubii, foot and horse',[25] which is probably the earliest example of this type of unit. It may be worth noting here that this Tiberian unit was recruited from the Ubii, a Germanic tribe distinguished for its loyalty to Rome.[26] In Gaul Caesar had employed Germanic horse warriors who could fight in conjunction with foot warriors, operating in pairs.[27]

Organized, disciplined and well trained, the pride of the Roman cavalry were obviously the horsemen of the *alae*, but more numerous were the horsemen of the *cohortes equitatae*. Having served for some time as infantrymen before being upgraded and trained as cavalrymen, these troopers were not as highly paid, or as well mounted as their brothers of the *alae*, but they performed much of the day-to-day patrolling, policing and escort duties.

Specialists

In addition, as in earlier times, there were specialists fulfilling roles in which Roman citizens, better utilized as legionaries, were traditionally unskilled. The best-known of these specialists were archers from Syria and slingers from the Baleares, weapon preferences that were solidly rooted in cultural, social and economic differences.

Among the Romans the bow seems never to have been held in much favour, though after the time of Marius it was introduced by Cretans serving Rome. During our period, however, archers were being recruited from amongst experienced people of the eastern provinces. Like slingers, it is possible they were equipped as regular auxiliaries rather than their exotic appearance on Trajan's Column would indicate (e.g. scene lxx depicts them with high cheekbones and aquiline noses, wearing voluminous flowing skirts that swing round their ankles). Certainly first-century tombstones show archers in the usual off-duty uniform of tunic with sword and dagger belts, *cinguli*, crossed 'cowboy' fashion.

Also likely is the possibility that individual soldiers within any given unit acquired the necessary ability to use bows, rather than simply relying on specialist units. In his military treatise, among other matters, Vegetius includes a recommendation that at least a quarter of all recruits should be trained as bowmen.[28] Yet, despite his sound advice here, Vegetius says it is the self-bow that will be used in training soldiers in the art of archery. It is assumed, therefore, that the standard of archery was obviously not expected to be the same as that provided by specialists units such as *cohors I Hamiorum Sagittariorum*, who were trained and experienced in precisely the sort of warfare in which the Principate army was decidedly deficient.

Appendix 4

Principate Army – Equipment

The Roman army is seen as rather standardized in terms of its equipment, especially its armour. This view, however, is rather misleading and we would probably be closer to the truth envisaging a situation where, as long as the soldier had fully functional equipment, then the army did not mind what type it was. I am not suggesting that Roman soldiers went into action looking like the crew of a pirate ship, but as long as their equipment did the job it was required to do and was well maintained, the pattern was of secondary importance. Besides, as with all professional, state-sponsored armies, improvements in equipment took place relatively slowly, necessitating the continued use of material that was of considerable age, even if certain older items, helmets in particular, were relegated to inferior grades of soldier. It may be said with truth of Roman arms that as long as a piece remained in serviceable condition, it continued to be used – generally speaking, given a minimum amount of daily care, weapons and equipment have a long life span. Thus, many soldiers would not have had top-of-the-line helmets and equipment. All the same, without going into too much detail, the Principate army was made up of a high proportion of armoured fighting men, men who were also as a rule individually more heavily armed and armoured than their adversaries, than any other.

It should be said at this juncture that the Romans were not at all resistant to technological innovation on cultural grounds because the innovation in question originated with a hated enemy; this was a luxury they fully understood that could not be afforded. Indeed, the Romans were adept at cultural borrowing, though they left their own unique stamp on each borrowed idea (and institution) in moulding it to their own purposes.

Finally, when we write of such things, we should not dissociate the weapon from the man who wields it, nor the load from the man who carries it. The legionary, like all professional infantry soldiers before his day and after, was grossly overloaded – alarmingly so according to some accounts. In the evening of his life, Cicero wrote of 'the toil, the great toil, of the march: the load of more than half a month's provisions, the load of any and everything that might be required, the load of the stake for entrenchment'.[1] Normally, perhaps, a legionary carried rations for three days, not the two weeks to which Cicero refers (a brilliant orator, yes, a practical soldier, no).[2] However, it has been estimated that the legionary was burdened with equipment weighing as much as thirty-five kilograms if not more. As Edward Gibbon justly says, this weight 'would oppress the delicacy of a modern soldier'.[3]

Helmet (*galea*)

Roman helmets, of Celtic inspiration, were made of iron or copper alloy (both bronze and brass are known). Bronze was a more expensive metal, but cheaper to work into a helmet: whereas iron helmets could only be beaten into shape, bronze ones were often 'spun' on a revolving former (a shaped piece of wood or stone) from annealed bronze sheets.

Whatever the material or type (viz. Coolus, Imperial Gallic, Imperial Italic),[4] however, the main features were the skull-shaped bowl, a large neck guard to provide protection from blows to the neck and shoulders, cheek pieces to protect the sides of the face – these were hinged so they could move freely – and a brow-guard, which defended against downward blows to the face. The helmet invariably left the face and ears exposed, since the soldier needed to see and hear to understand and follow battlefield commands. Soldiers often punched or scratched their names and those of their centurions onto their helmets to prevent mistaken ownership or indeed theft.[5]

Unlike infantry helmets, cavalry helmets had extensions of their cheek pieces to cover the ears. Often shaped as simulated ears themselves, the extra protection to the face was clearly considered to be more important than some loss of hearing. Also the neck guard was very deep, reaching down to close to the shoulders, but not wide, since this would have made the rider likely to break his neck if he fell from his horse. The cavalry helmet, therefore, protected equally well against blows to the side and the back of the head, vital in a cavalry mêlée when the two sides soon become intermingled.

Hobnailed boots (*caligae*)

The standard form of military footwear for all troop types, *caligae* consisted of a fretwork upper, a thin insole and a thicker outer sole. The twenty-millimetre thick outer sole was made up of several layers of cow or ox leather glued together and studded with conical iron hobnails – evidence from Kalkriese, the probable site of the Varian disaster in AD 9, suggests 120 per boot. Weighing a little under a kilogram, the one-piece upper was sewn up at the heel and laced up the centre of the foot and onto the top of the ankle with a leather thong, the open fretwork providing excellent ventilation that would reduce the possibility of blisters. It also permitted the wearer to wade through shallow water, because, unlike closed footwear that would become waterlogged, they dried quickly on the march.[6]

There is that well known story from Josephus relating to the tragic death of a centurion during the siege of Jerusalem in AD 70. Of Bithynian origin, centurion Iulianus was bravely pursuing the enemy across the inner court of the Temple when the hobnails of his *caligae* skidded on the smooth marble paving and he crashed to the deck, only to be surrounded and eventually despatched by those he had audaciously chased.[7] This was a possible danger of course, but in most circumstances the hobnails served to provide the wearer with better traction. Not only that, they also served to reinforce the *caligae*, and to allow the wearer to inflict harm by stomping. More to the point, the actual nailing pattern on the sole was arranged ergonomically and anticipated modern training-shoe soles designed to optimize the transferral of weight between the different parts of the foot when placed on the ground. Experiments with modern reconstructions have demonstrated that, if properly fitted of course, the *caliga* is an excellent form of marching footwear, and can last for hundreds of kilometres. Much like all soldier's equipment past and present, *caligae* would have needed daily care and attention, such as the replacement of worn or lost hobnails or the cleaning and buffing of the fretwork upper.

If there is one thing of importance to an infantryman, it is his feet. Tacitus represents the Flavians during the civil war as demanding *clavarium*, or 'nail money', that is, money to buy hobnails for their boots.[8] At the time of the claim the Flavian legionaries were making their long march to Rome. Suetonius seems to be alluding to a similar claim when, referring to marines (*classiarii*), who had regularly to march from Ostia or Puteoli to Rome, they demanded of Vespasianus *calciarium*, or 'boot-money'.[9] The emperor, famed for his sardonic wit (and measures), is said to have suggested to them they make the journey barefoot, a practice that was still being continued in Suetonius' day. Soldiers were charged, amongst other things, for their rations, clothing and boots by stoppages debited to their pay accounts and these demands must have been for extra pay to offset the expense of boot repairs.

With such footwear fully laden Roman soldiers could 'yomp' for miles, provided of course that they adapted themselves to local conditions. In cold weather, for instance, *caligae* could be stuffed with wool or fur, while one piece of sculptural evidence depicting a parade of praetorians, namely the Cancellaria Relief, suggests that thick woollen socks (*undones*), toeless and open at the heel, could also be worn with the boot. We also have that well-known writing tablet from Chesterholm-*Vindolanda*:

> I have sent (?) you... pair of socks (*undones*). From Sattua two pairs of sandals (*soleae*) and two pairs of underpants (*subligares*), two pairs of sandals... Greet... ndes, Elips, Iu..., ... enus, Tetricus and all your messmates (*contubernales*) with whom I hope that you live in the greatest of good fortune.[10]

Written in colloquial Latin, this letter was evidently sent to a soldier serving at Chesterholm-*Vindolanda* as the author refers to his *contubernium*, one of which, Elpis, bears a Greek name (literally Hope).[11] The recipient was probably a member of one of three *auxilia* units known to have been stationed here at the end of the first century, namely *cohors III Batavorum*, *cohors VIIII Batavorum*, or *cohors I Tungrorum*. The mention of socks (and underpants) strongly suggests the writer is a close relative or friend whose concern for the recipient's material comfort led him or her to send a parcel from home. Even if socks and underpants were not standard issue, provision of additional clothing of this kind is abundantly paralleled in the papyri from Egypt. What is more, evidence of this sort promotes the commonsense idea that Roman soldiers adapted to local conditions, however extreme. Finally, it is interesting to note that the Chesterholm-*Vindolanda* texts show us how swiftly auxiliary soldiers acquired literate habits and how proficient they became in Latin, a language that was not their native tongue but their Roman military service forced them to acquire.[12] As a point of comparison, Charlemagne was distinguished among his peers because he could write his name; however, there is no evidence that he could read at all.

As a final point, cavalrymen could attach spurs, of iron or bronze, to their *caligae*. Prick spurs had been worn by Celts of the La Tène period, being evident in late Iron Age Gaulish and central European graves and settlements, and were known in Greece from the late fifth century BC onwards.[13] They were sporadically used by Roman cavalry throughout the empire, especially by troopers on the Rhine and Danube frontiers.

Body armour (*lorica*)

The Romans employed three main types of body armour: mail (*lorica hamata*), scale (*lorica squamata*), and segmented (*lorica segmentata*).[14] All body armour would have been worn over some kind of padded garment and not directly on top of the tunic. Apart from making the wearer more comfortable, this extra layer complemented the protective values of each type of armour, and helped to absorb the shock of any blow striking the armour. The anonymous author of *De rebus bellicis*, an amateur military theoretician writing in the late fourth century, describes the virtues of such a garment:

> The ancients [i.e. the Romans], among the many things, which... they devised for use in war, prescribed also the *thoracomachus* to counteract the weight and friction of armour... This type of garment is made of thick sheep's wool felt to the measure... of the upper part of the human frame...[15]

The author himself probably coined the term *thoracomachus* (cf. Greek *thorâx*, breastplate), which seems to be a padded garment of linen stuffed with wool. One illustration on Trajan's Column (scene cxxviii) depicts two dismounted troopers on sentry duty outside a headquarters who appear to have removed their mail-shirts to expose the padded garment.

Lorica hamata: Mail was normally made of iron rings, on average about a millimetre thick and three to nine millimetres in external diameter. Each ring was connected to four others, each one passing through the two rings directly above and two directly below – one riveted ring being inter-linked with four punched rings. The adoption of *lorica hamata* by the Romans stems from their having borrowed the idea from the Celts, among whom it had been in use at least since the third century BC, albeit reserved for use by aristocratic warriors only. This early mail was made of alternate lines of punched and butted rings. The Romans replaced the butted rings with much stronger riveted rings, one riveted ring linking four punched rings.

The wearer's shoulders were reinforced with 'doubling', of which there were two types. One had comparatively narrow shoulder 'straps', and a second pattern, probably derived from earlier Celtic patterns, in a form of a shoulder-cape. The second type required no backing leather, being simply drawn around the wearer's shoulder girdle and fastened with S-shaped breast-hooks, which allowed the shoulder-cape to move more easily. The shoulder-cape is indicated on numerous grave markers belonging to cavalrymen, which also show the mail–shirt split at the hips to enable the rider to sit a horse.

Although mail had two very considerable drawbacks – it was extremely laborious to make, and while it afforded complete freedom of movement to the wearer, it was very heavy, weighing anywhere between 10 and 15 kilograms, depending on the length and number of rings (at least 30,000) – such armour was popular. A mail–shirt was flexible and essentially shapeless, fitting more closely to the wearer's body than other types of armour. In this respect it was comfortable, whilst the wearing of a belt helped to spread its considerable weight, which would otherwise be carried entirely by the shoulders. Mail offered reasonable protection, but could be penetrated by a strong thrust or an arrow fired at effective range. It was also vulnerable to bludgeoning weapons such as clubs or maces. Worn underneath the *lorica hamata* was undoubtedly some form of leather or padded protection, without which mail was relatively useless, to dissipate further the force of a blow.

Lorica squamata: Scale armour was made of small plates (*squamae*), one to five centimetres in length, of copper alloy (occasionally tinned), or occasionally of iron, wired to their neighbours horizontally and then sewn in overlapping rows to linen or leather backing. Each row was arranged to overlap the one below by a third to a half the height of the scales, enough to cover the vulnerable stitching. The scales themselves were thin, and the main strength of this protection came from the overlap of scale to scale, which helped to spread the force of a blow.

A serious deficiency lies in the fact that such defences could be quite readily pierced by an upward thrust of sword or spear; a hazardous aspect of which many cavalrymen must have been acutely aware when engaging infantry. This weakness was overcome, certainly by the second century, when a new form of semi-rigid cuirass was introduced where each scale, of a relatively large dimension, was wired to its vertical, as well as its horizontal, neighbours.

Scale could be made by virtually anyone, requiring patience rather than craftsmanship, and was very simple to repair. Though scale was inferior to mail, being neither as strong nor as flexible, it was similarly used throughout our period and proved particularly popular with horsemen and officers as this type of armour, especially if tinned, could be polished to a high sheen. Apart from those to cavalry, most of the funerary monuments that depict scale armour belong to centurions.

Lorica segmentata: This was the famous laminated armour that features so prominently on the spiral relief of Trajan's Column. Concerning its origins, one theory suggests that it was inspired by gladiatorial armour, since these fighters are known to have worn a form of articulated protection for the limbs. Part of a *lorica segmentata* was found at Kalkriese, the probable site of the Varian disaster in AD 9, making this the earliest known example of this type of armour. It is last seen (in a carving) sometime around AD 230 in the time of Severus Alexander – a good run, but of only perhaps two-and-half centuries as opposed to the six centuries many book illustrations and epic films (and, unfortunately, television documentaries) would have us believe.

The armour consisted of some forty overlapping, horizontal curved bands of iron articulated by internal straps. It was hinged at the back, and fastened with buckles, hooks and laces at the front. As the bands overlapped it allowed the wearer to bend his body, the bands sliding one over another. The armour was strengthened with back and front plates below the neck, and a pair of curved shoulder pieces. In addition, the legionary would wear a metal studded apron hung from a wide leather belt (*cingulum*), which protected the belly and groin. Round the neck was worn a woollen scarf (*focale*), knotted in front, to prevent the metal plates from chafing the skin.

Superior to mail with regard to ease of manufacture and preservation, but most particularly in view of its weight, this could be as little as 5.5 kilograms, depending on the thickness of the plate used. It was also more resistant to much heavier blows than mail, preventing serious bruising and providing better protection against a sharp pointed weapon or an arrow. Its main weakness lay in the fact that it provided no protection to the wearer's arms and thighs. Also full-scale, working reconstructions of *lorica segmentata* have shown that the multiplicity of copper-alloy buckles, hinges and hooks and leather straps, which gave freedom of movement, were surprisingly frail. It may have been effective against attacking blows or in impressing the enemy, but with its many maintenance problems we can understand why *lorica segmentata* never became standard equipment in the Principate army.

Body shield (*scutum*)

Legionaries carried a large dished shield (*scutum*), which had been oval in the republican period but was now rectangular in shape. Besides making it less burdensome, the shortening of the *scutum* at top and bottom was probably due to the introduction into the army of new combat techniques, such as the famous Roman 'tortoise' (*testudo*), a mobile formation entirely protected by a roof and walls of overlapping and interlocking *scuta*.[16] On the other hand, auxiliaries, infantrymen and horsemen alike, carried a flat shield (*clipeus*), with a variety of shapes (oval, hexagonal, rectangular) recorded.

Shields, *scuta* and *clipi* equally, were large to give their bearer good protection. To be light enough to be held continually in battle, however, shield-boards were usually constructed of double or triple thickness plywood made up of thin strips of birch or plane wood held together with glue. The middle layer was laid at right angles to the front and back layers. Covered both sides with canvas and rawhide, they were edged with copper-alloy binding and had a central iron or copper-alloy boss (*umbo*), a bowl-shaped protrusion covering a horizontal handgrip and wide enough to clear the fist of the bearer.

An overall central grip was probably adopted from the Celts, who certainly used such an arrangement at an early date. More specifically, however, such a grip was to encourage parrying with the *scutum* and not, as mentioned earlier in this book, the *gladius*. When the *scutum* was used offensively, the horizontal handgrip allowed for a more solid punch to be delivered as the fist was held in the correct position to throw a 'boxing jab'. It also meant that the legionary's elbow was not over extended as the blow was delivered. Such an arrangement, however, provided less balance to the *scutum* as a whole. If, for instance, the *scutum* were struck above or below its central plane, it would have been very difficult to prevent the shield from pivoting upon its axis. The resulting movement would have thus created an opening in the legionary's defence. The vertical handgrip, on the other hand, was more reliable in terms of blocking blows. The vertical orientation of the hand would have enabled the legionary to keep the *scutum* as straight as possible, even if the *scutum* were struck above or below the shield-boss. Of course, a less solid punch can be delivered with the fist in a vertical position as compared to the horizontal position.

When not in use shields were protected from the elements by leather shield-covers; plywood can easily double in weight if soaked with rain. Oiled to keep it both pliant and water resistant, the cover was tightened round the rim of the shield by a drawstring. It was usual for it to have some form of decoration, usually pierced leather appliqué-work stitched on, identifying the bearer's unit. A cavalryman had the luxury of carrying his shield obliquely against the horse's flank,[17] slung from the two side horns of the saddle and sometimes under the saddlecloth.[18]

So much for the defensive equipment employed by the Romans. Now we must turn our attention to their weaponry. Throughout our chosen period, the main weapons in use were the bow, the sling, the javelin, the spear, the sword, and the dagger. The first three were missile weapons, and the rest were used in the close-quarter mêlée. We will examine each, in the Roman context of course, in turn.

Shafted weapons

Few ancient civilizations eschewed the spear in their arsenals, and in its simplest form, a spear was nothing more than a stout wooden stick with a sharpened and hardened business end, the latter being achieved by revolving the tip in a gentle flame till it was charred to hardness. Beyond that, it was a long, straight wooden shaft tipped with a metallic spearhead, although the sharpened stick with the hardened tip could be quite an effective killing weapon too. Ash wood (as frequently mentioned in the heroic verses of Homer and Virgil) was the most frequently chosen because it naturally grows straight and cleaves easily. Moreover, it is both tough and elastic, which means it has the capacity to absorb repeated shocks without communicating them to the handler's hand and of withstanding a good hard knock without splintering. These properties combined made it a good choice for crafting a spear.

Heavy javelin (pilum)

Since the mid-third century BC the *pilum* had been employed by legionaries in battle as a short-range shock weapon; it had a maximum range of thirty metres or thereabouts, although probably it was discharged within fifteen metres of the enemy for maximum effect.[19] The maximum range of any thrown or shot weapon is irrelevant. Man is capable of running a sub-four minute mile, but this does not mean the average man is so able. Similarly, it may be of academic interest to know that a legionary was capable of launching a *pilum* more than thirty metres. What is of greater interest is the fact that the enemy had to be within twenty metres before the legionary had any real chance of scoring a hit.

By our period the *pilum* had a pyramidal iron head on a long, untempered iron-shank, some sixty to ninety centimetres in length, fastened to a one-piece wooden shaft, which was generally of ash. The head was designed to puncture shield and armour, the long iron shank passing through the hole made by the head.

Once the weapon had struck home, or even if it missed and hit the ground, the soft-iron shank tended to buckle and bend under the weight of the shaft. With its aerodynamic qualities destroyed, it could not be effectively thrown back, while if it lodged in a shield, it became extremely difficult to remove.[20] Put simply, the *pilum* would penetrate either flesh or become useless to the enemy. Modern experiments have shown that a *pilum*, thrown from a distance of five metres, could pierce thirty millimetres of pine wood or twenty millimetres of plywood.[21]

Continuing the practice of the late Republic, there were two fixing methods at the start of our period, the double-riveted tang and the simple socket reinforced by an iron collet. With regards to the tanged *pilum*, however, there is iconographical evidence, such as the Cancellaria Relief and the Adamklissi Monument, to suggest that a bulbous lead weight was now added under the pyramid-shaped wooden block fixing the shank to the shaft. Presumably this development was to enhance the penetrative capabilities of the *pilum* by concentrating even more power behind its small head, but, of course, the increase in weight would have meant a reduction in range.

Light spear (lancea)

Auxiliary foot and horse used a light spear (*lancea*) as opposed to the *pilum*. Approximately 1.8 metres in length, it was capable of being thrown further than a *pilum*, though obviously with less effect against armoured targets, or retained in the hand to thrust overarm as shown in the cavalry tombstones of the period.

Even though such funerary carvings usually depict troopers carrying either two *lancae* or grooms (*calones*) behind them holding spares, Josephus claims Vespasianus' eastern cavalry carried a quiver containing three or more darts with heads as large as light spears.[22] He does not say specifically where the quiver was positioned but presumably it was attached to the saddle. Arrian confirms this in his description of an equestrian exercise in which horsemen were expected to throw as many as fifteen, or, in exceptional cases twenty light spears, in one run.[23] Presumably infantrymen carried more than one *lancea*; a low-cut relief recovered from the site of the fortress at Mainz-*Mogontiacum* depicts an auxiliary infantryman brandishing one in his right hand with two more held behind his *clipeus*. Analysis of the remains of wooden shafts shows that ash and hazel were commonly used.

The simple term 'spearhead', however, embraces a great range of shapes and sizes, complete with socket ferrules (either welded in a complete circle or split-sided) to enable them to be mounted on the shaft and often secured with one or two rivets and/or binding. Head lengths can vary from six to eight centimetres all the way up to forty centimetres, whilst socket lengths range from seven to thirteen centimetres in length. For use as a stabbing weapon, practical experience tells us that the width of the blade was important, for a wide blade actually prevents the spearhead from being inserted into the body of an enemy too far, thus enabling the spear to be recovered quickly, ready for further use. In our period of study the most common designs were angular blades, with a diamond cross section, and leaf-shaped blades, with a biconvex cross section.

Edged weapons

The modern infantryman is no longer armed exclusively with the rifle and bayonet. His tactical repertoire has expanded to include hand grenades, pistols, daggers, and sharpened entrenching tools. If he is a specialist, he also masters a machine gun, a light mortar, or an anti-armour weapon. The Roman legionary, on the other hand, was a specialist with one weapon only, the *gladius*.

Short sword (gladius)

It would be a pointless sort of exercise to debate the relative importance of the different swords of the fighting forces throughout the period of Rome's domination of the Mediterranean world, whether it was single or double edged, short or long, heavy or light, straight or curved, and so forth, which played the most vital rôle, but certain it is that, as Rome expanded, the *gladius* was making an increasing contribution to the winning of empire. Against the unarmoured formations frequently met with by Roman legions it was a most potent weapon.

Of all the weapons man has seen fit to invent, the spear was probably the one most universally used during our period of study. Not so, however, with the Roman legionary, who was primarily a swordsman trained in the science and skill of a very singular sword. It goes without saying that the use of weapons has transformed man's capacity to inflict violence. The capacity of man-as-animal to deliver violence is very limited, as a psychologist appropriately named Gunn describes vividly:

It is extremely difficult for one naked unarmed man to kill another such man. He has to resort to strangulation, or to punching him hard enough to knock him over so that he may gash open an important vessel with his teeth, or break his head open by dashing it against the ground ... Weapons magnify the aggressiveness of a creature many times.[24]

It had been back in the third century BC when the Romans had adopted a long-pointed, double-edged Iberian weapon, which they called the *gladius Hispaniensis* ('Iberian sword'), though the earliest specimens date to the turn of the first century BC. In our chosen period the *gladius* was employed not only by legionaries, but by auxiliary infantrymen too.

Based on *gladii* found at Pompeii and on several sites along the Rhine and Danube frontiers, Ulbert has been able to show that there were two models of *gladius*, the one succeeding the other.[25] First was the long-pointed 'Mainz' type, whose blade alone could measure sixty-nine centimetres in length and six centimetres in width,[26] and is well-evidenced in the period from Augustus to Caius Caligula. The 'Pompeii' type followed this, a short-pointed type that replaced it, probably during the early part of Claudius' principate. This pattern was shorter than its predecessor, being between forty-two and fifty-five centimetres long, with a straighter blade 4.2 to 5.5 centimetres wide and short triangular point. Whereas the 'Mainz' type weighed between 1.2 and 1.6 kilograms, the 'Pompeii' type was lighter, weighing about a kilogram. The blade of both types was a fine piece of blister steel with a sharp point and honed down razor-sharp edges and was designed to puncture armour.[27] It had a comfortable bone handgrip grooved to fit the fingers, and a large spherical pommel, usually of wood or ivory, to help with counterbalance. In the hands of the trained soldier it was a formidable instrument of destruction.

This sword lacked a typical cross hilt, which tells us it was not a parrying weapon. There is little doubt, therefore, that the *gladius* was designed primarily as a short-range thrusting weapon, that is, the intention was to deliver the fatal blow by a thrust. Accordingly, the sword blade was straight and the handle short, while the main design feature was the point. The short length of the weapon allowed for ease of control, while its comparative lightness enhanced the swordsman's reaction time. It was weighted more closely to the actual hilt than a standard sword so as to discourage the slash and to encourage the thrust.[28] This arrangement also helped to increase the speed of the thrust. In addition, the oversized pommel increased the weight at the back end of the sword, thus increasing the power behind the thrust. Finally, the oval-shaped cross-guard just above the handgrip allowed the swordsman to apply maximum pressure to the thrust, and this, combined with a contoured grip to fit the hand snugly, increased the potency of the thrust.[29] The handgrip itself was some 7.5 to 10 centimetres in length, that is, slightly longer than the width of a hand. This arrangement allowed for better efficiency and control in weapon handling.

Unusually, legionaries and auxiliaries carried their sword on the right-hand side suspended by the *cingulum* worn around the waist. The wearing of the sword on the right side goes back to the Iberians, and before them, to the Celts. The sword was the weapon of the high status warrior, and to carry one was to display a symbol of rank and prestige. It was probably for cultural reasons alone, therefore, that the Celts carried their beloved weapon, the long slashing sword, on the right side. Customarily a sword, when not in the right hand, was worn on the left, the side covered by the shield, which meant the weapon was hidden from view. However, the Roman soldier wore his sword on the right hand not for any cultural reason. As opposed to a scabbard-slide, the four-ring suspension system on the scabbard enabled him to draw his weapon quickly with the right hand, an asset in close-quarter combat. Inverting the fighting fist to grasp the hilt and pushing the pommel forward drew the *gladius* with ease. More to the point, it also meant the sword arm was not exposed when doing so.

For the Roman soldier, the *gladius* fitted his temperament perfectly. It was a close-quarter weapon and the Roman was never one to stand around, engaging in distant firefights, but rather he sought every opportunity to engage his foe in a mêlée. Surely another sword type would never take the place of the Queen of Death, the *gladius*.

Long sword (spatha)

Cavalrymen, on the other hand, used a longer, narrower double-edged sword, the *spatha*, which followed Celtic types, with a blade length from 64.5 to 91.5 centimetres and width from four to six centimetres. The middle section of the blade was virtually parallel-edged, but tapered into a rounded point. It was intended primarily as a slashing weapon for use on horseback, and it usually was so employed, though the point could also be used for thrusting if need be.

In spite of its length, the *spatha* was worn on the right side of the body, as Josephus says,[30] and numerous cavalry tombstones confirm, suspended from a waist belt or baldric whose length could be adjusted by a row of metal buttons. At the turn of the second century, however, the *spatha* started to be worn on the left side, although not exclusively so.

Military dagger (pugio)

The *pugio* – a short, edged, stabbing weapon – was the ultimate weapon of last resort. However, it was probably more often employed in the day-to-day tasks of living on campaign. Carried on the left-hand side and suspended on the same *cingulum* that carried the sword (though two separate belts crossed 'cowboy' style was a dashing alternate), the *pugio* was slightly waisted in a leaf-shape and some 20 to 25.4 centimetres long. The choice of a leaf-shaped blade resulted in a heavy weapon, to add momentum to the thrust. Like the *gladius*, the *pugio* was borrowed from the Iberians and then developed; it even had the four-ring suspension system on the scabbard, characteristic of the *gladius*.

The *pugio*, worn by legionaries and auxiliaries alike, was obviously a cherished object. Soldiers seldom wasted time on aesthetics. Their equipment, whether it belonged to an individual or to the state, remained functional, the *pila, gladii, scuta* –

all such equipage were primarily utilitarian. Not so, it seems, the *pugionis*. The highly decorative nature of Roman daggers of our period, and particularly their sheaths, suggests that even common soldiers were prepared to spend considerable sums of money on what could be classified as true works of art. Though remaining an effective fighting weapon, the *pugio* was plainly an outward display of its wearer's power.

Missile weapons

Bow

Whereas bows of self-wood construction were made exclusively of wood in one or more pieces, the composite bow had an elaborate network of sinew cables on its back to provide the cast, with a horn belly to provide the recovery of the bow. The whole was built up on a wooden core with bone strips stiffening both the grip and the extremities (the 'ears'), and then covered with skin or leather and moisture-proof lacquers. The back of the bow was that side away from the archer, which was stretched in stringing and stretched even more when the bow was drawn. The belly was the side nearest the archer when drawn, which was compressed by stringing and compressed even more by drawing.

The design of a composite bow thus took full advantage of the mechanical properties of the materials used in its construction: sinew has great tensile strength, while horn has compressive strength. When released the horn belly acted like a coil, returning instantly to its original position. Sinew, on the other hand, naturally contracted after being stretched. This method of construction and the materials employed thus allowed the bow to impart a greater degree of force to the arrow when fired, compared with the wooden self-bow of the same draw weight. This latter characteristic enabled the archer to choose between two tactical options, depending on the need of the moment. He either could deliver a lightweight projectile over a distance twice what a wooden self-bow could shoot, or deliver a projectile of greater weight or force at short range when the capacity to pierce armour or to thoroughly disable an opponent was needed.

The actual range and performance of the composite bow is open to debate, and a number of varied figures have been suggested. Vegetius recommended a practice range of 600 Roman feet (*c.* 177 metres), while later Islamic works expected an archer to display consistent accuracy at 69 metres.[31] Modern research tends to place an accurate range up to 50 to 60 metres, with an effective range extended at least 160 to 175 metres, and a maximum range at between 350 and 450 metres.[32] Range is as much dependent upon the man as the bow and coupled with this was bow quality – the better made the composite bow; the more tailored to the individual archer's height, draw weight and length, the better the performance.

That is not to say that the composite bow was the 'ultimate weapon'. Draw weights of 150 pounds or more taxed even a very strong man and a high rate of fire could not be sustained indefinitely. Unlike firearms or weapons such as the crossbow, which store chemical or potential energy and, by releasing this, propel their missile, a bow converts the bodily strength of the firer into a force propelling the arrow. This skill is much harder to learn than the use of a crossbow or a firearm such as an arquebus, which only has to be loaded and aimed to be effective. Indeed, where a few hours sufficed to teach an ordinary fellow to draw and aim a crossbow, many years of constant practice and a whole way of life were needed to master the use of the composite bow. Archery did not consist of a series of mechanical movements that anyone could be trained to execute, but of a whole complex cultural, social and economic relationship.

Other externalities to consider are those of the accuracy and the effectiveness. The target's size and rate of movement, as well as the skill of the individual archer, governed accuracy. In actuality the archer would have practised shooting at a stationary target. A trained archer, when fresh, could get off six aimed shots in a minute with ease. Perhaps the best modern estimate of his long-range accuracy comes from W.F. Paterson, himself an experienced archer. Paterson concludes that a good shot on a calm day could be expected to hit a target the size of a man on horseback at 280 yards about once every four shots.[33] At a hundred metres such an archer would have been able to pick his man. At fifty he would have been sure of death.

However, whilst this level of accuracy – the ability to pick-off individuals – would have been useful in the archer's role as a skirmisher his main task was to stand behind his own infantry and shoot, indirectly, at a unit rather than an individual. In this case accuracy was more concerned with all of the arrows arriving on the target area at the same time, than with individual marksmanship. Thus, an effective shot was not necessarily an accurate one, and in pitched battle a murderous barrage was possible even without aiming.[34] When Titus formed a fourth rank of archers behind three of legionaries,[35] these men could have had little or no opportunity of seeing their target. They would have been firing blind, over the heads of the men in front, hoping to drop their arrows down from a high trajectory onto the general area occupied by the enemy and spread death and injuries amongst their ranks.

Arrow

The arrow penetrates because of the concentration of its kinetic energy behind a narrow cutting edge. The types of arrowheads used by the Principate army reflected these different penetrative requirements. Bodkin heads or flat-bladed types were used for armour piercing, be the target shield or body armour, acting on the same principles as the *pilum*.[36] On the other hand, trilobate, triple- or quadruple-vaned were more effective against unarmoured horses and men. A bow relies on sending an arrow deep into the body of its victim. As the arrow passes through it severs blood vessels and major arteries. Since arrows ordinarily kill by bleeding, projectiles that could open up a large wound on an unarmoured opponent were useful. A third category was designed to carry incendiary material, such as a naphtha-soaked ball of twine with wood splints.[37] Five such arrowheads were recovered from the fort at Bar Hill, Antonine Wall. They have three projecting wings that form an open iron framework capable of holding inflammable material.

In terms of arrow technology heads were mainly tanged, although the Romans also employed socketed types as well, and were glued and bound to the shafts. The shafts were made from wood,[38] cane or reed. The latter is one of the best materials, having a combination of lightness, rigidity and elasticity ideal for shafts. Reeds are also already well adapted to their aerodynamic role as shafts by their need while growing to maintain an evenly round profile to reduce wind drag, as well as by having the elasticity and strength to bend and return to upright position. This latter adaptation is critical as shafts need to be able to bend round the bow during shooting, and flex so the tail swings clear of the bow before swinging back into line as the arrow travels along the line it was aimed at the moment of release.[39] Where cane or reed was used the arrowhead was first attached to a wooden pile, which was then glued onto a cane or reed shaft. The piles reduced the risk of the cane or reed splitting on impact, which would, if it occurred, reduce the arrow's penetrative power. The remains of cane or reed arrows from Doura-Europos show that the surface of the shaft was roughened and the fletching glued onto this surface. The lower portions of three shafts actually bear painted markings, and it has been suggested that the arrows were marked to identify their owners or to denote a matching set.[40]

Because human ribs are horizontal and the bow held vertically, the head of a war arrow is often perpendicular to the plane of the notch, so that the point may pass more easily between the ribs. For the same reason, the plane of the head matches that of the notch in hunting arrows. Modern experiments have shown that socketed arrows tended to break behind the socket itself. Whether this action was deliberately intended or simply an accidental by-product of manufacture is hard to ascertain.[41] Tanged arrowheads proved less likely to break on impact, the sinew binding required to hold the head in place limiting their degree of penetration. These field trials were conducted against all known forms of Roman armour. Not surprisingly, *lorica hamata* proved to be the easiest to penetrate, followed by the *lorica segmentata* and finally the *lorica segmentata*, in which none of the arrowheads penetrated to a depth sufficient to cause a fatal wound even at a range of seven metres. Somewhat surprisingly the wooden shield, especially if covered with leather, almost provided as much defence.[42]

Sling

Slingers normally served as a complement to archers; the sling not only outranged the bow but a slinger was also capable of carrying a larger supply of ammunition than an archer. Slingshots were not only small stones or pebbles, but also of lead, acorn or almond shaped, and weighing some eighteen to thirty-five grams.[43] Unique to the Graeco-Roman world, these leaden bullets, the most effective of slingshots, could be cast bearing inscriptions, such as symbols – a thunderbolt emblem was popular – or a short phrase, usually only a few letters. Some of these may be an invocation to the bullet itself or invective aimed at the recipient – AVALE, 'swallow this'. Doubtless the last had a double meaning as the Latin term for lead sling bullet is *glans* (pl. *glandes*), which literally means 'acorn' but can also refer to the head of the penis. Other inscriptions, usually cut by hand in longhand writing rather than impressed into the two-part moulds from which the bullets were made, bear witness to the soldier's jesting filth.[44]

The sling itself, as deadly as it was simple, was made of a length of non-elastic material such as rush, flax, hemp or wool. It comprised a small cradle to house the bullet, and two braided cords, one ending in a knot and the other with a loop. In all techniques of slinging, the slingshot was placed in the centre of the cradle, the loop was secured to the second finger of the throwing hand and the knot between the thumb and forefinger of the same hand. In the Mediterranean world the common casting technique was the horizontal whirl, as described by Vegetius.[45] The sling was held with the throwing arm raised above the shoulder. The slingshot was placed in the cradle, and the hand and sling allowed to drop backwards over the head, and whirled around the head clockwise (from the slinger's point of view) a number of times (Vegetius only allows a single whirl around the head) until sufficient momentum was built up. The knot was then released perpendicular to the body so the slingshot flew out straight ahead, its range being related to the angle of discharge, the length of the whirling cords and the amount of kinetic energy imparted by the thrower.

The potential range of the sling has been a the subject of considerable debate and speculation. The problem lies with the testimony of the soldier-scholar Xenophon, who claimed that the leaden missiles of the Rhodian slingers carried 'no less than twice as far as those from Persian slings', the latter slinging a stone 'as large as the hand can hold'.[46] The more conservative estimates are around the 200 metres mark,[47] while 350 metres,[48] 400 metres,[49] and even 500 metres,[50] have been suggested as possibilities for the maximum range of a leaden bullet.[51] On the practical side, Korfmann observed for himself Turkish shepherds, males who grew up in a sling-using milieu, sling ordinary pebbles. In five out of eleven trials the pebbles reached 200 metres, and three of the best casts were between 230 and 240 metres.

Fast-moving slingshot could not be seen in flight and did not need to penetrate armour to be horrifically effective. Vegetius writes that slingshot was more effective than arrows against armoured soldiers in armour, since they did not need to penetrate the armour in order to 'inflict a wound that is still lethal'.[52] A blow from a slingshot on a helmet, for instance, could be enough to give the wearer concussion.[53]

Extra slings were normally carried, and those not employed were normally tied round the head or the belly.[54] Slingshot was carried in a bag slung over the shoulder.

Appendix 5

What Roman Soldiers Ate

T he axiom, commonly attributed to Napoléon, 'an army marches on its stomach' applies to all armies of all periods, and the Roman army was certainly no exception. Certainly the best tribute to the army of the early Principate, on campaign or in peacetime or even during the rare mutinies, is that there is no recorded complaint about the Roman military diet, and it appears that the soldier fed better than or at least as well as many civilians of a similar social background. Even the *auxilia* stationed in frontier forts had a varied and well-balanced diet.

The iron rations carried in the field were bacon-lard, hardtack, salt, sour wine and wheat,[1] the latter being milled by the soldier himself and then made into various dishes such as porridge or soup, the latter in combination with meat and vegetables, though it was commonly eaten in the form of unleavened bread.[2] The grain ration was probably issued on campaign in the form of hardtack, what later sources refer to as *bucellatum*.[3] In our period of study the elder Pliny mentions *panis militaris castrensis*, soldiers' bread, what poor Cicero once experienced as *cibarius panis*, ration bread.[4] Obviously for campaign consumption, soldiers' or ration bread was in all probability hardtack, which could be ground and used as flour, broken into pieces and boiled with water to make porridge, or softened with *posca* and eaten immediately. Pliny, who ended his days as the *praefectus* of the *classis Misenensis*,[5] mentions too *panis nauticus*,[6] presumably the navy's version of hardtack, ship's biscuits.

Of course we must not fail to remember that warfare creates its own famine as it moves. It is a simple matter of logistics. If your army is in garrison somewhere on the frontier, you can set up stable supply lines so your soldiers do not have to forage, 'living off the land', which means, basically, getting food from the locals at sword point. It is standard military practice, but it is neither clean nor pretty. After all, for these luckless locals an army of scrounging soldiers must have amounted to a fair-sized town in their midst. In the year of four emperors, for instance, we can scarcely imagine the suffering endured by those civilians unfortunate enough to be living in the Po basin. There is a limit to the number of times the same region can be foraged, and their fields and barns would have been visited and picked clean not by one or two hungry armies but by four (viz. Vitellian and Othonian, Vitellian and Flavian).

The diet in garrison was still based on wheat,[7] though it could be rich and varied, as animals were kept on land assigned to the garrison, levied, brought or hunted. Milk and cheese could again be obtained from the unit's own herds, exacted or purchased. A variety of local fruit and vegetables were also eaten. Analysis of the sewage at Bearsden on the Antonine Wall has confirmed that the military diet was high in fibre and primarily vegetable based, although documentary and archaeological evidence does demonstrate that meat was consumed too. The sewage from the fort contained fragments of wheat, barley, bean, fig, dill, coriander, opium poppy (possibly used on bread as today), hazelnut, raspberry, bramble, strawberry, bilberry, and wild celery. Fig, dill, coriander and wild celery, the seeds of which were used medicinally, were most likely shipped in from the Mediterranean. The sewage also tells us that the soldiers suffered from dangerous intestinal parasitic diseases such as whipworm and roundworm, and some of their grain appears to have been contaminated with weevils.[8]

An excellent picture of the meat soldiers ate can be seen from the analysis of animal bones from butchered-animal refuse pits excavated at Roman forts in Britain and Germany.[9] Ox, sheep and pig were most popular, in that order, but goat, red and roe deer, wild boar, hare, fowl both domesticated and wild, fish and shellfish were also eaten.[10] Of these supplementary commodities, seafood was probably very popular. A private letter to a *decurio* stationed at Chesterholm-*Vindolanda* states that the sender had received fifty oysters from a friend.[11] The Chesterholm-*Vindolanda* ink writing-tablets refer to a wide range of vegetables, including cabbage, garden peas, broad beans and horse beans, carrots, radishes, and garlic, not to mention pulses such as lentils and chickpeas. Fruits consumed included apples, pears, plums, cherries, peaches, grapes, elderberries, damsons, apricots, olives, and pomegranates, as well as nuts such as sweet chestnuts, walnuts, and beechnuts. Eggs should not be forgotten, nor spices and salt (*salaria*).

By our standards, even for those of us who are not too conscious of what we eat, the Romans consumed a great deal of salt, partly because food was preserved in it. In addition to this, or perhaps because of it, the Romans loved salty food. Just to give one, albeit extreme, example, Apicius cooks *porcellum Traianum* – 'Suckling pig à la Trajan' – in a pot with its own weight of salt.[12] If we measure the salt consumption by the amount the elder Cato says he gave to his slaves (one *modius* per annum), it amounts to a staggering twenty grams per day.[13] On the other hand, a lack of salt could be a real problem. In 151 BC Roman soldiers, physically exhausted and lacking sleep, had fed on the local fare and excessive amounts of meat boiled without salt, all with consequent ill effects upon their digestive system.[14]

To sweeten their food soldiers, just like civilians, used honey, and like all Romans they were fond of using highly salted fish sauces, especially *garum*, to flavour their food. The sauce was made from a variety of fermented sea creatures, such as prawns, oysters, anchovies, sardines, mackerel, tuna, salmon and red mullet. It was sometimes flavoured with herbs and spices. It was also mixed with wine. However, *garum*, which was somewhat akin to the popular Thai delicacy of *nam pla*, was very expensive, and the soldiers used a cheaper but inferior variety called *muria*. Besides being listed in the ink writing-tablets,[15] *muria* was once stored in one of the amphorae unearthed at Chesterholm-*Vindolanda*.

Normally two square meals were eaten each day, *prandium* eaten around midday, and *cena*, which was eaten around the tenth or eleventh hour on the Roman sundial. Army life began at dawn so the soldiers had little time to prepare breakfast, *ientaculum*. They nibbled a bit of bread, perhaps dipped in undiluted wine. Besides, Romans in general consider a heavy breakfast unhealthy and vulgar, though it is interesting to note that those poor citizen legionaries who went into battle breakfastless on the frigid forenoon of the Trebbia were to suffer dearly for it.[16]

In theory each soldier was provided with a daily ration of food, which he cooked himself, there being no central cookhouse,[17] but we should not assume that each soldier literally cooked for himself. The Carvoran-*Magnis* grain measure from the Stanegate fort of the same name holds the equivalent of seven daily rations and suggests that the grain be disbursed weekly.[18] As each soldier slept eight to a barrack room or tent, we can assume that they pooled their daily rations with one man taking on the food preparation and cooking for his *contubernium*, mess-group. This is supported by the discovery of cooking implements and millstones marked with the name of *contubernia*,[19] whilst in the Chesterholm-*Vindolanda* ink writing-tablets we read of references to a soldier's messmates, *contubernales*. Josephus implies too that food was cooked and eaten communally by *contubernia*,[20] whilst Appian states that when Scipio Aemilianus reintroduced military discipline to the army at Numantia when he took command of it in 134 BC, he ordered that the only way soldiers could eat their meat was by roasting or boiling it. It was for this purpose that he reduced the number of cooking utensils to the standard three common to our period of study: an iron spit (*trulleus*) for roasting, a bronze camp kettle (*veru*) for boiling, and a bronze mess tin (*patera*) for eating.[21] Thus, two opposites were required for cooking, water and fire.

A fresco from Pompeii depicts a soldier holding in an outstretched hand a tall vessel. He says to the innkeeper, who is just about to pour something into this, 'just a dash of water!' As already mentioned, the iron rations a soldier carried when on active service included *acetum*, a sour wine.[22] This, as opposed to good wine, *vinum*, was the drink of the ordinary soldier as proffered in an act of mercy to Christ on the cross.[23] Made by reusing wine spoiled by faulty storage, sour wine was less acidic than vinegar, and still retained some of the aroma and texture of wine. It had important dietary advantages too. As well as a source of liquid, it provided calories and was a valuable antiscorbutic, helping to prevent scurvy by providing vitamin C. It could be mixed with water to make the time-honoured tipple of the proletariat, *posca*.[24] In some cases, flavouring herbs, honey or eggs were also mixed.

Popular with travellers too, *posca* was a refreshing drink on the road. Like soldiers, they carried the sour wine in a flask, ready to dilute when they found water. Its acidity not only meant it took longer to spoil but it also killed harmful bacteria, a bonus when the only available water came from a dubious source. Its flavour helped to overcome the bad taste of these dodgy water supplies too.

As well as purifying water, wounds could be washed clean with it, and the elder Pliny gives a long list of applications, including its use as an eye salve and for the treatment of diarrhoea.[25] Obviously, inadequate hygiene made diarrhoea a frequent comrade on campaign; soldiers no doubt often ate with their hands but they were not always able to observe the nicety of washing their hands before and after every meal. At the site of the legionary fortress at Caerleon an amphora with the graffito AMINE – 'Aminean (wine)' – was found. This medication was a kind of panacea, devised for the treatment of diarrhoea and for the common cold too.[26]

From the graffiti on wine amphorae found on military sites we also have an indication that some soldiers, the officers presumably, drank more than just plain old *acetum*. The best collection comes from the first-century legionary fortress at Windisch-*Vindonissa*, Germania Superior. Here, examples have been discovered mentioning 'very mature' wine from Surrentum (Sorrento) in southern Italy,[27] wine from Messana (Messina) in Sicily,[28] and a third old wine is also attested, perhaps a form of fruit cocktail of wine infused on fruit.[29] Wine was also imported from Gallia Narbonensis and the Iberian peninsula.[30] Further information is provided by graffiti on amphorae discovered in Britain. One written in ink, on the neck of an amphora found in the wine cellar of the army supply depot at Richborough-*Rutupiae*, mentions wine from Mount Vesuvius, which was presumably produced before AD 79. An amphora from Newstead had 'good wine' scratched on one of its handles to identify its contents,[31] and graffiti on amphorae from Mumrills and Wallsend record 'sweet wine' and 'honey sweetened wine' respectively.[32] Known as *conditum*, honeyed wine, which was probably akin to our Martini, would be served as an *apéritif*. It was also the most popular drink, both as a refreshment and as a social drink, at the taverns (*popinae*).

Clearly beer (*cervesa*) was also popular with certain soldiers, especially so when you consider the Celtic or Germanic origins of those serving in the *auxilia*. An inscription mentions an ex-marine of the *classis Germanica* who had set himself up sometime in the late first century to supply local beer to the military market in Germania Inferior.[33] A number of military sites in northern Britain have shown evidence for the widespread use of barley. This grain may have been animal feed or punishment rations as literary sources suggest.[34] Alternatively, there was a demand for large quantities of beer, for which barley would have been used,[35] as can be seen from several of the Chesterholm-*Vindolanda* ink writing-tablets. One of them records the procurement, for a week, of more than forty-six litres of wine, including Massic, an Italian vintage of high reputation, some sour wine, and sixty-nine litres of Celtic beer, along with 187 litres or so of barley (*hordeum*).[36] Another letter refers to some 1,715 litres of threshed *bracis*, another cereal known to have been used in the production of Celtic beer.[37] That the brewing itself might well have been done at or near Chesterholm-*Vindolanda* is strongly suggested by a reference to a *cervasarius* (brewer) named Atrectus, and to a maltster (*braciarius*) named Optatus.[38]

This thirst for beer is epitomized in a postscript in a communiqué, that written by the *decurio* Masclus to his garrison commander the *praefectus* Flavius Cerialis, adding, 'the comrades have no beer, which I ask that you order to be sent'.[39] Having been detailed to collect winter wheat for the garrison, perhaps from the supply base at nearby Corbridge-*Coria*, Masclus and his troopers were thus absent from the fort and obviously missing their creature comforts.

Regardless of the weapon and equipment in hand, the proficiency and life span of a the Roman soldier (as much as any other soldier) was often more dependent upon what he had in his stomach. The site of the legionary fortress of Neuss-*Novaesium* on the lower Rhine in Germany has produced a catalogue of plant remains ranging from the obvious items such as grain to numerous examples of medicinal herbs.[40] At nearby Xanten-*Vetera*, a comparison was made between plant remains from military and civilian contexts, and it was found that the army had access to a wider range of soft fruits and pulses, which must have contributed to a healthy diet.[41]

In the poem, the *Moretum*,[42] ascribed to the Augustan poet Virgil, the rustic husbandman Simylus certainly dines much more simply than a common soldier: 'For ruddy onion, and a bed of leek / For cutting hunger doth for him subdue / And cress which screws one's face with acrid bite / And endive, and the colewort which recalls / The lagging wish for sexual delights.'[43] Although epicures might not have envied what soldiers are, the Roman military diet of our period must have been an added attraction to those poorly nourished civilians who were considering whether or not to take the emperor's *sesterius*.

Appendix 6

How Many Legions?

Augustus (or Octavianus as he was then known) had some sixty legions under his command shortly after Actium, far more than he needed or indeed could afford. In his *Res Gestae* he proudly boasts of having set up some 120,000 discharged soldiers in veteran colonies,[1] which amounts to twenty-four legions or thereabouts. Augustus, as emperor, then went on to establish clear and definite conditions of service for the army and eventually brought an end to the rather invidious practice of confiscating land for retired veterans. Typical of Augustus, he carried through his military reforms on a shoestring budget, and the simple cost of the exercise thus governed the size of the Principate army. The number of legions was established at twenty-eight, a level which Augustus saw fit for the army to do its job and be paid without exhausting the treasury. Nonetheless, it should be emphasized that the Principate army was the largest consumer not only of the empire's human resources, but also of imperial revenues.

According to Tacitus there were twenty-five legions in service in AD 23 – eight on or near the Rhine (*I Germanica, II Augusta, V Alaudae, XIII Gemina, XIIII Gemina, XVI Gallica, XX, XXI Rapax*), four in Syria and on the eastern frontier (*III Gallica, VI Ferrata, X Fretensis, XII Fulminata*), three each in Iberia (*IIII Macedonica, VI Victrix, X Gemina*) and Pannonia (*VIII Augusta, VIIII Hispana, XV Apollinaris*), two each in Egypt (*III Cyrenaica, XXII Deiotariana*), Moesia (*IIII Scythica, V Macedonica*) and Dalmatia (*VII Macedonica, XI*), and one in Africa (*III Augusta*) – around 125,000 citizen soldiers all told,[2] with probably an equal number of auxiliaries; three legions (*XVII, XVIII, XVIIII*) had been lost with Varus in Germania (AD 9) and were never replaced nor their numbers reused.[3] No new legions had been raised in the latter part of Augustus' principate, and it is generally agreed that there were twenty-eight as far back as 15 BC, when the brothers Tiberius and Nero Drusus campaigned north of Alps. Two new legions were raised by Caius Caligula (*XV Primigenia, XXII Primigenia*),[4] one by Galba (*VII Galbiana*), two by Nero (*I Italica, I Adiutrix*), and one more under Vitellius but accepted by Vespasianus (*II Adiutrix*). Four legions were disbanded by Vespasianus after the insurrection of Civilis (*I Germanica, XV Primigenia, IIII Macedonica, XVI Gallica*), the last two being replaced by two re-formed units (*IIII Flavia felix, XVI Flavia firma*). Thus, the total now stood twenty-nine, increased to thirty by Domitianus in AD 83 by the creation of *I Minervia pia fidelis*. One legion, *V Alaudae*, was lost probably by AD 92, so that when Trajan raised *XXX Ulpia* for the Dacian wars, as it number implies, there were thirty legions. However, Trajan also raised *II Traiana* and this probably replaced *XXI Rapax*, which had disappeared also by AD 92.

We may conveniently step beyond the chronological limit of this monograph to complete this account. An inscription from Rome, datable to the start of the principate of Marcus Aurelius, lists twenty-eight legions in a west-to-east-to-west order (i.e. Britannia to Iberia) with *VIIII Hispana* and *XXII Deiotariana* missing.[5] The first may have been lost on the Danube or in Cappadocia in AD 161 and the last in the final messianic Jewish revolt of Simon-bar-Kochba in AD 132–135. In AD 165 Marcus Aurelius himself raised two new legions in Italy, thereby putting the total number back up to thirty. These two legions, *II Italica* and *III Italica*, stationed in Noricum and Raetia respectively,[6] have been added at the end of the inscription. Thus, for over a century and a half between twenty-five and thirty legions were judged sufficient for the security of the emperor and his empire.

The distribution according to the unmodified inscription is three legions in Britannia, two in Germania Superior, two in Germania Inferior, three in Pannonia Superior, one in Pannonia Inferior, two in Moesia Superior, three in Moesia Inferior, one in Dacia, two in Cappadocia, three in Syria, two in Iudaea, and one each in Arabia, Egypt, Numidia and Iberia. To this we may add Marcus Aurelius' two 'Italic' legions, one in Noricum and the other in Raetia. A comparison with Tacitus' list shows that the Rhine has lost four legions, Iberia two, Syria and Egypt one each. Of the armed provinces not yet in existence in AD 23, Britannia still claims three, and after its revolts Iudaea has reached a level of two. But the most striking change is the increase of legions along the Danube. So the major changes had been the reduction of the garrison in Iberia from three legions to one, the sending of four legions to Britannia, to be reduced to three by Domitianus, and temporarily, after the outbreak of the Jewish revolt under Nero, the presence of three legions in Iudaea, to be reduced to one when it was over. But by the end of Trajan's Dacian wars, the Rhine was down to four legions, while the Danube, including the new province of Dacia, had twelve legions. In the east, with four legions under Augustus, all in Syria, had now gone to six, divided between Syria, Iudaea and Cappadocia. The two legions in Cappadocia, put there by Vespasianus, illustrate the increased importance attached to Asia Minor, partly as a continuation of the Danube frontier.

Appendix 7

Key to Legionary Titles

Numbers identified legions, like modern military units. However, they were not numbered sequentially or exclusively, such inconsistencies dating from the late Republic when new legions were created, as occasion demanded, and this tended to persist into the Principate. The consequence is that some legions have the same number. Yet each legion had a title, helping to distinguish it, that reflected its origin, very much like a modern military unit, which tends to have a character of its own, an identity comprising its history and traditions and the personality of its commander.[1] The title itself may reflect one of the following: a nickname; a god; a geographical area; a success; or an origin.

Adiutrix	'Supportive'
Alaudae	'Larks'
antiqua	'ancient' – in the sense of proven calibre
Apollinaris	'Sacred to Apollo' – this god was considered by Augustus to be his protecting deity
Augusta	'Augustan' – reconstituted by Augustus
Claudia	'Claudian' – loyal to Claudius
concors	'united'
Cyrenaica	from service in province of that name
Deiotariana	'Deiotarian' – belonging to Deiotarus (d. *c.* 40 BC), tetrarch of part of Galatia
Equestris	'Knightly'
Flavia	'Flavian' – belonging to Vespasianus
felix	'lucky one'
Ferrata	'Ironclad'
fidelis constans	'true and constant'
firma	'steadfast'
fortis	'courageous'
Fretensis	after naval victory over Sextus Pompeius in *Fretum Siculum* (straits of Messina)
Fulminata	'Thunderbolt-carrier'
Galbiana	'Galban' – belonging to Galba
Gallica	'Gallic' – served in Gaul
Gemina	'Twin' – one legion made out of two
Germanica	'Germanic' – served on the Rhine

Hispana	'Iberian' – served in Iberia
Hispaniensis	'Stationed in Iberia'
Italica	recruited from Italians
liberatrix	'liberators'
Macedonica	'Macedonian' – served in Macedonia
Macriana	'belonging to Macer'
Martia	'Sacred to Mars'
Minervia	'Sacred to Minerva'
paterna	'paternal'
pia fidelis	'loyal and true'
Primigenia	'First born' – of a new breed of legions
Rapax	'Greedy' – in the sense of sweeping all before it
Sabina	'Sabine' – raised in Sabine country
Scythica	'Scythian' – served in Scythia
Traiana	'Traianic' – belonging to Marcus Ulpius Traianus (Trajan)
Ulpia	'Ulpian' – belonging to Marcus Ulpius Traianus (Trajan)
Urbana	'Urban'
Victrix	'Victorious'

It takes time to build history and traditions, and military organizations with no history and traditions are generally ineffective. During the mutiny of the Pannonian legions in AD 14, the mutineers wanted to merge the three legions into one. 'But jealousy wrecked this suggestion', said Tacitus, 'because everyone wanted it to take his own legion's name.'[2] Quite right too. To illustrate this noteworthy *esprit de corps*, that religion of the soldier, let us pick one legion out of many, an old friend in fact, *legio VI Victrix pia fidelis*. Raised by Octavianus, perhaps in 41/40 BC for it is attested at his winter siege of Perusia (Perugia),[3] this was the younger sister of Caesar's *VI Ferrata*, currently serving under Marcus Antonius in the Roman Near East,[4] and it is possible that veterans who had fought under Caesar signed up for service with Octavianus' new legion. In 31 BC both these legions would come face to face at Actium.

As we know well, this was the legion that hailed Galba by the imperial title in AD 68. The title *Victrix* may refer to an outstanding victory in Iberia (the legion originally bore the title *Hispaniensis*),[5] where it had been stationed since 30 BC, while *pia fidelis Domitiana* would be awarded by Domitianus for staying loyal during the Saturninus rebellion (AD 89),[6] the last epithet being dropped after his death when he suffered *damnatio memoriae* (AD 96). In or around AD 122,[7] at the time Hadrian was planning his wall, the unit was transferred from Germania Superior to Britannia, being based at York-*Eboracum*,[8] and was still present there at the end of the fourth century according to the document known as the *Notitia Dignitatum*.[9]

Artillery Shield of *IIII Macedonica*

The legion was formed as part of Caesar's consular series of 48 BC (as was *III Gallica*), and served in Macedonia (47–44 BC) before being transferred to Italy by Marcus Antonius, then consul (44 BC). It was one of the two legions (the other was *legio Martia*) that defected to Octavianus,[1] fighting against Marcus Antonius at the two Mutina battles (43 BC), where it was severely mauled by *legio V Alaudae*,[2] but alongside him at Philippi (42 BC). From that time on the legion remained with Octavianus, thus it saw action at the winter siege of Perusia (40/41 BC) and possibly at Actium too (31 BC). It then did a long stint in Hispania Tarraconensis (30 BC – AD 43), before being transferred to the Rhine frontier (AD 43–69) to replace one of the legions earmarked for the invasion of Britannia. It fought for Vitellius at both Cremona battles, only to be disbanded by Vespasianus after the quelling of Civilis' insurrection (AD 70). It was quickly resurrected as *IIII Flavia felix*.[3] Its emblem, the bull and the capricorn (clearly depicted on the artillery shield), indicates its Caesarian origin (the bull was the zodiacal sign associated with Venus, divine founder of the Iulii) and reconstitution by Octavianus (the capricorn was the zodiacal sign under which he was conceived), while its title *Macedonica* reflects its service in Macedonia.

The inscription on the embossed bronze sheet, which was originally attached to the front of an artillery shield, reads:

LEG(ionis) IIII MAC(edonicae) / M(arco) VINICIO II TAVRO STAT[ili] O CORVINO [co (n)]S(vlibvs) C(aio) VIBIO RVFINO LEG(ato) / C(aio) HORATIO [......]O PRINC(ipe) P[r(ior)]

(Property) of *legio IIII Macedonica*. (Made) in the consulship of Marcus Vinicius (for the second time) and Taurus Statilius Corvinus; during the legateship of Caius Vibius Rufinus and while Caius Horatius ... was the centurion-overseer of legionary headquarters.[4]

So, the artillery piece, which was in all likelihood the three-span *scorpio* bolt-shooter as described by Vitruvius,[5] was constructed in AD 45, presumably in Germania Superior of which the legion (based at Mainz-*Mogontiacum*) formed part of the garrison. Vibius Rufinus was then legate governor, *legatus pro praetore*, of that province. The centurion Caius Horatius was *princeps prior* of the legion, that is to say, the centurion second in seniority to the 'top soldier', the *primus pilus*.

Imperial Succession

Calm and venomous, conscious of power, Vespasianus insisted that the Senate designate his two sons, Titus and Domitianus, as Caesars, a title that would increasingly mean heir apparent. It was probably in response to negative noises from the Stoic philosopher Helvidius Priscus (who was shortly to meet his maker) that Vespasianus was said to have remarked 'either my sons succeed me, or nobody', apparently on leaving the Senate. Titus and Domitianus were useful assets, two adult sons that Vespasianus was able to rely upon. However, among the Iulio-Claudian emperors we discern a curious, common factor, namely the absence of sons, reliable or otherwise. Though there was neither rule nor clear precedent for succession, would the availability of a natural heir have eased this anxious process? How did the Iulio-Claudian emperors arrange for transfer of power (*designatio*) from emperor to emperor-elect? And finally, how did a new emperor secure his legal position and authority with regards to the Senate, the army, and the people of Rome, as well as those who had a vested interest in the system, the Praetorian Guard and the imperial advisors?

Whichever way we look at it, there is always a certain air of ambiguity that surrounds Augustus and his establishment of the Principate. Some would say that it combined the survival of the past with preparation for the future. According to his own propaganda Augustus claims in his sixth and seventh consulships (28 BC, 27 BC) that he, in a grand gesture, transferred the Republic from his power to the control of the Senate and people of Rome, who, in their turn, were good enough to delegate him as their leader: 'After this time I excelled all in influence (*auctoritas*), although I possessed no more official power (*potestas*) than others who were my colleagues in the several magistracies'.[1] After this, the position of Augustus did not remain static for the rest of his long life, for he himself had to shift his position in the course of his forty-four years of supremacy, leaving his successors a legacy which (like Lenin's) was open to interpretation: 'back to Augustus' sounded all good and well, but could mean many things. Nonetheless, as Tacitus says, 'he gradually increased his power, and drew into his own hands the functions of the Senate, the magistrates and the laws'.[2]

In the end Augustus, as the first citizen, *princeps*, held a bundle of constitutional powers dissociated from republican magistracies. These included the *tribunicia potestas*, by which he could pose as champion of the lower orders and also veto any action in the city of Rome;[3] the *consulare imperium*, or power to command armies;[4] the *imperium proconsulare*, renewed every five or ten years, over half the provinces (viz. the military provinces, the Senate appointing proconsuls or propraetors each year to the other, senatorial provinces);[5] and sundry other honours and religious posts. These are all the titles and powers whose accumulation express what we understand by 'emperor', but it was the *tribunicia potestas* and the *imperium proconsulare*, without the inconveniencies and limitations of the magisterial offices, which became the legal basis of the Principate. Outwardly, his administration adhered broadly to a republican framework. He still used the Senate as a legislative and judicial body, and instituted six-monthly consultative committees, using a small number of leading senators as a cabinet (*consilium principis*) to formulate proposals that would then be put before the Senate as a whole. Yet in truth it was a new political order dressed up as a restoration, an autocracy with republican trimmings. As Fergus Millar so aptly puts it, 'the emperor was what the emperor did'.[6]

So, beneath the surface Augustus was absolute master, but in outward guise he – and his successors – could celebrate the resuscitation of constitutional order. Yet herein lay a grave defect that always weakened the roots of the Principate, namely the absence of a satisfactory method of ensuring the peaceful transition from one emperor to another. As we can gather from above, when Augustus had founded the Principate, his ill-defined job had comprised an agglomeration of powers, not one of which, formally speaking, could be passed on to any heir or successor. That is why Tacitus began his *Annales* with a detailed account of the critical tension that arose immediately after Augustus' death. For although Augustus had in practice taken the necessary steps, over a number of previous years, to ensure a smooth succession after his death, the historian wanted to stress the potentially catastrophic perils of such moments of transition.

Vespasianus' new powers

We have preserved for us in the Musei Capitolini, Rome, the last tablet of what must have been a series of bronze tablets on which was inscribed the text of a law bestowing powers upon Vespasianus.[7] This law, the *lex de imperio Vespasiani*, was passed by the Senate in the last days of December AD 69. The preserved section gives Vespasianus the power to make treaties, call and preside over the Senate, appoint magistrates, and extend the sacred boundaries of the city. He also has exemption from the laws, and finally the right to do whatever he thinks beneficial. In effect, by passing this law the Roman people gave over to the new emperor the powers that are theoretically theirs, and this act formed the legal basis of the emperor's powers.

Some modern commentators think that similar laws had been passed for earlier emperors as well, and that early provisions contained the grant of *tribunicia potestas* and *imperium maius*. This view seems incorrect. With the Iulio-Claudian dynasty ended and the Sabine *novus homo* Vespasianus now in power it was no longer enough for the emperor to rely on his *auctoritas*, which was precisely what Vespasianus lacked. As a 'clean break' his rule needed to be spelt out, and accordingly provision was made in the *lex de imperio Vespasiani* for Vespasianus' chosen magisterial candidates to be voted on first, so that there would be room for them and the Senate would have to vote them down in a yes–no vote if it did not want them elected, that is to say, they could not fail to be elected simply by getting fewer votes than the other candidates. What is more, this important law constantly defines the powers that were being granted to Vespasianus as the same as those of Augustus, Tiberius and Claudius (only Claudius in the case of extending the boundaries, since he alone did so). If this law is simply a new version of older but similar laws, there would be no need for these references to the Iulio-Claudian past. In fact, the powers of the earlier emperors (especially Augustus) were never neatly laid out like this at all but grew up gradually over time as the emperors' autocracy resulted in their gradual assumption of the functions of the state. Only with the establishment of a new man who had no dynastic claim to earlier powers was it thought necessary to formulate the position explicitly by enactment. The face of autocracy was thus recognized by law.

It is noteworthy that only Augustus, Tiberius and Claudius are cited as precedent. This means that the clearly disreputable Caius Caligula and Nero were not taken into account and that the other three claimants of the year of four emperors were conspicuously (and conveniently) brushed aside. This is interesting, because it reflects a purely constitutional position. A second-century document proves that a record was maintained in Rome of all imperial grants of Roman citizenship, and it included grants by Caius Caligula, Nero and Galba, but not Otho and Vitellius, and a response by Vespasianus himself to a petition shows him upholding all imperial favours granted from Augustus to Galba. Thus, it would seem that in terms of favours granted, those of all the Iulio-Claudians and Galba were recognized by Vespasianus, but as a matter of constitutional practice, only the usage of the 'acceptable' Iulio-Claudians were recognized. Not only were the practices of the unacceptable Caius Caligula and Nero considered unworthy of imitation, but also for this purpose any innovations of the recent usurper Galba were apparently not suitable.

This whole practice of passing a law to grant the emperor his power reflects the theory that would be laid out fully in the third-century jurists: the emperor held a legal position and was bound by the laws (even if he was in fact granted an exemption from them). While to some extent this legalistic interpretation is claptrap, it nonetheless forms an integral part of the peculiar conception the Romans had of their autocracy. Nonetheless, it is of interest to note that Vespasianus, a usurper (and we must call him by that blunt name), placed his *dies imperii*, the day of his elevation to the throne, on 1 July AD 69, the date he had been acclaimed by the soldiers in Egypt, rather than on 22 December AD 69, the date when his powers were formally voted by the Senate – Helvidius Priscus alone, so far as the record goes, expressing dissent. In effect he was emperor the moment he had the support of his provincial army and was prepared to back up his intentions with armed force; the political niceties could be sorted out later. And so they were, and the immediate advantage for our new emperor was that the brute facts of life had been ratified and agreed up front. The contents of the surviving tablet deserve our attention for this reason alone.

... that he shall have the right, just as the deified Augustus and Tiberius Iulius Caesar Augustus and Tiberius Claudius Caesar Augustus Germanicus [i.e.

Tiberius and Claudius respectively] had to conclude treaties with whoever he wishes;

And that he shall have the right, just as the deified Augustus and Tiberius Iulius Caesar Augustus and Tiberius Claudius Caesar Augustus Germanicus had, to convene the Senate, to put and refer proposals to it, and to cause decrees of the Senate to be enacted by proposal and division of the house...

And that at all elections especial consideration shall be given to those candidates for a magistracy, authority, *imperium*, or any post whom he has recommended to the Roman Senate and people or to whom he has given and promised his vote...

And that he shall have the right, just as the deified Augustus and Tiberius Iulius Caesar Augustus and Tiberius Claudius Caesar Augustus Germanicus had, to transact and do whatever things divine, public and private he deems to serve the advantage and the overriding interests of the state... to not be bound by those laws and plebiscites, which were declared not binding upon the deified Augustus and Tiberius Iulius Caesar Augustus and Tiberius Claudius Caesar Augustus Germanicus...

That whatever was done, executed, decreed or ordered before the enactment of this law by the Emperor (*imperator*) Caesar Vespasianus Augustus, or by anyone at his order or command, shall be as fully binding and valid as if they had been done by order of the people or plebs.[8]

We shall give the final word to Tacitus, who neatly wrapped it all up in one laconic phrase: 'At Rome the Senate awarded Vespasianus all the usual (*omnia solita*) imperial titles.'[9]

Galba's adoption speech

When Servius Sulpicius Galba, the legate governor of Hispania Tarraconensis, revolted, the Senate proclaimed Nero a public enemy. On his suicide no one of the Iulio-Claudian family qualified for the succession, and in any event the generals of the empire had fallen into a bloody contest to see who would gain the purple of the Caesars. On New Year's Day, AD 69, Galba took office as consul for the second time. That same day, the legions of Germania Superior refused to renew their oath of allegiance to him, and two days later joined the legions of Germania Inferior in proclaiming Aulus Vitellius, the newly appointed legate governor of that province, as emperor.

When the news reached Rome Galba, who was a childless old man, adopted as his colleague and heir the thirty-one-year-old Lucius Calpurnius Piso Frugi Licinianus, of impeccable pedigree, a descendant of Pompey and Crassus, highly acceptable to the Senate, but unknown to the provincial armies. He was the son of the distinguished consul of AD 29 who had formulated a very close relationship with Claudius, but he himself had yet to hold public office, having been forced into exile by Nero.[10] According to Tacitus there were a number of rival candidates in Galba's camp,[11] but the emperor picked the young Piso Licinianus – possibly as a fillip for the senatorial order – and then made a grand speech, the gist of which is given to us by Tacitus:

1.15 So it seemed that Galba took Piso's hand and spoke to him in terms which may be paraphrased as follows: 'If I were a private citizen (*privatus*) adopting you in the traditional way before the pontiffs with due legislative forms, it would have been gratifying to me to have a descendant of Cnaeus Pompey (Magnus) and Marcus (Licinius) Crassus entering my family, and you in your turn would have found it an honour to enhance your own distinctions with those of the Sulpicii and Lutatii [the paternal and maternal side of Galba's descent]. But as things are, the unanimous will of heaven and earth has called me to supreme power, and it is rather your character and patriotism which have impelled me to offer you the Principate. For this power, our forefathers fought on the battlefield, and I myself won it by the sword. But I now give it to you in time of peace, following the precedent set by the Divine Augustus. He it was who promoted to a position immediately below his own his sister's son (Caius Claudius) Marcellus,[12] then his son-in-law (Marcus Vipsanius) Agrippa,[13] later his own grandsons [Caius and Lucius],[14] and finally Tiberius Nero, his stepson.[15] But Augustus looked for a successor within his family: I have done so in the country at large. This is not because I have no relatives or army colleagues. But it was not from selfish motives that I accepted office myself, and the nature of my present choice should be plain from the fact that, for your sake, I have passed over the claims not only of my relatives but also of yours. Your brother is as nobly born as you are, and older. He, too, could worthily fill the part, were you not the better man.

'You are old enough now to have escaped the waywardness of youth, and you have nothing to apologise for in your past. Until today, misfortune was all you had to bear. But success probes a man's character more keenly. Men put up with bad times, but prosperity spoils us. Loyalty, independence and friendship are the finest flowers of human character. These qualities you will of course continue to display as sturdily as ever. But others will seek to weaken them by a cringing attitude. You will have to face up to flattery, honeyed words and the poison most fatal to sincerity – individual self-interest. Even if you and I are today conversing with perfect frankness, the world will prefer to address us as emperors, not as ourselves. Persuading a ruler to adopt the right course is a fatiguing business, but to flatter him regardless of his character is a mechanical exercise, which presupposes no real affection.

1.16 'If it were possible for our gigantic empire to stand erect and keep its balance in the absence of a ruler, I should be the right sort of person to hand over power to a republican form of government. But in fact we have long ago reached a point where drastic measures are necessary. Hence my declining years can make Rome no greater gift than a good successor, nor your youth any greater gift than a good emperor. Under Tiberius, Caius and Claudius, the Principate was the heirloom of a single family, so that the introduction of the principle of choice will mean liberty. The dynasty of the Iulii and Claudii has come to an end, and the process of adoption will discover the best man. To be born and bred of emperors is a matter of chance and is valued accordingly. But adoption implies the unfettered exercise of judgement. Moreover, if one wants guidance in this choice, public opinion points the way. Remember Nero, who prided himself on being the heir of a long line of Caesars. It was not Vindex [Caius Iulius Vindex, governor of Gallia Lugdunensis] with his undefended province, nor I with my one legion [*VI Victrix*, which had saluted Galba as emperor], who dislodged this incubus from the shoulders of Rome. His own monstrous excesses and life of pleasure did so, though there was no precedent at that time for the condemnation of an emperor. We ourselves, who owe our promotion to armed force and critical scrutiny, are bound to be the target of envious glances, whatever our merits. However, you must not lose confidence if two legions [*IIII Macedonica* and *XXII Primigenia* in Germania Superior] have not yet recovered their steadiness after the shock, which the Roman world has suffered. My accession too was far from tranquil. Besides, once men hear of your adoption they will cease to view me as an old man [he was seventy-three years of age] – the only criticism they can level at me now. Nero will always be missed by the riffraff. It is your task and mine to see to it that good men do not miss him as well.

'This is not a good moment for further words of advice, and indeed every precaution has been taken if I did right in choosing you. The most practical and also most rapid criterion of good and bad policy is to reflect what actions you would yourself approve or disapprove of if another were emperor. Rome is not like primitive countries with their kings. Here we have no ruling caste dominating a nation of slaves. You are called to be the leader of men who can tolerate neither total slavery nor total liberty.'

Such was the tenor of Galba's remarks. They sounded as if he were still in the process of creating an emperor. But the tone the rest took towards Piso showed that they regarded the process as complete.[16]

To no avail, this majestic speech. As the adoption came about at the time when the Rhine legions were refusing to play ball, Galba was obviously trying to present a brave front to his newly established principate by demonstrating all was well. That it failed to bring peace and stability to the Galban régime is further illustration of the fact – if such is needed – that there is often a great gulf between theory and reality, between the expectations of men and their realisation.

This process of adoption was new, and would come into its own after the death of Domitianus, when it became a vital issue.[17] The actual importance of adoption is pretty straightforward, for it held out to the senatorial order as a whole the idea that any one of them could win the lottery of becoming the next emperor. But of course it did not cure the problem of resentment felt by those overlooked in the game of thrones.

Appendix 10

The Cult of Iuppiter Dolichenus

oman soldiers expected special protection from a whole pantheon of powers called the *dii militares* (military gods) who aided them in their daily routine, in particular on the training ground, and even more so in battle. The deities worshipped by Roman soldiers may be divided for convenience into two main groups. The first group comprises the gods of the established state religions whose worship was regulated by the official calendars such as the *Feriale Duranum*. These naturally included the Capitoline triad of Iuppiter Optimus Maximus, Iuno Regina and Minerva, the war god Mars and the personification of victory, Victoria, not forgetting of course personified martial virtues such as Disciplina and Virtus. The second group, which concerns us here, included other cults, mainly non-Roman, which were adopted and encouraged by military units, but which were not included in the official calendars.

The god Iuppiter Dolichenus is said to have numerous origins. Some associated him with the Hittite-Hurrian god of thunder and fertility Teshub, while others said he came from Doliche (Dülük-Baba Tepesi, southeast Turkey), a place where iron was apparently born. Doliche was a small town in Commagene situated at a crossing of several roads leading from Asia Minor to the great towns of northern Syria. There were indeed ferruginous deposits near Marash, northwest of Doliche, and though the priests of the cult associated it with various other deities, its popularity within the Principate army may be connected with the role of iron in the lore surrounding Dolichenus, the metal from which the working tools, so to speak, of soldiers were forged. Thus, in various dedications from Roman soldiers the god is described as 'born where iron is born'.[1]

If we think of Iuppiter at all we are accustomed to thinking of him as devious-devising, the omnipotent ruler of the Olympian gods, spoiled members of a dysfunctional family. Yet Dolichenus, now a romanized soldier god of the Universe, embraced the heavens, safety, success, and military triumph. In this way, he was generally depicted wearing Roman military uniform, standing on a bull, and holding a three-pronged thunderbolt and a double-headed axe. The bull symbolizes the brute power of nature, the god on the bull his authority over the animal – as a sacrificial victim himself, the bull, symbol of brutality, is doomed. The thunderbolt and axe symbolize the power over weather. He usually formed with a consort a divine pair, romanized as Iuppiter Dolichenus and Iuno Dolichena.[2]

In the century or so between AD 120 and AD 230 or thereabouts, the cult of Iuppiter Dolichenus boomed in popularity, particularly in the army and especially along the empire's northern frontiers.[3] Originally it was argued that this mystery stellar cult was carried westward by Syrian merchants, slaves and soldiers,[4] but more recent research suggests otherwise. Social networks linked officers of the Principate army, military kinship that often involved geographical distance, and it is by this sympathetic means that the cult spread through the army rapidly,[5] a curious manifestation perhaps of Juvenal's *in Tiberim defluxit Orontes*.[6]

Appendix 11

Ancient Authors

Books are marvellous, crossing cultures and centuries, defeating ignorance and finally, cruel time itself. Yet one of the faults of most historians is that they take too much for granted. At the time of writing they naturally assume that the reader must know the common things they know; therefore, they tell only the uncommon things, details ferreted out of archives containing great files of dry-as-dust manuscripts and from private correspondence. It is frustrating to read most history, because so many times the reader (who is usually searching for quick answers) can see the author hovering on the verge of explaining some important fact and then shying away out of fear of dullness; everyone knows *that*, the author says to himself, and I will not bore the reader (and myself) by telling him what he already knows. But, as you and I well know, if a historian is writing to be read a hundred years from now or, with good fortune (and a continued interest in one's period of study), even a thousand years, like our five principal ancient authors, Tacitus, Plutarch, Suetonius, Cassius Dio and Josephus,[1] then all those things we take so much for granted today will be quite unknown to those who come after. There, I have said it. I too hunger for immortality!

What can be more solid than established facts? Well, to quote the words of Hegel: reason becomes unreason. In his classic work, *What is History?*, the English historian E.H. Carr said that historical facts are 'always refracted through the mind of the recorder' and that you should 'study the historian before you begin to study the facts'.[2] By that he meant that the telling of history cannot be separated from the viewpoint, political or otherwise, both of the writer and of the reader and of the times they live or lived in. It is often said that history is written by the victors. In other words, the selection and interpretation of historical events are shaped by the actual outcome of those conflicts as they affect the historian and in turn his or her perception of what the reader will want to read. Despite the pretensions of historians to an alleged objectivity, the writing of history inevitably reflects a personal point of view. It is impossible to escape having some sort of perspective on the events described. To claim otherwise is to attempt to defraud the reader.

Tacitus

Is there such a thing as the public interest? Is history over? In short, yes and no. For historians such as Thucydides and his Roman counterpart Tacitus endure through history, and so also their works. Tacitus, our concern here, brilliantly illuminates later times as well as his own. He helps us to understand the human condition. To put it simply, he is by far the best source we have for our period of study. But it is critical that we unravel the evidence he provides very carefully as he often tries to imply things not warranted by his own facts. At times he even seems unaware of his own contradictions. But first, a potted history of our principal historian.

Born (*c.* AD 58) to an equestrian family in Gallia Narbonensis, perhaps at Vasio (Vasion-la-Romaine),[3] Tacitus (Publius or Caius Cornelius Tacitus) passed the early years of his life in (for us at least) complete obscurity. Not even his praenomen is known with certainty. His father was perhaps the equestrian procurator of Gallia Belgica and the Two Germanies mentioned by the elder Pliny who served as an officer on the Rhine from around AD 46 to AD 58.[4] In the opening paragraph of the *Historiae*, Tacitus states quite clearly that his own public career 'owed its beginnings to Vespasianus, its progress to Titus, and its further advancement to Domitianus'.[5]

Studying oratory at Rome in AD 75, Tacitus was granted the *latus clavus*, that is, the right to wear the broad purple stripe of senatorial rank by Vespasianus. Shortly thereafter, in AD 77, he married a local girl, the (unnamed) daughter of Cnaeus Iulius Agricola, a native from Forum Iulii (Fréjus), a colony and naval station on the coast of Gallia Narbonensis, perhaps while serving his initial military service as *tribunus laticlavius*. It is possible that Tacitus visited Britannia with his father-in-law in the late seventies when serving as a young military tribune. If so, he saw for himself some of the fringes of empire on which his first literary work, the panegyrical *Agricola*, is famously centred. As a matter of interest we should note that whereas his father had followed an equestrian military career, the younger Tacitus opted for a senatorial one. This meant of course coming to the notice of the emperor, especially so when one needed the emperor's patronage to follow a senatorial career. So when Tacitus says his public career was started by Vespasianus and so on, he means it.

Evidently Tacitus passed quickly through the junior magistrates of a senatorial career, because he is next attested as praetor in AD 88 (at an early age for a *novus homo*). While holding office, he would have presided over a law court and heard speeches by some of Rome's great orators, an art in which he too was to excel. In the same year he served on the priestly board of the *XV viri sacris faciundis* with Domitianus, who used his position in the college to organize and celebrate the Secular Games, which notionally represented the beginning of each new hundred year cycle in the life of Rome. It is pertinent to note that Tacitus thus reached the peak of his public career under Domitianus, and as one of the *XV viri* would have been heavily involved in the Secular Games, which of course promoted the greater glory of Domitianus. He was abroad (probably as a provincial governor) when his beloved father-in-law Agricola died on 23 August, AD 93. Later in his writings Tacitus hints, on very slight evidence, that the death was by the hand of Domitianus, but he himself would survive the last years of the emperor's principate, which by all accounts was a reign of terror of Stalinist proportions.

On returning to Rome after an absence of three years or more, he was the *consul suffectus* in the second half of AD 97, but whether he was nominated by Domitianus or Nerva must remain a mystery. As consul he delivered the funeral oration for Lucius Verginius Rufus,[6] the suppressor of the Vindex revolt, an honour befitting his reputation as one of the foremost orators of the day.[7] In AD 100 he, along with his good friend the younger Pliny, successfully prosecuted Marius Priscus, the former *proconsulare* of Africa, for bribe taking.[8]

Thereafter our information on his activities is meagre. We surmise from Pliny (eleven of whose letters are addressed to him) that Tacitus was at work on the *Historiae* in or around AD 106,[9] and the chance discovery of an inscription in Asia Minor informs us that Tacitus reached the summit of a senatorial career, *proconsulare* of Asia, in AD 112/13. A passage in the *Annales* alluding to the extension of Roman dominion to the Sinus Arabicus (Red Sea),[10] territory first conquered during Trajan's Parthian campaign of AD 115/16, provides a definite *terminus post quem* for his death. The succession of Tiberius, which opens the *Annales*, seems to elude the succession of Hadrian in AD 117, although this is a point of contention.[11] Whether he lived to complete his greatest work, we do not know.[12] We do know, on the other hand, that his literary career began during the principate of Trajan, for he emphatically informs his readership that he could not write under Domitianus because 'all the most energetic have fallen victims to the ferocity of the emperor'.[13] Like everyone else, Tacitus probably preferred to avoid undue distress at the hands of a tyrant. His first literary work, the *Agricola*, does of course contain ferocious criticism of the now damned Domitianus, and there was nothing more loved by a reigning emperor than rancorous rumblings about a predecessor's rule. It appears that Tacitus was one of those writers imbued with their tradition who could hit back and damn a ruler, if not to his face, at least after his death.

But what sort of historian was Tacitus? Well, he noticeably comes from the Graeco-Roman tradition of historical writers whose purpose was as much to promote a moral agenda using rhetorical flourishes as it was to elucidate facts. In Rome, as we know, Tacitus studied oratory, including Cicero, and may have written oratorical treatises before his four best known historic/ethnographic pieces, *Agricola*, *Germania*, *Historiae*, and *Annales*. Despite his political success, he lamented a century's worth of continually reduced aristocratic power, that is, of the Senate. Naturally he made the conventional claim of historians to be unbiased, saying though he owed his career to the emperors he was not about to flatter them. As he says at the beginning of the *Annales*, 'I shall write without indignation or partisanship.'[14] Unquestionably, Tacitus was not alive under Tiberius, Caius Caligula or Claudius, and much too young under Nero, which meant he had no personal contact with the Iulio-Claudian emperors at all. No matter, Tacitus aimed at supplanting the previous bias accounts of the Principate – he believed that previous historians had either flattered the Iulio-Claudian emperors too much or written with hatred in mind – and on reading him we soon notice that the history of the Principate revolves entirely around the person of the emperor. He was also very interested in the traditional matters of the Republic and its history, actually aping the polished style of late republican writers such as Cicero and Sallust.

Tacitus' works are infused with apparently unequal power relations (rulers/ subjects, emperors/aristocrats, Romans/non-Romans, men/women), relations that he sees as constructed through the negotiation of continuing discourses, with force, consent, hegemony and other technologies of power all on display. In this regard, his interests obviously extended towards the Senate and its relationship with the emperor. It is clear that he must have known how the once prestigious organ functioned. Wishing to preserve what dignity remained to it, Tacitus liked those emperors who allowed the Senate to retain a certain amount of independence.[15] In fact, a lot of abuse heaped upon those so-called 'bad' emperors stems from the belief that they – viz. Caius Caligula, Nero, and Domitianus – treated the Senate and its members like dirt. Even Tacitus' bogeyman Tiberius found it very difficult to cooperate with the Senate, and the reader notices the constant tension that exist between the two in the first six books of the *Annales*. Tacitus was truly fascinated with the psychology of this struggle, and the reader can almost see him squirm when he records senators behaving in a servile manner. He emphasizes the value of *libertas*, liberty (as his admirers in the French Revolution recognized).

However, we must not believe that Tacitus was tinted with a republican sentiment, far from it, for he was a product of the imperial system. His preference was for a modest, accessible and sane emperor who would leave the Senate a little space for business and would not be a moral disgrace. In present-day terms, he was a great believer in the politics of consensus rather than of confrontation. Besides, any attempt to restore the long defunct Republic on the death of an emperor had always failed, and by the principate of Trajan, when he was writing, the fantasy ceased to be a cause of plots and rebellions against the Principate. Tacitus' fellow senators had long ago lost confidence in the possibility of restoring the Republic, and did no more than jealously hold onto their perquisites and privileges. He sees the danger in one man's rule, but he hopes only to temper it, not to overthrow the system itself. In short, Tacitus lived under the full maturity of the Principate and his histories merely look back over its tortured beginnings.

The historian selects his materials in accordance with his specific aim. Thus, Tacitus omits many military and topographical details that a modern reader with a military bent might expect or desire. According to the magisterial Mommsen, Tacitus was 'the most unmilitary of historians'.[16] One wonders if Mommsen had ever read any of Livy's military gobbledygook.[17] Certainly with the *Historiae* the reader is repeatedly puzzled or irritated because the details of chronology, topography, logistics, strategy and tactics are not always there, and certainly the puzzlement and irritation factors increase because Tacitus takes every opportunity offered for dramatic narrative and vivid presentation.[18] But there is no real indication that he is not in control of his material. Besides, he was not writing a regimental history or a monograph of a campaign, and he was (inevitably) including military history in the framework of a history of the period. He is not interested in the nitty gritty and frequently boring details of war.

Of much more interest to Tacitus was the nature of human relationships, the personalities, destructive ones particularly, and in the issues and effects of military action, which were important for that history. He was writing for an audience whose knowledge and interests were sometimes very different from ours. Military experience must have been widespread among his intended audience. Tacitus was too good an author to disappoint his audience. Thus it was that he provided a narrative to hold a reader's attention, and so his vivid style often reveals his own strong opinions and prejudices. He presents crises and highlights rather than an accumulation of detail, which in fact, if carried too far, can itself be a distortion of the historian's material. In this way, he compresses his military material, but his accounts are basically comprehensible and reliable. Taken all around, we need to hold in mind as we read the *Historiae* that we cannot be condescending about Tacitus, since he knows more than we do.

All of which is to say that we feel, reading the *Historiae*, as if we are dancing with a partner who distinctly hears a different music. The speed of the telling leaves us frequently lagging well behind. Misfortune succeeds misfortune and cruelty is heaped on cruelty at a pace that seems to a contemporary ear, headless and abrupt. Syme, whose extraordinary credentials need not be repeated here, has argued convincingly that in the *Historiae* Tacitus used a variety of sources, including eyewitness reports and official records, and achieved an independent historical description that includes the historian's own views and comments on the crisis.[19] Tacitus was interested in what happened when the stable and organized relationship between emperor and army broke down and the restraints of military discipline were removed. He was appalled at the violence and brutality of the soldiers, and the description of the murder of Galba early in the *Historiae* is designed to create the worse possible impression of them. Galba, defenceless, old, and isolated in his own capital, was butchered like a pig in the Forum in front of the temple of the gods.[20] Traditional military discipline had collapsed – 'once they had emulated each other in valour and obedience, so now there was a rivalry in insubordination and insolence'.[21]

Almost alone of the major classical historians, Tacitus wrote about a world of absolute monarchy, a dark world of decline and corruption. Hence the subject matter of the *Annales* emphasizes Tacitus' hatred for the great concentration of power in the hands of the Iulio-Claudian emperors. However, though he hated the Principate and in his writings tries to paint every emperor as a corrupt despot, he hated civil war and anarchy even more. He had a particularly heavy bias against Tiberius, whom he portrayed as a sinister and cruel emperor, purging his opponents from the Senate by having them tried for treason and executed. He showed scorn for Claudius and Nero, and even his writings about Augustus contained some belittling innuendoes and snide remarks.

If we return to Tacitus' characterization of Tiberius, it should be noted that his idea of what Tiberius was like probably came from the author's own experiences of life under Domitianus. It is fairly clear he saw both of them as similar characters, and in fact there was a rumour current at the time that Domitianus modelled himself on Tiberius and had even read his speeches. This is particularly obvious when we read what Tacitus has to say about Domitianus in *Agricola* 39–43, the main theme here being one of play-acting, that is to say, the doubletalk, the suspicion, the jealousy, and of course the hatred. Court life was a sort of humourless pantomime performed before an aphasic audience, and for each performance 'the emperor had his hypocrite's part prepared'.[22] But as Tacitus points out, 'even under bad emperors men can be great'.[23] Yet there is one issue, of course, which he does not (or cannot) resolve. Can good men serving a bad emperor – for whatever reasons – still be good men?

Well armed with arch remarks and catty asides, Tacitus' writing is full of tales of corruption, government scandal, and innocent people being destroyed or having their good names ruined because of the emperor's lust for power. Returning once more to Tacitus' *bête noir* Tiberius, the emperor got worse as time wore on. Initially his cruel behaviour, his twisted contorted mind, his moroseness, envy and hatred were all kept in check by the presence of his advisors, and even his *eminent grise* Sejanus, according to Tacitus, holds Tiberius back. We witness unrestrained crime and infamy once these advisors exit the stage one by one, and Tacitus sees the year AD 23 as a turning point in Tiberius' principate, which is why he introduces Sejanus at this point. This is a convention of historiography found also in the works of Polybios and Sallust; power corrupts and matters go from bad to worse. Of course it is an artificial division, but it does serve a useful purpose for Tacitus who is working away at blackening Tiberius' character. It is clear that in Tacitus' mind Tiberius was a bad lot, a nasty character from the very beginning of his career. What to us appears as change (and hence needing explanation) was, to Tacitus, merely the progressive uncovering of qualities which, though always present, had not at first been revealed.[24] Various restraints had checked the unhealthy elements in Tiberius' nature at first, namely in the guise of strong characters such as Livia, Augustus and Sejanus. Tiberius aside, it was Tacitus' firm belief that an emperor had so much power in his hands that no man could occupy the throne without being corrupted by that power.

Lord Acton's renowned observation, though often misquoted, put the matter succinctly: 'Power tends to corrupt, and absolute power corrupts absolutely'.[25] For us moderns, wherever there is consensual government, we witness our politicians, MPs and ministers, getting used to power, and it is hard for them to lay it down. It only takes a little persuasion, some argument to let them justify keeping it. Power is more addictive than opiates. For Tacitus, on the other hand, wherever there was a throne, one was likely to observe in rich detail every folly and wickedness, of which man is capable, enamelled with manners and gilded with hypocrisy. Today, we have politicians who are a psychotic form unto themselves. They must gain power to serve. They live on power, by power, for power. They greedily accept it, thriving on it the way that a vampire bat thrives on blood, but it must be 'sold' to the ordinary mass of people because they are myopic and parochial, interested in only preserving their own power. An affective sales tool is fear, fear of differences the politicians will establish and then focus on selectively and accentuate. Wearing the mask that grins and lies, the policy then becomes In The National Interest, or The Terrorist Threat, or such like. Slogans such as 'Us or Them', 'State-Sponsored Terrorism', 'Axis of Evil', 'Perverse Leaders', and so on, pepper the language of our politicians in their endless, rehashed speeches that refer to conflict as it were like the daily weather forecast: unstoppable and inscrutable. Lies and pretences, after all, always require more lies and pretences.

As always happens when political doubletalk is intensified to the limit but the moment of explosion has not yet come, in these speeches there is a certain amount of conscious spreading of panic, threats are here dressed up in the form of prophecies. But the art of government requires something beyond an attitude of scaremongering. These shabby speeches of our politicians, rhetoric for all reasons, expose not so much a personal bankruptcy, as the bankruptcy of modern, violent liberalism (with its expensive exported 'democracy').[26] They lied, lie and will lie to the people.

Nowadays style in speaking is everything, content nothing, and if we meekly accept the pabulum offered, then politicians smile on you. With scant sincerity it seems, they cannot think beyond their term of office, they are incapable of thinking past the immediate, of becoming concerned by the remote. They always aim at immediate splendid results, forcing things either too quickly, or else do nothing at all, the twin tyrannies of the instant and the inert. Beware: when politicians try to shock, to frighten, to hypnotise, in order the more easily to convince us that the country's security is threatened, they probably do so because they need that to keep them in power and us in the dark, to divert our attention from the real problems facing us, problems more often than not much closer to home, such as gross prosperity of some and the grinding poverty of others. Maybe they sell fear because they have nothing else to sell.

The people may want peace and prosperity for all, but it is assailed by predatory and adventurous politicians in the quest of some colossal plunder or some dazzling diversion from their domestic difficulties. Thence the eagerness for foreign wars and colonial adventurers. People see themselves subjected to the state and forced to serve it with their money (and occasionally, their blood), but they do not feel that they are a vital and organic part of it, and generally take no interest in its affairs.

Everything conspires to make us acquiesce in the world as it is, to discourage the belief that it can be radically reordered on more just and equal lines. There is a grim constant in this matter, and it is incredible how we all fall for that old chestnut. It works just about every time. It is not a new trick. If we go backward from the present day, we shall have no difficulty in finding similar uses of doubletalk in all sorts of religious, national, philosophical and of course political disguises, beginning with biblical times and still earlier. After all, this is how one bunch of primates keeps itself together, by hating another bunch of primates in the next tree. It is the law of the jungle, gentle reader, if you are in the trees you have got to swing. It is that simple.

Most of our politicians, with their inattention to the 'ordinary people' (a much-love phrase amongst them) and domestic affairs, are ham actors – worse, they are well-heeled lawyers – who bandy impudent phrasemongering in answer to protests and cries of despair. In fact, being ordinary we prefer to be asked and not told, and so it would be nice to be courted, not to be taken for granted. They should understand that. But having acquired a scorn for us, what they give in return is a climate of fear. And I think this needs to be said, because too often it is forgotten – our politicians need to be reminded from time to time that the country does not exist apart from the individuals (you and I) who comprise its citizenry. As a source of government, the parliamentary democratic system might be all right – it is by no means free from the faults of every representative system, which are unavoidable so long as that system is unavoidable – but its weakness lies in that the men (and women) in charge of it are often appalling, and by extension one would be tempted to share completely the view of Machiavelli that human beings in general 'are ungrateful, fickle, false, cowardly, covetous'.[27] Its strength, on the other hand, is freedom of speech. This is precious and should not be taken all for granted.

Even so, if we choose to accept the parliamentary system (what we think of as 'democracy'), it is pointless to protest about the consequences. This is not the place to enter into a discussion concerning the relative aesthetics of political left, right and centre, about which everyone is entitled to hold an opinion. However, a mere state of mind is not sufficient for the attainment of a goal, for having a sense of protest is clearly not the same as the constitutional remedy of relevant action (the precise cure I leave to the reader's imagination, though it isn't exactly an assault on the Winter Palace). Life would be simpler if we could choose our duties and responsibilities, but we can't, we shouldn't. Of course, good citizens should be partisans but never zealots, respecters of the facts that attend each situation but never benders of those facts, uncomfortable in positions of leadership but rarely able to turn down a responsibility once it has been thrust upon them.

So, as good citizens who do not want to be the playthings of self perpetuating oligarchies or giant transnational monopolies, who cherish the ideals of the greatest good of the greatest number, we must remove the plastic wrap of fear and let reality breathe freely. It may demand of us civic courage;[28] it may demand of us being shaken loose from the mundane existence of our inactive urbanite lives too. But that way our politicians would stop peddling the politics of fear and start taking a long view of things, look to the next generation and not just the next election. People in authority are good at putting things back in order all at one stroke, solving everything the same way Alexander solved the Gordian knot – by cutting it in two with a sword. Parliamentarians seem an innately frivolous breed, preferring brilliant declarations to unostentatious planning, liking first nights but not rehearsals. And so, at the risk of repeating myself, I believe we, the ordinary people, very much prefer the idea of long-term efficiencies as opposed to short-term frenzies.

It is an old truth that an army does not act in accordance with anything except its orders. It bows neither to commonsense nor to necessity nor to anything else.

That is what distinguishes if from any other institution. Once upon a time I myself subscribed to the soldier's credo of 'ours is not to reason why'. I do not subscribe to this any longer. At the same time I also thought that politicians, our representatives in democracy, were on my side. I do not think this any more. They breathe neither compassion nor goodness, and appear to doubt neither themselves nor their politics. For them, democracy is a device nothing more, a Greek drollery – to coin a phrase. It sometimes looks as if it exists not so much to benefit the people, but to bring prestige, position, and prosperity to our politicians. They are often very close to the big banks and monolithic monopolies. Money, as they say, has a soft surface and it rubs off on those who handle it.

I am sure that my readers will pardon me for my political grandstanding. Still, we may all live the normality of our daily lives – humdrum even at the best of times – in the confines of manufactured fear, but in Tacitus' day the terrorism of fear was rather more scary, for it was the fear induced by the knowledge that men's lives and fortunes could be taken away from them at one careless nod of the imperial head. Power like that was frightening, and even the best of emperors often behaved with the grimmest cynicism and brutality. Good or bad, an emperor had the absolute power to decapitate anybody offending his highness or his favourites. Tacitus provides a valuable insight into the age-old debate about the very nature of power itself.

Plutarch

Born during the reign of Claudius, around AD 46, at Chaironeia in Boiotia, the hugely learned and prolific Plutarch was an aristocratic Greek who moved in the cultured Roman circles of his day, and may have held some imperial posts under the emperors Trajan and Hadrian. He also served as a life member of the college of priests at Delphi. Greece was then a comfortable, demilitarized backwater of the empire and Athens itself, where Plutarch studied philosophy as a young man (he was there when Nero made his artistic incursion into Greece in AD 66), a self-satisfied university town and cultural centre. No matter they had been dead for centuries, Athens was still the city of Plato and Aristotle, and for any philosophically and academically inclined student it had status, class and a reputation that other places of learning could never equal. As an exponent of Platonism, he vigorously denounced the position of the Stoics and Epicureans.

Written in Greek (he did not get around to learning Latin until late in life), his *Parallel Lives* – *Bioi paralleloi* – are an extremely useful source for Roman (and Greek) history as he collected much detail and various traditions. However, Plutarch can be fairly uncritical. Although his main aim is to moralize about the nature of the man, he does make a fair stab in some of the *Lives*, which were written in pairs of Greeks and Romans of similar eminence (e.g. Agesilaos and Pompey, Alexander and Caesar, Demetrios and Marcus Antonius), at producing some sort of history. Interestingly, however, the two of his biographies that concern us (viz. *Galba* and

Otho) are unpaired. It is believed that the first biographical work written by Plutarch was a series of single lives of Roman emperors from Augustus to Vitellius, and of these only *Galba* and *Otho* survive. This early work was probably published under the Flavian emperors.

Suetonius

A Latin biographer, Caius Suetonius Tranquilius was probably born in AD 69, the tragic year of four emperors. His father was the equestrian Suetonius Laetus, one of the military tribunes (*tribuni militum angusticlavii*) of *legio XIII Gemina*, which had fought bravely for Otho at First Cremona on 14 April AD 69,[29] while his grandfather had been one of the drones on the fringes of Caius Caligula's overblown court (the emperor had installed in his palace a rabble of sword fighters, charioteers, grooms, actors, jugglers and other hangers-on). Suetonius himself was in Rome as a teenager during the eighties,[30] doubtless completing his education in the capital in the normal manner of the sons of the municipal aristocracy who had some kind of public career in view.

From the surviving correspondence of his good friend the younger Pliny, Suetonius appears to have attracted attention in Rome as an author and scholar by AD 97, and also gained experience in advocacy. Perhaps intending to pursue the equestrian military career like his father had done, Suetonius secured through Pliny's patronage a military tribunate in Britannia sometime around AD 102, which in the event he declined to hold.[31] In AD 110 he travelled with Pliny to Bithynia-Pontus as a member of the provincial governor's retinue (*cohors amicorum*). In the later years of Trajan's principate and under Hadrian, Suetonius held three important posts in the imperial administration, as a fragmentary inscription found in 1952 at his home town of Hippo Regius (Bône) in Numidia records.[32] As such, he was likely to have accompanied Hadrian to the three Gauls, Germania Superior and Inferior and Britannia in AD 121/22.

However, apparently for discourteous behaviour towards the empress Sabina, he was then dismissed from office when Hadrian simultaneously deposed as his praetorian prefect Caius Septicius Clarus, to whom Suetonius' biographies of the first twelve emperors (including Iulius Caesar) were dedicated to.[33] It obviously pays not to annoy an empress. Anyway, having done so and paid the price, this might explain why in the first four *vita* Suetonius quotes actual letters from the emperors, correspondence that he could have only secured via access to the imperial archives. After *Divus Claudius*, however, there are no further quotations from such letters bar one example,[34] but this could be just another example of an anecdote and does not actually mean that he saw Nero's letter. The date of Suetonius' death is unknown, but it is probably later than AD 132, since he makes a reference to Domitianus' widow, Domitia Longina, who survived until then, as though she were no longer alive.[35]

A striking feature of the *vita* is their thematic, rather than the strictly chronological arrangement, which Greek fellow-biographer Plutarch (who was about twenty years older than Suetonius) tended to favour.[36] In writing about the lives of the first Roman emperors and their families, Suetonius concentrated on the private lives of the people he wrote about, while Tacitus, his contemporary, dealt with political events and the emperors' conducted affairs of state. All the same, Suetonius and Tacitus have both a histrionic attitude to facts and a healthy interest in sex, power and politics, writing a great deal as they did about scandalous events and the immoral and pleasure-seeking lifestyles of the Roman aristocrats of the time. On the other hand, Suetonius, unlike Tacitus, did try to report events fairly and did not attempt to paint every emperor as a power hungry tyrant who ruled at the expense of traditional Roman rights and freedoms. He thus judges his subjects against a set of popular expectations of imperial behaviour that had taken shape by the time his biographies were composed. Tiberius, Tacitus' *bête noir*, is repeatedly criticized for having failed to live up to expectation, whereas even Nero and Domitianus, rulers on whom Suetonius' final judgement is damning, can nevertheless be commended for having successfully met some of their imperial responsibilities.

Cassius Dio

A Greek-speaking senator and author of a monumental eighty-book history of Rome from the foundation of the city to his own retirement from office in AD 229,[37] Cassius Dio was born in AD 164 at Nicaea in Bithynia. He was related to the Stoic orator Dio Chrysostom. On the death of his father, who had been a proconsular governor of Cilicia, Cassius Dio came to Rome in AD 180, entered the Senate, and, under the emperor Commodus, was an advocate. A close friend to several emperors, his senatorial career was distinguished. He was praetor in AD 194, and *consul suffectus* probably around AD 204. For ten years from AD 218 he was successively *curator* of Pergamum and Smyrna, *proconsulare* of Africa and *legatus* first of Dalmatia and then of Pannonia Superior. In AD 229 he crowned his career by holding a pukka consulship with the emperor Severus Alexander as colleague and then, in failing health, retired to Nicaea. He died there around AD 235. Cassius Dio lived through turbulent times: he and his fellow senators quailed before tyrannical emperors and lamented the rise of men they regarded as upstarts, and in Pannonia Superior he grappled with the problem of military indiscipline.[38] These tough experiences are vividly evoked in his account of his own epoch and helped shaped his view of earlier periods.

Like its author, the work is an amalgam of Greek and Roman elements. It is written in Attic Greek, with much studied antithetical rhetoric and frequent verbal baggage from the classical authors, above all Thucydides. The debt to Thucydides is more than merely stylistic: like him, Cassius Dio is constantly alert to discrepancies between appearances and reality. However, in its structure his work revives the Roman tradition of annalistic record of civil and military affairs arranged by consular year, although naturally this did not prevent him from manipulating chronology and including digressions where he saw fit. It is a veritable achievement to say the least, though he understood the imperial system of his own day more so than that of the late Republic and the early Principate. Interestingly, he does say that the history of the Principate was rather more difficult to research than that of the Republic, the first being of a more secretive nature,[39] but this could have been a statement made for the sake of mere convention.

It is clear that Cassius Dio thoroughly approves of the Principate, or 'monarchy' as he rightly terms it,[40] liking benevolent rulers naturally, with Augustus serving as the author's role model. On the whole he follows the Tacitean slant on Tiberius, though Cassius Dio does tend to make him more of a puzzle. In particular, he has great difficulty in accepting Tacitus' view that absolute power corrupts absolutely, preferring instead to state that if an emperor was 'bad' it was because he was not up to the job in the first place. He makes his moral position on civil war clear too, explaining that 'there is no doubt in civil wars the state is injured by both sides'.[41]

As regards his general attitudes, he has all the weaknesses that us moderns find in ancient historians, namely he is too rhetorical, too verbose, too dramatic, and naturally he fails to quote his sources. We also face chronological problems with Cassius Dio. He is, however, very useful in that he has preserved anecdotes and details otherwise unavailable, one interesting instance of this being his obvious hostility towards that 'Stoic Saint', Seneca. He may not have Tacitus' vast intellect or power of expression or rich rhetoric, but his treatment of the principates of individual emperors is important to us as it reflects the values and interests of the Roman senator.

Josephus

It is indeed curious that Joseph ben Matthias, better known to history as Josephus (Titus Flavius Iosephus), wrote the best descriptions of the Principate army in war and peace. A pro-Roman historian but also a member of the priestly aristocracy of the Jews (on his mother's side he was descended from the Asmonaean princes) with a largely rabbinic education, he had been chosen by the Sanhedrin, the Jewish council of state, to defend Galilee in the revolt of AD 66 against Rome. It was there that Josephus witnessed firsthand the legions of Vespasianus and his son Titus in action against his Jewish countrymen.

The following year, when a large Roman force invaded Galilee, his army ran away and he retreated into the town of Iotapata (Mizpe Yodefat). The siege of that strongly fortified and fanatically defended fortress lasted for forty-seven days and ended with Josephus' capture, but his life was spared, after an act of shocking duplicity,[42] and he was taken hostage by Vespasianus. Hearing his prisoner had the gift of prophecy, Vespasianus requested that his own fortune be told. Claiming to be God's messenger to him, the Jew assured the Roman that the empire should one day be his and his son's.[43] Clearly the prophecy, like that of the witch sisters given to a Scottish usurper married to a murderess, was one that had a tendency to fulfil itself. Vespasianus, apparently, was greatly impressed.[44]

So God too was recruited to oversee the victory of the Flavian cause. In the meantime, Josephus was held under gentle duress and persuaded to act as interpreter and mediator, in which role he witnessed the six-month agony of Jerusalem from the Roman side. He was thus seen as a collaborator by his fellow Jews.

After landing, however involuntarily, in the Roman camp, Josephus turned his captivity to his own advantage, and benefited for the rest of his days from his change of side. Given Roman citizenship, a pension for life and land in Iudaea, Josephus spent most of his life in or around Rome as an advisor and historian to the Flavian emperors, Vespasianus, Titus and Domitianus. Like Polybios before him, as a defeated foreigner Josephus was very much interested in seeking the primary factors that contributed to the superiority of Roman arms.

For centuries, the works of Josephus were more widely read in Europe than any book other than the Bible, especially the *Jewish Antiquities* (*Antiquitates Iudaicae*), a monumental history of the Jewish people all the way from Adam down to the eve of the Jewish revolt of AD 66. For us, however, his *Jewish War* (*Bellum Iudaicum*), originally written in Aramaic (this version is no longer extant) but later appearing in an amplified Greek translation (Greek had not only been the *lingua franca* of the east for more than three centuries but was also a language accessible to educated Romans), is an invaluable account based on eyewitness testimony and probably the campaign diaries (*commentarii*) of Vespasianus and Titus. Josephus certainly considered that they were valuable sources for the war and, more to the point, failure to use them could have been held against him (it certainly does not do to upset your saviour and patron). His profane flattery of father and son, especially the latter who he often simply addresses as Caesar,[45] is both frequent and obvious. But what may jar today was then admirable, and Josephus had his hour of fame. After all, if Tacitus owed his brilliant career to the Flavians,[46] then Josephus surely owed them his life.[47]

Notes

Maps and graphics
1. The ancient name of Rosinos de Vidriales is as yet unknown.
2. As Josephus records, it was here that the Philistines had once hung up the dismembered bodies of Saul and his sons 'on the walls of the city of Beth Shan, which is now called Scythopolis' (*Antiquitates Iudaicae* 6.14.8, cf. 1 Samuel 31:9–10 NIV).

Prologue
1. *RIC* I Otho: 3–6. Of course, passive power over the entire *orbis* in the hands of the Roman emperors was a common imperial theme.
2. Tacitus *Historiae* 1.40.2.
3. These are the words of the nineteenth-century Piedmontese artist and writer turned soldier and statesman, Massimo d' Azeglio (*Things I Remember*, (1966) p. 180).
4. Gibbon (1737–94) was, after Edmund Burke, the greatest prose writer of his generation. Edward Gibbon took for subject *The Decline and Fall of the Roman Empire*, a vast work published at intervals between 1776 and 1788. As an historian he was learned, truthful, and as well-informed as it was possible to be in his day. He was, moreover, an artist who could compose admirable descriptive pictures and who knew how to bring them into the narrative of events.
5. We may frown now on stereotypes, especially those that contain a tinge of truth. Yet in more recent conflicts involving British troops, 'our boys' are always incomparable heroes; their adversaries are always braggarts, cowards, false and perjured traitors. Take, for example, the one I am more familiar with, the Falklands/Malvinas War, when the daily papers (there was no live coverage) went to war too with their crude, stereotyped newspaper headlines, which were invariably massive and sloganized. One example will suffice, indeed the most notorious by far, 'GOTCHA' (*The Sun*, 3 May 1982).

Introduction
1. Thucydides 2.8.1. Likewise Pindar: 'War is sweet to the inexperienced, / but an experienced man fears it as it approaches with all his heart, extraordinarily' (fr. 110).
2. As Mama says in Oliver Stone's film *Heaven & Earth* (1993): 'If war produces one thing, it's many cemeteries. And in cemeteries, there are no enemies.' True words indeed.
3. By basing the calculations on 2004 estimates, it can be reckoned that some 1.49 per cent of males between the ages of fifteen and forty-nine (viz. military-age males) are serving in the British Armed Forces.
4. Brunt 1971: 28. Conscription often appeals to governments, because it is a quick and cheap way of getting troops, but its application is limited in that it demands either an efficient administrative system (viz. universal conscription), or a willingness to press-gang (viz. strong-arm conscription). In Rome both existed, though it must be stressed that the latter method was much more a feature of the Principate rather than the Republic. In this day and age, the advantage of conscription is that it can foster a sense of duty, and can keep the army tightly integrated into society, the military becoming part of the mainstream. On the other hand, however, conscription tends to produce not volunteers but evaders. In Rome I believe this condition did not exist.

5. Livy 22.49.15. To put it more bluntly, this figure, if correct, meant that the army at Cannae had suffered no less than 80 per cent casualties. The casualty rate suffered by Britain and its colonial allies on 1 July 1916, the date of the opening of the British offensive on the river Somme, does not compare with this shocking figure (19,240 killed, 35,493 wounded, 2,152 posted as missing and 585 captured). What is more, unlike Rome and its Cannae nightmare, Britain has never really recovered from this, its first experience of continental warfare in the industrial age.
6. Polybios 3.107.9.
7. Brunt 1971: 419–22.
8. Plutarch *Pyrrhos* 19.7. Hopkins (1978: 33) calculates that at the height of the war with Hannibal in 213 BC 29 per cent of Rome's male citizens were serving in the legions.
9. The term Principate is used by modern commentators for the thinly disguised monarchy established by Augustus.
10. Juvenal *Satire* 10.81 Green.
11. Vegetius *Epitoma rei militaris* 3 *praefatio*. This is the earliest expression in Latin of the classic paradox, *si vis pacem, para bellum*, 'If you want peace, prepare war'. Of course the idea was not new, and the Thucydidean parallel does not preclude a preemptive strike: 'So much more have we [the Boiotians] to fear from this neighbour [imperial democratic Athens] than from another. Besides, people who, like the Athenians in the presence instance, are tempted by pride of strength to attack their neighbours, usually march most confidently against those who keep still, and only defend themselves in their own country, but think twice before they grapple with those who meet them outside their frontier and strike the first blow if opportunity offers' (Thucydides 4.95.5).
12. A myth about peace did exist at Rome (*vide* Ara Pacis), but only as the consequence of victory. After all, the principate of Augustus was an age of peace that succeeded generations of war and also one that saw an attempt to resuscitate the of the stern but superannuated moral code that had seemingly made the early Republic a nation of dedicated farmer soldiers and faithful, fertile wives. These are cultural issues that have much resonance in our age. Of course, this was a myth already propagated by Augustan literary sources.
13. Plutarch *Caesar* 15.3. Today we would call this genocide, but the deliberate extermination of a whole people or nation by another is as old as the human race, and perhaps the first ever genocide was committed by *Homo sapiens sapiens* against *Homo sapiens neanderthalensis*. The last Neanderthals were found in cul-de-sacs such as the Iberian peninsula or the valleys of the Alta Garrotxa region, on infertile land, such as Banyoles lake, far from the great valleys, hemmed in as a result of pressure from our species. The data is clear, but the thing that is missing is a workable hypothesis explaining what happened. There are no remains of a single battlefield. Ecologists assert that there is a norm in biology according to which the species that encroaches on another species' territory always ends up eradicating this species. Other, more tangible examples from man's distant past are Melos by Athens, Thebes by Alexander the Great, Carthage by Rome, though some scholars of antiquity prefer to call these atrocities examples of gendercide, in which adult males were killed and women and children (especially girls) were enslaved, rather than genocide. The word itself was first coined in 1944 by the Polish lawyer Raphael Lemkim (1900–59) who constructed the noun by combining the rooted words *génos* (Greek: family, kindred, tribe, race) and *caedês* (Latin: a killing, slaughter, murder, massacre). Here we can note too, Agamemnon's tirade to his brother Menelaos in Homer's *Iliad*: 'Transgressors will pay the price, a tremendous price, / with their own heads, their wives and all their children. // Yes, for in my heart and soul I know this well: / the day will come when sacred Troy must die, / Priam must die and all his people with him, / Priam who hurls the strong ash spear!' (lines 186–91 Fagels). And then there is the Bible, where men, women, children, and sometimes even their livestock are exterminated. Their very existence is to be extinguished. One example will suffice, namely Samuel to Saul in the Old Testament: 'Now go and attack the Amalekites and totally destroy

everything that belongs to them. Do not spare them; put to death men and women, children and infants, cattle and sheep, camels and donkeys' (1 Samuel 15:3 NIV). As Moses sang after the complete destruction of the Egyptian army in the Red Sea, 'The LORD is a warrior' (Exodus 15:3 NIV). It all depends on what you think about the Bible, naturally.

14. The two principal exceptions of course were Mutina 43 BC and Perusia 41/40 BC.

15. Caesar *Bellum civile* 3.57.4.

16. Confucius (551–479 BC) promoted the ideal of 'humaneness', which required people to 'love others' (*Analects* 12.22, 17.6). He was the first to promulgate the Golden Rule: 'Do not do unto others as you would not have done unto you' (ibid. 12.2).

17. As Tacitus writes, 'from the time that the Divine Augustus consolidated the power of the Caesars, the wars of the Roman people had been in remote places, and had caused anxiety or brought honour to but one man' (*Historiae* 1.89.2).

18. Tacitus *Historiae* 3.11.2. Tacitus had good reason to be horrified by all this anarchy, since Iulia Procillia, his father-in-law's mother, had been killed in cold blood on her estate by a band of marauding Othonian sailors during an attack on Intimilium (modern Ventimiglia) in March AD 69 (Tacitus *Agricola* 7.1).

19. Livy 1.7.3.

20. Dionysios of Halikarnassos 1.85.6–86.4. 'Here Remus watched in vain, while the Palatine birds / gave his brother the first omens' (Ovid *Fasti* 5.151-2).

21. Livy offers us two versions of Remus' death. In one, 'more common version', Remus belittles Romulus' wall, and in a final insult to the new city and its founder, leapt over it. Romulus cut him down in anger, adding the threat, 'So perish, then, whoever else will jump over my walls' (Livy 1.7.2, cf. Ennius *Annales* 96 Skutsch, Dionysios of Halikarnassos 1.87.3, 4, Plutarch *Romulus* 10.2, 34.1). Ovid (*Fasti* 5.461), also writing under Augustus, has Romulus inaugurate the festival of Lemuria (or Lemuralia) to appease Remus' resentful ghost. This was the festival in May when Romans performed rites to exorcise the noxious spirits of the dead from their houses.

22. Burkert (1984: 21) compares Remus' murder with the Jewish myth of Cain and Abel. After Cain had slain his brother, he fled and founded the first city in mankind's history (Genesis 4:17 NIV). So the first man to build a city was also the first murderer. In both cases, the new beginning of society is based on *la violence fondatrice*.

23. Tacitus *Historiae* 3.25.2. If this event is not completely fictional, then it is exceptionally macabre. Or should it be put down to artistic licence? Then again, Tacitus specifically names his source for this incident, the eyewitness Vipstano Messalla. Anyway, what follows is Tacitus' story. A young soldier, recruited into *legio VII Galbiana* in Iberia, inflicted mortal injuries upon an older soldier of *legio XXI Rapax*. As he looked more closely at the prostrate and semi-conscious figure, he recognized his own father, Iulius Mansuetus, who had left home years before to serve at Windisch-*Vindonissa* in Germania Superior. Though stationed there since AD 43, having transferred from Xanten-*Vetera* in Germania Inferior, in the Claudian-Neronian period *XXI Rapax* drew recruits from Iberia and northern Italy – of the five other recruits to it whose origin is known, four came from northern Italy and one from Hispania Tarraconensis (Forni 1953: 56, 226). Thucydides' celebrated account of the civil war at Corcyra (Corfu) in 427 BC naturally includes a reference to 'fathers [who] killed their sons' (3.81.5). On the motive of close relatives killing each other as synecdoche for self-destructive civil war, see Woodman 1983: 116-19.

24. Tacitus *Historiae* 3.51.1.

25. Antoine de Saint-Exupéry, L'Espagne ensanglantée (3) Une guerre civile, ce n'est point une guerre, mais une maladie, *L'Intransigeant*, 14 August 1936. Thucydides (3.82.1–2) had likened the civil conflict, *stasis*, which afflicted many Greek states of his day to a kind of virulent illness.

26. Ignatieff 1998: 46. Modern examples of close relatives fighting against each other tend to be uncommon but not entirely unknown. One renowned example will suffice in this context.

The Chissano brothers found themselves in opposite camps during Mozambique's war of independence (1962–75). Joaquim Chissano was a high-ranking leader of the rebel group FRELIMO (*Frente de Libertação de Moçambique*), who went on to become the country's second president (1986–2005), while his brother served as a lieutenant in the Portuguese army. For this and other examples, see Kalyvas 2006: 331 n. 3.

27. Genesis 4:3–5 NIV.
28. The concept of the feral child continues with Edgar Rice Boroughs' Tarzan and Rudyard Kipling's Mowgli.
29. Livy 1.4.9.
30. Cf. Hesiod *Theogony* 26 Howie: 'Country shepherds! Evil disgraces! Mere bellies.'
31. Lévi-Strauss, C., 1980. *Mythos und Bedeutung*, 8, 30.
32. See Fields 2011B: 18–29.
33. Livy 2.16.3–5, Dionysios of Halikarnassos 5.40.3.
34. Livy 1.9.1–13.8.
35. Plutarch *Romulus* 15.7.
36. Lévi-Strauss, C., 1980. *Mythos und Bedeutung*, 87.
37. According to tradition, Remus chose the Aventine not the Esquiline hill. However, local archaeology tells us that in the beginning there were two separate and distinct palisaded settlements, one on the Palatine and one on the Esquiline. The Palatine was the supposed site of Romulus' city, and his thatched hut, the *casa Romuli*, was preserved there down to Livy's day as a sort of museum piece (Livy 5.53.8, Dionysios of Halikarnassos 1.79.11, Cassius Dio 48.43.4). Its postholes are still visible on the southwest corner of the Palatine, a spot Plutarch names (wrongly) as 'the so-called Steps of Fair Shore' (*Romulus* 20.4), which gave access to the hill from the Tiber riverbank. Indeed, investigations have proved the existence of Iron Age dwellings of wattle-and-post and pit burials (*a pozza* cremations) on this spacious hill at the time of the traditional foundation, and even earlier. As with the Palatine, archaeological evidence exists for Iron Age settlement on the Esquiline. See Fields 2011B: 4–6.
38. Remus' death suggests the Biblical custom of sacrificing a royal prince at the foundation of a city (1 Kings 16:34, 2 Kings 16.3 NIV).
39. Romulus is believed by at least one notable scholar, namely Count Andrea Carandini, to have been a historical figure, the first king of Rome even. Carandini bases his controversial hypothesis on his 1988 discovery of an ancient wall on the north slopes of the Palatine hill at about where the slope itself levels off and meets the Via Sacra. He dates this structure to the mid eighth century BC and names it the *murus Romuli*. The *murus Romuli* was the name given to a wall built to protect the Palatine hill, and ancient tradition held that this wall was built by Romulus (e.g. Tacitus *Annales* 12.24). See Roberto Sucro, Newly Found Wall May Give Clue To Origin of Rome, Scientist Says, *The New York Times*, 10 June, 1988.
40. Nietzsche, F.W., 1980. *Kritische Studienausgabe*, vol. 9, p. 73, n. 3[98].

Chapter 1

1. Pliny *Historia Naturalis* 7.8.45, *Sibylline Oracles* 5.490–520.
2. Roger of Hovedon *Chronica*, 'The Letter of William, archbishop of Sens, to our lord the pope, against the king of England, in relation to the death of the blessed Thomas'.
3. Warmington 1981: 11, Grant 1989: 6.
4. Suetonius *Nero* 6.1, cf. Cassius Dio 61.2.3.
5. 'Plantagenet, I will; and like thee, Nero / Play on the lute, beholding the towns burn' (Shakespeare *Henry VI, Part 1* 4.iv).
6. De Quincey, T.S., 1838. *The Caesars*.
7. Merivale, C., 1865. *A History of the Romans under the Empire*, vol. VII, chap. LV, p. 2.
8. In English: 'Where are you going?' or 'Wither goest thou?'. This Latin phase refers to a Christian tradition regarding Peter. Apparently when Peter was fleeing Rome and likely crucifixion he is met along the road by a risen Jesus. Peter asks his master '*Quo vadis?*', to

which he replies, '*Romam vado iterum crucigi*' – 'I am going to Rome to be crucified again' (Vercelli Acts 35, cf. John 13:36 NIV). Peter thereby gains the courage to return to Rome and his ministry, eventually to be martyred by being crucified upside down. The first text to suggest that Nero killed an apostle is the apocryphal *Ascension of Isaiah*, a Christian writing from the second century. It says: 'the slayer of his mother, who himself is king, will prevent the plant which the Twelve Apostles of the Beloved have planted. Of the Twelve one will be delivered into his hands' (*Ascension of Isaiah* 4.2). Thereafter it is Eusebius (d. AD 338/9), bishop of Caesarea in Palestine, who first claims (*Ecclesiastical History* 2.25.2) that Nero's persecution of the Christians led to the deaths of Peter and Paul, though the emperor did not give any specific orders. As for the manner of death, the bishop only mentions the beheading of Paul. As for Peter, he is said to have been crucified upside down in Rome during the reign of Nero in the apocryphal *Acts of Peter*, which was written around AD 200. By the fourth century, a number of Christian writers were claiming that Nero personally ordered the apostles' deaths (e.g. Sulpicius Severus *Chronica* 2.28–29). Which brings us to three contentious points about Peter: there is little evidence for the claim that he was bishop of Rome, it is debatable that Jesus had given him primacy over his other apostles (the apostles themselves seem to have been unaware of it), and no one can pretend that Jesus had said anything about Peter and his successors – if they were his successors – becoming rulers of earthly states, the so-called Patrimony of Saint Peter.

9. *Quo Vadis: A Historical narrative of the Time of Nero*.
10. Tacitus *Annales* 15.39. Tacitus also adds here that Nero playing his lyre and singing at the time of the fire was only a rumour.
11. The suspicions were certainly unfounded, as were similar charges in 1666 against James Duke of York.
12. Tacitus *Annales* 15.44.3–8, cf. Suetonius *Nero* 16.2. For Tacitus the Christians were guilty, and so got their just deserves at the hands of Nero, for their 'abominations' and their 'mischievous superstitions' and their 'hatred of mankind' (*Annales* 15.44.4, 5). Here we can compare the observations on the Christians made by Tacitus' friend, the younger Pliny. As legate governor of Bithynia-Pontus Pliny wanted to keep a careful eye on local politics to stop any illegal political organizations springing up. This why he held an investigation into the Christian sect, in order to establish whether their practices were criminal or not. Some renegades gave him the following account (*Epistulae* 10.96.7) of their weekly gatherings:

> They all did reverence to your statue and the images of the gods in the same way as the others, and reviled the name of Christ. They also declared the sum total of their guilt or error amounted to no more than this: they had met regularly before dawn on a fixed day to chant verses alternatively amongst themselves in honour of Christ as if to a god, and also to bind themselves by oath [*sacramentum* – Pliny obviously misunderstood its Christian connotation as 'sacrament'], not for any criminal purpose, but to abstain from theft, robbery, and adultery, to commit no breach of trust and not to deny a deposit when called upon to restore it. After this ceremony it had been their custom to disperse and reassemble later to take food of an ordinary, harmless kind; but they had in fact given up this practice since my edict, issued on your instructions (*mandata*), which banned all political societies. This made me decide it was all the more necessary to extract the truth by torture from two-slave women, who they call deaconesses. I found nothing but a degenerate sort of cult carried to extravagant lengths.

Trajan replies (*Epistulae* 97) that it is impossible to lay down a fixed rule, and Christians are not to be hunted out (*conquirendi non sunt*). However, he does add, 'if they are brought before you and the charge against them is proved, they must be punished'.

13. E.g. 'the vicissitudes of battle', wrote Tacitus, 'take over and stimulate the readers' imagination' (*Annales* 4.33.3). Likewise, the architect Vitruvius (5 *praefatio* 1) declared that the essence of history was to retain the reader's interest, and the younger Pliny (*Epistulae* 5.8.4) said that history provides entertainment no matter how it is written. But without a doubt it is Cicero, in his well-known letter to Lucceius, advising his friend how to write history, who says it all when he emphasizes its entertainment potential no less than nine times (*Epistulae ad familiares* 5.12.4–5, cf. *De oratore* 2.53, 63, 66). Nowadays, just to be entertained is the populist position much derided by academics as simpleminded and unsophisticated, proof of questionable analytical and critical acuity. For academe, of course, history is a true record of what happened, how people lived and died, what they did and what they said, and so forth and so forth. That is the *proper* way to write history. An epic theme merely distorts the record, and generals' eve-of-battle speeches, to take a suitable example, are agreeable as oratory but disagreeable as history. A good general could not possibly deliver a studied oration on the eve of battle, even if he had one prepared. For his lips would inevitably speak as his heart prompted, a few words honest and sincere, spoken in a firm but modulated voice, without excessive emotion or grand gestures. Besides, what soldier in his right mind would want to listen to a highfaluting harangue on the eve of a bloody battle? In truth, young soldiers, for most soldiers in all armies are not far beyond their boyish years, do not enjoy listening to lengthy speeches loaded with rhetorical flourishes. Happiest in the cocoon of close comradeship, for them there is no point in lengthy battlefield harangues.
14. Tacitus *Annales* 12.58.
15. As usual our sources vary, but many of them claim Agrippina poisoned Claudius (Tacitus *Annales* 12.66, Suetonius *Divus Claudius* 44.2, Cassius Dio 61.34.2–3, cf. Josephus *Antiquitates Iudaicae* 20.8.1, who is less sure). According to Tacitus it was a humble mushroom that defied Claudius, 'the poison was infused into some mushrooms, a favorite delicacy' (*Annales* 12.67). It is not known whether or not Nero knew of his mother's crime, or if he was even involved, Suetonius (*Nero* 33.1) and Cassius Dio (61.35.4) claiming that he knew, while Tacitus (*Annales* 12.65) and Josephus (*Antiquitates Iudaicae* 20.8.1) only mention Agrippina. Then mushrooms were not cultivated but gathered in forests. Their harvest could be as dangerous as hunting wild animals: 'Mushrooms grow on the ground and some are edible. Most of them cause death by asphyxiation' (Athenaios *Deipnosophistae* 2.60e). However, the Romans, like my *belle-mère*, were so familiar with mushrooms that they attributed mushroom poisoning to stupidity or skulduggery. Poisoners were keen on mushrooms.
16. Tacitus *Annales* 13.16, Suetonius *Nero* 33.2, Cassius Dio 61.7.4, Josephus *Antiquitates Iudaicae* 20.8.2.
17. This is clearly shown in a scene depicted on a decorative panel from the north portico of the Sebasteion at Aphrodisias. The deeply carved relief shows Agrippina crowning a youthful Nero with a laurel wreath. She is in the guise of Tyche, carrying a *cornucopia*, the symbol of fortune and plenty, and he is in guise of a Roman general, wearing cuirass and cloak, while a helmet rests at his feet. The Sebasteion was a privately funded, grandiose temple complex dedicated to Aphrodite and the Iulio-Claudian emperors.
18. Tacitus *Annales* 12.7.5–6.
19. Cassius Dio 61.3.3–4.
20. *RIC* I Nero: 1–3, 6–7.
21. Suetonius *Nero* 26.1. For tavern Suetonius employs the most commonly used term *popina*, and *popinae* were often associated with prostitution. In the small provincial town of Pompeii, where some 118 have been excavated, they are to be seen with a little upper room that contained only a simple bed. The bill would specify not only food and drink, but the company of a lady. According to Juvenal (*Satire* 8.171–8 Green) all *popinae* attracted bad company.
22. Suetonius *Nero* 26.2, cf. Tacitus *Annales* 13.25.3, who names the senator, one Iulius Montanus.

23. Tacitus *Annales* 13.25.2.
24. Suetonius *Nero* 28.1. Sporus was the unfortunate boy's name. Soon after Nero's demise, Sporus was taken into the household of the praetorian prefect Nymphidius Sabinus, who treated him as his partner in marriage, and even went as far to call him by the name Poppaea (Plutarch *Galba* 9.3). After the prefect's death he became the 'toy boy' of Otho. To the victor the spoils, and the next emperor of this long year, Vitellius, planned for Sporus to play the starring role of *The Rape of Persephone* for the delectation of the spectators during one of the gladiatorial shows. Sporus, no doubt tired of being used and abused, took his own life to avoid the public humiliation (cf. Suetonius *Nero* 46.2, Sporus' gift to Nero of a ring engraved with the rape of Persephone). He was probably under twenty years of age at the time of his death.
25. Tertullian (d. *c.* AD 225) was the first to call Nero the first persecutor of Christians. He wrote, 'examine your records [does he mean Tacitus here?]. There you will find that Nero was the first that persecuted this doctrine' (Tertullian *Apologeticum* ap. Eusebius *Ecclesiastical History* 2.25.4). Lactantius (d. *c.* AD 320) follows suit, saying that Nero 'first persecuted the servants of God' (*De mortibus persecutorum* 2), as does Sulpicius Severus (d. *c.* AD 424) (*Chronica* 2.28).
26. In AD 422, Augustine of Hippo commented on 2 Thessalonians 2:1–11, where he believed Paul was referring to the coming of the Antichrist. Though he himself rejected the hypothesis, he did say that many Christians believed that Nero was the Antichrist or would return as such. He wrote: 'so that in saying, "For the secret power, of lawlessness is already at work" [2 Thessalonians 2:7 NIV], he alluded to Nero, whose deeds already seemed to be the deeds of Antichrist' (*Civitas Dei* 20.19.3).
27. Nero's maternal grandmother was Antonia minor, the second daughter of Marcus Antonius and Octavia, while his father, Cnaeus Domitius Ahenobarbus (*cos.* AD 32), was the son of Antonia maior, the first daughter. As Nero's maternal uncle, Caius Caligula also traced his lineage to Marcus Antonius via Antonia minor, his paternal grandmother.
28. Tacitus *Annales* 14.47.3.
29. Ibid. 15.42.
30. It was said by Suetonius (*Nero* 38) and Cassius Dio (62.18.1) that Nero sang the *Sack of Ilium* (a Greek epic now lost) from beginning to end in stage costume while his capital burned; unlike Tacitus, both these authors favour Nero as an arsonist, so he could construct his palatial complex, the *domus aureus*. It is significant that the Flavian emperors later ostentatiously returned much of the area to public use with the construction of the first concrete amphitheatre in Rome, the Colosseum, a building designed to house the gladiatorial games and wild beast hunts, which were the favourite entertainment of the people.
31. Tacitus *Annales* 14.20–21, Suetonius *Nero* 12.
32. It is usual, in writing about Augustus, to refer to him as Octavianus up to 27 BC and as Augustus thereafter (Suetonius *Divus Augustus* 7.2, Cassius Dio 53.16.7–8).
33. In 29 BC Virgil finished his *Georgics*. Ostensibly a didactic poem on farming – in truth, few working farmers would have been readers of poetry – the *Georgics* is the great poem of united Italy. Others, including Varro in his contemporary and more serviceable prose manual, had praised the variety, fertility, self-sufficiency and temperate climate of Italy (Varro *De re rustica* 1.2.3–7), and the elder Cato, who wrote the first agricultural treatise in Latin in the second century BC, had praised the sturdy qualities of its sons who were by turns farmers then soldiers (Cato *De agri cultura* preface 4). As Mao Tse-tung once said: 'There is no profound difference between the farmer and the soldier' (*On Guerilla Warfare* (1937) chap. 5), and it is interesting to contrast (not to draw any parallels) the fact that most recruits today are much more likely to be from an urban environment rather than an agrarian one, the tough countryman, for whom the rigours of field service differed little from the grinding hardship and privation of everyday life, is a vanished commodity in the western world. Anyway, I digress. Virgil's famous eulogy of Italy is the Augustan apogee

in that it adds a new dimension, the association of this land with the greatness of Rome (Virgil *Georgics* 2.136–76). This virtuoso set piece ranges far beyond the workaday realm of agriculture and sometimes even of sober truth. Virgil, of course, was a poet and one for whom embellishment was no vice. Yet his allegory of a conscious and united Italy, where Romans are Italians and Italians are Romans, was to be an overture to the glorification of Augustus and his new régime, and an assertion of Rome's imperial destiny. The Augustan poets, Virgil chief among them, consciously revealed attitudes and ideals (and sometimes even policies), which are the greatest importance for our comprehension of the more intangible aspects of Augustus' régime. In his *Republic*, which is an admirable piece of argument, Plato was for keeping all poets whatsoever out of his ideal state: he reckoned that they were all liars, the peerless Homer included. Virgil was a rather dull fellow who tried to be a Homer and could not do it: Virgil was merely a remarkable verse-craftsman. Catallus, acquaintance of Caesar, was the last of the true Roman poets: poetry and liberty go in concert, and under a monarchy true poetry dies. As we know, when one talks of liberty everything seems beautifully simple.

34. Returning from the east in the summer of 29 BC, Octavianus entered Rome on 13 August, and during three successive days the capital witnessed the pomp of three triumphs, for his Illyrian wars, for Actium, and for Egypt – all wars of Rome against a foreign enemy (Suetonius *Divus Augustus* 22.1, Cassius Dio 51.21.5–9, cf. *Res Gestae Divi Augusti* 4.1.)

35. E.g. 'the wild Queen …/ with her squalid / Pack of diseased half-men' (*Horace* Odes 1.37).

36. Suetonius *Divus Augustus* 68.1.

37. Cf. Martial *Epigrammata* 11.20, where he claims that even Octavianus could turn his hand to writing lewd verse.

38. Umbricius, in Juvenal *Satire* 3.60–5 Green. The Orontes (Nahr el-Asi) was the largest river in ancient Syria; it rose in the hills near Damascus and flowed northwards by Epiphania and Apamea, turning sharply southwest by Antioch to the Mediterranean Sea. The name Umbricius is Etruscan, and much has been written about this (in every sense) shadowy character (Umbricius, *umbra*): real person or fictional *alter ego*? Most scholarship has leaned towards an Umbricius who was probably real, though not, as formerly suggested, the official soothsayer, *haruspex*, mentioned by the elder Pliny (*Historia Naturalis* 10.6.19), Tacitus (*Historiae* 1.27.1), and Plutarch (*Galba* 24.2).

39. In Latin: *Graeculi*, Juvenal *Satire* 3.77 Green. Obviously a Roman term of abuse, the patronizing diminutive *Graeculus* – Greekling – is best defined as an insignificant or contemptible Greek, a wretched Greek, if you will.

40. From the second century BC onwards, the ideal of *mos maiorum* (lit. 'customs of our ancestors') became a statement of the key virtues of the Roman citizen, which included valour (*virtus*), prestige (*gloria*), greatness of spirit (*magnitudo animi*), praiseworthiness (*dignitas*), authority (*auctoritas*), seriousness (*gravitas*), standing (*honos*), and nobility (*nobilitas*). The literati of Rome, it seems, were keen to reconstruct the glories of a semi-mythical past, those good old days of uncorrupted simplicity, the tug of heroic nostalgia set against the harsh realities of the present. See Lind 1979: 28–41.

41. In Latin: *Graecia capta ferum victorem cepit*, Horace *Epistulae* 2.1.156. This clever play on words is frequently found in the speeches and writings of the elder Cato (e.g. Livy 33.4.3).

42. Pliny *Epistulae* 10.40.2.

43. Ibid. *Panegyricus* 13.5.

44. Tacitus *Historiae* 3.47.2.

45. Cassius Dio 62.21.1, cf. Suetonius *Nero* 22.2.

46. Suetonius *Nero* 24.2. The portraits of Nero on his coinage depict him wearing his front hair 'set' and 'crimped' in steps, like a charioteer's.

47. Tacitus *Annales* 15.65 (Piso), 16.21 (Thrasea).

48. At first, Nero too performed only in private, but in AD 64 at Greek-speaking Neapolis (Naples) he made his first public appearance (Tacitus *Annales* 15.33, Suetonius *Nero* 20.2).

The next public performance that we know of was his appearance at the second *quinquennial Neronia* the following year (Suetonius *Nero* 21.1). Nero apparently worked hard to develop his singing voice, following the then usual procedures, such as lying on his back with a lead weight on his chest, and using enemas to keep his weight down (ibid. 20.1). Vegetables of the onion family were believed to be good for the voice, and Nero added these to his diet. Suetonius reports (ibid. 51.1) that the emperor suffered from body odour as well.

49. The Romans had deep-seated qualms about the ethical standing of various sorts of tradesmen (cf. Cicero *De officiis* 1.150), and those who pursued dishonourable professions included *infames* much favoured by Nero, such as actors, dancers, gladiators and charioteers.
50. Chaucer *Canterbury Tales*, The Monk's Tale, Shakespeare *Hamlet* 3.ii.
51. Tacitus *Annales* 14.7.
52. Ibid. 14.8, cf. Cassius Dio 62.13.5. Feisty to the very end, when the marine centurion bared his sword Agrippina cried out *Ventrem feri*, 'Smite my womb!'
53. What are we to make of Lucan's ironic assertion (*Pharsalia* 1.33–7) that all the death and destruction of the civil and triumvirate wars were worthwhile because it led to the advent of Nero?
54. Tacitus *Annales* 16.18.1.
55. Ibid. 14.4–7, cf. Suetonius *Nero* 34, Cassius Dio 62.13.1–5.
56. Josephus *Bellum Iudaiacum* 20.153.
57. Tacitus *Annales* 13.3.2.
58. For such abuses *after* Nero's principate, see Tacitus *Historiae* 1.37.
59. Tacitus *Annales* 13.4, cf. 11.2, 5 (Claudius' closed door style of government).
60. Ibid. 13.5.1.
61. Ibid. 13.48 (riots), 49 (gladiators), 14.42–45, cf. 13.32.1 (slaves).
62. Aurelius Victor *Epitome* 5.
63. Martial *Epigrammata* 7.34. The real importance of Nero's baths in the Campus Martius, like that of the *domus aurea*, was the use they made of the new techniques of construction in concrete.
64. Tacitus *Annales* 15.65.2, 16.21.2.
65. Claudius, for example, was a very unmilitary figure, but he kept the soldiers well paid and was briefly present on a campaign that added a new province to the empire. He also accumulated twenty-seven *imperator* acclamations, the title used to designate a victorious general whose success had been acknowledged by his own soldiers. Augustus had only managed twenty-one, and Tiberius, who surely was a pukka general, eight.
66. Sumner 2002: 22, 46, pl. F1.
67. An inscription (*CIL* iii 7591) tells us that Nero gave *I Italica* its *aquila* and *signa* on (by our reckoning) 20 September (viz. *dies natalis*), which confirms Cassius Dio 55.24.2. But was this in the early autumn of AD 66 or AD 67?
68. While the legion's initial *dilectus* recruited only six-foot Italians, further recruits were to be found outside of Italy. Out of eight later inscriptions left by members of *I Italica* in Moesia, where it was based for at least 350 years after Second Cremona, two legionaries are from Italy (*CIL* iii 12352, v 7667), one from Gallia Narbonensis (ibid. iii 8198), two from Macedonia (ibid. iii 7441, 6144), while four are of Thracian descent (ibid. vi 2803, 2601, 2785, xiv 3631).
69. At this time Nero was planning a great military enterprise against the Albani, who lived *ad Caspias portas*, the Caspian Gates.
70. Suetonius *Nero* 19.2. In our period of study the Roman foot measured 295.7 millimetres as opposed to the modern imperial foot of 304.8 millimetres. Incidentally, Vegetius says that 'men of six (Roman) feet [1.77m] or at least five (Roman) feet ten (Roman) inches [1.72m] were approved for service in the *alae* or the *prima cohors* of the legion' (*Epitoma rei militaris* 1.5). Incidentally, whether or not Nero himself cared much about the greatest leader of antiquity, Alexander was the one Greek whom the Romans considered their equal in the art

of war and imperial dominion, in exploration and the founding of cities in barbarous lands, and as the bringer of civilization.

71. Tacitus *Annales* 14.51 (Burrus), 53 (Seneca). Tacitus provides two reasons for Burrus' demise, natural causes or poison, with the emphasis of course on the second. But it is worth noting that Tacitus is the only authority who suggests any doubt at all. Suetonius (*Nero* 35) and Cassius Dio (62.13.3) both state simply that Nero disposed of Burrus by poison.

72. Tacitus *Annales* 13.2.

73. See Tacitus *Historiae* 1.72 where he writes a character sketch of Ofonius Tigellinus, 'a man of obscure birth, steeped in infamy from his boyhood, and shamelessly profligate in his old age'.

74. Tacitus *Annales* 14.60.1.

75. Cassius Dio 62.13.1.

76. Tacitus *Annales* 14.60. In the *Octavia*, the historical drama that details the downfall of Nero's first wife, the disgruntled populace attacks the images of Poppaea as surrogates for assaulting her living body (lines 684–7, 794–9).

77. Tacitus 14.60.2–4.

78. Ibid. 14.62.3. It had been Anicetus' marines that had put to death Agrippina.

79. Ibid. 14.62.5.

80. Ibid. 14.64.

81. The Calpurnii Pisones, linked by adoption or by marriage to the descendants of those republican warlords Pompey and Crassus, came to be the nearest there was to an alternative dynasty. They furnished three men who died for their prominence between AD 65 and AD 70, including the conspirator against Nero, a proconsul of Africa (murdered in Vespasianus' interests), and Lucius Calpurnius Piso Frugi Licinianus, adopted by Galba only to die with him (see Appendix 9). Still later, Caius Calpurnius Piso Crassus Frugi Licinianus conspired against Nerva and Trajan, was exiled, and was killed under Hadrian.

82. Seneca and members of his family – Gallio, Mela, and Lucan – were all suspected of involvement to kill Nero the year after the great fire – apparently Lucan at least had played a major role – and with the detection of the plot came the downfall not only of Seneca, but most of Seneca's close circle of family and friends. Anyway, guilty or not, Seneca's suicide took on an exemplary quality and was narrated in detail by Tacitus (*Annales* 15.63.4–64.5). Seneca's magnificent exit (one of a number described in the *Annales*) is presented by Tacitus in ways that recall other famous deaths, not only that of Sokrates but also of the younger Cato, who was celebrated for committing suicide in preference to living under the tyranny of Iulius Caesar. Likewise, Thrasea Paetus was invited by the emperor to commit suicide (ibid. 16.34–35). Seneca had changed since the time of his death. Like Cato, who had died a human-sized defender of tradition and political propriety only to rise again as a titanic advocate of liberty, so Seneca, in his grave, had both swelled and altered. Tacitus had played his part in Seneca's posthumous inflation.

83. Cassius Dio 62.2.1.

84. Tacitus *Annales* 13.42.3.

85. Ibid. 15.67. Tacitus says he has given us the actual words of the good soldier Flavus.

86. Seneca *Hercules Furens* 922–24. Seneca wrote nine tragedies, mostly based on originals by Sophokles and Euripides, but designed for recitation rather than performance, and burdened with exaggerated rhetorical effects.

87. Cassius Dio 63.17.5–6.

88. Frontinus *Strategemata* 2.9.5, 4.1.21, 28, 2.3, 7.2. Sextus Iulius Frontinus (d. AD 103) himself had a distinguished ancestry and a distinguished career – thrice consul, legate governor of Britannia (AD 73/4–77/8). He also had an interest in technical matters unusual in his class, having written a lost treatise on surveying and an extant treatise on aqueducts, *De aquis urbis Romae*. On military matters he wrote a theoretical treatise entitle *The Art of War*, which is lost, and followed it with the more practical *Strategemata*, which of course survives.

89. In its extreme form, what *la Légion étrangère* calls *le cafard*, armed men with nothing to do become so obsessed with being bored stiff that they can resort to suicide, or murder, or desert, or plot mutiny.

90. Tacitus *Annales* 13.8.3.

91. In Greek: *áxios* (literally right and proper), Cassius Dio 62.17.6. Generally it was used in acclaiming a hero, this Greek expression is still used today, an acclamation made by the faithful when bishops, priests or deacons are ordained in the Orthodox and Eastern Catholic churches. In this case, *áxios* is best translated as 'he is worthy'.

92. Here we are following Suetonius, who says that when Nero heard of the defection of 'other armies' (*ceteri exercitus*, *Nero* 47.1) – he does not identify them – it threw the emperor into a panic that immediately preceded his suicide.

93. Cassius Dio 63.29.2. Epaphroditos would survive the day and subsequently become a trusted aide to Vespasianus, Titus and Domitianus, until the latter would have him done away with at the end of his principate. And the emperor's reason for this? Well, apparently for failing to prevent Nero's suicide (Suetonius *Domitianus* 14.1, Cassius Dio 67.14.4).

94. Here, I offer the most popular English translation. In Latin: *Qualis artifex pereo*, Suetonius *Nero* 49.1.

95. Tacitus *Historiae* 2.8–9 (AD 69), Cassius Dio 66.19.3b–c (AD 79), Suetonius *Nero* 57.2 (AD 88). According to Cassius Dio it was during the reign of Titus that a certain Asiatic by the name of Terentius Maximus, who resembled Nero in face and voice and also played the lyre, received the support of the Parthian king Artabanus IV. This king, who had some cause of quarrel against Titus, made preparations for securing the pretender's return to Rome. On the other hand, Suetonius says it was the third pretender, the one who cropped up during the reign of Domitianus, who had the support of the Parthians, who only reluctantly gave him up, and Tacitus (*Historiae* 1.2) adds the matter almost came to war.

96. Marcus Cocceius Nerva was a sinister character who had been involved in the suppression of the Piso conspiracy against Nero, which won him political honours equalled in Nero's principate only to those of Ofonius Tigellinus (Tacitus *Annales* 15.27.1, *ILS* 273) and was probably played a part in Domitianus' death.

97. Tacitus *Historiae* 1.4, cf. Suetonius *Nero* 57.1, Cassius Dio 63.29.1.

98. Philostratos *Vita Apollonii* 5.41, cf. Dio Chrysostom *Discourse* 21, On Beauty.

99. Suetonius *Nero* 40.3.

Chapter 2

1. Suetonius actually says 'on the anniversary of Octavia's murder' (*Nero* 57.1).

2. Gibbon *Decline & Fall* vol. I, chap. III, p. 69.

3. His great-grandfather, Servius Sulpicius Galba, was the legate of *legio Martia* (its numeral is unknown) in the consular army of Aulus Hirtius and had fought against Marcus Antonius in the first of the Mutina (Modena) battles, that fought on 14 April 43 BC at Forum Gallorum (now Castelfranco) on the line of the Via Aemilia. The story of the battle is narrated in a marvellous letter penned the day after to his friend Cicero (*Epistulae ad familiares* 10.30). In another letter to Cicero touching upon the same dramatic events outside Mutina, that from Caius Asinius Pollio, '*legio Martia* has been destroyed' (ibid. 10.33.4). Severely cut up, *legio Martia*, in fact, survived the day at Forum Gallorum only to come to a tragic end the following year. During a crossing of the Adriatic, allegedly on the very day the first battle at Philippi (26 October 42 BC), the transports carrying the legion were intercepted by warships and its personnel mostly drowned (Appian *Bellum civilia* 4.115). Anyway, previously, Galba had been a *praetor urbanus* (54 BC) and had successfully served in Gaul as the legate of Caesar's *legio XII* (Caesar *Bellum Gallicum* 3.1–6). In 49 BC he was a candidate for the consulship, but, to the annoyance of his friend Caesar, he was not elected 'despite his far greater popularity and larger number of votes, because he was closely associated with Caesar both as a friend

and as a legate' (ibid. 8.50.6). According to Suetonius (*Galba* 3.2, cf. Appian *Bellum civilia* 2.113), he turned sour and consequently was party to the conspiracy of Brutus and Cassius, the self-styled 'Liberators'.

4. Suetonius *Galba* 7.1. Ruthlessness certainly ran in his blood, at least on the maternal side, for Galba's mother was the illustrious Mummia Achaica, a grand-daughter to Quintus Lutatius Catulus (*cos.* 78 BC), a steadfast partisan of Sulla, and a great-granddaughter of Lucius Mummius (*cos.* 146 BC), the destroyer of wealthy Corinth.

5. Suetonius *Galba* 8.1. The *Augustales* was a special priesthood created to minister (and pay for) a cult to the dead (and subsequently deified) Augustus, first in Rome, and then in the provinces. The vast majority of *Augustales* were freedmen (85 to 95 per cent of those attested in inscriptions) and they served other deified emperors in due course.

6. The governor of Gallia Aquitania was certainly hostile to him (Suetonius *Galba* 9.2).

7. Vindex's father was a Roman senator, a position probably achieved as a result of Claudius' policy of AD 48. Claudius, in his role as censor, had given 'trousered, long-haired Gauls', chieftains from the area of Gaul conquered a century earlier by Caesar, the right to hold public office at Rome. What is more, one of the most striking initiatives was the Senate's decision to admit to membership a number of these Gaulish nobles. Tacitus tells us that the momentous decision followed Claudius' personal intervention in the senatorial debate, and all the available evidence strongly suggests that he was very much acting on his own initiative and not as a mouthpiece for others. Of particular interest here is the Lyons Tablet (*CIL* xiii 1668 col. 2). This bronze tablet from Lyon (Lugdunum, the capital of the Three Gauls), discovered in November 1528, immortalizes a *verbatim* copy of the speech the emperor made before his fellow senators in AD 48. The speech, an argument in favour of enlarging the Senate by opening its hallowed portals to 'foreigners', is also recorded by Tacitus (*Annales* 11.24), who does not reproduce it exactly or faithfully but brings out the main points.

8. Tacitus *Historiae* 2.94.

9. Plutarch *Galba* 4.3 (100,000), 6.3 (20,000). To believe the first figure you would have to surmise that Vindex armed butchers, bakers, bath attendants and suchlike, slaves even. However, you cannot make a slave into a soldier by simply tying a breastplate on him, putting a spear in his hand, hanging a sword round his middle, and telling him to fight. Slaves masquerading as soldiers is not the solution.

10. Cassius Dio 63.22.1a.

11. Ibid. 63.22.2–3.

12. Ibid. 63.22.6.

13. Vindex had the support of Aedui, Sequani, and Arverni (Tacitus *Historiae* 1.51.6, 4.17.5, cf. Pliny *Historia Naturalis* 4.106, 109), and of the city of Vienna, titular colony and capital of the Allobroges (Tacitus *Historiae* 1.65). We do know of two Gallic tribes that actually sided with Verginius Rufus during the revolt of Vindex, the Treveri and the Lingones (ibid. 4.69.2).

14. *OGIS* 669 = McCrum-Woodhead 328. A contemporary copy of the edict was found in El-Khârga Oasis in Upper Egypt, some 660 kilometres to the south of Alexandria, a lengthy Greek inscription comprising sixty-four lines carved on the east face of the north jamb of the outer gateway to the temple of Hibis. It should be realized that the province of Egypt was organized differently from all other provinces. It was the emperor's private possession, and no senator was allowed to set foot in it without his authority. Consequently there could be no *legatus Augusti pro praetore* nor *legati legionum* in the province, and, while the governor was called a *praefectus Aegypto*, the commanders of the legions stationed there had the title of *praefectus legionis*, and performed exactly the same rôle as their senatorial counterparts. These *praefecti* were all trusted men of equestrian rank. A senator in Egypt, it was believed by Augustus, might harbour dangerous, 'republican' ambitions; as well as its garrison of two legions, there were a further three or four legions in Syria. There is some justification for such a view in Tacitus (*Historiae* 1.11.1) who thought that Augustus wished to control tightly

a province, which was populous, wealthy and fertile. So what was once Cleopatra's Egypt became the crown of an equestrian career.

15. Although Plutarch (*Galba* 4.3, 5.3) and Cassius Dio (63.23) have Vindex proclaim Galba emperor, Suetonius has him urge Galba to 'make himself the liberator and leader of mankind' (*Galba* 9.2). This does seem much more plausible, as Vindex needed to win general support and thus could not afford to cause unnecessary jealousy by committing himself irrevocably to one candidate.

16. Apparently Agrippina wanted to marry Galba, though he was already married to a lady of the Lepidii. He was perfectly satisfied with his wife and behaved as coldly as possible towards Agrippina as his loyalty to her brother the emperor permitted. Agrippina persisted in her pursuit of Galba and there was a great scandal one day at a reception given by Galba's mother-in-law, which Agrippina gatecrashed. The mother-in-law called her out in front of all the nobility assembled, abused her roundly as a shameless and lascivious hussy and actually struck her with her fists (Suetonius *Galba* 5.1). Agrippina, it should be understood, was a direct descendent of Augustus, of Livia, of Marcus Antonius, a daughter of Germanicus, a sister of the present emperor. Fortunately for all concerned, Agrippina was implicated in a plot against Caligula's life and banished to a rock off the north African coast.

17. Suetonius *Galba* 5.2. Galba's father, apparently an ugly hunchback, had married a second wife, the beautiful and wealthy Livia Ocellina, from a distant branch of Livia's own family, and by all accounts, Galba got on very well with his stepmother, whose name he took and carried for a time (ibid. 3.4, 4.1).

18. Germania Superior was home to three legions, *IIII Macedonica* and *XXII Primigenia* (Mainz-*Mogontiacum*), and *XXI Rapax* (Windisch-*Vindonissa*).

19. The praenomen of Verginius Rufus is in some doubt, as we find in inscriptions, in which his different consulships are recorded, both Lucius and Titus. But since he is expressly stated by the younger Pliny (*Epistulae* 2.1.1) to have been thrice consul (AD 63, AD 69, AD 97), it is more likely that there is an error in one of the inscriptions than that they refer to a different person. Besides, Pliny surely should know, as Verginius Rufus had formerly been his guardian (ibid. 2.1.2).

20. Cassius Dio 63.24.2. Most modern commentators now see Verginius Rufus as in sympathy with Vindex's movement, and thus guilty of having broke his oath of loyalty to Nero (e.g. Brunt 1959: 537–9, Daly 82–5, *contra* Chilver 1957).

21. No pitched battle has ever been won by fantastically bedizened volunteers against disciplined and well-trained soldiers, and Vindex's men proved to be no exception to this old truth. They were in all probability militia made up of farmers, artisans and tradesmen, many armed with only bills, hoes and mattocks. If so, then these were men not bred for war, and, panicky and undisciplined; the only thing they knew of battle was how to run from it. The Gaulish aristocrats alone could be called warriors, men who could ride and fight, and, if we can believe Cassius Dio, Vindex himself 'was powerful in body and of shrewd intelligence, was skilled in warfare and full of daring for any great enterprise' (63.22.1b), a true classical hero.

22. Hobbes, T., 1651. *Leviathan*, II.17.2.

23. Tacitus *Historiae* 1.8.2, 'late to revolt from Nero (*tarde a Nerone desciverant*)'. Also, Suetonius says that when Nero heard of the defection of *ceteri exercitus* (*Nero* 47.1) – he does not identify them – it threw the emperor into a panic that immediately preceded his suicide. If the army of Verginius is included, his defection came late in the day. Plutarch's version (*Galba* 6.1–2), on the other hand, is that Verginius Rufus abandoned Nero before the battle, and when his soldiers saluted him emperor, he declared that he would not except, nor would he allow anyone else to take power except as the nominee of the Senate. The offer was renewed, and declined once more, after the battle. One important point needs to made here: each of our authors is writing and selecting from the material before him for his own purposes; he has his own timescale, within which he speeds up or slows down as the material interests him more or less.

24. Tacitus *Historiae* 1.52.3. We know from Pliny (*Epistulae* 2.1.8, with *ILS* 982) that Verginius Rufus hailed from Mediolanum (Milan), and thus was not just a simple *equites* but a provincial one to boot. His birth and origins may have been lowlier than Galba, but not noticeably inferior to the eventual victor of AD 69, Vespasianus (with the permission of the constant reader I will retain his natural name; to mangle it into Vespasian seems quite unnecessary). It seems that in the long run birth and origins no longer mattered after all. Life is funny like that.

25. Tacitus *Historiae* 1.8.2, *nec statim pro Galba Verginius*.

26. Ibid. 3.62.2.

27. Pliny *Epistulae* 2.1.2.

28. Verginius Rufus was thus born in AD 13 or AD 14, the very last year of Augustus' principate.

29. In Latin: *Hic situs est Rufus, pulso qui Vindice quondam / imperium adseruit non sibi, sed patriae*, Pliny *Epistulae* 6.10.4 = 9.19.1, cf. Cassius Dio 68.2.4. This was the year the emperor Nerva made him consul for the third time, along with himself. During his consulship he was reciting a speech, which he was about to pronounce in honour of Nero, when a large volume he had his in hand slipped from his grasp, and in an effort to retrieve it, he fell and broke his thigh. The bone was badly set, and death soon followed. He was awarded a public funeral, and his funeral oration was delivered by Tacitus, who was then consul, which, as Pliny says, crowned the good fortune of a prosperous life (ibid. 2.1.6). Incidentally, his second consulship, which, though it lasted only a month (March AD 69), followed immediately upon the consulships of Otho himself and his brother, with the emperor sacrificing a month of his own to accommodate Verginius Rufus (Tacitus *Historiae* 1.77.2, Plutarch *Otho* 1.2). Under the Flavians there would be no public offices for Verginius Rufus.

30. Pliny *Epistulae* 9.19.5. Cluvius Rufus was a born survivor with a talent for political acrobatics. He had been a member of Nero's entourage, had served in Iberia under Galba as the legate governor of Hispania Tarraconensis and remained there in control until his retirement under Vespasianus. He had promptly recognized Otho in January and as promptly gone over to Vitellius (Tacitus *Historiae* 1.8.1, Suetonius *Nero* 21.2, Cassius Dio 63.14.3). We do not know the names of all the historians of the year AD 69, but three prime candidates can be brought forward as the source that supplied material to our extant historians: the elder Pliny, Fabius Rusticus, and Cluvius Rufus. Tacitus rarely mentions the sources of his information, but though he speaks rather patronisingly of Cluvius Rufus – 'an eloquent man, who had all the accomplishments of civil life, but who was without experience in war' (*Historiae* 1.8.1) – it is believed that he was one of those used by him.

31. Initially, Galba had only this legion, along with the auxiliaries of two *alae*, and three *cohortes* (Tacitus *Historiae* 5.16.3, Suetonius *Galba* 10.2, Josephus *Bellum Iudaicum* 2.375). However, as soon as he had declared against Nero Galba set about raising a new legion, *VII Galbiana* (Suetonius *Galba* 10.2, *ILS* 9125).

32. The struggle against Sextus Pompeius and the climatic naval engagement off Actium had given the Roman navy a greater political importance than it had hitherto enjoyed, and it was impossible for Augustus to overlook it. From Augustus onwards there were two main fleets, the largest one was based at the northern end of the Bay of Naples at Misenum, the *classis Misenensis* (established *c.* 30–20 BC to replace Portus Iulius, which Marcus Agrippa had created in 37 BC for the naval campaign against Sextus Pompeius), and the other one, perhaps half as large, based in the Adriatic at Ravenna, the *classis Ravennas* (Suetonius *Divus Augustus* 49.1). Both fleets were commanded by high-ranking equestrian officers (*praefecti classis*) responsible only to the emperor. In addition, there was a minor fleet based at Forum Iulii (Fréjus) east of Massilia (Strabo 4.5.1, Tacitus *Annales* 4.5.1). Independent fleets were soon established on all the major waterways and seas: the Channel (*classis Britannica*), the Rhine (*classis Germania*), the Danube (*classis Pannonica* to the west and *classis Moesica* to the east), the Black Sea (*classis Pontica*), off the coast of Syria (*classis Syriaca*), et cetera. These

provincial fleets were commanded by more junior *praefecti*, responsible to their respective provincial governors.

33. Tacitus *Historiae* 1.5.1, Plutarch *Galba* 8, cf. Cassius Dio 63.27.2b.

34. Tacitus *Historiae* 1.35. The praetorians were probably given the usual harangue, consisting of threats and pleading, and it is not difficult for us to imagine Sabinus' baritone ringing out across the parade ground of *castra praetoria*: 'You will all receive your reward. All of you.' When all duties have been attended to, soldiers turn their attention to the things of interest to all soldiers, namely the three Rs – rations, remuneration, and recreation.

35. Tacitus *Historiae* 1.5.

36. Ibid. 1.30.2.

37. Cassius Dio 63.3.4.

38. According to Cassius Dio (63.29.6), however, Galba effectively accepted the imperial power, titles or not, when he met a senatorial deputation at Narbo (Narbonne) in July.

39. E.g. *RIC* I Galba: 24, 39, cf. 237, 275, 370, etc. (LIBERTAS PVBLICA, 'Liberty of the State').

40. E.g. ibid. 2, 26, 41, 161.

41. E.g. ibid. 207, 209, 211, 214.

42. Suetonius *Galba* 9.2, cf. Plutarch *Galba* 4.4. The elder Pliny, on the other hand, describes Vindex himself as a 'restorer of liberty' (*adsertor libertatis*, *Historia Naturalis* 20.57.160).

43. *Res Gestae Divi Augusti* 1.1.

44. E.g. *RIC* I Galba: 7, 8. This coin issue recalls a *denarius* of Brutus, which was struck after Caesar's assassination, which shows a *pilleus* and two daggers, and bears the slogan EID(ibvs) MAR(tiis) ('The Ides of March').

45. Two passages in Tacitus (*Histories* 1.11.2, *Africa ac legiones in ea* – 'Africa and its legions' – and 2.97.2, *In Africa legio cohortesque delectae a Clodio Macro* – 'In Africa, the legion, and the auxiliary infantry levied by Clodius Macer') make it certain that a second legion existed temporarily in Africa.

46. *RIC* I Civil Wars: 5–6, 12, 19–20. In fact, Clodius Macer issued a series of *denarii* paying tribute to both his legions. These silver coins are extremely rare today, about eighty-five are known to exist, of which only twenty bear his portrait bust.

47. Ibid. 1–4, 7–11.

48. Meaning 'by the decree of the Senate', indicating that body's responsibility for the issue of the coins, e.g. ibid. 6, 15, 17, 20, 31, etc.

49. Ibid. 32–42. Officially, as the emperor's representative in Africa, Clodius Macer was *legatus Augusti propraetore Africae*.

50. Clodius Macer surely had the backing of the rich landowners, six of which reputedly owned half of Africa Proconsularis (Pliny *Historia Naturalis* 18.35).

51. Plutarch *Galba* 13.3.

52. In Latin: *domini minoris*, Tacitus *Histories* 1.11.2.

53. Ibid. 1.7.1.

54. Op. cit., Suetonius *Galba* 11.1, Plutarch *Galba* 15.2.

55. In Latin: *magistra libidinum Neronis*, Tacitus *Historiae* 1.73.1.

56. In Greek: `epitropeían tìn perì `esthêta, Cassius Dio 62.12.4.

57. Tacitus *Historiae* 1.73.1.

58. Her husband was Sextus Traulus Montanus, who may well have been related in some way to the handsome young *eques* of the same name, whom Messalina made her lover for one night (Tacitus *Annales* 11.36.2). Following her death (AD 48), he was executed. Anyway, olive oil amphorae recovered from Ptju-*Poetovio* bear stamps with her name – [C] AL(viae) CRISPINILLAE – or Calvia and Traulus Montanus together – TRAVL(I) ET CRIS[PINILLAE] (*ILS* 8574a–b, *CIL* iii 12020.7, 14371.7). Incidentally, Ptju-*Poetovio* was the Pannonian home of *legio XIII Gemina*.

59. Tacitus *Historiae* 1.73.1.
60. Morgan 2000: 467–8.
61. In Latin: *omnium consensu capax imperii nisi imperasset*, Tacitus *Historiae* 1.49.2.
62. For the theme of Galba as a disciplinarian, see ibid. 1.18.2, 1.23.2, 1.35.2, Plutarch *Galba* 26.2, Suetonius *Galba* 19.2, Cassius Dio 63.6.2.
63. Tacitus *Historiae* 1.5.3, Plutarch *Galba* 18.2, Suetonius *Galba* 16.1, Cassius Dio 63.3.3. The colleague of Ofonius Tigellinus, Nymphidius Sabinus, had promised the praetorians 7,500 *denarii* per man for their deserting Nero for Galba (Plutarch *Galba* 2.2). This was a small fortune when you consider an ordinary guardsman was receiving 750 *denarii* per year in pay, which in itself was three times the 225 *denarii* a legionary was earning. The Praetorian Guard, it must be noted, were recruited almost entirely from 'Etruria and Umbria or ancient Latium and the old Roman colonies' (Tacitus *Annales* 4.5.5). This restriction remained in force down to the time of the *Historiae*, for we find Otho addressing the praetorians as 'sons of Italy, the true youth of Rome' (*Italiae alumni Romana verè juventus*, ibid. *Historiae* 1.84). A modern study has suggested that at the turn of the second century Italy (as a whole) still provided 86.3 per cent of these soldiers (Passerini 1939: 141–89).
64. The soldiers themselves offer us the best testimony for the impact of Galba's rigorous régime on the Rhine when they sang the jingle, *disc miles militare, Galba est non Gaetulicus* ('learn to be a soldier, soldier / don't make a fuss / Galba is here / not Gaetulicus', Suetonius *Galba* 6.2), Gaetulicus being the lax and very popular former legate governor.
65. In the saying of Goethe about reason becoming nonsense – '*Vernunft wird Unsinn*' (*Faust*, part 1, line 1653) – this same thought is expressed about the impersonal Zeus of the historical dialectic.
66. Suetonius *Galba* 8.1. An *aureus* was a gold coin worth twenty-five *denarii*, so according to Suetonius' reckoning, Galba's pocket money was equivalent to 1,111 years' pay for a legionary. Tacitus, in a short obituary for Galba, has this to say of the emperor with regards to money: 'Other men's money he did not covet, with his own he was parsimonious, with that of the State avaricious' (*Historiae* 1.49.2).
67. Tacitus *Historiae* 1.37.3 (list of those liquidated apparently on Galba's orders, including Petronius Turpilianus, Fonteius Capito and Nymphidius Sabinus), Plutarch *Galba* 15.1, Suetonius *Galba* 14.1 (resentment against Galba), Tacitus *Historiae* 1.6 (sham trials).
68. Tacitus *Historiae* 1.48.
69. Suetonius *Galba* 22.1.
70. Tacitus *Historiae* 1.13.1, Suetonius *Galba* 14.2.
71. *RE* 89, cf. *PIR*² A 866.
72. Antonius Primus was expelled from the Senate for conspiring to forge a will with Valerius Fabianus, Vinicius Rufinus, and others, and was banished from Rome (Tacitus *Annales* 14.40.5, Cassius Dio 64.9.3).
73. Tacitus *Historiae* 2.86.2. Tacitus calls it so (ibid 2.86.1), in all probability to distinguish it from the older *legio VII Claudia pia fidelis*, but this appellation is not found on any surviving inscriptions. The *dies natalis* of *VII Galbiana* was 10 June AD 68 (*ILS* 9125), the day after Nero's suicide.
74. Caius Nymphidius Sabinus had certainly come a long way in his thirty-odd years. He was born around AD 35 the son of an imperial freedwoman, Nymphidia. Some speculate that his father was a certain Martianus, a gladiator, but Plutarch reports (*Galba* 9.1) there were also claims he was the bastard son of the emperor Caius Caligula.
75. Plutarch *Galba* 13.1. Normally, the Praetorian Guard were under the command of two senior officers, who were styled *praefecti praetorio* (Tacitus *Historiae* 1.46, 2.92).
76. Tacitus *Historiae* 1.20.
77. Suetonius *Galba* 12.1.
78. Tacitus *Historiae* 1.6, Suetonius *Galba* 12.2, Plutarch *Galba* 15.3, Cassius Dio 55.24.2.

79. The navy was not dissimilar to the *auxilia*. The rowers were generally free non-citizens, the captains often freedmen, and the admirals of the two great fleets, based at Misenum and Ravenna, equestrian. When it came to the sea soldiers, marines, they too were recruited from outside Italy (e.g. Tacitus *Historiae* 3.12.1), enjoyed inferior pay and service conditions than legionaries, and were glad to be incorporated in a legion if the opportunity presented itself (e.g. ibid. 3.50.3). Grave stele show us that seamen of the Roman navy called themselves *milites* (soldiers), *milites classiarii* (fleet soldiers), *propugnatores* (defenders), or *remiges* (rowers), rather than *nautae* (sailors). See Starr 1960.

80. Suetonius *Galba* 12.2, Plutarch *Galba* 15.3–4 (though he does not mention the act of decimation), cf. Tacitus *Historiae* 1.6.2, 37.2.

81. Tacitus *Historiae* 1.36.4, cf. 31.2, 37.2, 87.1, 2.11.3. When one thinks of this 'nautical' legion it is easy to imagine the greater part of its first recruits as being slightly damaged, that is to say, they had lost minor parts of their bodies through the perils of naval life: a bit of ear or nose, a few fingers or toes, et cetera, et cetera. Anyway, despite its rather shaky start and modest origins, *legio I Adiutrix* went on to have a long and successful career. For instance, after the murder of Pertinax in AD 193 – twenty years previously the emperor had been *legatus legionis* of *I Adiutrix* – the legate governor of Pannonia Superior, Septimius Severus, was proclaimed emperor by the legions of the Danube, backed by those of the Rhine. Our legion was among his staunchest supporters and a sizable *vexillatio* took part in his march on Rome against Didius Iulianus, another candidate for the throne. The situation was not dissimilar to the military crisis of AD 69. We do know of one member of the legion at this particular time, a certain Aurelius Surus. His grave stele (Istanbul, Arkeoloji Müzesi, inv. 5826 T), dated AD 210–215, bears an inscription (Campbell 37) informing us that he was a *bucinator* in *legio I Adiutrix pia fidelis*, having served for eighteen years he died age forty – he perhaps joined the legion around AD 194/5, the time Septimius Severus was in Syria just prior to his Parthian campaign. The inscription also tells us that the grave stele was put up by his comrade and heir, Septimius Vibianus, a fellow Syrian. On it Surus is depicted holding the tool of his trade, the *bucina* or trumpet. As for the later award of *pia fidelis* (e.g. *ILS* 1029, 1061), this title was courtesy of Trajan in recognition of the legion's backing during the tense period leading up to Nerva's adoption of him as his heir and successor. The legion is last recorded for the year AD 444 (*Codex Iustiananus* 12.30.6, 52.3.2 with John Lydus *De magistratibus* 3.3), when it was stationed at Szöny-*Brigetio* in Pannonia.

82. On the soldiers' annual oath to the emperor as commander-in-chief, see Pliny *Epistulae* 10.52.

83. *Iliad* 14.98 Fagels.

84. Tacitus *Historiae* 1.41.2, Suetonius *Galba* 20.1.

85. So goes one version. Another version (Plutarch *Galba* 27.2) has it that it was a soldier of *legio XV Primigenia* from Xanten-*Vetera* who did the dirty deed, while Tacitus says 'about the actual murderer nothing is clearly know' (*Historiae* 1.41.3), a soldier of *XV Primigenia* being one of the possible candidates for this dubious honour.

86. Suetonius (*Galba* 20.2, cf. Tacitus *Historiae* 1.41.3, 44, Plutarch *Galba* 27.2–3) tells us that after Galba was dispatched a soldier decapitated him, but because the emperor was bald the soldier could not carry the head by its hair and instead simply stuffed it into his cloak. He then presented it to Otho, 'with his thumb thrust into the mouth', and the new emperor then gave the trophy to his servants who promptly put it on a spear and mocked it. A former freedman of Patrobius Neronianus purchased the head for a hundred gold pieces, only to hurl it to the ground at the exact spot where Patrobius had been murdered on Galba's orders. Unusually, head and corpse were eventually reunited in decent burial. Perhaps Suetonius has touched up the story of Galba's end with gory colours supplied by his own imagination, or indeed that of his father.

Chapter 3

1. Suetonius *Divus Claudius* 13.2.
2. Suetonius even goes so far as to hint not only that 'Nero and Otho were birds of a feather', but also 'that their relationship was decidedly unnatural' (*Otho* 2.2, cf. 12.1, Martial *Epigrammata* 6.32.2). Make of that what you will, but if Otho was truly a Nero-clone then the sexual relationship between the two was not only 'unnatural' but narcissistic too.
3. Tacitus *Annales* 13.46, cf. *Historiae* 1.13.
4. Suetonius *Otho* 3.2.
5. Galba had married Aemilia Lepida, the daughter of Manius Aemilius Lepidus (*cos.* AD 11), who bore him two sons, but both his wife and sons died and he never married again.
6. See Appendix 9.
7. Is Umbricius the *haruspex* (Tacitus *Historiae* 1.27.1, Pliny *Historia Naturalis* 10.6.19, Plutarch *Galba* 24.2) Umbricius the xenophobe of Juvenal's third satire? That gentleman, remember, was responsible for those immortal and immoral lines: 'For years now Syrian Orontes has poured its shit into our native Tiber / its lingo and manners, its flutes, its outlandish harps / with their traverse strings, its native tambourines, / and the whores who hang out round the racecourse' (*Satire* 3.62–5). The name is Etruscan, a people celebrated for their soothsaying skills, and more recent scholarship favours the idea that Juvenal's Umbricius was real enough though not the *haruspex* who warned Galba. There are those, however, who argue that Umbricius the xenophobe was merely a fictional *alter ego*.
8. Tacitus *Historiae* 1.27.1, cf. Suetonius *Galba* 19.1.
9. Suetonius *Galba* 4.1. Tacitus (*Annales* 6.20), on the other hand, puts these words into the mouth of Tiberius not Augustus.
10. Tacitus *Historiae* 1.13.3.
11. Plutarch *Otho* 3.2, Suetonius *Otho* 7.1, cf. Tacitus *Historiae* 1.78.2.
12. Tacitus *Historiae* 1.76, 2.6.1.
13. Ibid. 1.46.
14. Suetonius *Otho* 8.1. The name of the daughter (by Vitellius' second wife, Galeria Fundana) is unknown, but she would have been around fourteen at the time.
15. The battle of 14 April is variously called Bedriacum or Cremona; it should be named after the latter location not the first, the battle site being much closer to Cremona, and the name First Cremona (Second Cremona being the battle of 24/25 October) will be used from here on to avoid confusing the reader. I believe the confusion over names arises because Tacitus says Bedriacum 'is a village situated between Verona and Cremona, and has now acquired an ill-omened celebrity by two great days of disaster to Rome' (*Historiae* 2.23.1). Tacitus, it can be assumed, never bothered himself to visit the two battlefields in question, though in his defence he does say, quite rightly, that the distance from the first battleground to Bedriacum, the site of the Othonian camp, was 'very great' (ibid. 2.44.1).
16. Tacitus *Historiae* 2.47. According to Plutarch (*Otho* 18.2, cf. 15.4) this was the most honourable deed ever performed by Otho. It was certainly his last. Incidentally, a number of the letters burnt by Otho would have been from Vitellius himself, for during the period leading up to the battle the two of them exchanged frequent missives, some containing sexual abuse (*mox quasi rixantes stupra ac flagitia in unicem obiectauere*, Tacitus *Historiae* 1.74.1).
17. Suetonius *Otho* 11.2.
18. Tacitus *Historiae* 2.11.2, cf. 1.87.1.
19. Fabius Valens had taken the Col de Montgenèvre (1,854m), Hautes-Alpes, which, though not the lowest of the Alpine passes, is comparatively sheltered and easy. This is the watershed pass Pompey used making his way to Iberia in 77 BC (Sallust *Historiae* 2.98) and Caesar used hotfooting it to Gaul in 58 BC (Caesar *Bellum Gallicum* 1.10.3–5). Gibbon (*Decline & Fall*, vol. I, chap. XIV, p. 314, n. 1) had Hannibal go this way. In the meantime, Caecina Alienus had taken the Col du Grand Saint-Bernard (2,469m), which in summer provided the quickest

communication between Rome and Rhine (Strabo 4.6.7). On 20 May 1800 First Consul Napoléon, as he then was, swept over the Alps into Italy, using this very pass, astride a sturdy grey mule and wearing a simple grey waistcoat. 'We have fallen like a thunderbolt,' he wrote four days later to his brother Joseph (*Correspondance*, vol. VI, no. 4836, p. 308). On 14 June, at the Piedmontese village of Marengo, he was to gain what turned out to be the most decisive victory of his career, a battle that he should have lost. This battle opposed 28,000 French soldiers against 31,000 Austrian soldiers under the command of General Mélas. At first dominated, the French had to retreat nearly twelve kilometres. Mélas believing victory was assured left the command to a subordinate and retired to Alessandria. The adversary's *faux pas* thus allowed Napoléon to concentrate his forces. The following year he had himself painted by Jacques-Louis David riding a white charger through the snows of the Col du Grand Saint-Bernard (Napoléon commissioned four versions, with David adding a fifth).

20. Tacitus *Historiae* 1.68. Though this tribe had once been famous for its fighting prowess (Caesar *Bellum Gallicum* 1.1.4), the Helvetii had long since gone soft through the so-called benefits of Roman comforts such as baths and banquets (cf. ibid. *Agricola* 21).
21. Tacitus *Historiae* 2.11.1. Tacitus of course is including *legio XIIII Gemina Martia Victrix*, which had originally come from Britannia, in his reckoning here, the legions of Dalmatia and Pannonia being one (*XI Claudia pia fidelis*) and two (*VII Galbiana, XIII Gemina*) respectively.
22. Tacitus *Historiae* 2.43.2.
23. Ibid. 2.32.4, cf. 2.66.1.
24. Ibid. 2.46.3, 85.1.
25. Ibid. 2.31.
26. Plutarch *Otho* 8.1.
27. Tacitus *Historiae* 2.24.2.
28. Whence the plural the Castors, *ad Castores*. The Dioscuri (Greek *Disokouri*) were, among other things, protectors of travellers and horsemen.
29. Tacitus *Historiae* 2.26.2.
30. Ibid. 2.32.
31. Of course there is nothing in the world as stirring as a parade of well-drilled soldiers, even for those of a pacific disposition, but soldiers with purely ceremonial duties in imperial capitals cannot be a model in anything but drill and turnout. And besides, endless drill and turnout simply deprives young men of their personalities. If the personal bodyguard to the emperor was to be a model of how to fight it had to be a fighting body. The Praetorian Guard were such an outfit. Once in the field with Otho, they soon threw off the fetters of the parade ground and, after a week or so of 'yomping', were equal to their opponents from the Rhine. 'Yomping' – calling it such is of course modern and has been used here only for the sake of convenience – transformed the guardsmen from the elegant *urbani milites* that went through neat evolutions in the *castra praetoria* into the rough-and-ready, round shouldered objects that route marched fully laden from Rome to Cremona. At First Cremona the praetorians may have been lacking in experience, but they were self-confident, highly trained, passionately devoted to the emperor's person and as rapacious as vultures.
32. Tacitus *Historiae* 2.37. However, it must be said that Tacitus merely reports this as a rumour, he himself dismissing the idea because he believed the soldiery had too much to gain from war to desire peace.
33. Tacitus *Historiae* 2.66.1.
34. Ibid. 2.33.
35. I have always wondered about the use of axes (Tacitus *Historiae* 2.42 clearly says *securis* here, a general Latin term for axe or hatchet) by the legionaries at First Cremona, an unusual weapon for them to wield in battle – more often used for hewing wood or even for animal sacrifice (e.g. Suetonius *Galba* 18.1). Perhaps they were carried by those ex-marines that now

made up the rank and file of *I Adiutrix*, an axe being a handy weapon for sea soldier during a boarding action.

36. In Latin: *circumventi plurium adcursa quartadecimani*, ibid. 2.43.1

37. Ibid. 2.53.

38. Fields 2008A: 37–42.

39. Vegetius *Epitoma rei militaris* 1.12.

40. Here it is important to note that the Roman style of fighting required less room to execute, which resulted in a much tighter tactical formation. In practical terms this meant when up against, for example, Celts, who required a fair amount of room to swing their long slashing swords effectively, at least two legionaries could face one Celt on the field of battle.

41. Tacitus *Annales* 14.36.3.

42. Connolly (1991) suggests that the crouch stance was a standard fighting position, but Goldsworthy (1998: 173) believes this was impractical, as it negates the protection of the *scutum* and places great strain on the left arm. However, by adopting a *very slight* crouch the legionary not only keeps the full protection of his shield but also gains an optimum position of balance. This type of fighting stance is clearly seen in the Mainz *principia* relief (Landesmuseum Mainz) showing two legionaries fighting in close order one behind the other, the front man hunkered down behind his *scutum* with his *gladius* drawn.

43. Adamklissi Tropaeum Traiani, Metope XVIII. As a matter of interest, the Romans were glad, it seems, to acknowledge as worthy foes the trousered and bearded Dacians, commemorating them in literature and in the lively sculptures that encircle the Adamklissi Tropaeum Traiani and the spiral up Trajan's Column.

44. *Iliad* 13.658 Fagels. Intra-abdominal infection, or secondary peritonitis, was first thoroughly described by Hippokrates of Kos (b. *c.* 460 BC). Secondary peritonitis is an inflammation (irritation) of the peritoneum (the membrane lining the abdominal cavity) caused by another condition, most commonly the spread of an infection from the digestive organs or bowels. Hippokrates describes (*Epidemics* 5.61) the case of a man from Aenea, struck in the upper back by a javelin at Delos, presumably during an athletic contest. Initially there was 'no pain in the wound', but by the third day the patient was suffering 'pain in the stomach'. The following day the pain, 'like a thunderclap', had moved towards the testicles. Lack of bowl movements, vomiting and loss of consciousness were the obvious symptoms, the patient dying after five days.

45. Engels, F., 1877. *Anti-Dühring*, part II, chap. III, published in *MECW*, vol. 25, p.153.

46. In Latin: *noscentes inter se*. These three innocuous words surely bring into sharp focus the notion that a civil war is an internal conflict between two societal camps, who share the same national identity. Whereas the Misenum sailors of *legio I Adiutrix* had never set eyes on the legionaries of *legio XXI Rapax*, who had been long stationed in Windisch-*Vindonissa*, Germania Superior, the contestants in the centre had probably trained side by side. The Othonian praetorians – substantially the praetorians of Galba and Nero – must surely have met or worked alongside those handsome fellows of *legio I Italica* (nee Nero's Phalanx of Alexander the Great) when both formations were training for Nero's Caucasus campaign in AD 67. Many will have recognized a comrade or two in the enemy ranks. It is perhaps Lucan who encapsulates the special horror of a Roman civil war when he refers to '*pila* threatening *pila*' (*Pharsalia* 1.7).

47. A body of gladiators from Rome commanded by the consul designate Titus Flavius Sabinus (a son of the city prefect of the same name?) had crossed the Po on galleys of the *classis Ravennas* to deliver a diversionary attack on the Vitellians from the south. As they left the safety of the riverbank, the gladiators were pounced upon by the Batavi under Alfenus Varus. In an earlier passage (*Historiae* 2.11.2), Tacitus tells us that 2,000 gladiators were included in the army of Otho.

48. Tacitus *Historiae* 2.42–43 Penguin edition, with revisions.

49. Very little had changed in this respect from the days of the middle Republic, for Polybios (1.37.7–10), a credible eyewitness, saw the Romans as rather old-fashioned in their straightforward and open approach to warfare, commenting that as a race they tended to rely instinctively on 'brute force' (*bía* in his Greek) when making war. The Romans had an excellent attack army; its whole advantage was attack and its weapons were weapons of attack. So for the Romans, as for the city-state Greeks before them, close-quarter confrontation was decisive and the objective was to bring that about as quickly as possible. Modern western armies are composed of men who are simply not capable of this duty, lacking either the stamina or right frame of mind to throw themselves enthusiastically into hand-to-hand combat. Besides, nowadays hand-to-hand combat is usually a sign that something has gone way wrong in the plan. In modern, high-tech warfare, the whole idea is to destroy your opponent before he gets even close enough to grapple with you. In general, as indeed during most periods before, the bayonet is used far more frequently in a domestic rather than a military context. It is used from time to time certainly, as a species of entrenching tool, but much more often it's is to be seen in the soldier's 'kitchen', opening, say, a tin of steak and kidney pudding or some similar article of Composite Rations (Rat-Packs or Compo) to be reheated prior to consumption by the owner of the weapon. Experience is a great thing and every soldier knows about ten such tricks. In truth, there have been very few actions in history when the combatants actually fought each other with the bayonet; either the attackers recoil before matters came to hand-to-hand fighting or the mere glint of an enemy bayonet caused the defenders to run away. To finish on a more personal note, I often said to my men that if I ever gave them the command to fix bayonets, then I have failed them as their leader – to fix bayonet and lead the attack may be the bravest of personal actions, but in my book it is not the most laudable. Martial virtue consists in finding the most efficient way of doing the job, not in the *beau geste* of a bayonet charge. Cold steel against high-tech weapons may be magnificent, but it is not war. Those who have been there, if only once, will understand, and those who have not can never be my judges. Even so, as General Sir Garnet Wolseley (later Field Marshal Viscount Wolseley) once said: 'The more helpless the position in which an officer finds his men, the more it is his bounden duty to stay and share their fortune, whether for good or ill' (in his review of the Court Martial findings of Lieutenant Harwood, February 1880).
50. Appian *Bellum civilia* 4.137 (Philippi, 42 BC).
51. Tacitus *Historiae* 2.42.4.
52. Ardant du Picq 1946: 90.
53. Ibid. 1946: 5.
54. Suetonius *Otho* 10.1.
55. Vegetius *Epitoma rei militaris* 1.13, quoting the lost (apart from a few fragments) *De re militari* (fr. 3 Jordan) of the elder Cato.
56. Plutarch *Otho* 18.2. A sentiment marvellously echoed by that master of the epigram, Martial, in a prim and proper testimonial: 'When civil still in the balance lay / And mincing Otho might have won the day, / Bloodshed too costly did he spare his land, / And pierced his heart with an unfaltering hand. // Caesar to Cato yields, while both drew breath: / Greater than both is Otho in his death' (*Epigrammata* 6.32). So Otho, until the moment of his selfless sacrifice, remains the antithesis of that great hero of Roman Stoicism, the younger Cato. Compare, for instance, Plutarch's parallel details in these two 'good' suicides (*Cato minor* 68–71, *Otho* 15–17).
57. Tacitus *Historiae* 2.11.3, cf. Suetonius *Otho* 12.1, where the author notes Otho 'was almost as fastidious about his appearance as a woman. His entire body had been depilated, and a toupee covered his practically bald head … He shaved every day, and since boyhood had always used a poultice of moist bread to prevent the growth of his beard'. In the speech he puts into the mouth of Piso Licinianus, Tacitus poses the question about Otho: 'Shall he earn

that empire now by his manner and his gait, or by those womanish adornments?' (*Historiae* 1.30.1). Otho's apparent womanishness is most graphically illustrated by Tacitus' friend, the social satirist Juvenal (*Satire* 2.99–109 Green), where he also describes Otho as Nero's *pathicus*, his passive homosexual partner. The phrase 'new annals and recent histories' (*novis annalibus atque recenti historia*, line 102) is very likely a not too subtle advertisement for the *Annales* and *Historiae*.

58. Tacitus *Historiae* 2.50.1. In an earlier passage Tacitus says 'it was by his death Otho gained high renown, as Vitellius incurred by his the foulest infamy' (ibid. 2.31.1).

59. Here we should note Seneca's recipe for survival in Nero's court, namely 'swallow insults and express gratitude' (*On Anger* 2.33.2, cf. Tacitus *Annales* 14.56). I suppose in a good cause, such as staying alive, hypocrisy becomes virtue, but then virtue is often just exhausted vices.

60. Tacitus *Historiae* 1.22.1. Martial (*Epigrammata* 6.32.2), who admired Otho a great deal, calls him effeminate (*mollis*) too, while Plutarch (*Galba* 19.2) likened him to the archetypal effeminate warrior Paris.

61. Tacitus describes Otho in Lusitania as 'a pleasure loving man when idle, and self-restrained when in power' (*Annales* 13.46.3). Though descended from an ancient Etruscan clan, Otho was not of the nobility, his grandfather having been the first member of the family to enter the Senate, his father the first to hold the rank of consul (AD 33).

Chapter 4

1. Of course, it is more than likely that Galba was afraid of the intentions of the ambiguous Verginius Rufus and thence had him come to Rome. On becoming emperor, Otho, anxious to conciliate the favour of the Rhine soldiers, raised him to the consulship for a second time.

2. Tacitus *Historiae* 1.52.1, cf. Suetonius *Vitellius* 7.1.

3. Tacitus *Historiae* 1.55.2. In addition to its other standards, the eagle (*aquila*) being the most familiar, each legion carried an *imago imperatoris*, bearing the portrait of the reigning emperor as a reminder to his soldiers of their oath and loyalty. This standard was carried on a separate pole by the *imaginifer*, and Tacitus (*Annales* 1.39.4) clearly implies that the *imago* shared the same honours as the *aquila*, and it too was under the personal care of the *primus pilus*, the legion's most senior centurion, the 'top soldier'.

4. Tacitus *Historiae* 1.56.3.

5. *Contra* Ash 1999: 108–10.

6. Tacitus *Historiae* 1.57.1.

7. Suetonius *Galba* 6.2–3.

8. Ibid. *Vitellius* 8.2.

9. Plutarch *Galba* 22.1–2, Suetonius *Galba* 16.2. These seven legions had been in the two Germanies for at least twenty-eight years, indeed one, *XV Primigenia*, had been based in Germania Inferior for fifty-nine years. It is quite obvious that the men of these units had formed local attachments of every kind.

10. According to Tacitus (*Historiae* 1.53.1), Caecina Alienus' personal presence was commanding, being as he was tall in stature, bonny in person, and upright in gait. He also possessed the gift of oratory, and was ambitious. Little wonder, therefore, he was popular with his men.

11. Besides the legate (*legatus legionis*), the other senior officers of a legion were six military tribunes, one of senatorial rank (*tribunus militum laticlavius*, 'with the broad purple strip on the toga') the others equestrians (*tribuni militum angusticlavii*, 'with the narrow purple strip on the toga'), and sixty (later fifty-nine) centurions. In the hierarchy of command the senatorial tribune always ranked next to the legate, by virtue of his noble birth, and thus acted as the second-in-command of the legion. He served a short term as tribune before he was twenty-five years of age, prior to entering the Senate as a quaestor, a junior magistrate who administered financial matters in Rome or out in one of the provinces. He could look forward to receiving full command of a legion later in his senatorial career.

12. Tacitus *Historiae* 1.56.1.
13. Ibid. 1.56, 59.1.
14. Ibid. 1.56.
15. In Germania Inferior, Neuss-*Novaesium* was garrisoned by *XVI Gallica* and in Germania Superior, Windisch-*Vindonissa* by *XXI Rapax*. Anyway, as the result of the rebellion in AD 89 of Lucius Antonius Saturninus, legate governor of Germania Superior, who induced the two legions (*XIIII Gemina Martia Victrix*, *XXI Rapax*) based at Mainz-*Mogontiacum* to support his cause, Domitianus issued a regulation forbidding in future more than one legion to occupying the same camp (Suetonius *Domitianus* 7.4). Thus, the two legions at Mainz-*Mogontiacum* were separated, and the fortress cut to one legion (*XIIII Gemina Martia Victrix*), and in general fortresses were reduced in size (*c.* 20–25 ha) to house a single legion. The one exception to Domitianus' empire-wide regulation was Egypt, where the two legions that formed its garrison (*III Cyrenaica*, *XXII Deiotariana*), were concentrated in one legionary camp at Sidi Gaber-*Nikopolis* just outside Alexandria, the second city in the empire for size and wealth, continuing to do so till at least AD 119 when one was transferred to allow the reinforcement of the garrison of ever troublesome Iudaea.
16. Tacitus *Historiae* 1.61. In some modern accounts *XXII Primigenia* is counted as a third full legion, *but* Tacitus only talks of two full legions, *V Alaudae* to Fabius Valens and *XXI Rapax* to Caecina Alienus.
17. Tacitus *Historiae* 1.61.2. Both these figures given by Tacitus are in all probability inflated and perhaps should be regarded as the approximate total strength of the Rhine army, viz. roughly 5,000 men per legion plus an equal number of auxiliary troops. Vitellius certainly did not want to strip the Rhine frontier of all its troops.
18. Tacitus *Historiae* 1.50.1.
19. Ibid. 1.64.1.
20. Ibid. 3.56.2, Vitellius is *ignarus militiae*.
21. Ibid. 2.68.2.
22. Ibid. 2.70.1. Usually burying the dead at the earliest opportunity was a priority, but at First Cremona, as Tacitus tells us, though the body of the legate Orfidius Benignus was recovered and cremated with full honours, only a 'few were buried by their friends; the multitude that remained were left above ground' (ibid. 2.45.4). As Toynbee notes: 'Soldier: killed on the battlefield were collectively cremated … or buried. The funeral expenses were paid by their comrades' (1971: 55). Later, by the turn of the second century if not before, one of the deductions from a soldier's pay would be a standard contribution to the burial-club organized by the standard-bearer of the soldier's century (Vegetius *Epitoma rei militaris* 2.22, cf. Onasander *Stratêgikos* 36.1–2). Should he die during service, this would then cover the cost of a basic funeral.
23. Tacitus *Historiae* 2.89.1.
24. Ibid. 1.62.2. This designation had first been awarded (posthumously) to Nero Drusus, the father of Claudius, because he had, allegedly, conquered Germania.
25. Tacitus *Historiae* 2.59.3, Cassius Dio 65.1.2a, cf. Plutarch *Galba* 22.7. The unfortunate child, after the fall of his father, was to be hunted down and liquidated on the orders of Caius Licinius Mucianus with the view of removing all dynastic obstacles to the elevation of Vespasianus (Tacitus *Historiae* 4.80.1).
26. Tacitus *Historiae* 2.52–53.
27. Ibid. 2.63. Dolabella had been banished from Rome by Otho not because of any crime, but 'for suspicion by his ancient name and by his relationship to Galba' (ibid. 1.88.1, cf. 2.63.1).
28. Ibid. 2.64.1.
29. *IGR* III 4, 37.
30. Tacitus *Historiae* 1.59.2.
31. Ibid. 3.39.1.
32. Ibid. 3.39.2.

33. Ibid. 2.51.1.
34. In Latin: *manebat admiratio viri et fama, sed oderant ut fastiditi*, ibid. 2.68.4.
35. Ibid. 2.66.1.
36. Ibid. 2.67, 3.44.1.
37. In AD 66 a former *primus pilus* of *XIIII Gemina Martia Victrix*, one Marcus Vettius Valens, set up a dedication at Ariminum (Rimini), presumably his home town, which recorded he had been decorated in the '*bello Britan(nico) torquibus armillis phaleris*' (*CIL* xi 395 = *ILS* 2648 = Campbell 90), apparently confirming the fact that the legion had been transferred to Italy. Vettius Valens had started his military career as an ordinary ranker in the Praetorian Guard, and having reached the rank of *primus pilus* (in two legions, *VI Victrix* and *XIIII Gemina Martia Victrix*) earned the right to be an *eques*. As in Caesar's day the post was normally a one-year appointment (Dobson 1974: 411), but under the Principate it automatically elevated the holder to the *ordo equester*. Invariably, therefore, a *primus pilus* went on to become *praefectus castrorum*, camp prefect, his last post before retirement. However, a man could be posted back to a legion to hold the position for a second term, viz. *primus pilus bis*. This was obviously what happened to Vettius Valens. Anyway, as his career inscription reports, Vettius Valens was currently serving Nero as the *procurator provinciae* of Lusitania. The procurator of a province, drawn, unlike its governor, from the equestrian order, was appointed by and directly responsible to the emperor, not the governor, a potent cause of friction within the provincial administration but means by which the emperor could keep tabs on his governor. The governor may have led the army of occupation, but the procurator, dealing as he did with all financial matters, paid the occupying soldiers. In that case, Vettius Valens must have been well acquainted with the current governor of Lusitania, Otho.
38. See, for example, the simple grave stele (Saintes, musée archéologique, inv. 49.475) of one Lucis Autius, son of Lucius, found in 1855 at Camp d'Aulney, north of Saintes (*département* of Charente Maritime), and dated to just after the Gallic revolt of AD 21/2. Born in Forum Iulii (Fréjus), Gallia Narbonensis, Autius was a legionary of *XIIII Gemini*. He died age thirty-five having served for fifteen years. His epitaph (*CIL* xiii 1121) reads: L(vcivs) AVTIVS L(vcivs) | ANI(ensi tribv) FOR(o) IVLI(i) MIL(es) | LEG(ionis) XIIII GEM(inae) ANNO | XXXV STI(pendorivm) XV H(ic) | S(itvs) E(st).
39. In Latin: *potissimos*, Tacitus *Historiae* 2.11.1.
40. On his career inscription (*CIL* xi 395 = *ILS* 2648 = Campbell 90), the procurator Marcus Vettius Valens reports '[*pr(imo)p(ilo)*] *leg(ionis) XIIII Gem(inae) Mar(tiae) Victr(icis)* ', which just happens to be the first attestation of the legion's full titles.
41. In Latin: *longa illis erga Neronem fides et erecta in Othonem studia*, Tacitus *Historiae* 2.11.1.
42. While stationed in Britannia eight *cohortes* of Batavi had been attached to *legio XIIII Gemina Martia Victrix*, and had departed with it in AD 66 as part of Nero's planned expedition to the Caucasus (Tacitus *Historiae* 1.6.4, 59.1, 66.2, 2.27.2, 4.12.3, 15.1). All Rome's eastern adventures had the same purposeless on-and-on to-and-fro adventure, unless very seldom, so seldom as almost to be never, an emperor fully committed himself to give purpose and direction to the flux. Trajan was such one, but he died before he could give full proof of his full genius. This much reminds us of Kipling's 'The Ballad of East and West' (1889): 'And the end of the fight is a tombstone white / with the name of the late deceased / And the epitaph drear: "A fool lies here / who tried to hustle the East".'
43. Tacitus *Historiae* 1.59.2, 3.44.1, cf. 2.86.4. Also, while his two lieutenants descended upon Italy and fought First Cremona, Vitellius was assembling *vexillationes* summoned from the three legions then stationed in Britannia (*II Augusta, VIIII Hispana, XX Valeria Victrix*), totalling some 8,000 men (ibid. 2.57.2), and these may possibly have been 'the flower of the army of Britannia' with Vitellius when he was in Italy (ibid. 3.1.2), and certainly it was these veteran *vexillationes* that formed the centre of the Vitellian army at Second Cremona. The only actual unit from Britannia known to have taken part in the first battle is a single *cohors* of Britons in the army of Caecina Alienus (ibid. 1.70.3).

44. Cassius Dio 64.6.2, Tacitus *Historiae* 2.60.1.
45. Suetonius *Vitellius* 10.1.
46. Tacitus *Historiae* 2.93.2. The praetorian cohorts, *cohortes praetoriae*, originally served generals in the late Republic as a small but select unit of soldiers acting as a bodyguard. For example, at the battle of Forum Gallorum (14 April 43 BC) the proconsular Marcus Antonius had two *cohortes praetoriae*. It was Augustus, however, who created at the very beginning of his reign the permanent Praetorian Guard (Cassius Dio 53.11.5), the collective name we commonly use for the *cohortes praetoriae*, initially nine in number (*cohortes* I to VIIII). For some time they continued to be a real bodyguard, inasmuch as Augustus kept them under direct control, but in 2 BC the command was entrusted to two *praefecti praetorio*, who were regularly of equestrian rank. In a latter part of his reign, Augustus increased the number of *cohortes praetoriae* from nine to twelve (*cohortes* I to XII), and reduced it to nine (*cohortes* I to IX) again by re-designating three as *cohortes urbanae* in AD 12 (*cohortes* X to XII). This according to Tacitus (*Annales* 4.2.1, 5.1, cf. Campbell 96) was the number in AD 23 when Lucius Aelius Seianus (Sejanus) concentrated them in the *castra praetoria* on the Viminal hill in Rome – sensibly, Augustus had not allowed more than three *cohortes praetoriae* in the city at any one time. Inscriptions show that the *cohortes praetoriae* were back up to twelve by the reign of Caius Caligula or that of Claudius, while the number of *cohortes urbanae* had been increased from three to six then seven. The task of the *cohortes urbanae* is defined by Suetonius: they had to be 'the guard of the city' just as the *cohortes praetoriae* were the 'emperor's guard' (*Divus Augustus* 49.1). They were basically a police force. In our period of study they were answerable to the city prefect, *praefectus urbi*, a person of senatorial rank, and housed in the same camp, the *castra praetoria*, as the Praetorian Guard. Like the praetorian cohorts, the urban cohorts were commanded by tribunes. Other urban cohorts were brought into being, and based at Puteoli (*cohors XV*) and Ostia (*cohors XVII*), to protect the grain warehouses, at Carthage (*cohors XIII*), the collection point for African grain before its shipment to Italy, and at Lugdunum (*cohors I*), to protect the imperial mint there.
47. Tacitus *Historiae* 2.93.2.
48. Ibid. 2.94.1.
49. As well as receiving three times as much pay as the legionaries, the praetorians enjoyed better conditions of service, serving for only sixteen years, promotion was that much quicker, and receiving greater rewards on retirement (legionaries received 12,000 *sestertii*, praetorians 20,000 *sestertii*). Furthermore, service in Rome could be more pleasant than military duties in a remote province close to the enemy. The praetorians lived on the fat of the land, and for them there was always wine, women and song during their off-duty hours.
50. There is the grave stele of Caius Vedennius Moderatus whose lengthy inscription (*CIL* vi 2725 = *ILS* 2034 = Campbell 63) informs us that he served ten years in *legio XVI Gallica* before transferring to *cohors VIIII praetoria* in which he served for eight years before being honourably discharged. He may have been one of the Rhine legionaries who were rewarded by Vitellius with a reassignment to the new, enlarged Praetorian Guard. If so, then he survived (unlike his former legion) the drama of the régime change to continue his military service as a praetorian under the emperor, Vespasianus. His inscription implies that the same emperor called him back to the 'colours' (*revocatus ab imperatore*), for Vedennius Moderatus re-enlisted as an *evocatus*. An *evocatus* would usually serve in a specialist rôle, and our man was to be no exception, serving a further twenty-three years as *architectus armamentarii imperatoris*, 'engineer in the emperor's armoury'. Thus, aged sixty or so, he finally retired from military service under Trajan in AD 100 (or thereabouts). His working life thus lasted forty-one years. The grave stele was found in Rome and is now housed in the Musei Vaticani.
51. Tacitus *Historiae* 2.67.1 Vespasianus urged the Danube legates to recruit praetorians hostile to Vitellius (ibid. 2.82.3, cf. 3.43.1).

52. E.g. Tacitus *Historiae* 2.62.1, 71.1, Suetonius *Vitellius* 13–14. Vitellius (b. AD 15) was the son of that famous consul of AD 34 Lucius Vitellius, who went on in the following year to command in the east as the legate governor of Syria. Vitellius had done very well out there, having surprised Artabanus III, the Parthian king, who was about to invade the province, by a forced march across the Euphrates – the boundary between Syria and Parthia. Caught on ground unfavourable for his mobile army, the Parthian king was obliged to sign a humiliating peace and give his sons up as hostages. On his return to Rome he gained a second consulship in AD 43 and a third in AD 47, finally capping his illustrious career by sharing the censorship with Claudius (he was a close friend of the emperor) in AD 48, the very same year his son was consul (Suetonius *Vitellius* 2.4). The trouble with Vitellius junior was that he suffered from all the inherent problems of having a celebrated father. There was a darker side to this fame too, for he was a consummate flatterer, setting the example, for instance, of recognizing Caius Caligula as a living god. Even those in Rome who believed his advancement not to his exploits but to his talent at flattery, intrigue and making himself popular at court. As the astute Tacitus pointed out: 'The man, I am aware, had a bad name at Rome, and many a foul story was told of him. But in government of provinces he acted with the virtue of ancient times' (*Annales* 6.32.4).
53. Josephus *Bellum Iudaicum* 4.651.
54. Kissinger, H., 1979. *The White House Years*, p. 1476.
55. Tacitus *Historiae* 2.89.3.
56. Philostratos *Vita Apollonii* 5.13, Tacitus *Historiae* 2.49.
57. Plutarch *Otho* 18.1.
58. Suetonius *Vitellius* 10.3. On this, see Morgan 1992.
59. Suetonius *Vitellius* 10.3. More than any other sensory recollection, it is the smell of a battlefield that lingers. In that truly memorable film, *Apocalypse Now* (1979), the havoc-wreaking Kilgore delivers those oft-(mis)quoted lines celebrating the unique chemical smell of napalm: 'I love the smell of napalm in the morning. You know, onetime we had a hill bombed, for twelve hours. When it was all over, I walked up. We didn't find one of 'em, not one stinkin' dink [derogatory term for the VC/NVA] body. The smell, you know that gasoline smell, the whole hill. Smelled like [sniffing, reflecting] victory. Some day this war's gonna end …' [strides away]. Of course, Lieutenant Colonel William 'Bill' Kilgore, 1st Squadron, 7th Air Cavalry Regiment commander and surfing buff, is a fictional character, albeit with nuances of the 'larger than life' General George S. Patton Jnr, but his napalm-glorifying remark rings true.
60. Tacitus *Historiae* 1.52.3. It is interesting to note that these two gentlemen are not at all mentioned by Suetonius, who is not interested in the complexities of Vitellius' meteoric but paradoxical rise to power. Likewise, although Plutarch does include them, they are noticeably absent from his description (*Galba* 22.3–5) of Vitellius' rise to power.
61. Suetonius *Vitellius* 3.2, 4.1. Caius Caligula had his own racing track, the *Caianum*, on his Vatican estate, and it was here that Vitellius suffered a spill when driving with the emperor, and had a permanent limp afterwards (ibid. 17.3).
62. In Latin: *deorum cibum*, Suetonius *Nero* 33.1. Though Suetonius claims the emperor was quoting a Greek proverb, Cassius Dio (61.35.4) imparts that the saying is original with Nero.
63. Since there was no intercourse between Rome and the Americas, the ancients were certainly unaware of the tomato and the potato, two staple commodities, which few in the West would now do without, and in the recent past the humble potato was for many, from Ireland to Siberia, the only staple food.
64. In Latin: *vinum vita est*, Petronius *Satyricon* 34.7. Almost universally known by this name since Fellini's film, Petronius' bawdy novel was probably originally called *Satyrica* or *Satyricon libri*.
65. The language of *De re coquinaria – On the Art of Cookery –* by one Apicius is 'vulgar' (perhaps more happily translated as 'vernacular') fourth-century popular Latin, which probably means

a cook rather than a noble wrote it. However, whoever he was he must have been highly regarded, because 'Apicius' was a nickname that meant something like gourmet. Tertullian wrote: '... just as artists name themselves after Erasistratus, philologists after Aristarcus and cooks after Apicius ...' (*Apologeticum* 3.6). So it looks as if our legendary Marcus Gavinus Apicius gave his name to cooks and gourmets, though we must be aware that there was an earlier namesake and fellow gastronome who lived in the nineties BC. Anyway, the cookbook itself slavishly describes the meals of the rich, to whom most of our information relates. The appearance of ostriches, peacocks, cranes and flamingos on their tables was largely due to the search for novelty. The book was composed not for the unflinching Stoic but for the Epicurean, perhaps even the hedonist, with the culinary resources of an empire to command. Apicius had access through Greek and Roman traders to the spice markets of southern Asia. Pepper, spikenard, cinnamon, ginger, nutmeg, cardamom, coriander, cumin, and cloves were transported by ship from India, Ceylon, the Spiceries (the Banda and Molucca island groups), and China with a frequency that was not to be matched until the voyages of the Portuguese caravels in the late fifteenth century. The drain on the imperial treasury was alarming, especially to conservatives like the elder Pliny who viewed the situation with distaste: 'At the lowest computation, India, China (Seres), and the Peninsula [of Arabia] carry off 100 million *sestertii* a year from our empire – such is the bill for our pleasure and our women' (*Historia Naturalis* 12.41.84). Pliny also provides prices for the various imported spices (Latin *species*, meaning a commodity of especial distinction or value), ginger (*zingiberi*), for example, being sold at six *denarii* a Roman pound (323 grams), long pepper (*piper longum*) at fifteen, white pepper (*piper album*) at seven, and black (*piper nigrum*) at four (ibid. 12.14.28). From a list of fifty-four items subject to import duty at Alexandria, twenty-three were spices from the Far East (The Alexandria Tariff, *Digesta* 39.4.16), and pepper, for instance, soon became the staple commodity of Roman trade with India. Over 90 per cent of the 478 recipes immortalized by Apicius call for costly imported spices, particularly pepper, which had supplanted the native but milder myrtle berry as the prime seasoning – Apicius frequently says 'sprinkle with pepper and serve'. In fact, by the end of the first century, the epithet 'Apicius' had already become a cliché for unlimited wealth (Martial *Epigrammata* 3.22, Juvenal *Satire* 11.2–3).

66. Seneca *Epistulae Morales* 87.3.
67. Petronius *Satyricon* 34.6. Romans greatly favoured the vineyards along the coast north of Neapolis, and it was here, on the slopes of Mount Falernus, Falernum was produced. It was a white wine with a relatively high alcohol content (15 per cent vol.). It was best drunk after ageing for ten to twenty years. Any older, and it gave the drinker a headache (Pliny *Historia Naturalis* 23.20, cf. 14.62–63). Readers of Plutarch's *Marcus Antonius* will recall that Quintus Dellius offended Cleopatra with the complaint 'that Antonius' friends were served sour wine, while at Rome Sarmentus, Caesar's little page (his *delicia*, as the Romans call it), drank Falernum' (59.4). This refers to Sarmentus, a former slave of Marcus Favonius, the loyal friend of Cato and Brutus executed after Philippi (Suetonius *Divus Augustus* 13.2), who was now serving Octavianus and whom enemies of Octavianus claimed to be his catamite (cf. Tacitus *Annales* 1.73.1).
68. See Appendix 5 for the Roman military diet.
69. Martial *Epigrammata* 5.78.
70. Suetonius *Divus Augustus* 74.1.
71. Ibid. 76.1.
72. Ibid. 77.1. The Raetian wine (*Raeticum*) that Augustus particularly liked came from the hills northwest of Verona (Pliny *Historia Naturalis* 14.67, cf. Martial *Epigrammata* 14.100), today's Valpolicello viticultural zone more or less, where the Octavii once had estates. The elder Cato praised Raetian wine (Servius *Commentary on the Georgics of Virgil* 2.95) and Strabo (4.6.8) confirms its reputation. On the other hand, Virgil, a native of these parts,

is studiously non-committal (*Georgics* 2.95–6). Raetian wine was matured in wooden vats treated with local pitch (Strabo 5.1.12, cf. Celsus *De medicina* 4.12.8). See Dalby 2000: 90.
73. Suetonius *Vitellius* 13.2.
74. Apicius *De re coquinaria* 4.2.133, 134.
75. Pliny *Historia Naturalis* 35.163. Tacitus reports that Vitellius, as emperor, 'is believed to have squandered nine hundred million *sestertii* in a very few months'(*Historiae* 2.95.3). Both these astronomical sums are found in Cassius Dio (64.3.2, 3) too, who adds that for his Shield of Minerva recipe Vitellius had a special vessel made of silver, which remained as a sort 'of votive offering, until Hadrian finally set eyes on it and melted it down' (ibid. 64.3.3).
76. In Latin: *patinarum paludes*, Pliny *Historia Naturalis* 35.164.
77. Cassius Dio 64.3.1.
78. Apicius *De re coquinaria* 5.3.189 and 193 (*pisam Vitellianam sive fabam* – peas or beans *à la* Vitellius), 8.7.371 (*porcellum Vitellianum* – Suckling pig *à la* Vitellius)
79. Suetonius *Vitellius* 16.1, cf. Tacitus *Historiae* 3.84.4.

Chapter 5
1. Cicero *De re publica* 3.23.35.
2. Suetonius *Vespasianus* 6.4.
3. Tacitus *Historiae* 2.77.3.
4. This unit had seen a little service at the end of Domitius Corbulo's Parthian campaign but lacked the experience of the other two legions in Iudaea. At twenty-seven years of age Titus was younger than most legionary legates and his appointment reflects the tradition of senators relying on family members to serve as their senior subordinates. Another of Vespasianus' subordinates was Marcus Ulpius Traianus, *legatus legionis* of *X Fretensis*. He was, of course, the father and namesake of the future emperor, Trajan.
5. Tacitus *Historiae* 2.1.1. Note, Tacitus makes Galba observe that 'the process of adoption will discover the best man' (ibid. 1.16.2). See Appendix 9.
6. Ibid. 2.4.1, cf. Suetonius *Titus* 5.1. A marble altar dedicated by Titus to Paphian Aphrodite, found in the temple precincts in 1888, bears testimony to his visit. A more curious relic of his visit, on the other hand, is a sardonyx gem found in the so-called House of Theseus at Nea Paphos. Engraved with an *aquila* and the legend LEG XV APOLLINARIS, it appears to have been the seal from a signet ring lost by the second centurion (*princeps prior*) of the first cohort (*cohors prima*) of this legion when he accompanied Titus on his voyage (Daszewski 1973). Titus, of course, was the current *legatus legionis* of *XV Apollinaris*, and the *princeps prior* perhaps his close protection bodyguard.
7. Both Vespasianus and Titus, as emperors, would issue silver *drachmae* (now extremely rare) depicting the temple of Aphrodite at Paphos (e.g. *RPC* II Vespasianus 1806 var, *RPC* II Titus 1809) on their reverse and bearing the Greek legend ETOYC NEOY IEPOY Θ, thereby spreading the fame of the Paphian goddess and her oracle.
8. An interesting character was Tiberius Iulius Alexander (*PIR*² I 139). By birth he was a Jew of Alexandria, by upbringing a Hellenized cosmopolitan, by status a Roman *eques*, by profession an administrator and general, always a faithful and efficient servant of Rome and of whoever might be Rome's ruler. Having first recognized Galba the previous summer, in February or March, Otho, and in May, Vitellius were likewise promptly recognized. His father, brother of the worthy religious thinker and philosopher Philo Iudaeus, had been one of the wealthiest Jews in Alexandria. To the disgrace of his family, Tiberius Alexander 'did not remain in his ancestral custom' (Josephus *Antiquitates Iudaicae* 20.5.2), and as an apostate entered the Roman government service to act as a procurator of Iudaea under Claudius (op. cit., ibid. *Bellum Iudaicum* 2.11.6), prefect of Egypt under Nero (ibid. 2.15.1), and would subsequently serve as Titus' chief-of-staff at the siege of Jerusalem (ibid. 5.1.6, 6.4.3). As the *praefectus Aegypto*, Tiberius Alexander had his residence in Alexandria, not just the city of his birth,

but a city founded by Alexander the Great as a Graeco–Macedonian city. It would retain its non-Egyptian, exclusive character throughout its pre-Arabic history, and in a sense we see this in the 'melting pot' personality of Tiberius Alexander. Indeed, in the opening phrase of his Great Edict of AD 68, it is Alexandria that he mentions first (*OGIS* 669 lines 3–4).

9. Tacitus *Historiae* 2.1–4, Suetonius *Vespasianus* 5.4–6. This hesitation on Vespasianus' part is given a dramatic twist by Josephus, for he tells us that 'the rank and file surrounded him sword in hand, and threatened to kill him if he refused the life that was his due' (*Bellum Iudaicum* 4.10.4).

10. Tacitus *Historiae* 2.7.2. Nonetheless, Vespasianus never got to like the man. Likewise Licinius Mucianus, who had the disputable reputation of being the passive partner in homosexual intercourse, treated the emperor with scant respect. For his part, Vespasianus never criticized Licinius Mucianus in public, but in private once uttered the words 'I at least am a man' (Suetonius *Vespasianus* 13.1).

11. Tacitus *Historiae* 2.77.1, Josephus *Bellum Iudaicum* 7.4.1.

12. Josephus says (*Bellum Iudaicum* 3.4.2) these three legions were supported by twenty-three auxiliary *cohortes*, of which ten were *peditatae milliariae* (viz. each ten *centuriae*, a total of 800 infantrymen commanded by a *tribunus cohortis*), the rest being *equitatae quingenariae* (viz. each six *centuriae* and four *turmae*, a total of 480 infantrymen and 128 cavalrymen commanded by a *praefectus cohortis*), along with six *alae* (viz. each sixteen *turmae*, a total of 512 cavalrymen commanded by a *praefectus equitum*). Josephus also says (op. cit.) *XV Apollonaris* was brought from Alexandria by Titus.

13. Incidentally, *legio XII Fulminata* was probably in origin the *legio XII* formed by Caesar in 58 BC for his Gallic campaigns and once commanded by Galba's great-grandfather (see chap. 2, n. 3). The legion served under Marcus Antonius during his Parthian campaign (36 BC), when it bore the name *antiqua*, and it was still with him for the Actium campaign (31 BC). In 27 BC the legion bore a new title, *paterna* (*CIL* xi 1058, *RE* col. 1705), which was perhaps an attempt by Octavianus to remind the veteran soldiers of the legion's earlier association with his adoptive father, the divine Iulius Caesar.

14. We should note that the legions under that 'Vicar of Bray', Tiberius Iulius Alexander, had declared for Vespasianus on 1 July (dating his regnal years from this date), while his own three legions in Iudaea did not proclaim him emperor until two (or ten) days later on 3 (or 11) July ('fifth day before the Nones' – Tacitus *Historiae* 2.79.1, 'fifth day before the Ides' – Suetonius *Vespasianus* 6.3, cf. Josephus *Bellum Iudaicum* 4.10.6). It is of interest to note too that many of the eastern (and Danube) *legati legionum* were later rewarded with consulships (e.g. Trajan, the father of the future emperor, in AD 70). Furthermore, the Danube legions and their legates had close relationships with the east, for example *legio III Gallica*, now stationed in Moesia, had moved there from Syria the previous year, its *legatus legionis* Titus Aurelius Fulfinus (grandfather of the emperor Antoninus Pius) having made the transfer too. Another possible connection to consider is the fact that many of these officers had served under the great Neronian general Cnaeus Domitius Corbulo, already known to us. This meant there existed a tight group of senior officers who knew each other and, more importantly, had served with each other under a top-flight general. To this select group can be added Tiberius Iulius Alexander, who had passed the years AD 63–66 as Corbulo's chief-of-staff (*minister bello datus*, Tacitus *Annales* 15.28.1), and another 'easterner', Caius Licinius Mucianus, who took part in Corbulo's campaigns in the years AD 58 and onwards. In a very real sense, Vespasianus' elevation to the purple was a cosy affair done and dusted between old army acquaintances.

15. *Iliad* 5.82–3 Lattimore: '... and the purple death and destiny the powerful took hold of both eyes'. This is a play on πορφύρεος as the colour of blood and of royalty. On 6 November AD 355, on the solemn occasion of being elevated to Caesar by his cousin Constantius II, Iulianus 'whispered to himself the line from Homer: "Wrapped in death's purple by all-

powerful fate'" (Ammianus Marcellinus 15.8.17). On 18 January AD 532, at the climax of the Nika revolt, Iustiananus decided on ignominious flight. At this crucial juncture Theodora, once Constantinople's leading courtesan and now empress who travelled with a magnificent court of her own, made her famous intervention: 'So now, if it is still your wish to save yourself, O Emperor, there is no problem. For we have plenty of money, the sea is there, and here are ships. Nevertheless, consider whether, once you have managed to save yourself, you might not then gladly exchange safety for death. But as for me, I take pleasure in an old expression that the purple is the noblest winding sheet' (Procopius *Wars* 1.24.37). The 'old expression', which Theodora shrewdly quoted so as to put backbone into her wavering husband, is derived from Isokrates' *Archidamos* §45 – 'royalty is a fair winding sheet' – but may have been transmitted by Diodoros 14.8.5, who repeats the saying verbatim. Evidently it is a glorious thing to die a king. On Tuesday 29 May 1453, at the Military Gate of St Romanos, Constantine XI Palaiologos, the eighty-eighth ruler to sit on the throne of Constantine, would dismount from his horse and go out to die valiantly alongside his men 'in the winding sheet of his Empire', earning himself a place in Greek folk legend and an unofficial seat alongside the saints of the Greek Orthodox Church.

16. Euripides *Phoenissae* 602. This was one of Augustus' favourite tags (Suetonius *Divus Augustus* 25.4).
17. Tacitus *Historiae* 2.81.
18. Ibid. 2.83.1. *XII Fulminata* was the legion sent to Jerusalem to attempt to re-establish control there (Josephus *Bellum Iudaicum* 2.18.9, 19.7), but was overwhelmed in the pass of Beth-horon, losing its *aquila* in the process (Suetonius *Vespasianus* 4.4), and thus no longer capable of a good fight for a long while thereafter. It was this surprising victory that irrevocably committed the Jews to war with Rome. The disgraced legion was to join Titus for his siege of Jerusalem (Tacitus *Historiae* 5.1.3), but it did not stay long, for Titus mistrusted the soldiers and so despatched *XII Fulminata* far away to Melitene (Malatya), a garrison town near the Euphrates on the Cappadocia-Armenia frontier (Josephus *Bellum Iudaicum* 7.1.3). It obviously did not pay to get trounced, let alone lose your eagle into the bargain.
19. Cf. Tacitus *Historiae* 3.8.2, 48.3, 4.52.2.
20. According to Tacitus the soldiers of *VII Claudia pia fidelis* and of *VIII Augusta* tore to pieces 'the colours which displayed the name of Vitellius' (*Historiae* 2.85.1, cf. Suetonius *Vespasianus* 6.3).
21. From Rome *legio VII Galbiana* had been dispatched by Galba to Petronell-*Carnuntum* on the Danube to take the place of *legio X Gemina*, transferred to its old stamping ground of Iberia.
22. Tacitus *Historiae* 2.86.1.
23. According to Tacitus (*Historiae* 3.8.3), Licinius Mucianus had written frequent letters to Antonius Primus outlining the Flavian strategy; he would have stressed therefore his boss' policy of no invasion of Italy as the peninsula (and the Vitellians along with it) would be conquered through famishment. It almost seems as if Vespasianus was still reckoning in weeks and months, while Antonius Primus was keeping his count in days. Prudence is a brake and not a motive force. Nobody ever made a journey on brakes, and nobody ever created anything out of prudence. Antonius Primus was a driven man.
24. Tacitus *Historiae* 2.96.1.
25. Surprised by *legio III Gallica* when laden with booty, the Rhoxolani had been cut to pieces (Tacitus *Historiae* 1.79, Tacitus also gives good details of Sarmatian equipment and methods of fighting).
26. Tacitus *Historiae* 2.85.2. Tettius Iulianus, warned in time, made good his escape and eventually appeared at Alexandria to court Vespasianus.
27. Tacitus *Historiae* 3.11.2.
28. Ibid. 3.50.2.

29. Ibid. 3.4.1, 10.2. Tacitus gives us no details about how the two men were related

30. Ibid. 2.86, 3.4.

31. Ibid. 3.10.3–4.

32. Pliny *Historia Naturalis* 9.8.26.

33. Tacitus *Historiae* 2.86.

34. Ibid. 2.86.

35. Ibid. 3.1.1.

36. Ibid. 3.2.

37. Machiavelli *The Prince*, chap. 25.

38. As Engels rightly said: 'There is but one good line of policy in war: to go at it with the greatest rapidity and energy, to beat your opponent, and force him to your terms' (Letter to H. J. Lincoln, editor of the *London Daily News*, 30 March 1854, published in *MECW*, vol. 39, p. 423).

39. Domitianus was to marry Corbulo's youngest daughter, Domitia Longina (Suetonius *Domitianus* 1.3, Cassius Dio 65.3.4). Born around AD 53, through her mother Cassia Longina, Domitia was a direct descent of Augustus and one of the last remaining Iulii. Domitianus was her second husband.

40. Tacitus *Annales* 13.9, *Historiae* 3.6.1.

41. Nine years later, *ala Gallorum Sebosiana*, was to find itself stationed at Carlisle-*Luguvalium* (Tomlin 1998: 74), while in AD 122 it was enjoying the delights of Szöny-*Brigetio* in Pannonia (*CIL* xvi 69), to be back again in Britannia by AD 262 at Lancaster (*RIB* 605).

42. Tacitus *Historiae* 3.6.3.

43. Ibid. 3.7.1.

44. Ibid. 3.8.1.

45. Ibid. 3.9.2.

46. Ibid. 3.9.3. Vipstanus Messalla, who Tacitus praises as 'the only man who had brought into that conflict an honest purpose' (opt. cit.), wrote a history of his time. It is his memoirs that Tacitus used to give us a more than usually accurate picture of the days leading up to Second Cremona – at 3.25.2, the author specifically names him as his source here. Tacitus obviously admired Messalla as a man and orator, for he appears as one of the speakers in the second part of Tacitus' *Dialogus de Oratoribus*. Incidentally, Messalla was a man who championed Antonius Primus and his point of view.

47. Tacitus *Historiae* 2.85.2.

48. Cf. Silius Italicus *Punica* 8.597, *Athesi circumflua*. Founded in 89 BC by Pompeius Strabo (Pliny *Panegyricus* 9.8, cf. Pliny *Historia Naturalis* 3.130), the father of Pompey the Great, the Roman colony of Verona was the birthplace of such literary luminaries as Catallus, Cornelius Nepos, Vitruvius, and the elder Pliny. It was noted for its wine too, the Raetian enjoyed by Augustus, and its splendid amphitheatre (still largely standing) had a seating capacity of 22,000. Traces of a rampart and ditch to the south of the neck of peninsula have been found near the Museo Maffeiano, and on this evidence the Flavian work would have run along the line Castel Vecchio-Via Pallone, a distance of over a kilometre.

49. Tacitus *Historiae* 3.11.4.

50. Arthur Conan Doyle *Songs of Action*, (1898) 'Cremona' 1.3–5. The reader interested in multi-period battle sites might be happy to hear that during the opening stages of the War of the Spanish Succession Cremona was the scene of an engagement. This was between the French under the duc de Villeroi, who occupied the fortified town as their winter quarters, and the Imperial Austrian Army under Prince Eugène of Savoy. During the small hours of 1 February 1702 the Imperialists took Cremona by a startling *coup de main*, and occupied the entire town before the alarm was raised. Villeroi and the French garrison were captured *tout ensemble*. However, a battalion of Dillon's Regiment of *La Brigade irlandaise*, led by Major Daniel O'Mahony – Jacobite Irish fighting under the standard of *La fleur de Lys* – refused

to surrender and held on to a fort in their possession, namely the one that commanded the Porta Po of Cremona. Eventually Eugène, being unable to dislodge the Irishmen from their strong point and with a relieving French army fast approaching Cremona, was forced to withdraw from the town he had won so easily. He is reported to have said, 'Taken by a miracle – lost by a still greater one'. Other known battles at Cremona date to 200 BC (Roman-Gaulish wars), 1431 (Venetian-Milanese wars), and 1648 (Thirty Years' War).

51. When Henri IV of France (r. 1589–1610) converted from Protestantism to Catholicism in a very public ceremony at the basilica of Saint-Denis on Sunday morning, 25 July 1593 – *realpolitik in extremis*, to say the least – he apparently uttered the words 'Paris is well worth a mass' (*'Paris vaut bien une messe'*).

52. Tacitus *Historiae* 3.35.1, cf. 46.3, *Vitelliano exercitu*. Illyricum was a general term for the provinces between the Adriatic, the Danube and the Black Sea, i.e. Noricum, Pannonia, Dalmatia, Moesia and Thrace. Thus, the Vitellian full legions, *I Italica* and *V Alaudae*, followed by the Flavian *VII Claudia pia fidelis*, were sent to Moesia. There, *I Italica* was stationed at Svištov-*Novae*, where it virtually settled until sometime in the reign of Valentinianus III (AD 425–455), *V Alaudae* perhaps at Silistra-*Durostorum*, and *VII Claudia pia fidelis* returning to its old base at Koštolac-*Viminacium*. As for the other Vitellian full legion, *XXI Rapax*, it appears to have returned to its old base at Windisch-*Vindonissa*, which had been entirely denuded of its legionary garrison.

53. Tacitus *Historiae* 3.12, 36.2, 40.1.

54. Ibid. 3.50.3, cf. 55.1.

55. Cf. ibid. 5.16.3, '… the men of *legio II* [*Adiutrix*] were in that battle first to consecrate their new standards and new eagle'.

56. Ibid. 3.57.1.

57. Aemilius Macer *De re militari* 2 apud *Digesta* 49.16.13 §3.

58. Sometime early in AD 71 Vespasianus reinstated Licilius Bassus as prefect of both fleets (*CIL* xvi 14, 15 = *ILS* 1990, 1991, cf. Tacitus *Historiae* 4.3.1).

59. Tacitus *Historiae* 3.57.2.

60. Starr 1960: 183–4.

61. Tacitus *Historiae* 3.58.1.

62. Ibid. 3.76.1.

63. Ibid. 3.77.1.

64. Ibid. 3.77.3. The other rebel leader, Apinius Tiro, had quitted Tarracina a few days before (ibid. 3.76.2).

65. Ibid. 3.43.1.

66. Ibid. 3.43.2. A *liburna* was a light, swift, two-banked galley with 144 oarsmen, ten to fifteen sailors and forty marines.

67. Tacitus *Historiae* 3.62.1.

68. Ibid. 2.92.1, 3.36.2.

69. Ibid. 3.55.1. Tacitus calls these '*e classicis legio*', and they were perhaps sailors recruited from the *classis Misenensis*.

70. Ibid. 3.58.1.

71. Ibid. 3.69.3.

72. Tacitus, in his account (*Historiae* 3.71) of this tragic incident, rather unusually does not point the finger at who was actually to blame for setting fire to the temple, the Vitellians or the Flavians. On the other hand, Josephus (*Bellum Iudaicum* 4.649), Suetonius (*Vitellius* 15.3) and Cassius Dio (64.17.3) all lay the blame squarely at Vitellius' door. By contrast, Tacitus acknowledges the difficulties of apportioning blame to this side or that. Besides, as he rightly points out, the question who threw the first torch is irrelevant: the temple would have never burned down if the two sides had not chosen the Capitol as a battleground in the first place.

For a discussion on who was responsible for the firing of the Capitol, see Wellesley 1972: 16–18.

73. Now in his late sixties, Flavius Sabinus' public career extended over thirty-five years. In AD 43 he had fought alongside his brother in Britannia, had governed Moesia for seven years (AD 49–56), was city prefect twice under Nero (AD 56–60, AD 62–68), and once again from Otho's succession onwards. During the seven years he had governed Moesia, and the twelve years he had served as city prefect, the only charge ever brought against him was his passion for long-windedness. It was universally agreed, that before Vespasianus became emperor, the dignity of the Flavians centred on Flavius Sabinus.

74. Tacitus *Historiae* 3.74.2.

75. Ibid. 3.74.1.

76. Ibid. 3.82.2.

77. Ibid. 3.83.1.

78. Ibid. 3.84.3. There were perhaps only three cohorts of praetorians left in Rome. Of the sixteen (ibid. 2.93.2), fourteen had been sent to hold the Apennines at Mevania under the praetorian prefects, Iulius Priscus and Alfenus Varus (ibid. 3.55.1), and two left in Rome under Lucius Vitellius, the emperor's brother (ibid. 3.55.2). Seven surrendered at Narnia to the Flavians (ibid. 3.58.1), seven having returned to Rome, rejoining the two there, making nine now in Rome. Of these nine, six were sent to Campania under Lucius Vitellius (ibid. 3.58.1) and eventually surrendered in their turn (ibid. 4.2.3). It was the three remaining in Rome that stormed the Capitol (ibid. 3.78.2), before fighting to the bitter end at the *castra praetoria*.

79. Letter to Marx, 3 April 1851, published in *MECW*, vol. 38, p. 326. Marx and Engels were not only radical thinkers but military ones too. Concepts of military strategy and tactics may seem alien to the spirit of these fathers of scientific socialism, whose declared policy was one of enmity towards the military machine, the military caste, and the military state, whose anticipated socialist order merged with the pacifist millennium. Engels particularly, in the last stage of his long career, came to see the triumph of proletarian revolution through the ballot box, rather than through the bullet and the bayonet. Proud of his early service in the Royal Prussian Army – he had been a bombardier (corresponding infantry rank of corporal) in the *landwehr* artillery – and especially of his active role in the Baden insurrection of 1849, Engels turned his attention to the study of military science during his many years of exile in Manchester, in order to prepare himself for the coming social revolution. An avid reader, his interest in military history was historical rather than physical.

80. The 'buddy-buddy' system, under modern combat conditions, works like this: one man will give covering fire while the other dashes forward to the nearest cover. Then he takes cover while his buddy rushes forward in turn. The section (or squad) to which these two men belong likewise operates on the same principle, the fire team concept allowing it to manoeuvre within itself. With the triple decentralization of firepower, manoeuvre and command (it is no longer sufficient for a small unit leader to be the bravest member of the battle line), the modern battlefield has disintegrated into thousands of miniature combats.

81. Tacitus *Historiae* 3.85.1.

82. According to Cassius Dio (64.21.2), Vitellius' severed head was paraded through the streets of Rome.

83. Suetonius *Vitellius* 9.1, 18.1, cf. Martial *Epigrammata* 9.99.

84. Tacitus *Historiae* 1.10. Licinius Mucianus was not only a general and statesman of the highest calibre, but a fluent orator and had literary and antiquarian ambitions. His powers of oratory are greatly praised by Tacitus (ibid. 1.80), who tells us that Licinius Mucianus could address an auditory even in Greek with great effect. This extraordinary man was a clever writer too, not only compiling a corpus of political speeches from the Republic but also a memoir chiefly dealing with the natural history and geography of the orient, which is often

quoted by the elder Pliny as a source of marvels such as the Greek-writing elephant (*Historia Naturalis* 8.3) .

85. Licinius Mucianus, who never wavered in his allegiance to Vespasianus and whose favour he retained in spite of his gross arrogance, was to be rewarded by the emperor with a further two consulships (*cos.* II AD 70, *cos.* III AD 72).

Chapter 6

1. Burne, A.H., 1952. *More Battlefields of England*, p. ix.
2. Tacitus *Historiae* 2.100.1.
3. Ibid. 2.100.3.
4. Ibid. 3.14.1.
5. Ibid. 3.14.3.
6. In Latin: *et fidus Vitellio Fabius nec militiae ignarus*, ibid. 3.15.1.
7. Ibid. 3.17.1. For Antonius Primus' action, compare that of Caesar at Dyrrhachium: 'when Caesar grabbed the standards of the men fleeing and ordered them to halt, some gave their horses rein and continued in their course of flight, while others in their fear actually let the standards drop, but no one halted at all' (*Bellum civilia* 3.69.4). All the same, both these generals relied on hands-on management, and luck. Both served them well.
8. Before appointing a general Napoléon would inquire, '*mais est-il la chance?* ' – 'but is he lucky?' We should also remember that if Napoléon had not been a gambler, he would not have achieved his place in history.
9. Moltke 1916.
10. In Latin: *ad quartum a Cremona lapidem*, Tacitus *Historiae* 3.18.1.
11. Op. cit.
12. Ibid. 3.18.2.
13. Ibid. 3.19.1, 2.
14. Ibid. 3.21.1.
15. Ibid. 3.21.2.
16. Ibid. 3.33.1.
17. Josephus *Bellum Iudaicum* 4.11.3.
18. Tacitus *Historiae* 3.23.1.
19. Ibid. 3.1.2.
20. Ibid. 2.43.1.
21. In Latin: *omnibus se manipulus miscreant*, ibid. 3.22.2.
22. Ibid. 3.21.2 (*septima Galbiana patenti campo stetit*), 23.1 (*sustinuit labantem aciem Antonius accitis praetorianis*).
23. However, it is not clear whether an entire legion shared a common shield device, or whether each cohort was distinguished in some way, perhaps by colour. For reenactors, at least, the stylized wing, thunderbolt and lightening flash design, the emblem of Iuppiter, is most popular.
24. Tacitus *Historiae* 3.23.2, cf. Cassius Dio 64.14.2. Note, the Latin text clearly says '*sextae decimae legionis*', not 'fifteenth legion' as in certain English translations. For this, see especially Wellesley 1972: 107–8.
25. Here Frontinus is alluding to his earlier treatise on the art of war. This was probably written after his return from Britannia in AD 77/8. This military work of a theoretical nature was used by Vegetius (*De re militari* 1.8), but it is now wholly lost, except in so far as Vegetius may have incorporated it in his own work.
26. Frontinus *Strategemata* 1 *praefatio*.
27. Campbell 1996: 325–31.
28. Onasander *Stratêgikos* 33.1.
29. Tacitus *Historiae* 3.24.1.

30. Ibid. 3.24.3.
31. Ibid. 4.77.2.
32. Arrian *Ektaxis katà Alanon* 10 DeVoto.
33. Made of gold or silver-gilt, the *aquila*, along with the unit's other standards, was an object of veneration (Tacitus *Annales* 1.39.7, cf. Tertullian *Apologeticum* 16.8) and the principal festival in honour of the *aquila* was the *natalis aquilae*, which celebrated the day on which the legion had been established.
34. Tacitus *Annales* 14.30.1.
35. Ibid. 14.30.2.
36. Ibid. *Historiae* 3.22.4.
37. Found in Gigen-*Oescus*, a stele of Caius Valerius Prudens records he was a '*milites* in *V Macedonica*, *centuria* of Atilius Verus' (*AE* 1912.188). Gigen-*Oescus*, Moesia, was the home of this legion before it left in AD 62 to take part in Corbulo's Parthian campaign.
38. Atilius Verus may have been the first *primus pilus* of *VII Galbiana*, in which case he is most likely to have been transferred not from *V Macedonica* but *VI Victrix*, the single established legion of Hispania Tarraconensis at the time of Galba's insurrection. If true, then he would have been transferred from *V Macedonica*, currently with Vespasianus in Iudaea, to *VI Victrix* before AD 68. During the principate of Trajan, Atilia Vera, a daughter of Atilius Verus, would set up a grave marker for her husband, Lucius Aemilius Paternus, centurion and *primus pilus* of the same legion. The inscribed stele (*CIL* ii 4461 = *ILS* 2661 = Campbell 172) was found at Avella in Spain, ancient Aeso in Hispania Tarraconensis. All the indications of the origins of Aemilius Paternus suggest that Atilia Vera at least had Iberian connections if not her father. For an excellent summary of Atilius Verus' career, see Summerly 1992: 17–18.
39. Tacitus *Historiae* 3.22.4, *sex primorum ordinum centuriones*. In the *cohors prima* its six centurions were collectively known as the *primi ordines* ('the first ranks') and enjoyed immense prestige. More so the *primus pilus*, who, as the legion's top soldier, commanded the first century of the *cohors prima* and had charge of the *aquila*.
40. Tacitus *Historiae* 3.13–14.1.
41. Frontinus *Strategemata* 1.1.9, Josephus *Bellum Iudaicum* 3.5.3, cf. 4.
42. E.g. Tacitus *Annales* 1.28.3, 68.3.
43. In Latin: *ita in Syria mos est*, Tacitus *Historiae* 3.24.3, cf. Cassius Dio 64.14.3. Millar (1995: 75, 522) doubts that sun worship was typical of Syria. Note, however, *IGR* III 1242 for a Syrian centurion's dedication to Sol.
44. Cassius Dio 64.14.3.
45. Tacitus *Historiae* 3.24.3–25.1.
46. The earliest recorded time for sunrise (in Milan) on 25 October is for the year 1695, when the sun rose at 06.43 hours. This is of course well before the introduction of Daylight Saving Time (DST), which was first implemented by the Germans (and their allies) on 30 April 1916 as a way to conserve coal during wartime. For 25 October 2014 the sunrise in Milan will be at 07.53 hours.
47. Anon. *Bellum Hispaniense* 30.9.
48. Appian *Bellum civilia* 4.117 only mentions one legion by name at Philippi, *IIII* (probably now with its title *Macedonica*), but according to Keppie (1998: 119) the other Caesarian formations were *VI* (soon to be *VI Ferrata*), *VII*, *VIII*, *X Equestris* and *XII*, and among the younger legions *III* (perhaps now with its title *Gallica*), and probably *XXVI*, *XXVIII*, *XXVIIII* and *XXX*, all of which provided veteran colonists at Philippi after the battles (e.g. *AE* 1924.55).
49. Plutarch *Marcus Antonius* 42.11, Tacitus *Historiae* 3.24.2.
50. Tacitus *Annales* 13.8.2, 15.6.5, 26.1, *Historiae* 3.24.2.
51. Josephus *Bellum Iudaicum* 2.3.1.

52. An inscription (*CIL* iii 217) from Cyprus belonging to the early Principate (Augustan/ Tiberian date) gives the cognomen *Gallica*, which should reflect service in Gaul (48–42 BC).

53. Ammianus Marcellinus (19.6.1) informs us that the fortress was still in commission in AD 359.

54. Tacitus *Historiae* 2.74.2.

55. Ibid. *Annales* 13.7.1, 35.3. We should also note the decision of the Flavian war council at Berytus, whereby the 'first business of the campaign was to levy troops and recall the veterans to service' (*prima bella cura agere dilectus, revocare veteranos*, ibid. 2.82.1). This surely suggests not only the normality of local recruiting into the army, but also the discharge of veterans and their settlement within local society. Josephus speaks of 'a centurion named Gallus, cut off with ten soldiers in the mêlée, crept into somebody's house. Like the others he was a Syrian …' (*Bellum Iudaicum* 4.1.5). Likewise, two inscriptions (*CIL* viii 2904, 4310) inform us of two soldiers transferred from *III Gallica* to *III Augusta* in Africa came from Syria. Conversely, another inscription (*CIL* viii 18084), informs us that *III Augusta*, the least peripatetic of Rome's legions for it was long stationed in Africa, had a number of Syrian veterans from all parts of the province – Apamea, Sidon, Tripolis, Tyre, Damascus, Emesa, and Berytus.

56. See Appendix 10.

57. Herodian 5.3.8–9, 12.

58. For the loyalty of Capua to Vitellius, see Tacitus *Historiae* 3.57.1: *Capua Vitellio fida*.

59. Tacitus *Historiae* 4.39.

60. Rafaniat-*Raphaneae* near Emesa (Homs) had been home for a good part of the legions stay in Syria, and would be until it left for the southern part of Phoenicia.

61. Pliny *Epistulae* 7.31.1, cf. 1.10.1, 3.11.2.

62. Cassius Dio 55.23.2. The last known reference to *III Gallica* has it still in Syria in AD 323.

63. Tacitus *Historiae* 2.21.4, cf. 1.84.3. Likewise, their general, Caecina Alienus, marches into Italy wearing a typically barbarian costume of trousers and multi-coloured cloak (ibid. 2.20.1).

64. Tacitus *Historiae* 3.22.3.

65. Today this would be called friendly fire, blue on blue, or fratricide.

66. Tacitus *Historiae* 3.27.2. For *falces muralis*, see especially Caesar *Bellum Gallicum* 3.14.5, Vegetius *Epitoma rei militaris* 2.25.

67. Tacitus *Historiae* 3.27.3.

68. Ibid. 3.29.1. As this part of Tacitus' narrative reads like an eyewitness' account, he is in all probability using that of Vipstanus Messalla, the acting legate of *VII Claudia pia fidelis* (cf. ibid. 3.28.1).

69. In Latin: *septimani dum nituntur cuneis … securibus gladiisque*, ibid. 3.29.1. The *cuneus* is defined by Vegetius as 'a mass of infantry who are attached to the line, which moves forward, narrower in front and broader behind' (*Epitoma rei militaris* 3.19, cf. 1.26, 3.17).

70. As well as the elder Pliny and Vipstanus Messalla, Tacitus also used the work of an otherwise unknown gentleman, Hormus, a freedman and confidante of Vespasianus (Tacitus *Historiae* 3.12.3, cf. 28.1).

71. Ibid. 3.29.2.

72. An alternative name for this military decoration was *corona castrensis* (Aulus Gellius *Noctes Atticae* 5.6.17, Festus *Castrensis corona* 49 Lindemann, cf. Valerius Maximus 1.8.6). Polybios, observing the republican Roman army of his day, has this to say: 'To the first man to mount the wall at the assault of a city, he [the general] gives a crown of gold' (6.39.3). See Maxfield 1981: 79–80.

73. Tacitus *Historiae* 3.30.1.

74. Ibid. 3.30.2.

75. Ibid. 3.31.4.

76. Ibid. 3.31.1.

77. Ibid. 3.32.2, cf. 2.67.3.

78. In Latin: ... *per quadriduum Cremona suffecit*, ibid. 3.33.2. Tacitus' grim narrative covering the rape of Cremona has been confirmed by archaeology. In the autumn of 2005 excavations conducted in Piazza Marconi revealed a thick layer of ash and butchered remains from Roman Cremona, jolly good evidence for the brutal sack of October AD 69. Piazza Marconi is not in the heart of Cremona but it does lie within the circuit of the old town walls and is close to what was the Porta Po.

79. Polybios tells us that he had witnessed the aftermath of the Roman sack of a city – probably when he had accompanied Scipio Aemilianus on campaign in Africa or Iberia (he was certainly present at the sacks of Carthage and Numantia) – and in the streets 'you may often see not only the corpses of human beings but dogs cut in half and the dismembered limbs of other animals' (10.15.6). The Roman sack of a city was pretty brutal even by the standards of Polybios' day, which assumed general massacre of men and rape of women.

80. Janowicz 1959: 48.

81. Rudyard Kipling, *Barrack-Room Ballads* (1892), 'Tommy' 4.4.

82. In Latin: *furore principum*, Tacitus *Historiae* 3.72.1.

83. Cf. Antonius Primus' speech to his dissatisfied troops at Carsulae: 'From our victory at Cremona sufficient glory has accrued to us, and from the destruction of that town only too much disgrace' (Tacitus *Historiae* 3.60.3).

84. Mao Tse-tung, 1937. *On Guerrilla Warfare*, chap. 3.

85. *Civitas Dei* 3.29.1. Rendered in English as the 'City of God', *civitas* rather means 'community' or 'society'. It was written to answer pagan taunts that God had allowed Rome, a Christian city, to be sacked on 24 August AD 410 by Alaric the Visigoth. Written over a period of fourteen years and finished in AD 427, it is a great work of political theory, philosophy and theology, which surveys the history of Rome from its traditional foundation by Romulus in 753 BC to Augustine's own day. The influence of Augustine (AD 354–430) on western thought has been profound, especially regarding Catholic belief, from the early mediaeval period to the present.

86. Letter to Marx, 7 January 1858, published in *MECW*, vol. 40, p. 241.

87. Tacitus *Historiae* 2.93, 99. By the end of Nero's principate nearly 40 per cent of the legionaries serving in the Rhine legions were being recruited from Gallia Narbonensis (Forni 1953: 157–212).

88. The only precise figure we have for the Vitellian forces are those three *vexillationes* from Britannia (*II Augusta, VIIII Hispana, XX Valeria Victrix*), totalling some 8,000 men (Tacitus *Historiae* 2.57.2). There were five other *vexillationes*, those from the Rhine, say 12,000 men. Then there were three legions (*I Italic, V Alaudae, XXI Rapax*), but two of these had been badly mauled and the survivors dispersed amongst the other Vitellian cohorts (ibid. 3.22.2), say 6,000 men. A grand total of 26,000 Vitellian legionaries.

89. Conrad, J., 1899. *Heart of Darkness*, part 1, p. 3.

Chapter 7

1. Vegetius *Epitoma rei militaris* 1.1.
2. Cicero *Tusculanae disputationes* 2.37.
3. Josephus *Bellum Iudaicum* 3.5.1.
4. Ibid. 3.5.7, cf. 3.10.2.
5. Cicero *Tusculanae disputationes* 2.38. Here we should note that the level of medical care afforded the Roman soldier did not generally improve until the use of penicillin.
6. In Latin: *exercitus, quod exercitando fit melior*, Varro *de lingua Latina* 5.87.
7. E.g. Frontinus *Strategemata* 4.1.1 (route marches), Aulus Gellius *Noctes Atticae* 6.3.52 (field exercises), Vegetius *Epitoma rei militaris* 1.9, 10 (physical training), 2.23 (weapons training), 2.22, 3.4, Tacitus *Annales* 3.33.3 (drill).
8. Arrian *Ars Taktika* 5 DeVoto.

9. Tacitus *Historiae* 4.71.6–9.
10. Ibid. 1.59.2.
11. Ibid. 4.13.1.
12. Suetonius *Galba* 12.2. When it came to protecting the emperor's person, the Iulio–Claudians employed a personal bodyguard of German warriors, a distinct unit quite separate from the Praetorian Guard. Their origin lay in the wars of the triumvirate, when foreigner mercenaries seemed to have been regarded as more reliable than a bodyguard of Roman citizens whose loyalties might be divided. Suetonius (*Divus Augustus* 49.1) tells us that as *triumvir* Octavianus had maintained a bodyguard of Calgurritani from Iberia, which he dismissed after the defeat of Marcus Antonius. As emperor Augustus kept a bodyguard of Germans until the Varian disaster (op. cit.). However, they were reintroduced under Tiberius (Tacitus *Annales* 1.24.2). Endowed as they were with ample physique and renowned ferocity, a Germanic bodyguard would discourage aspiring assassins. This did not help Caius Caligula of course, but his *Germani corporis custodes* did go on the rampage searching for the murderers of their esteemed 'king', 'killing several of the assassins and a few innocent senators into the bargain' (Suetonius *Caius* 58.3). Nero placed special trust in these foreigners precisely because they were outsiders (Tacitus *Annales* 15.58.1). A *sestertius* of Nero (Campbell 126), issued at Rome around AD 64–66, possibly designates his Germanic bodyguard as a *cohors*, which suggest that at least during his principate the *Germani corporis custodes* numbered around 500 men. Suetonius reveals that under the same emperor they had their own camp 'near to the Gardens of Cnaeus Dolabella' (*Galba* 12.2), perhaps where their cemetery has been discovered near San Giovanni Laterano.
13. Spiculus the gladiator had been showered with wealth by the emperor (Suetonius *Nero* 30.2). According to Plutarch (*Galba* 8.5), he came to a nasty end, being lynched as one of 'Nero's men'. The mob threw him to the ground in the Forum and he was crushed beneath toppled statues of Nero.
14. Tacitus *Historiae* 4.16.1, 32.2. For Batavians in the *Germani corporis custodes* under Caius Caligula, Claudius and Nero: Suetonius *Caius* 43.1, *ILS* 1717, 1725, 1727, 1729, 1730, Campbell 76. For a Batavian in the Praetorian Guard, *ILS* 2040.
15. Tacitus *Historiae* 1.59.1.
16. Ibid. 2.17, 27.
17. Ibid. 2.43.
18. Ibid. 2.28.
19. Ibid. 4.12.3. The 'German wars' were those campaigns of Germanicus east of the Rhine in AD 14–16 (ibid. *Annales* 2.8, 11, 16).
20. See Appendix 3.
21. See Appendix 4.
22. Tacitus *Annales* 2.16, *Agricola* 36.2, *Historiae* 4.20, 33, 5.16.
23. Tacitus *Agricola* 36.1, 2, cf. *Annales* 2.14.2.
24. E.g. Trajan's Column scenes xxiv, lxvi, lxxii. For his two seasons (AD 82–83) north of the Bodotria (Forth), Agricola had mustered *vexillationes* from the four legions, *II Adiutrix pia fidelis*, *II Augusta*, *VIIII Hispana* and *XX Valeria Victrix*, of Britannia. These were supported by some 8,000 auxiliary infantry and 5,000 auxiliary cavalry. Of the *auxilia*, we know of four *cohortes* of Batavi, two *cohortes* of Tungri, and an unspecified number of Britons recruited from the tribes in the south. If the *auxilia* were organized as *quingenaria* units, then Agricola would have had some sixteen *cohortes* and ten *alae* all told. See Fields 2009: 66, 79–80.
25. Tacitus *Historiae* 2.66.
26. Ibid. 2.69.2.
27. Ibid. 2.97.2.
28. Ibid. 4.14.3.

29. According to Tacitus (ibid. 4.13), Civilis was urged by a letter from Antonius Primus, and by a personal request from Hordeonius Flaccus, to prevent the Rhine legions from marching into Italy to the support of Vitellius, by an appearance of a Germanic insurrection. If true, then Civilis converted the appearance into a reality.

30. Tacitus *Historiae* 5.26. No doubt the two had fought together in Britannia in the years AD 43–47, when the emperor was *legonis legatus* of *II Augusta*.

31. Ibid. 4.36.3.

32. There was also the issue of the oath to 'the empire of Gaul' (*pro imperio Galliarum*, ibid. 4.59.1, cf. 58 (speech of Dillius Vocula, *legonis legatus* of *XXII Primigenia*).

33. Ibid. 4.78.3. A number of coins were issued by the rebels, including one naming the unfortunate *legio XV Primigenia* (*RIC* I Civil Wars: 130). None of these coins show the portrait or titles of a living emperor, indeed their legends stress *Fides, Concordia, Gallia, Libertas* (ibid. 130–134).

34. Tacitus *Historiae* 4.16, 66.

35. Ibid. 4.13.1, 32.1. Tacitus puts it well when he says Civilis 'was wont to represent himself as Sertorius or Hannibal, on the strength of a similar disfigurement of his countenance'. The leader of the Cherusci in AD 9, Varus' nemesis Arminius, had also twenty-five years' service in the Roman army, had become a Roman citizen and had achieved the status of *eques*.

36. Ibid. 4.61.1, cf. *Germania* 31.1–2. Red hair was apparently fashionable among the Germans, and those denied it by nature could acquire it by means of a preparation of animal fat and beechwood ashes (Pliny *Historia Naturalis* 28.51). Which brings us to a marvellous little ditty from the pen of Martial: 'I am the fancy of the potter, the mask of a red-haired Batavi. This countenance, at which you smile, is an object of terror to children' (*Epigrammata* 14.176).

37. Ibid. 4.68.3, cf. 5.14.1. As well as *XIIII Gemina Martia Victrix* legions included *II Adiutrix, VIII Augusta, XI Claudia pia fidelis, XIII Gemina*, all belonging to the victorious Flavian army, *XXI Rapax*, which had previously belonged to the Vitellian army, and from Iberia the Othonian *I Adiutrix* and Galban *VI Victrix*. Later, Petilius Cerialis' army was strengthened by *X Gemina* (ibid. 5.19.1), the last of the three Iberian legions, so that his total force on the Rhine consisted of nine legions, not counting of course the legions that had gone over to the rebels.

38. Tacitus *Historiae* 5.16.3.

39. Ibid. 3.59.2.

40. Ibid. 3.59, 78–79.

41. Ibid. 5.21.3.

42. Ibid. 4.74.1.

43. It may appear rather odd to us, but one deity often honoured by military men, particularly commanders, was Fortuna, frequently enough in fact to make it seem a semi-official cult. A rather curious example of this was found against the south wall of the apodyterium of the bathhouse inside the Antonine Wall fort at Balmuildy. For here was erected an altar dedicated by a certain Caecilius Nepos, a tribune of an unnamed auxiliary cohort, to Fortuna (RIB 2189). Nearby were scattered counters and parts of a gaming-board.

44. Tacitus *Historiae* 4.75–78.

45. One of the notable events of the Boudican rebellion took place when a *vexillatio* of *legio VIIII Hispana*, under the command of its legate Petilius Cerialis, quickly marched south to the rescue, but it was ambushed and destroyed (Tacitus *Annales* 14.32.2). Those legionaries who were unlucky to have been cut down in what seems a carefully planned ambuscade probably numbered around 2,000, which is the number Tacitus (ibid. 14.38.1) later tells us were needed to bring the legion back to full strength. The impetuous legate got away with whatever cavalry survived, probably to the fortress at Longthorpe on the Nene near Peterborough. Excavations there have revealed that he got his much reduced legion to hastily throw up a smaller fort ('Longthorpe II') within the original fortress. Petilius Cerialis, no

doubt thinking his military career was over, and his command would now sit tight and await events.

46. Tacitus *Agricola* 8.2. Petilius Cerialis also departed for Britannia with *legio II Adiutrix*, which would serve in the province until circa AD 86, being based first at Lincoln-*Lindum* and then at Chester-*Deva*.

47. Tacitus *Agricola* 7.2.

48. Agricola had served under Caius Suetonius Paulinus as a senior military tribune, *tribunus militum laticlavius*, believed to have been awarded this commission by the legate governor himself. We do not know exactly in which legion he served in, but a case could be made for *legio II Augusta*, nor does Tacitus record any direct personal involvement by Agricola in the squashing of the Boudican rebellion, but his skill as a writer certainly leaves the reader with the impression Agricola had been involved.

49. Tacitus *Agricola* 17.1.

50. Ibid. *Historiae* 4.77–78.

51. Ibid. 5.16–18.

52. Ibid. 5.22.2.

53. Ibid. 5.23.3.

54. Ibid. 5.26.1. The Nabalia has yet to be identified; two possible candidates are the Utrechtse Vecht and the Hollandse IJssel.

55. Tacitus *Germania* 29.2. It is known that in AD 356 Iulianus, then Caesar, added Batavi to his legions in Gaul, 'of whose discipline we still make use' (Zosimus 3.13.1).

56. Two of these legions, *I Germanica* and *XV Primigenia* (whose shameful surrender was celebrated on rebel coinage) are never heard of again. The two other legions were reformed and renamed: *IIII Macedonica* became *IIII Flavia felix* and was immediately transferred to Dalmatia; *XVI Gallica* became *XVI Flavia firma* and was transferred to Cappadocia by AD 72. It was once believed that *V Alaudae* shared the same ignominious fate as *I Germanica* and *XV Primigenia*, but an inscription (*IMS* VI 33) reports a veteran colonist at Scupi (Skopje) under Domitianus. See Appendix 5.

Chapter 8

1. Tacitus *Historiae* 1.4.1.

2. Suetonius *Vespasianus* 2.1.

3. Ibid. 5.3. See also ibid. 2.3, Cassius Dio 59.12.3 for Vespasianus' military tribuneship, quaestorship and praetorship. For the early career of Vespasianus and the attendant problem of dating, see Nicols 1978: 2–7.

4. The triumph, which had once been open to every member of the Senate, was now a mere family rite of the Caesars. According to Cassius Dio (54.11.6–7), Marcus Vipsanius Agrippa was granted a triumph by the Senate in 19 BC, but in deference to Augustus, to whom he was completely devoted to, refused to hold it. Five years later he again refused the same illustrious honour and Cassius Dio (54.24.7) believed that this was the reason why no other senator was given a full triumph (*iustus triumphus*) after this date. From now on only the emperor (or a member of his family) celebrated the *iustus triumphus*, lesser mortals making do with an award of *ornamenta triumphalia*, which consisted of the decorations and dress usually associated with a *triumphator* but excluded the grand street parade. But triumphal trappings were only a poor substitute for the real thing, a day of glory when the triumphator entered the city of Rome in solemn procession, riding high in a splendid four-horse chariot and decked out in the dress of Iuppiter Optimus Maximus (viz. Iuppiter Best and Greatest), accompanied by his soldiers, booty, captives, and tableaux or pictures of his glorious exploits. He then made his offering at Iuppiter's temple on the Capitol (the temple of Iuppiter Optimus Maximus was situated on the highest point of the *capitolium*, the southern summit of Rome's Capitoline hill), and then feasted the populace. Augustus, as founder of a military monarchy, had robbed the senatorial aristocracy of its day of glory, and Tacitus, describing

the *triumphalia* of his father-in-law Agricola, scoffs 'and whatever is given in place of a triumph' (*Agricola* 40.1). The last private citizen (viz. non-member of the imperial family) to triumph was Lucius Cornelius Balbus in 19 BC. Augustus was by nature an autocrat. No one was to be a rival to his power, and no one was going to challenge the emperor's post as Rome's military supremo.

5. Suetonius *Vespasianus* 4.1, cf. Josephus *Bellum Iudaicum* 3.1.2: 'by force of arms he had added Britannia, till then unknown, to the empire, so enabling Nero's father Claudius, who had not lifted a finger himself, to celebrate a triumph'. Here the author deliberately plays up the rôle of Vespasianus in Britannia, which is an obvious flattering exaggeration, since he commanded only one of the four legions that made up the invasion army.

6. Suetonius *Vespasianus* 4.4, 14. Tacitus (*Annales* 16.5.3) places the transgression in Rome (AD 65) and not Greece (AD 68).

7. Suetonius *Vespasianus* 4.5.

8. Tacitus *Historiae* 2.5.1. Much like his father, Titus was 'famous for his soldiering' (ibid. 5.1.1).

9. Cassius Dio 57.2.3.

10. Kissinger, H., 1979. *The White House Years*, p. 113.

11. Cassius Dio 59.1.3.

12. Orosius 7.3.7, cf. 7.9.8–9. For Vespasianus' building programme, see Levick 1999: 126.

13. *Res Gestae Divi Augusti* 13, cf. Cassius Dio 54.36.2, Orosius 6.22.1. As Tacitus tartly said, Augustus 'seduced every one by the delights of peace' (*Annales* 1.2.1), and 'it was in the interest of peace that all power should be conferred on one man' (*Historiae* 1.1.1), a couple of comments that would no doubt have appealed to Augustus' mild vanity.

14. On coins of around AD 64, Nero announces to the world a forthcoming closure of the temple of Janus, because through his general Domitius Corbulo, he had tackled and solved the perennial problem of Armenia, interminably disputed between Rome and Parthia. Finally, in AD 66, the ceremony took place. Romans saw the unprecedented sight of Tiridates, the brother of the Parthian king, officially visiting Rome to pay homage to Nero – who fortified him with an enormous daily cash handout – and to receive the diadem of Armenia from him (Tacitus *Annales* 15.24, 29, Suetonius *Nero* 13, 30.1).

15. This was a small rectangular shrine with doors at both ends and the statue of the god facing both ways within. It stood in the Forum near the Curia, at the entrance to the Argiletum. The doors stood open in times of war, and the antiquarians of the late Republic held that they had been closed only twice in Roman history before Augustus' time, once in the reign of Numa and once in 235 BC (Varro *De lingua latina* 5.165, cf. Livy 1.19.1–3). They were closed again in 29 BC and 25 BC (Cassius Dio 51.20.4, 53.26.5) after the ending of the Alexandrian and Cantabrian wars respectively. The third occasion is unidentified but guaranteed by Augustus himself (*Res Gestae Divi Augusti* 13); the Christian writer Orosius puts it in 2 BC but activity at that time on the Rhine and Danube frontiers makes this implausible and besides he was suggesting that when Christ was born 'no war or battle's sound / was heard the world around' (6.22.1). Syme (1978: 26) makes cases for 18 BC, 13 BC, or sometime before 8 BC and 1 BC, which seem much better guesses.

16. E.g. *RIC* II Vespasianus: 181, 241, 243, 273, 378, 512 etc., cf. 1407, 1413, 1426, 1433 (PACI ORB(is) TERR(arvm) AVG(vsti), 'Augustan Peace of the World'). In fact, it has been noted that nearly one-third of all coins minted in Rome under Vespasianus celebrated military victory of world peace (Jones 1971). See also Levick 1999: 70.

17. Tacitus *Historiae* 2.5.2, Suetonius *Vespasianus* 16.1.

18. Suetonius *Vespasianus* 23.2, Cassius Dio 65.14.5. Forget what you have seen on the television, for public urinals were mainly big pots standing at street corners, which the fullers and tanners used to carry away, when the contents reached a certain level, to use in their respective trades.

Incidentally, that phrase soon acquired wings, and even to this day Vespasianus' name is still attached to public urinals in France (*vespasiennes*), Italy (*vespasiani*), and Romania (*vespasiene*).

19. Suetonius *Vespasianus* 9.2.

20. Ibid. 23.4, Cassius Dio 66.17.3.

21. In Latin: '*Vae, puto deus fio*', Suetonius *Vespasianus* 23.4. It will be a very different story with his second son, Domitianus. He was one of the megalomaniacal monsters of Roman history, who styled himself in official documents as *dominus et deus*, 'lord and god' (ibid. *Domitianus* 13, Martial *Epigrammata* 5.8.1, 7.34.8, 10.72.8).

22. There are also the two 'miracles' performed by Vespasianus while he was waiting in Alexandria for the right weather to cross over to Italy. The first *miraculum* involves a blind man, who begs to be cured with Vespasianus' spittle, and the second a crippled man, who wants the future emperor to heal him by standing on his maimed hand. And so the eyes see the light of day and the hand is restored to its full use (Tacitus *Historiae* 4.81, cf. Suetonius *Vespasianus* 7.2, where the second man is lame in one leg).

23. Of relevancy here is surely the picture that the Romans had of the end their very founder met, which combines self-interested deception practised by a powerful group of men with the enlightened deception then resorted to by one of them. Livy (1.15.8–1.16) says that Romulus, who was less loved by the senators than by the army and people, disappeared in a cloud during a sudden storm that broke out while he was reviewing his troops. Senators standing beside his throne said he had been carried aloft. Although a few initial cries that he was now divine led to the general multitude praying to him as a god for his favour, some quietly suggested he had been torn to pieces by the senators (viz. assassination and dismemberment by the senators, each man taking away a piece of the victim). Unease and suspicion persisted until the respected Iulius Proculus conceived the plan of appearing before the people and announcing that Romulus had descended from heaven and that, before going back up into the sky, he had commanded him to 'tell the Romans that by heaven's will my Rome shall be the capital of the world. Let them learn to be soldiers. Let them know, and teach their children, that no power on earth can stand against Roman arms' (Livy 1.16.7). The people than took heart, and believed in Romulus' divinity. This story come from a part of Livy's work (books 1–5) completed between 27 BC and 25 BC, a critical time in the development of the Principate.

24. *Divus*, an epithet implying something like deification, was officially applied to some (viz. Augustus, Claudius, Vespasianus, Titus, Nerva), but not all emperors after death. In the competition to heap up privileges upon the emperor, deification was the ultimate honour the state could bestow. The worship of a ruler as divine or semi-divine had long been the regular expression of loyalty, affection, respect, etc. in the Near East.

25. It is properly said that detailed supervision can only lead to dependence, and will in time kill the use of initiative. Under Vespasianus it would become even more obvious that the powers of the emperor were continuing to grow at the expense of the Senate, and at the end of his reign of ten years, it was discovered that during this time Vespasianus had held eight consulships, Titus seven and Domitianus five.

26. The power of praetorian prefects was a potential source for revolt, as was demonstrated by Sejanus under Tiberius, the removal of Caius Caligula in AD 41, and the Piso conspiracy of AD 65. It might be argued that the Praetorian Guard brought about the fall of Nero, but as we have already seen, it was Nero who let the praetorians down with his dithering, and not vice versa (Tacitus *Historiae* 1.30.2, speech of Piso Licinianus).

27. A damaged papyrus (*P. Hib.* II 215) from Egypt refers to Titus' army buddy Tiberius Iulius Alexander as holding the post of *praefectus praetorio* (ἐπάρχου πρα[τωρίου], fr. B line 7). Now, it is possible to interpret this in two ways. First, this was the rank Tiberius Alexander held during the siege of Jerusalem, viz. when he was serving as Titus' chief-of-staff (Josephus *Bellum Iudaicum* 5.1.6, 6.4.3). Second, and more contentious, he did indeed become a prefect

of the Praetorian Guard in Rome, which in latter years certainly became the ultimate career berth for former prefects of Egypt (Turner 1954: 61–4). In either case, not bad for a man of Jewish birth who also carried the extra stigma of being an *Aegyptius*. For those of you who, like me, wish to believe Tiberius Alexander rose to the esteemed rank of *praefectus praetorio*, perhaps during the principate of Titus, then take a quick look at Juvenal's first satire at the point when the satirist has his xenophobic speaker pointing out the triumphal statues in the Forum of Augustus, 'including a jumped-up Egyptian Pasha's, / whose effigy's only fit for pissing on – or worse' (*Satire* 1.130–1 Green). For Green's 'Pasha', however, read 'Arabarches' in the Latin (Greek ἀραβάχης, an officer of customs in Roman Egypt), though the title in reality was borne by Tiberius Alexander's father, Alexander Lysimachos. See Turner 1954: 63.

28. Caecina Alienus had betrayed in succession Nero, Galba, Vitellius and, apparently, Vespasianus. In civil war, with its shifting allegiances, oaths of fidelity are but feeble bonds. After all, that paragon of Tacitean virtue, Tacitus' own father-in-law Agricola, held office under Galba and Otho at Rome, and after being called away by his mother's death quickly transformed himself into a Flavian.

29. Cassius Dio 65.16.3, Suetonius *Titus* 6. According to Aurelius Victor (*Epitome* 10) Caecina Alienus was put to death by Titus because he suspected him of scheming with his Jewish mistress Queen Berenice (daughter of Herod Agrippa, widow of Herod of Anjar, and sister of Herod Agrippa II).

30. Unfortunately, when it was Titus' turn to be emperor Mount Vesuvius erupted, wiping off the map the Campanian towns of Pompeii and Herculaneum; there was a horrific plague on the Italian peninsula; and an inferno consumed parts of Rome. In all cases, Titus responded generously to the victims. One bright moment in his brief reign was the opening of the Flavian Amphitheatre (Colosseum), which his father had begun building on the site of Nero's grotesque Golden House, *domus aurea*. Titus died suddenly, aged forty-two, of a fever at Acquae Cutiliae – the same place his father had passed away a few years earlier. The meaning of his final words, 'I have made but one mistake' (Suetonius *Titus* 10.2), is unknown. In no time stories began circulating that he had been killed by Domitianus, who felt he had been waiting far too long for the throne of the world.

Chapter 9

1. Gibbon *Decline & Fall* vol. I, chap. III, p. 73.
2. Cassius Dio 53.17.1.
3. The eloquent Seneca, working for the young emperor Nero, was happy to call it what it was, 'a monarchy' (*De beneficiis* 2.20.2).
4. Take for instance Tacitus, who begins the *Annales* proper with the principate of Tiberius, the section on Augustus being only introductory. In these chapters (*Annales* 1.1–10) he examines Augustus as the first of a line of autocrats and conveys some sense of the inevitability of the Principate, an approach that does not reveal the opportunistic nature of Augustus' early career. There was one man, however, who was under no illusion about the young Octavianus, and that was Nero's advisor Seneca. In *Clementia*, Seneca extols before the young emperor the virtue of mercy, the failure to use the absolute power you hold in your hands. As for the clemency of the deified Augustus, well Seneca puts this down to *lassa crudelitas*, 'weariness of cruelty' (*Clementia* 1.11.2).
5. Tacitus *Annales* 1.5.
6. Adopted by Caesar's will (Suetonius *Divus Iulius* 83.2), Octavianus in the usual Roman style took his adoptive father's name, with his own name added in a modified form (he had been born Caius Octavius), becoming Caius Iulius Caesar Octavianus. Not long after he was to add to his nomenclature the title *imperator*, thus becoming Caius Iulius Caesar Octavianus Imperator. Early in January 42 BC the Senate proclaimed Caesar a god (Cassius Dio 47.18.3).

The young Octavianus now conveniently found himself *Divi filius*, 'a son of a god', which brought him, so to speak, halfway to apotheosis, and by 38 BC at the very latest his name was thence finessed into the quite extraordinary form Imperator Iulius Divi f. Caesar, more divine appellation than human nomenclature. Without it, he had nothing. Cicero reports an angry Marcus Antonius as shouting in the Senate 'you, boy, owe everything to your name' (*Philippic* 13.11.24). He was right, of course. To the victor went the spoils, and the spoils in this case were the components of Caesar's vast legacy – political, legal, financial, and genetic. In 27 BC Octavianus would receive from the Senate the equally exalted and unparalleled *cognomen* 'Augustus', a word with profound religious connotations, meaning 'venerable' or 'majestic', almost 'sacred', in recognition of his position of supreme power. On 16 January 27 BC his name thus took on its final and definitive form Imperator Caesar Divi f. Augustus. Not bad for a boy who started life as plain old Octavianus. But there again, the Iulii did claim it was descended from Aeneas, celebrated as the ancestor of the Roman people, and in doing so it also added his mother, the goddess Venus, to the family tree.

7. Livia's first husband had been Tiberius Claudius Nero (Suetonius *Divus Augustus* 62.2), a blue-blooded follower of Marcus Antonius. Livia Drusilla, to give her full name, was also of Claudian stock: her father, who fought against the triumvirs at Philippi and committed suicide after the battle, was a Claudius who had been adopted into the family of the Livii Drusi. She was actually pregnant (with Nero Claudius Drusus, Tiberius' younger brother) when she wed Octavianus on 17 January 38 BC. She was nineteen at the time, seven years younger than Octavianus. She was his third and last wife. The marriage is said to have been a love match, but this is not the whole truth. Octavianus, as Augustus, ruled the world, but Livia ruled Augustus, or so it was said by those having an utter contempt for petticoat politics. As is well known, in chess each king is accompanied by his queen, who proves to be the most active and vicious fighter on the field. This, I believe, is a fitting analogy for the ruling partnership of Augustus and his tough and capable wife, Livia.

8. In practice Tiberius, a mature and experienced general, had served Augustus loyally for years, and already shared his *tribunicia potestas* (6–1 BC, AD 4–14) and his *imperium* in all the imperial provinces. At Tiberius' adoption in AD 4 Augustus said 'I do this for the sake of Rome' (Velleius Paterculus 2.104.1). However, it would be pertinent to note that he was the eighth choice in Augustus' succession plans. Rumour blamed his mother, Livia, whom Caius Caligula later dubbed 'Ulysses in a frock' (Suetonius *Caius* 23.2), for the premature deaths of the other imperial candidates (the picture popularized by Robert Graves with a little help from the master, Tacitus). Whatever the truth of the matter, she was determined that her son should succeed, but he was unenthusiastic about becoming emperor and ended up loathing his position. Tiberius was much happier (and more confortable) playing the part of a soldier than a sovereign.

9. Tacitus *Annales* 3.28.1.

10. This, the first part of the story of Claudius' elevation to the throne, reflects the version given by Josephus' in his detailed but rather jumbled account (*Antiquitates Iudaicae* 19.2.1–3.4). However, his follow-on account (*Antiquitates Iudaicae* 19.4.1–2) of Herod Agrippa's part in all this is clearly a Jewish tradition glorifying Herod Agrippa, which does not harmonize with the Roman tradition.

11. This, the second part of the story of Claudius' elevation, reflects the version in the accounts of both Suetonius (*Divus Claudius* 10) and Cassius Dio (60.1.1–3a).

12. By the end of his reign, Claudius had been hailed as *imperator* twenty-seven times (e.g. *CIL* vi 1256 = *ILS* 218), more than any emperor until Constantine the Great. This may seem surprising to us, but one of Claudius' great achievements was in foreign affairs. There was, of course, the conquest of the southern part of Britannia in AD 43, which had first been 'invaded' by Iulius Caesar, thereby initiating the full-scale annexation of Britannia as a province. The inscription from his (lost) triumphal arch (Arch of Claudius), now in a courtyard of the Musei Capitolini in Rome, declares that 'he received the surrender of

eleven British kings who had been defeated without loss in battle, and was the first to bring barbarian peoples from across the Ocean under the sway of the Roman people' (*CIL* vi 920 = *ILS* 216). There were other military actions. Claudius had inherited a war in Mauretania from Caius Caligula's reign and, once fighting subsided, organized the former kingdom into two provinces, Mauretania Tingitana and Caesariensis, perhaps as early as AD 43. He subdued trouble in Lycia and annexed the region as a province, probably around AD 47 or AD 48. He saw some serious fighting along the Rhine and the Danube.

13. Gibbon *Decline & Fall* vol. I, chap. III, p. 68.
14. Suetonius *Divus Claudius* 10.1–3, Cassius Dio 60.1.3a, Josephus *Antiquitates Iudaicae* 19.4.3, *Bellum Iudaicum* 2.11.2–3.
15. Suetonius *Divus Claudius* 10.4, cf. Josephus *Antiquitates Iudaicae* 19.4.2 gives 5,000 *drachmae* (= 20,000 *sestertii*).
16. Cassius Dio 60.12.4.
17. *PIR²* A 1140.
18. Suetonius *Divus Claudius* 13.2, Cassius Dio 60.15.3, cf. Tacitus *Annales* 12.52.1, *Historiae* 1.89.1, 2.75.1. The two legions of Dalmatia, *VII* and *XI*, were each to earn for themselves the laudatory title *Claudia pia fidelis* for repenting of their actions after their five-day rebellion (Cassius Dio 55.23.4, 60.15.3–4). Do note, however, Cassius Dio calls him Furius Camillus Scribonianus, which is technically correct as he was the *biological* son of Marcus Furius Camillus Scribonianus (*cos.* AD 8) and the *adopted* son of Lucius Arruntius (*cos.* AD 6), the noble who chose to commit suicide rather live under Caius Caligula (Tacitus *Annales* 6.48). Apparently, in his last conversation with Tiberius, Augustus described Arruntius as 'not unworthy of the Principate and would have boldness enough to seize it should the opportunity arise' (ibid. 1.13.1).
19. Suetonius *Otho* 7.1.
20. Tacitus *Historiae* 1.78.3, Plutarch *Otho* 3.1–2, cf. Suetonius *Otho* 12.1.
21. As Augustus says in the virtuoso opening sentence of the *Res Gestae*: 'at the age of nineteen on my own initiative and at my own expense I raised an army, with which I successfully championed the liberty of the Republic when it was oppressed by the tyranny of a faction' (*Res Gestae Divi Augusti* 1.1). Of course, as he puts it, he is simply professing a concern for the 'liberty of the Republic'. The *Res Gestae* is in essence a Roman eulogy in the republican tradition (*vide* the self-aggrandizing inscriptions from the Tombs of the Scipiones, *ILLRP* 311–16), and thus would hardly contain any directly untrue claims, since there would be too many people who could disprove them. This imposed limitations on the author who obviously wishes to represent his actions in the best possible light for posterity. However, the account of his achievements might be highly selective, and indeed they are. For example, in the *Res Gestae* Augustus' opponents do not appear by name; Marcus Antonius heads 'the tyranny of a faction' (op. cit.), Brutus and Cassius are 'murderers of my father' (2), and it is implied that Sextus Pompeius is a nothing other than a pirate (25.1). Of course, the *Res Gestae* was a great public monument designed to present a particular image of Augustus' reign.
22. The terms triumvirate and triumvirs are modern inventions. In Latin, Marcus Antonius, Octavianus and Marcus Aemilius Lepidus (a rich but sluggish noble who did not really count, in spite of the ancient glories of the Aemilii) were sinisterly titled *tresviri rei publicae constituendae*, 'three men with responsibility for settling the state', with the clear implication that the state had broken down. In essence, the three men, who commanded armies, had agreed to form what amounted to a military junta for five years.
23. Tacitus *Historiae* 1.50.4.
24. Suetonius *Vespasianus* 8.3.
25. Ibid. *Divus Augustus* 35.1.
26. Ibid. 35.2, cf. 19.1.
27. Ibid. 49.1.
28. Cicero *pro Murena* 52.

29. Ibid. *In Catilinam* 2.20.
30. See Fields 2008B: 72–6, 182, 185.
31. Helvidius Priscus has frequently been characterized as an uncompromising republican, but his main point of opposition appears to have been concerned not with the presence of the emperor *per se* but with the rôle of the Senate in relation to the emperor. For a good account of his opposition, see Levick 1999. By contrast, his father-in-law, Thrasea Paetus, had always distinguished himself by republican sentiments, paying, for instance, especial honours to the images of Brutus and Cassius, the murderers of Caesar, and celebrating their birthdays in grand style.
32. Tacitus *Agricola* 42.5.
33. As Syme shrewdly observed, 'As a Roman historian, Tacitus had to be a republican: in his life and in his politics he was a monarchist' (1956: 517).
34. As Tacitus puts into the mouth of a senator, 'while I pray for good emperors, I can endure whomsoever we may have' (*bonos imperatores voto expetere, qualiscumque tolerare, Historiae* 4.8.2).
35. E.g. Suetonius' bold assertion that Otho, 'avoiding all promises, told the troops merely that he would welcome whatever powers they might give him, but claim no others'(*Otho* 6.3), or that of Tacitus when he says 'everything was then ordered according to the will of the soldiery' (*Historiae* 1.46.1).
36. Tacitus *Historiae* 1.80–82.
37. At the root of the psychology of war is the myth of glory, first introduced into western thought by the ancient Greeks and sustained by almost all national and religious authorities of every nation-state ever since. Even today, where modern technology has usurped the traditional role of the individual soldier, the myth that war provides an opportunity for unique virtue still remains true. No army, to my knowledge, has yet abandoned the custom of awarding battle decorations even though the level of personal combat required to kill, in the main, has dropped almost to zero. At the same time, military institutions remain cluttered with a vast array of trophies from past conflicts and the promise that the brave acts of the soldier will live on in the collective memories of the people remains, especially for the young, as seductive as ever. The myth of glory and its accompanying promise of virtue and eternal memory seem out of place, false, and unrealistic in modern warfare as the chariot and the bow. And yet it continues as a powerful social custom whose utility lies in its ability to initiate the green recruit into the military tribe. Its presence remains a serious obstacle to unlearning the art of war.
38. In Latin: *legiones classes provincias, cunta inter se conexa,* Tacitus *Annales* 1.9.1.
39. In German: *Unglücklich das Land, das Helden nötig hat,* Brecht *Leben des Galilei,* (1939) scene 12, p. 115. The poetry and plays of Bertolt Brecht are especially noted for their political content, pungent satire and teasing irony. In Brecht's view, man, the thinking being, has a greater influence on history than those who claim to be in charge. But, paradoxically, the thinking man is under the disposal of those with power. Power can control and dominate the world for a brief period but the thinking makers of history will, sooner or later, break the chains and emerge as the supreme force that decides the course of human history. For Brecht, as a committed Marxist, those with power are mere puppets in the hands of history.
40. Carlyle, T., 1841. *On Heroes, Hero-Worship, and the Heroic in History,* p. 1. Thomas Carlyle (1795–1881), who was both a satirist and prophet, represented Calvinism secularized. He vehemently denounced the evils of the present, even while he dealt with the past. He expounded his doctrines on the conduct of the individual man and the organization of society. As he aged he became more and more hostile to democracy, which he feared and flouted. To the egalitarian idea he opposed that of hero worship, and in doing so comes very close to the worship of mere strength: 'might is right'.
41. Dio Chrysostom *On Wealth* 79.6.
42. Spinoza, B., 1670. *Tractatus Theologico-Politicus, praefatio.*

Epilogue
1. Tacitus *Historiae* 2.86.1, 2, cf. Velleius Paterculus' description of Marius 'as excellent in war as he was the worst man in peace' (2.11.1).
2. There can be no test of a soldier but that of war, and 'war', said General Wolfe, 'is in its nature hazardous and an option of difficulties' (Letter to Major Rickson, Blackheath, 5 November 1757).
3. Martial *Epigrammata* 10.23.3.
4. Martial's death is mentioned by the younger Pliny (*Epistulae* 3.21.1), but his charming homily to one of his dearest friends gives us no fixed date.
5. Martial *Epigrammata* 10.32.
6. Ibid. 9.99. In this epigram Martial honours Antonius Primus as 'the undeniable glory of Palladia Tolosa' (In Latin: *Marcus Palladiae non infitianda Tolosae*, ibid. 9.99.3). It was Domitianus who had awarded Tolosa the title of *Palladia*, a reference to the emperor's favourite goddess, Pallas Athena (Roman Minerva), who he worshipped passionately.
7. Martial *Epigrammata* 10.23.
8. Ibid. 10.73.3. The gastronomic Apicius we have already met. Fabricius, on the other hand, was Aulus Didius Gallus Fabricius Veiento, the adopted son of Didius Gallus who was legate governor of Britannia AD 52–57. An honours-broker (and praetor) under Nero, he was expelled from Italy in AD 62 for perpetrating a libellous mock-will (Tacitus *Annales* 14.50). He was recalled by Vespasianus, and by AD 83 had been consul three times. Under Domitianus he was an informer, but contrived to remain on good terms with Domitianus' successor Nerva. References to him (e.g. Juvenal *Satire* 3.185, 4.133, Pliny *Epistulae* 4.22.4–5) are not very flattering, and his wife (who was actually called Attica) may have been the Eppia who ran off with a gladiator (Juvenal *Satire* 6.82, 110–13).
9. In Latin: *hoc est / vivere bis, vita posse priori frui*, Martial *Epigrammata* 10.23.7–8.
10. *ILS* 9199 = McCrum-Woodhead 335 = Campbell 95.
11. Named for the Canaanite god Baal, Baalbek is not mentioned in the extant texts from ancient Assyria nor in the Bible. Furthermore, Assyrians, Babylonians, Persians and Macedonians all passed through the Massyas (Beqaa) valley, but none record a sanctuary at the source of the Orontes and Leontes (Litani). It is possible that the site is identical to the town called Triparadeios, where in 320 BC the warring generals of Alexander met in conference and carved up his empire (Diodoros 18.39.1–7, cf. Arrian *FGrHist* 56 F9 §§34–38). The Greeks, who identified Baal with the sun-god Helios, translated Baalbek into Heliopolis, and the Romans, in their turn, spoke of Iuppiter of Heliopolis. Some argue that Augustus settled some of his veterans in the town. However, the Roman jurist Ulpianus says (*Digesta* 50.15.1§2) that Heliopolis became a *colonia* during the principate of Septimius Severus after the civil war with Pescennius Niger in AD 193/194.
12. The name of the emperor has been mutilated in the inscription, but it is presumed to be Nero. For a good description of an award ceremony in the field, see Josephus (*Bellum Iudaicum* 7.1.3, cf. Polybios 6.39.2–6), where he describes Titus Caesar presiding over such a parade after the fall of Jerusalem in AD 70.
13. *Corona vallaris*, a crown made of gold and ornamented with a rampart and given to the man (usually restricted, but not always, to centurion rank and above) first over the enemy rampart or *vallum*. However, Maxfield (1981: 64) reckons that all crowns bar the prestigious *corona civica* of oak leaves, which was awarded to a soldier irrespective of rank for saving the life of a fellow citizen on the field of battle (Pliny *Historia Naturalis* 16.3), had now lost all connection with the deeds that they originally were contrived to commemorate.
14. *Corona aurea*, a plain gold crown, originally awarded for killing an enemy in single combat and holding the ground to the end of the battle, but now probably awarded for gallantry and invariably restricted to centurion rank and above.
15. *Vexillum*, a miniature flag or banner mounted on a silver base, which served as a general award for officers of senatorial and equestrian status.

16. *Hasta pura*, a blunt-headed, miniature spear possibly with a silver shaft, originally awarded for killing an enemy in single combat, but now probably served as a general award for officers of senatorial and equestrian status.

17. The new Roman urban centres of client tribes were called *civitates* (sing. *civitas*), and were usually re-founded on or close to the site of an old pre-Roman capital. Tacitus scathingly describes how the Britons of his day embraced the new urban centres: 'All this in their ignorance, they called civilisation, when it was but a part of their servitude' (*Idque apud imperitos humanitas vocabatus, cum pars servitutis esset, Agricola* 21.4).

18. On retiring from the post of *primus pilus*, Antonius Naso would have been elevated to the *ordo equester*, which therefore qualified him for those two *vexilla* and two *hastae purae*.

19. Created by Augustus in AD 6, the *vigiles urbani*, watchmen of the city, served as a permanent fire brigade and a night-time police force. Recruited from freedmen who served for six year, there were seven cohorts in all, each cohort responsible for tackling fires in two of the fourteen *regiones* into which Rome was now divided. Headed by the *praefectus vigilum*, who was of equestrian status, the *vigiles* were under military command, their tribunes having seen service as *primi pili* in the legions, and their centurions were former praetorians who had become *evocati* (viz. retained after their sixteen-years' service). However, the *vigiles* carried no weapons. Claudius had one *cohors vigilum* stationed at Puteoli and another at Ostia (Suetonius *Divus Claudius* 25.6), the two large seaports through which grain supplies went to Rome.

20. As the inscription is somewhat illegible here, others (e.g. Wellesley 2000: 2–1 following McCrum-Woodhead 335) have stated that he was the *legatus legionis* of this legion. If so, then Antonius Naso, as far as I know, would be the first example of an *eques* commanding a legion outside of Egypt. A *legatus legionis* was appointed from the senatorial order by the emperor to command in his name, and by the end of the Iulio-Claudian period only a senator who had already served as praetor was eligible. The command of a legion, therefore, now had a definite place in the hierarchy of the senatorial order, and was usually held for a period of about three years. At a later stage, after having held a consulship, a senator would have become a provincial governor and, if in an armed province, ranked as a *legatus Augusti pro praetore*, praetorian legate of the emperor, and had control over the legions stationed there. In this way the emperor governed through his senatorial *legati*, who held delegated power or *imperium*.

21. For an excellent summary of Antonius Naso's career viz. centurionate and tribunate, see Summerly 1992: 16–17. For his subsequent career, see Dobson 1978: 75.

22. *CIL* 6693 = *ILS* 253 = McCrum-Woodhead 421. Also, there are two very rare coins struck the same year in the name of Antonius Naso as procurator of Bithynia-Pontus. On both, the obverse shows a portrait bust of Domitianus, the reverse bears the Greek legend EΠI Λ ΑΝΤΩΝΙΟΥ ΝΑΣΩΝΟΣ ΕΠΙΤΡΟΝΟΥ (*RPC* S2-II–631A, B).

23. This is merely speculation on my part, and perhaps I am reading too much into it, but perhaps a Syrian ancestor of Antonius Naso adopted the *nomen* of the *gens Antonia* when he was enfranchised by the most famous of the Antonii, Marcus Antonius, when the *triumvir* was in that part of the world preparing for his Parthian campaign.

24. There is nothing to suggest that outside of official government circles Latin ever became an accepted language, let alone the normal language of daily speech. Nor did it ever supplant Greek as the literary language of the Roman Near East (the *Res Gestae* of Ammianus Marcellinus, a native of Antioch, being the exception of course).

Appendix 1

1. The region was initially conquered by Tiberius, the future emperor, in 12–9 BC, following operations by Marcus Vinicius (*cos.* 19 BC) and Agrippa in 14 BC and 13 BC, but revolted in AD 6 and was not finally subdued by Tiberius until AD 9.

Appendix 2

1. E.g. *Res Gestae Divi Augusti* 13, 30.1, 32.3.
2. Tacitus *Annales* 1.17.3.
3. Cassius Dio 52.27.1.
4. *Sub vexillo,* hence *vexillarii*, a corps of veterans, a reserve.
5. Apparently they were not to be called upon to take part in entrenching the marching camp, in keeping guard, et cetera.
6. Cassius Dio 54.25.6, 55.23.1.
7. Ibid. 55.25.2, cf. Suetonius *Divus Augustus* 49.2, Tacitus *Annales* 1.78.2.
8. *Res Gestae Divi Augusti* 17.2.
9. Tacitus *Annales* 1.6.
10. Ibid. 1.17. Once again, according to Tacitus, such bribes were still being 'paid as a kind of annual tribute' (*Historiae* 1.46, cf. 58.1) to centurions by common soldiers in AD 69. One policy that was to outlast Vitellius was the ending of this invidious practice, a change Tacitus describes as being adopted by 'all good emperors'.
11. Tertullian *ad Martyras* 3.
12. Tacitus *Annales* 1.17.6.
13. Suetonius *Domitianus* 7.35, 12.1. The next pay rise for the army was not to occur until the principate of Septimius Severus, when legionary pay rose to perhaps 1,800 *sestertii* (450 *denarii*) – Herodian (3.8.4–5) does not give the actual amount but the figure given is based on the next pay rise throughout the army, that made by Caracalla (ibid. 4.4.7). In the two centuries between Augustus and Septimius Severus, there was an increase of 100–200 per cent in legionary pay, a rate well below that of even the most budget-conscious modern governments.
14. Cassius Dio 67.3.5.
15. E.g. Campbell 24, 25.

Appendix 3

1. In Latin: *cedo alteram*. This fellow, who enjoyed a well-earned hatred, was one of the first victims of mutiny of the army in Pannonia after the death of Augustus (Tacitus *Annales* 1.23).
2. Tacitus *Annales* 1.23.1.
3. Forni 1953: 157–212.
4. Called such because an *optio* was *adoptandum*, 'adopted', by his centurion (Varro *de lingua Latina* 5.91, Festus 201.23).
5. In Latin: *contubernales*, literally 'tent-mates'.
6. *Digesta* 50.6.7.
7. *RIB* 481.
8. Josephus *Bellum Iudaicum* 3.68.
9. Tacitus *Annales* 14.32.6.
10. Tacitus *Historiae* 3.44.1, Suetonius *Vespasianus* 4.1, Cassius Dio 60.20.3, *ILS* 2696, *AE* 1924.78.
11. *CIL* v 7165, *RIB* 292, 294, 296.
12. *ND Occ.* XXVIII$_{13, 19}$: 'At the disposal of the respectable man, the count of the Saxon Shore in Britannia ... the prefect of *legionis secundae Augustae* at *Rutupiae* (Richborough).'
13. *CIL* iii 6580 = *ILS* 2304 = Campbell 249. For a different theory with regards the term *origo castris*, see le Bohec 2000: 80–1.
14. Tacitus *Annales* 15.8–17.
15. Ibid. 14.32.2.
16. Ibid. 14.38.1.
17. Ibid. *Germania* 29.1.

18. Ibid. *Historiae* 1.59.1, 2.27.2, 66.2, 4.12.3, 15.1, cf. *Annales* 2.8, 11. It has been calculated that the total population of the Batavi was no more than 35,000 (Willems 1986: 234–8), which looks as if one son from every family may have 'signed up' for service with Rome. The earliest known use of these warriors was in AD 16, when we hear of a unit of Batavi under their own chieftain Chariovalda supporting a Roman expedition across the Rhine under Germanicus (Tacitus *Annales* 2.11). Living, as they did, on the '*insula Batavorum*' (Caesar *Bellum Gallicum* 4.10.1), an island in the Rhine-Meuss/Maas (*Rhenus-Mosa*) delta system, the Batavi were unsurprisingly renowned for their prowess at swimming, and the *ala* of Batavi were 'a picked cavalry force specially trained for amphibious operations' (Tacitus *Historiae* 4.12.4, cf. 2.35.1, 5.14.2, *Agricola* 18.4, Cassius Dio 55.24.7, 60.20). Soranus, a trooper of *cohors III Batavorum milliaria equitata*, had performed on manoeuvres, in front of the emperor Hadrian, what he claims in his epitaph (*ILS* 2558 = Campbell 47) was a unique feat. After swimming the Danube in full battle kit, he shot an arrow in the air and hit it with a second one before the first fell to earth. The unit was not bow-armed (*sagittaria*) and Soranus displayed a skill of little practical use in battle, but he did this, as Cassius Dio (69.9.6) confirms, on manoeuvres.
19. Tacitus *Annales* 4.47.4.
20. Ibid. *Historiae* 2.89.2, cf. 1.68.2, 70.3, 2.14.1 for cohorts of Thracians, Germans, Raetians, Gauls, Lustianians, Britons, Ligurians, Tungrians. Our author of course paints this particular Vitellian episode with Rome as a symbol of culture trampled under the boots of barbarism.
21. *RIB* 109.
22. Hyginus 16, cf. *CIL* iii 6581.
23. Fink 80, cf. Arrian *Ars Taktika* 18.3 DeVoto.
24. Hyginus 26–27.
25. *ILS* 2690.
26. Tacitus *Germania* 28.
27. Caesar *Bellum Gallicum* 7.65.5, 8.36.4, cf. Tacitus *Germania* 6.2.
28. Vegetius *Epitoma rei militaris* 1.15.

Appendix 4

1. Cicero *Tusculanae disputationes* 2.37.
2. Cicero was practically without military experience – as a young man he had served for a very short time in the army of Cnaeus Pompeius Strabo, father of Pompey the Great, during the Social War (Cicero *Philippic* 12.27, cf. *ILS* 8888) – and anything but a soldier. It was not that he had so little experience in war; the truth of the matter was that he was uninterested in war.
3. Gibbon *Decline & Fall* I.1.28. His allusion to the soldier of his own day is very reminiscent of Guibert's in his famous *Essai général de Tactique* where he draws attention (1775: II.307) to the habits of the French soldier as he found him on the eve of the Revolution, a squanderer, impatient, physically weak, addicted to material comforts, all of which he ascribes to the exclusive adoption of the magazine system to provide the maintenance of an army in times of war. This was the epoch of the professional mercenary armies of eighteenth-century absolutism, which marched and manoeuvred in a sort of detached world, detached, that is, from the populations of the territories through which they passed. Of course, unlike Gibbon's 'modern soldier', the infantryman is still the heaviest laden fighting animal in the world and, by nature of his role in combat as the 'Queen of Battles', must remain so into the indefinite future. Today's infantrymen operate as beasts of burden, as the legionaries had done, and those who think otherwise are fooling themselves. Infantry has formed the bedrock of the art of warfare since time immemorial. Through the ancient ages and recent history it has evolved itself. The evolution has been a journey of adaptability to survive every advent in technology that hoped to replace it. For all the talk of precision munitions and autonomous weapons, the very ground war remains human bodies.

4. As a matter of interest, a bronze Imperial Italic 'C' helmet was recovered from Cremona, and is now in the Museo Stibbert, Florence. This pattern would have been worn anytime between AD 60 and AD 120, and it therefore possible that this particular helmet was lost at one of the battles of Cremona in AD 69. The main difference between Gallic and Italic patterns was one of ornamentation, the former being generally more ornate than the latter. Imperial helmets might be made of iron or bronze, although the latter is far more common for the Gallic type.

5. An excellent example of this habit is to be found in the Museo di Storia ed Arte di Trieste, for here is displayed a Buggenum type helmet (inv. 3648), dated to the time of the triumvirate wars. On the large neck guard of this bronze helmet are scratched two inscriptions, one above the other: the external (older) one reads 7 • POSTVMI • M • VALERI • BACINI (Marcus Valerius Bacinus (or Bacenus) century of Postumus); the internal (newer) one reads 7 • CAESIDIENI • C • TOMIVS (Caius Tomius century of Caesidienos). Thus, the helmet served two legionaries (with Celtic *cognomina*), one after the other.

6. Immersion foot, what was once known as trench foot, is a painful disorder resulting from prolonged exposure in a damp or wet environment in which the skin wrinkles and creases then layers begin separating, leaving the foot raw and putrid with fungal infections. Just to take one example I am familiar with, during the war on the Falkland Islands, despite socks being regularly changed for dry ones and wet socks being dried out inside combat jackets with body heat during the day, 2 PARA lost nearly as many from trench foot and frostbite as from enemy action.

7. Josephus *Bellum Iudaicum* 6.1.8.

8. Tacitus *Historiae* 3.50.3.

9. Suetonius *Vespasianus* 8.3.

10. *Tab. Vindol.* II 346. In March 1973 at the fort of Vindolanda, just south of the Tyne–Solway frontier, a wooden writing-tablet was discovered. Since then, thousands more have followed. Their deposition dates vary from AD 90 to AD 125 (Hadrian's Wall was begun in AD 122). They include letters and documents, both private and administrative, which cast much needed light upon aspects of Roman life: military, social, private, economic etcetera.

11. Such evidence warns us not to assume that Greek names necessarily indicate either servile status or an origin in the Greek east. Though we are more familiar with the idea of the adoption of Roman names by auxiliary soldiers, Greek names were not uncommon, for example, among members of the *custodes corporis Germani*. Other Greek names are evident in the ink writing-tablets, such as Paris and Corinthus (*Tab. Vindol.* II 311) and Hermes (*Tab. Vindol.* II 186). Of some relevance here is the 1916 study of the *cognomina* of legionaries conducted by L.R. Dean. Despite its age, Dean's study is still of value because it was based on a truly representative sample of 5,700 cases. Unsurprisingly, at the top there are fifty-six Latin names (except for one, Alexander/Alexandrus) with a frequency rate of more than twenty. Though it reveals only 192 names for 328 men, the second most frequent category is Greek (Dean 1916: 97–9). On the military list of AD 194 at Alexandria mentioned before (*CIL* iii 6580 = *ILS* 2304 = Campbell 249), nineteen of the names are Greek, ten of which (out of the twenty-four) are *origo castris* (Dean 1916: 98).

12. In the Roman army no orders were given in Greek, Egyptian or Aramaic, the languages of the defeated. So, not only did a soldier need to speak Latin, he also needed to be able to read it. He might enter the army as an unlettered provincial: he left not only with Roman citizenship but also with two-and-a-half decades' experience of literacy and numeracy in Latin. By way of a comparison, in the final decades of its existence, the Soviet Union consisted of fifteen sub-national Soviet republics, and the natives of each of these republics invariably spoke different languages and some republics had even more than one language. As a native of Siberia had great difficulty communicating with a native of Georgia, the Soviet army was thus considered a crucible into which young men would go in as Siberians or Georgians and

come out as Russians. One scheme to develop friendship between the peoples and to foster national understanding, was to put men from different republics into the same regiment, an idea that seemed admirable in theory but in practice it meant a platoon of soldiers very often did not understand either their platoon commander or one another. Unlike the Roman army, the Soviet army did not have the benefit of an official universal language. On top of that, the multilingual Soviet Union was also, along with seven other communist states, a member of the Warsaw Pact.

13. E.g. Xenophon *Peri Hippikes* 8.5, 10.2.
14. Readers of Roman texts will notice that nowhere do Roman authors use the term *lorica segmentata*. In fact, the term was first coined during the Renaissance.
15. Anon. *De rebus bellicis* 15.1–2.
16. E.g. Josephus *Bellum Iudaicum* 3.273.
17. Ibid. 3.96.
18. Trajan's Column scenes v, xlii, xlix, lxxxix, civ.
19. Junkelmann 1991: 188.
20. Caesar *Bellum Gallicum* 1.25.3.
21. Bishop–Coulston 1993: 48.
22. Josephus *Bellum Iudaicum* 3.96.
23. Arrian *Ars Tactica* 40.10–11 DeVoto.
24. Gunn 1973: 43.
25. Ulbert 1969.
26. Connolly 1997: 49–56.
27. Unlike bronze, iron was worked by forging rather than casting. All bronze weapons were cast from molten metal. Contrastingly, iron weapons had to be beaten into shape as it was impossible to obtain sufficient temperature from the casting of iron. Beaten weapons were far stronger than cast ones, but the early technology of iron did not produce a commodity superior to bronze until a form of carburisation was tried, leading to the production of a steel-like metal. It was the cheapness and comparative abundance of iron ores that was the root of its popularity over bronze, which, after all, was a strenuous merger of copper and tin. Anyway, it is controversial whether the Romans used steel. According to Manning (1976: 148) 'there is no evidence for widespread, regular, intentional production of steel in the Roman Empire'. The problem is that the only essential difference between iron and steel is the amount of carbon in the metal. Regular wrought iron has a carbon content of about 0.5 per cent and steel has a carbon content of 1.5 per cent. It is possible that this much carbon was imparted to the blade by the charcoal used to heat the metal as the smith forged the blade. This contact between the metal and charcoal created a sort of outer layer of steel in a process called carburisation (Manning 1976: 148). It is doubtful that the Romans were aware that this process was taking place, but the end product was 'blister steel', so called because of its blistered surface.
28. The balance point of a standard sword was some ten centimetres above the hilt. The fulcrum, therefore, is so positioned to effectively encourage the swing using the pommel in a pendulum like fashion to add weight to the slash.
29. This oval shape allows for the use of the whole hand for the thrust. Compared with medieval cross-hilts, which were comparatively thin, the ovular type was essentially in contact on all points with the hand. This meant that when the thrust was delivered, the legionary could bring to bear with equal force his entire hand and arm.
30. Josephus *Bellum Iudaicum* 3.96.
31. Vegetius *Epitoma rei militaris* 2.23.
32. McLeod 1965: 8.
33. Paterson 1966: 83.
34. E.g. Josephus *Bellum Iudaicum* 3.152.

35. Ibid. 5.135.
36. Coulston 1985: 282.
37. Pollux (*Onmasticon* 1.137) mentions fire-arrows as a well-recognized class of missile, and Cassius Dio relates that, in the crisis of the battle of Actium, Octavianus endeavoured to set Marcus Antonius' ships ablaze by a shower of 'fiery shafts' (50.34.2).
38. Birch, hornbeam, some oak, and some ash being both strong enough to stand in a bow, but also light enough to fly.
39. Technically known as the archer's paradox.
40. Coulston 1985: 266–7.
41. According to the physician, Paulus Aegineta (6.88.2), this was done with the intention of complicating the extraction, or, according to Ammianus Marcellinus (31.15.11), to prevent the enemy from reusing one's own arrows. These two passages are salutary reminders of how an author's intellectual background and the contents and the aims of his work can influence his view of things.
42. See especially, Massey 1994: 36–9.
43. This is the weight range of the best known find of lead sling bullets, the group of 500 from Olynthos excavated in the late nineteen-twenties and early nineteen-thirties (Korfmann 1973). Olynthos, head of the Chalkidic *poleis*, was besieged and sacked by Philip II of Macedon in 348 BC. In fact, Philip so thoroughly levelled Olynthos as to excite the comment of one Athenian contemporary, the statesman Demosthenes (*Philippic* 3.117), that a visitor to the place would never realize that there had been a city there.
44. Many of the so-called *glandes Perusinae*, the lead sling bullets recovered from Perugia and dating to the siege of Perusia of winter 41/40 BC, exhibit brief obscenities, denigrating the leaders of opposing armies, emphasizing their physical defects, doubting their sexual orientation, and are envisaged as being aimed directly at them to strike them in particularly tender parts of the male or female anatomy. Thus, L(vcivs) A(ntonivs) CALVE (et) FVLVIAE CVLVM PAN(dite) – 'bald Lucius Antonius and you too, Fulvia, open up your arsehole' (*CIL* xi 6721.14) – on a bullet slung by one of Octavianus' soldiers in the besieging army, which evoked a matching response PETO OCTAVIA(ni) CVLVM – 'I'm heading for Octavianus' arsehole' (*CIL* xi 6721.7) – from the besieged army of Fulvia, loyal wife of Marcus Antonius, and Lucius Antonius Pietas (*cos.* 41 BC), his younger brother. As is common in any war of words, accusations are for the most part baseless. However, it is interesting to note that Lucius Antonius' receding hairline is known from his consular coinage (e.g. Sydenham 1185). For the *glandes Perusinae*, see Griffiths 1989: 267–9.
45. Vegetius *Epitoma rei militaris* 3.14.
46. Xenophon *Anabasis* 3.3.16, 17.
47. Ferrill 1985: 25.
48. Connolly 1998: 48–9.
49. Korfmann 1973: 37.
50. Demmin 1893: 876.
51. For reported ranges achieved for casts by slings, see especially Brown Vega-Craig 2009: Table 1, p. 1265.
52. Vegetius *Epitoma rei militaris* 1.16.
53. Celsus *De medicina* 5.26.5, 7.5.4.
54. Diodoros 5.18.3, Strabo 3.5.1, Florus *Epitomae* 1.43.5.

Appendix 5

1. Iron rations on active service are usually mentioned in connection with second-century generals who are considered authoritarian, for instance Avidius Cassius, who 'forbade the soldiers when on campaign to carry anything except bacon, hardtack, and sour wine' (*SHA* Avidius Cassius 5.3), or Caius Pescennius Niger, who 'gave orders that no one was to drink [good] wine on

campaign, but that they should be content with sour wine' (*SHA* Pescennius Niger 10.3). If we can actually trust the notoriously untrustworthy *SHA*, the latter emperor (a usurper, in truth) was the living personification of severity itself, especially when it came to his soldiers and their understandable fondness for wine, *vinum*, of course, not *acetum*. Once, when his soldiers in Egypt asked for wine, he curtly replied 'do you ask for wine when you have the Nile?' (ibid. 7.6). Another time, when his unhappy soldiers exclaimed 'we get no wine, we cannot fight', he replied 'then blush, for the men [Saracens] who defeated you don't drink wine' (ibid. 7.8). He himself was apparently 'very fond of wine' (*vini avidus*, ibid. 6.6).

2. Yeast made its debut in the days of the Republic, but conservatism meant a resistance to eat the light bread as it was considered unhealthy. For the soldier then 'bread' was unleavened crust. The elder Cato had called this 'kneaded bread', *panis depicius*, which he made as follows: 'Wash your hands and a bowl thoroughly. Pour into the bowl, add water gradually, and knead thoroughly. When it is well kneaded, roll out and bake under a crock' (*De agri cultura* 74). His flour, *farina*, was wholemeal spelt flour, and the resulting loaf looked more like a modern pitta and is the ancestor of the pizza. Another form of unleavened bread was 'quick bread', *panis strepticus*, which was rolled into wafer-thin sheets then baked quickly, probably on a hot stone or in the ashes of a fire. This was probably the daily bread of our soldier. Reference to the behaviour of Caracalla on campaign, living the life of one of his soldiers, states that he 'would grind enough grain for himself with his own hands and make a *mâza* (literally 'kneaded thing') which, after baking in the ashes, he would eat' (Herodian 4.7.5, cf. Cassius Dio 62.5.5). Normally in peacetime fresh bread was eaten.

3. E.g. *SHA* Avidius Cassius 5.3, *SHA* Pescennius Niger 10.4, Ammianus Marcellinus 17.8.2. The Latin word *bucellatum* was derived from *buccella*, a small mouthful. In the late Roman empire the term *bucellatum* would lend itself to soldiers known as *bucellarii* (sing. *bucellarius*), biscuit-eaters, hired bands of private retainers attached to military magnates, warlords such as Stillicho and Aëtius. In effect private armies, *bucellarii* could be relied upon to follow their commanders wherever they went and, due to the need for mobility, they were exclusively horsemen. The court-poet Claudian (*In Rufinum* 2.76–77) tells us that Arcadius' praetorian prefect Rufinus maintained an armed retinue of barbarians, and we learn from another source (*Chronica Minora* 1.650) that this corps was composed exclusively of Huns. The term *bucellarius* neatly reflects the fact that the commander himself supplied his *bucellarii* their daily rations. Liebeschuetz (1991: 45) makes the valid point that the men who joined these fighting retinues perhaps did so because their Roman paymaster could guarantee them long-term employment and full bellies. For his African campaign Count Belisarios (d. AD 565), the outstanding general of the age, enlisted around 1,100 *bucellarii*, including 300 Huns, horse-warriors who had made a private contract with him, albeit supplemented by the *sacramentum* oath to the emperor (Procopius *Wars* 3.17.1, 3, 19.24, 4.18.6, cf. 7.1.18–20, *Anékdota* 4.13). It was with his *bucellarii* that he put down the Nika revolt of AD 532 in Constantinople, slaughtering possibly 30,000 citizens in the process. As an institution the *bucellarii* are found during the barbarian invasions/migrations of the late fourth century, while the usage of the term was common by the twenties of the fifth century when Olympiodoros notes that 'in the days of Honorius, the name *bucellarius* was borne not only by Roman soldiers, but also by some Goths' (fr. 7.4). This development, however, meant the emperors lost their monopoly of violence, and so, by the late sixth century, the *bucellarii* had been taken over and were henceforth paid for by the state and fully incorporated into the imperial army.

4. Pliny *Historia Naturalis* 18.67, Cicero *Tusculanae disputationes* 5.97, cf. *SHA* Divus Aurelianus 9.6.

5. Pliny *Epistulae* 6.16.4, cf. 20.1. The elder Pliny was a polymath who died in the eruption of Mount Vesuvius in August AD 79 as he was making observations on the event. He was the younger Pliny's maternal uncle, and mother and son were both staying at Misenum at the time of his death.

6. Pliny *Historia Naturalis* 22.138.
7. It has been calculated that the 300,000 soldiers of the Roman army required about 100,000 tonnes (or 15 million *modii*) of wheat annually – including an addition allocation for cavalrymen (Garnsey/Saller 1987: 88–90).
8. Knights *et al.* 1983.
9. Davies 1989: 192 Table I, 194 Table II, 195 Table III.
10. Polybios (2.15.3) once observed that in Italy acorns were used to feed a large number of swine, which were slaughtered not only for private consumption but also to feed the army. Whereas cattle fulfilled all kinds of practical functions, sheep provided wool, goats gave their milk, geese and chickens likewise their eggs, the only animal that had no other use than for the spit or the pot was the pig. Pork was succulent, sumptuous meat. Only the pig lives to be eaten. Indeed, the Romans ate every bit of the pig, apart from the bones and the eyes: the ears, the cheek, the jaw, snout and tongue were all considered delicacies. Just as the elder Pliny once said: 'No other animal produces so much material for cooking' (*Historia Naturalis* 8.77).
11. *Tab. Vindol.* II 299. According to the elder Pliny (*Historia Naturalis* 9.169), oysters were plentiful on the coasts of Britannia, Richborough-*Rutupiae*, much like nearby Whitstable today, being a particularly well-known source. Indeed, oysters were discovered stored in the cellar at Richborough-*Rutupiae*, and Juvenal refers to oysters raised 'on the sea-beds of Rutupiae' (*Satire* 4.143 Green); it is not absolute certain, but it is possible that our satirist was once a tribune in command of *cohors I Dalmatarum* in Britannia (*CIL* x 5382 = *ILS* 2926, cf. *RIB* 1795). Believe it or not, oysters do travel well and are quite commonly found at military sites in Britain and Germany. See especially, Davies 1989: 193–4.
12. Apicius *De re coquinaria* 8.7.380.
13. Cato *De agri cultura* 58.
14. Appian *Iberica* 54.
15. E.g. *Tab. Vindol.* II 190.27.
16. Polybios 3.72.4.
17. Sixth-century papyri (*P. Oxy.* 1920, 2046, cf. 2013, 2014, Polybios 6.39.3) from Egypt record a daily ration of 1.4 kilograms of bread, 0.45 kilograms of meat, one litre of *acetum* and five centilitres of olive oil per soldier.
18. *RIB* 2415.56. The measure holds 9.82 litres up to the gauge mark, which is a more or less equivalent to the common Roman measure of capacity, the *modius* (pl. *modii*). The Carvoran-*Magnis* grain measure carries an inscription to Domitianus and is dated to AD 90/91 and actually states its capacity to be 17.5 *sextarii* (9.54 litres). Is this for reasons of natural error, or because fraud was integrated into the design so as to shortchange the locals? Note, one *modius* = sixteen *sextarii*.
19. E.g. a small millstone (42cm ø) from Saalburg bears the inscription CON(tvbernivm) BRITTONIS, 'mess-group of Britto' (*CIL* xiii 11954a). Here it should be noted that Britto was merely the logistical/administrative leader of his mess-group, not a small unit commander. Due to its small size, this Saalburg millstone was probably for campaign use too. Hand-mills or querns were to be found amongst the equipment necessary for a campaigning army simply because they were, as the Greek soldier Xenophon explains, 'the least heavy amongst implements used for grinding corn' (*Kyroupaideia* 1.2.11). This meant that the troops could carry ungrounded grain and thus reduce the risk of spoilage, as well as allowing them to take advantage of grain collected on the march.
20. Josephus *Bellum Iudaicum* 3.85.
21. Appian *Iberica* 85, cf. Plutarch *Moralia* 201C, Frontinus *Strategemata* 4.1.1, 2, Polyainos *Strategemata* 8.16.2.
22. Appian *Iberica* 54, *SHA* Hadrian 10.2, Vegetius *Epitoma rei militaris* 3.3.
23. John 19:29.

24. Plautus *Miles Gloriosus* 837, *Truculentus* 610, Suetonius *Vitellius* 12.1, cf. 10.3.
25. Pliny *Historia Naturalis* 23.27.
26. Celsus *De medicina* 4.5.4, 4.26.3, 9.
27. SVRRE(ntinvm) PERV(etvs), Callender 1965: 37–41. According to Athenaios (d. AD 230), the Greek gastronomic chronicler from Naukratis in Egypt, Surrentine wine began be good 'after twenty years' (*Deipnosophistae* 1.26).
28. MES(sanivm amphora) XIII, Callender 1965: 37–41.
29. COND(itvm) TINC(tvm vinvm) VET(vs), Callender 1965: 37–41.
30. Davies 1989: 196.
31. VIN(vm), Curle 1911: 269.
32. GLVK(vs oinos), Davies 1989: 198.
33. *AE* 1928.183.
34. Polybios 6.38.2, Suetonius *Divus Augustus* 24.2, Frontinus *Strategemata* 4.1.25, 37, Plutarch *Antony* 39.7, Vegetius *Epitoma rei militaris* 1.13. Barley was generally known as 'fodder for slaves' (Athenaios *Deipnosophistae* 7.304b) and considered far less nourishing than wheat, so much so that by the four century BC the preference for wheat and the bread made from it, in affluent circles at least, had ousted barley from its prominent position in the Mediterranean diet. Wheat therefore became the 'corn' or staple cereal in the Mediterranean basin, and barley the cheaper but lowly alternative. In the Bible we read 'a *choinix* of wheat for a *denarius*, and three *choinikes* of barley for a *denarius*' (Revelations 6:6 NIV), the measure of wheat being sufficient for a man for one day at a price equivalent to a labourer's daily wage.
35. Hops, which give beer its bitter taste, were not used in brewing until the thirteenth century. In fact, beer is the oldest alcoholic drink known to man. The Mesopotamians and Egyptians were the first beer-drinkers of ancient times. Apart from water, beer was the main drink for the Egyptians, and was brewed in the household from barley or emmer wheat. The brewing process was short and went hand-in-hand with the baking of bread, and the final product seems to have been a thick, soupy liquid, which, although not always strongly alcoholic, was highly nutritious. The Egyptians began their brewing process with the preparation of partially baked cakes of barley bread. These were placed on a screen over a vat or jar, and water was poured over them until they dissolved and drained into the vessel, whereupon the resultant mixture was left in a warm place to ferment. Often a variety of flavourings were added to the brew, including date juice, myrtle, cumin, ginger and honey. The sugar from date juice or honey would also have speeded up the fermentation. It was sometimes drunk warm.
36. *Tab. Vindol.* II 190.
37. Ibid. II 343.
38. Ibid. II 182.14, III 581.4, 17, 646.2.
39. Ibid. III 628. After he had put down the revolt of the Batavi, it is surmised that Quintus Petilius Cerialis (*cos.* AD 70) rewarded those among the loyal Batavian nobles who were not yet Roman citizens with this status, and they assumed the family name (*gentilicium*) of Vespasianus (viz. Flavius). One of them, it is further inferred, gave his son, perhaps born shortly afterwards, the *cognomen* of his benefactor: he would be called Flavius Cerialis, future *praefectus* of *VIIII cohors Batavorum* in which capacity he would occupy the *praetorium* at Chesterholm-*Vindolanda* in the years around AD 100 (*Tab. Vindol.* II 225–290). See especially, Birley 2002: 44–5.
40. Knörzer 1970.
41. Ibid. 1981: 158–60.
42. The Latin word *moretum* best translates as 'a dish of herbs and cheese', which describes a sort of cheese spread or paste to put on bread that Simylus makes by grinding together garlic, fresh green herbs (Apicius *De re coquinaria* 1.21.38: 'mint, rue, coriander, fennel, all fresh') and curd cheese.

43. Pseudo–Virgil *Moretum* 84–7 Mooney.

Appendix 6

1. *Res Gestae Divi Augusti* 15.3. The great inscription from the temple of Rome and Augustus at Ancyra (modern Ankara) in Galatia, known as the *Res Gestae* or the *Monumentum Ancyranum*, was Augustus' own numeration of his achievements. This is actually a copy (Latin text and a Greek paraphrase of it) of the text set up on two bronze pillars outside the emperor's mausoleum in Rome. Two other sources for this invaluable document are the fragments of the Greek text discovered at Apollonia in Pisidia (Greek was the common literary language of the Near East), and the fragments of the Latin text discovered at Antioch. Despite very minor variations of the text preserved in our three sources, it is clear all three spring from a common origin.

2. Tacitus *Annales* 4.5.2–5, cf. Cassius Dio 55.23.2. See also the researches of Parker (1958) and Syme (1933).

3. Tacitus *Annales* 1.43.2, Suetonius *Divus Augustus* 23.1, Cassius Dio 56.20.5.

4. Though the first literary reference to these two new legions is in connection to the events surrounding Vitellius in January AD 69, epigraphic evidence *(CIL* x 4723 with xiii 11853–6) points to their presence on the Rhine during the principate of Caius Caligula. We also know that the new legate governor, Galba, after his appointment to Germania Superior by Caius Caligula, was involved in training 'old campaigners as well as raw recruits' (Suetonius *Galba* 6.3).

5. *ILS* 2288.

6. Cassius Dio 55.24.4.

Appendix 7

1. In the British Army, for instance, a section becomes the extension of the section commander, a platoon a compromise of the platoon leader and the platoon sergeant, and the company, the body of the major who leads it. Battalion tends to be the last level where the brunt of a commander's (a lieutenant colonel) whims, likes and dislikes are felt by the individual soldier; yet even at brigade level the brigadier marks the collective personality of the units below (viz. 3 Commando Brigade under Brigadier Julian Thompson during the Falklands/Malvinas War).

2. Tacitus *Annales* 1.18.2.

3. A significant number of lead sling bullets found at Perugia, obviously manufactured during the siege itself, are inscribed with the legionary numerals, including that of *legio VI* (*CIL* xi 6721.10, 20–23).

4. It is possible, if *'ékti Makedonikí* (viz. *VI Macedonica*) mentioned in an Greek inscription from Ephesos (*ILS* 8862) is identical with *VI Ferrata*, then it will have fought at Philippi (42 BC) as one of Marcus Antonius' eight veteran legions (Appian *Bellum civilia* 5.3). The inscription belongs to the decade before Actium, and the title could reflect a short-lived commemoration of Philippi, fought within the province of Macedonia.

5. The title *Victrix* is first attested during the principate of Nero (*CIL* xi 395 = *ILS* 2648 = Campbell 90), as is its original title *Hispaniensis* (*AE* 1917/1918.2). The first inscription, dated to AD 66 and describing the career of Marcus Vettius Valens, notes a recent victory *contra Astures*, perhaps in the early part of Nero's principate.

6. *ILS* 2279.

7. Though legion is first attested at Haltonchesters on Hadrian's Wall between AD 122 and AD 126 (*RIB* 1427), the fact that it came from Germania Inferior, the same place as the new legate governor Aulus Platorius Nepos, suggests it probably escorted him. He came to Britannia not long before 17 July AD 122, for an auxiliary soldier discharged by the previous legate governor of Britannia, Quintus Pompeius Falco, received a *diploma* with that date and on it Platorius Nepos is named as legate governor (*CIL* xvi 69).

8. Late second-century inscriptions demonstrate that punitive campaigns were conducted north of Hadrian's Wall by the garrison units of Britannia. Hence the altar, found near

Stanwix fort on Hadrian's Wall, erected by a *legatus legionis* of *VI Victrix* to give thanks for 'the successful outcome of action conducted beyond the Wall' (*RIB* 2034).

9. *ND Occ.* XL$_{18}$: '*Praefectus legionis sextae*'. The unit of course was now part of the *limitanei*, territorial army.

Appendix 8

1. Cicero *Philippic* 14.27.
2. Ibid. *Epistulae ad familiares* 10.33.4.
3. Cassius Dio 55.24.3.
4. *ILS* 2283.
5. Vitruvius 10.10. A three-span machine shot a bolt three times a hand span, which was equivalent in length to twenty-seven Roman inches (69cm). This was a popular size, combining as it did portability with power. There is a very fine frontal view of a *scorpio* depicted on the grave stele of Caius Vedennius Moderatus discovered in Rome. Contemporary writers generally employ three terms when describing types of Roman artillery: *scorpio* (pl. *scorpiones*), a light bolt-shooter; *catapulta* (pl. *catapultae*), a heavy bolt-shooter; *ballista* (pl. *ballistae*), a stone-thrower. Then there is a change in artillery terminology, perhaps around AD 100, when writers transfer the term *ballista* from stone-thrower to bolt-shooter, with *onager* (pl. *onagri*) now being the term for stone-thrower (e.g. Ammianus Marcellinus 23.4.1–7, Vegetius *Epitoma rei militaris* 4.19, Procopius *Wars* 1.21.14–19). This change corresponds to technological changes in Roman artillery, probably connected with Apollodoros of Damascus, Rome's chief engineer under Trajan and Hadrian until his banishment in AD 129. As we know, Vedennius Moderatus himself served as an *architectus armamentarii imperatoris*, 'engineer in the emperor's armoury' (*CIL* vi 2725 = *ILS* 2034 = Campbell 63), which meant he would have been well acquainted with engines of war. Coincidentally, he probably retired from this position around the time of the innovative alterations in Roman artillery design.

Appendix 9

1. *Res Gestae Divi Augusti* 34.1. The 'restoration' of the Republic was widely referred to by Augustan writers (e.g. Velleius Paterculus 2.89.3–4, Ovid *Fasti* 1.589). By contrast with these contemporary and perhaps partly 'inspired' views, Cassius Dio (52.1.1, 53.11.4) dates the autocracy from this moment, and Tacitus everywhere implies that Augustus' position was monarchical. In retrospect, what Augustus had done, by his singular victory over Marcus Antonius and subsequent constitutional settlements, was to bring a period of freedom from threat by internal (and external) enemies. Peace, and a measure of *de facto* political stability, allowed the normal organs of government, the consuls, Senate and people, to resume their accustomed roles. Augustus came to occupy a somewhat special place, and Cassius Dio is right when he remarks that 'from his time a monarchy, strictly speaking, was established' (53.17.1). For this contrary view, see Millar 1973.
2. Tacitus *Annales* 1.2.
3. Augustus accepted *tribunicia potestas* when he abdicated from the consulship of 23 BC (*Fasti Capitol* E–J^3 36), and reckoned the years of his reign by it – on his imperial coinage you will see the legend *trib. pot.* followed by the relevant Roman numeral. The powers of this ancient office were: 1) *auxilium*, the right to intervene on behalf of citizens who were being unfairly treated by other magistrates; 2) *intercessio*, the right to veto the acts of other magistrates; 3) *coercitio*, the right to compel reluctant citizens to obey his orders, and impose sanctions if necessary; and 4) *ius agendi cum populo et ius consulendi senatum*, the right to summon the people, address them, and put legislation to them, and the right to summon the Senate and put motions to it.
4. As Octavianus he had held the consulship continuously from 31 BC to 27 BC. As Augustus he was granted consular power and insignia (viz. the *fasces* and sit between the consuls) in

19 BC (Cassius Dio 54.10.5), so that after this date he held *imperium* equal to the consuls' in Rome and greater than anyone else's outside the city. This grant, though not essential to his position, conveniently allowed him to exercise *imperium* in his own right in the city and it gave him the formal prominence that the Roman people evidently desired him to have.

5. In the Senate meetings of 13 and 16 January 27 BC, Augustus was granted ten-year proconsular commands over Egypt (which he administered virtually as a private estate), Cyprus, and the three great military provinces of Iberia (except Baetica), all Transalpine Gaul, and Syria (including Cilicia). These provinces are conventionally termed 'imperial'. The 'senatorial' provinces were Africa, (including Numidia), Illyricum, Macedonia, Achaea, Asia, Bithynia with Pontus, Crete with Cyrene, Sicily, Sardinia with Corsica, and Baetica (Cassius Dio 53.12.4–8). From the first, most of the army was in his provinces, though there were legions in Africa, Illyricum and Macedonia, how many we do know. Later, Augustus would surrender the peaceful provinces of Gallia Narbonensis and Cyprus, which would then be made senatorial, while in 11 BC Illyricum would be taken under his control (Strabo 17.3.25, Cassius Dio 54.4.1, 34.4). In AD 6 Sardinia became imperial (Cassius Dio 55.28.1), and the new province of Moesia took over the legions hitherto stationed in Macedonia (probably around AD 3). In the end only one legion, in Africa, was left under the command of a proconsul: all other legions were under commanders who had been picked by Augustus, for loyalty as well as talent. Other new provinces, all imperial, created after 27 BC were Galatia (25 BC), Raetia, Noricum (both 15 BC), and Iudaea (AD 6). The governor of a senatorial province was called *proconsul*, of all imperial, *legatus Augusti pro praetore* – unless he was the equestrian governor of Raetia, Noricum, Iudaea, or Sardinia, when his title was *praefectus* (or from Claudius' principate, *procurator*).

6. Millar 1992: 6.

7. Before his famous tribunate of 1347, Cola di Rienzo (d. 1354), searching for the long neglected documents of ancient Rome, came across this large bronze tablet in the basilica of San Giovanni in Laterano where it had been used by Boniface VIII (pope 1294–1303) in the construction of an altar. In 1576, the venerable relic was transferred to the Palazzo dei Conservatori on the Capitol, where it now rests. Incidentally, the basilica derives its name from the patrician family of Plautius Lateranus, who, having, been implicated in the Piso conspiracy against Nero in AD 65, was deprived of his life and property, the latter being expropriated by the emperor.

8. *CIL* vi 930 = *ILS* 244.

9. Tacitus *Historiae* 4.3.

10. Ibid. 1.48.1. The brothers of Piso Licinianus, Magnus and Crassus, had suffered worse fates, having been put to death by Claudius and Nero respectively.

11. Ibid. 1.13.1.

12. The son of Octavia (*c.* 66–11 BC) and her first husband, Caius Claudius Marcellus senior (*c.* 93–41 BC, *cos.* 50 BC).

13. Augustus' oldest friend and greatest commander, who had married his daughter Iulia (39 BC – AD 14), the issue of Augustus' second marriage, that to Scribonia. Agrippa (63–12 BC, *cos.* 37 BC, *cos.* II 28 BC, *cos.* III 27 BC) was Iulia's second husband, her first being Caius Claudius Marcellus (42–23 BC), the son of Octavia.

14. Augustus' grandchildren by Iulia and Agrippa. He adopted Caius (20 BC – AD 4) and Lucius (17 BC – AD 2) as his own sons while they were still infants. It was common practice among the Roman nobility to adopt (even adults) to prevent a name dying out. Augustus himself owed everything to his adoption by Caesar, and wished his two grandsons similar good fortune. There was a third boy, Agrippa Postumus (12 BC – AD 14), so called because he had been born posthumously, Agrippa having died suddenly in 12 BC, but Augustus did not adopt him too, but left him to carry on Agrippa's name. However, in AD 4 he was adopted along with Tiberius by Augustus, only to be disinherited two years later.

15. Viz. the first son of Livia (58 or 57 BC – AD 29) and her first husband, Tiberius Claudius Nero (c. 78–33 BC). The other issue of this marriage was Nero Claudius Drusus (38–9 BC), the father of the future emperor Claudius (10 BC – AD 54). The genealogical tree of the Iulio-Claudian family rivalled in complexity that of the Olympian gods.
16. Tacitus *Historiae* 1.15–16 Penguin edition, with revisions.
17. Pliny *Panegyricus* 7.

Appendix 10

1. E.g. *ILS* 4301–3.
2. E.g. *ILS* 4320–22.
3. E.g. *RIB* 1022, 1131, 1330, 1725. A sanctuary to Iuppiter Optimus Maximus Dolichenus was erected in AD 191 on the Aventine hill in Rome. From this sanctuary we have an inscribed relief: 'In honour of Iuppiter Optimus Maximus, of Doliche, where iron is born, Caius Sempronius Rectus, *centurio* of the *frumentarii* gave this gift' (*ILS* 4302). Another addresses him as 'eternal preserver' (*AE* 1940.75), and again, but more fulsome, 'Iuppiter Optimus Maximus Dolichenus Eternal, preserver of the firmament, preeminent divinity, invincible provider' (*ILS* 4316). All in all there are around 430 dedications to Iuppiter Dolichenus, many inscribed.
4. Cumont 1956: 105–8.
5. Collar 2011.
6. Juvenal *Satire* 3.62. Juvenal's third satire was issued shortly after the accession of Hadrian (r. AD 117-138), while the earliest datable evidence for the god's worship outside of Doliche is the dedication (*CIL* viii 2680 = 18221 = *ILS* 4311a) of a temple to Iuppiter Dolichenus in Lambaesis, Numidia, in AD 125 by the *legatus pro praetore* Sextus Iulius Maior (*cos.* AD 126), a senator from Nysa in Asia Minor.

Appendix 11

1. Only the most frequently cited ancient authors are listed here. Further details about them, and information about other sources, is most conveniently available in *The Oxford Classical Dictionary* (3rd edition).
2. Carr 1990: 23.
3. Vasio had also been the origin of an earlier significant historian, Pompeius Trogus (c. 65–15 BC). Originally the tribal capital of the Vacontii, it had been rebuilt in 20/19 BC by Marcus Vipsanius Agrippa, greatest friend and son-in-law of Augustus.
4. Pliny *Historia Naturalis* 7.76.
5. Tacitus *Historiae* 1.1.3.
6. Pliny *Epistulae* 2.1.6. Tacitus' home province of Gallia Narbonensis was noted for producing high-calibre rhetoricians.
7. Ibid. 7.20.
8. Ibid. 2.11.3.
9. Ibid. 6.16.1. Probably the most famous line from Pliny's correspondence to his literary brother is the following: 'I predict, and my predictions do not fail me, that your histories will be immortal' (ibid. 7.33).
10. Tacitus *Annales* 2.61.2.
11. Interestingly, his friend Pliny makes no mention of the *Annales* in his letters; he died in AD 113 and we assume therefore that this work was written after his death.
12. The *Annales*, whose composition began promptly after the *Historiae*, survive in part only: books one to six (parts of five are missing), books eleven to fifteen breaking off in the middle of book sixteen two years before the demise of Nero. Tacitus may well have stopped at this point, died and thus not completed the work. Syme convincingly argues that the *Annales* extended to eighteen books, or three hexads of differing tones, the first six, for example,

covering the long reign of Tiberius, the ruler whose psychology and published utterances intrigued Tacitus and led him to his masterly representation of austerity, dissimulation and eventual depravity. The *Historiae* starts from AD 69 and Jerome claims that Tacitus wrote the lives of the Caesars in thirty books, *triginta volumina* (Jerome *Commentary on Zechariah* 3.14). Indeed, coupled together the two works cover from Tiberius to Domitianus and represent an impressive achievement by anyone's standards.

13. Tacitus *Agricola* 3.
14. Ibid. *Annales* 1.1.
15. On this particular subject, see especially Pliny *Epistulae* 8.6.
16. Mommsen 1881: 181.
17. To be brief, each Livian battle is a series of disjunctive actions at which all soldiers act and think in unison, with much emphasis given to their emotional reactions and to the personal achievements of generals, all described in epic and poetic terms, with slight attention paid to topography or tactics.
18. Of this masterpiece we have only the first four and quarter books out of (probably) twelve. However, it is this precious third of the whole work that covers the military anarchy and chaos immediately following Nero's death, considerably more space to a year-and-a-half period than to the twenty-seven-year period between AD 69 and AD 96 in the *Historiae*.
19. Syme 1985: 1.176ff; Appendix 29. Look at, for example, Tacitus *Annales* 1.81 (imperial archives), 3.65, 6.7, 15.74 (the *acta senatus*, the records of senatorial meetings), 1.69, 13.20 (other historians, such as the anecdotal, cynical and scandalous Cluvius Rufus), 4.43 (memoirs, such as those of the fearsome Agrippina minor or the great general Corbulo).
20. Tacitus *Historiae* 1.40–43.
21. Ibid. 3.11.2.
22. Tacitus *Agricola* 42.
23. Ibid.
24. There was a tendency of ancient thought to see a man's character as something fixed and 'given' at birth. See, for instance, Tacitus' comments on Tiberius' character in *Annales* 6.51.5–6. Suetonius delivers a similar judgement: 'but after he had acquired the freedom of seclusion away from the public gaze, all his vices, *long imperfectly concealed*, were at last indulged together' (*Tiberius* 42.1).
25. Letter to Bishop Mandell Creighton, 5 April, 1887, published in Figgis, J.N., & Laurence, R.V., (eds.), 1907. *Historical Essays and Studies*. London: Macmillan.
26. The style of British politicians' comments is often imbued with the faded cartographic pink of a long-gone imperial confidence. It was not always so. 'What the devil is it to you', Milton demands of Salmasius, 'what the English do among themselves?' The English, he declares in another passage, 'were born free, they stand in need of no other nation, they can make what laws they please for their own good government'. Claudius Salmasius was the Latin name of Claude Saumaise (1588–1653), a French classical scholar who was a prolific writer and textual critic. In his *Defensio Regio pro Carolo* he had vigorously argued that the 'rebels' led by Cromwell were guilty of regicide. In response, Milton's vitriolic blast was his Latin polemic *Pro Populo Anglicano Defensio [First Defence]* (1651), from which come the two quotes above.
27. Machiavelli *The Prince* 17.
28. 'A man', as Aristotle notes on civic courage, 'should not be brave because he is forced to be, but because courage is itself a noble thing' (*Nicomachean Ethics* 3.8.5).
29. Suetonius *Otho* 10.1. This legion may go back to Caesar's *XIII* formed in 57 BC (Caesar *Bellum Gallicum* 2.2.1), and if so, then it was this single legion that was with him when he audaciously crossed the Rubicon on the night of 10 January 49 BC (ibid. *Bellum civile* 1.7–8).
30. Suetonius *Domitianus* 12.2: 'As a boy (*adulescentulus*), I remember once attending a crowded Court …'.
31. Pliny *Epistulae* 3.8, cf. 5.10, 9.34.

32. *AE* 1953.73. These posts included *a bibliothecis*, librarian, and *ab epistulis*, chief secretary to the emperor, which was the summit of his official career.
33. That is, if we can believe the writer of the Hadrian (11.3) in the problematical *SHA*. It appears that on Pliny's death Septicius took over the role of Suetonius' patron. The *De vita Caesarum* survive complete, except for the beginning of *Divus Iulius*.
34. To be found at Suetonius *Nero* 23.1.
35. Ibid. *Titus* 10.2.
36. Plutarch is very specific in divorcing his craft, biography, from that of history: 'I am not writing history, but biography, and in most deeds there is not always a revelation of virtue or vice. In fact a little thing like a saying or a joke often reveals character more clearly than murderous battles, or vast musterings of armies, or sieges of cities' (*Alexander* 1.2).
37. Most of what remains is not Cassius Dio's complete text, only a brief epitome. We possess books thirty-six to sixty (thirty-six and fifty-five to sixty have gaps), which cover the years 68 BC to AD 46. The missing portions are partly supplied, for the earlier gaps, by Zonaras, and for some later gaps (book thirty-five onwards) by Xiphilinos, two Byzantine epitomators who wrote *Reader's Digest* versions of Cassius Dio's work. There are also many excerpts.
38. Cassius Dio's experiences in Pannonia made him especially sensitive to the power of obstreperous armies, and at one point he reflects that 'the soldiers indulge in such wantonness, licence and lack of discipline, that those in Mesopotamia even dared to murder their commander, Flavius Heracleo, and the praetorians denounced me in the presence of Ulpianus because I controlled the soldiers in Pannonia strictly' (80.4.2).
39. Cassius Dio 53.19.1–3.
40. Ibid. 44.2.
41. Ibid. 41.14.2.
42. In our version of the *Bellum Iudaicum* the fact that Josephus was one of the two last survivors of a suicide pact was put 'down to divine providence or just to luck'(3.8.7). On the other hand, the Slavonic version, perhaps translated into old Russian around 1250, blandly gives what the cynical reader probably suspect was the truth anyhow: 'he counted the numbers cunningly so managed to deceive all the others'. If true, then this piece of sharp practice was later suppressed as too ignoble for the gallant Jewish commander and esteemed pensioner of the Flavians.
43. Josephus *Bellum Iudaicum* 3.399–404, 6.390–393, cf. 3.7, Tacitus *Annales* 15.47, *Historiae* 5.13, Suetonius *Vespasianus* 4.5. Josephus himself is our main authority for the events of his life, a circumstance obviously not without its drawbacks, especially as he is by no means averse to self-laudation.
44. We know from Tacitus that 'Vespasianus was not immune to such superstition' (*Historiae* 2.78.1, cf. Suetonius *Vespasianus* 5.1), a trait normally associated with common soldiers not supreme commanders, what Cicero called 'a groundless fear of the gods' (*De natura deorum* 1.42.117). Whether you choose to believe in them or not, prophecies are much like clothes. There they hang in the tailor's shop; many men pass them, many a man they would fit. One comes along and takes the garment. And so it is made for him and for him alone. A good tailor makes clothes that will fit many men.
45. The title 'Caesar' was conferred on both Vespasianus' sons when he became emperor.
46. Tacitus *Historiae* 1.1.3.
47. Josephus *Bellum Iudaicum* 3.396–397, 5.541.

Abbreviations

AE	*L'Année Épigraphique* (Paris, 1888 onwards)
Campbell	J.B. Campbell, *The Roman Army, 31 BC – AD 337: A Sourcebook.* (London, 1994)
CIL	T. Mommsen *et al.*, *Corpus Inscriptionum Latinarum* (Berlin, 1862 onwards)
Fink	R.O. Fink, *Roman Military Records on Papyrus* (New Haven, 1971)
FGrHist	F. Jacoby, *Die Fragmente der griechischen Historiker* (Berlin & Leiden, 1923–58)
IGR	R. Cagnat *et al.*, *Inscriptiones Graecae ad res Romanas pertinentes* (Paris, 1911–23)
ILLRP	A. Degrassi, *Inscriptiones Latinae Liberae Rei Publicae* (Firenze, 1963–5)
ILS	H. Dessau, *Inscriptiones Latinae Selectae* (Berlin, 1892–1916)
IMS VI	B. Dragovejić-Josifovska, *Inscriptions de la Mésie Supérieur* VI (Beograd, 1982)
McCrum-Woodhead	M. McCrum and A.G. Woodhead, *Select Documents of the Principates of the Flavian Emperors, AD 69–96* (Cambridge, 1961)
MECW	*Marx / Engels Collected Works* (London/New York, 1975–2005)
ND Occ.	O. Seeck, *Notitia Dignitatum in partibus Occidentis* (Berlin, 1876)
OGIS	G. Dittenberger, *Orientis Graecae Inscriptiones Selectae* (Leipzig, 1903–5)
P. Hib. II	E.G. Turner and M.-Th. Lenger, *The Papyri Hibeh* II (London, 1955)
P. Mich.	C.C. Edgar *et al.*, *Papyri in the University of Michigan Collection* (Ann Arbor, 1931 onwards)
P. Oxy.	B.P. Grenfell *et al.*, *The Oxyrhynchus Papyri* (London, 1898 onwards)
PIR²	E. Groag and A. Stein, *Prosopographia Imperii Romani* (Berlin, 1933)
RE	A. Pauly *et al.*, *Real-encylopädie des Classischen Altertumswissenschaft* (Berlin, 1894 onwards)
RIB	R.S.O. Tomlin, *Roman Inscriptions of Britain²* (Stroud, 1995)
RIC I	H.V. Sutherland, *Roman Imperial Coinage* I (London, 1984)
RIC II	H. Mattingly and E.A. Sydenham, *Roman Imperial Coinage* II (London, 1926)
RPC II	A. Burnett, M. Amandry and I. Carradice, *Roman Provincial Coinage* II (London/Paris, 1999)
RPC	A. Burnett, M. Amandry, P.P. Ripollès and I. Carradice, *Roman Provincial Coinage*, supplement II (www.uv.es/=ripolles/rpc_s2, 2006)
SHA	*Scriptores Historia Augusta*
Sydenham	E.A. Sydenham, *The Coinage of the Roman Republic* (London, 1952)
Tab. Vindol. II	A.K. Bowman and J.D. Thomas, *The Vindolanda Writing-tablets:* Tabulae Vindolandenses II (London, 1994)
Tab. Vindol. III	A.K. Bowman and J.D. Thomas, *The Vindolanda Writing-tablets:* Tabulae Vindolandenses III (London, 2003)

Bibliography

Adams, J.N., 1995. 'The Language of the Vindolanda writing tablets: an interim report'. *Journal of Roman Studies* 85: 86–134.

Aldhouse-Green, M.J., 2006. *Boudica Britannia: Rebel, War-leader and Queen*. Harlow: Pearson Education.

Alston, R., 1994. 'Roman military pay from Caesar to Diocletian'. *Journal of Roman Studies* 84: 93–104

Ardant du Picq, Ch., 1903 (trans. Col. J. Greely and Maj. R. Cotton 1920, repr. 1946). *Battle Studies: Ancient and Modern*. Harrisburg: U.S. Army War College.

Ash, R.E., 1999. *Ordering Anarchy: Armies and Leaders in Tacitus' Histories*. London: Routledge.

Ash, R.E. (ed.), 2007. *Tacitus. Histories Book 2*. Cambridge: Cambridge University Press.

Baazt, D., 1980. 'Ein katapult der Legio IV Macedonica aus Cremona'. *Mitteilungen des Deutschen Archaeologischen Instituts, Römische Abteilung* 87: 283–99.

Baillie Reynolds, P.K., 1926 (repr. 1996). *The Vigiles of Imperial Rome*. Chicago: Ares.

Baldwin, B., 1975. 'Vespasian and freedom'. *Rivista di Filologia e di Istruzione Classica* 105: 306–8.

Baldwin, B., 1983. *Suetonius*. Amsterdam: Hakkert.

Ball, L.F., 2003. *The Domus Aurea and the Roman Architectural Revolution*. Cambridge: Cambridge University Press.

Barnabei, F., 1887. 'Frammenti di una cassa militare della Legione IV Macedonica, scoperti in Cremona'. *Notizie delgi Scavi di Antichità* 12: 209–21.

Barrett, A.A., 1989. *Agrippina: Sex, Power and Politics in the Early Empire*. New Haven: Yale University Press.

Bengston, H., 1979. *Die Flavier: Vespasian, Titus, Domitian*. München: Beck.

Bergman, C.A., McEwen, E. and Miller, R., 1988. 'Experimental archery: projectile velocities and comparison of bow performances'. *Antiquity* 62: 658–70.

le Bohec, Y., 1989. *La Légion Troisième Auguste*. Paris: Centre national de la recherche scientifique.

le Bohec, Y., 1994 (trans. R. Bate 2000). *The Imperial Roman Army*. London: Routledge.

le Bohec, Y., 2005 (3e éd.). *L' armée romaine sous le Haut-Empire*. Paris: A & J Picard.

Birley, A., 2002. *Garrison Life at Vindolanda: a Band of Brothers*. Stroud: Sutton.

Birley, R.E., 1977. *Vindolanda: a Roman Frontier Post on Hadrian's Wall*. London: Thames & Hudson.

Bishop, M.C. and Coulston, J.C.N., 1993. *Roman Military Equipment from the Punic Wars to the Fall of Rome*. London: Batsford.

Bouchier, E.S., 1916. *Syria as a Roman Province*. Oxford: Blackwell.

Bowman, A.K., 1994 (repr. 2003). *Life and Letters on the Roman Frontier: Vindolanda and its People*. London: British Museum Press.

Bowman, A.K., 1994. 'The Roman Imperial Army: letters and literacy on the northern frontier', in A.K. Bowman and G.D. Woolf (eds.), *Literacy and Power in the Ancient World*, 109–25.

Breeze, D.J., 1969. 'The organization of the legion: the First cohort and the *equites legionis*'. *Journal of Roman Studies* 59: 50–5.

Brown Vega, M. and Craig, N., 2009. 'New experimental data on the distance of sling projectiles'. *Journal of Archaeological Science* 36: 1264–8.

Brunt, P.A., 1959. 'The revolt of Vindex and the fall of Nero'. *Latomus* 18: 531–59.

Brunt, P.A., 1971. *Italian Manpower, 225 BC–AD 14*. Oxford: Oxford University Press.

Brunt, P.A., 1977. '*Lex de imperio Vespasiani*'. *Journal of Roman Studies* 67: 95–116.

Brunt, P.A. and Moore, J.M. (eds.), 1967 (repr. 1986). *Res Gestae Divi Augusti: the Achievements of the Divine Augustus*. Oxford: Oxford University Press.

Burkert, W., 1984. *Anthropologie des religiöse Opfers: Die Sakralisierung der Gewalt*. München: Carl Friedrich von Siemens Stiftung.

Callender, M.H., 1965. *Roman Amphorae: with an Index of Stamps*. London: Oxford University Press.

Campbell, J.B., 1984 (repr. 1996). *The Emperor and the Roman Army, 31 BC–AD 235*. Oxford: Clarendon Press.

Carandini, A., 2006. *Remo e Romolo: Dai rioni dei Quiriti alla città dei Romani (775/750–700/675 a.C. circa)*. Torino: Einaudi.

Carandini, A., 2007 (trans. S. Sartarelli 2011). *Rome: Day One*. Princeton, NJ. Princeton University Press.

Champlin, E., 2003. *Nero*. Harvard: Harvard University Press.

Charlesworth, M.P., 1938. 'Flaviana'. *Journal of Roman Studies* 27: 54–62.

Cheesman, G.L., 1914 (repr. 2010). *The Auxilia of the Roman Imperial Army*. Milton Keynes: Leonaur.

Chilver, G.E.F., 1957. 'The army in politics, AD 68–70'. *Journal of Roman Studies* 47: 29.

Chilver, G.E.F., 1979. *A Historical Commentary on Tacitus' Histories I and II*. Oxford: Clarendon Press.

Cicatrix, J. and Rowson, M., 1995. *Imperial Exits*. London: Macmillan.

Collar, A. 2011. 'Military networks and the cult of Jupiter Dolichenus'. *Asia Minor Studien* 64: 217–46.

Connolly, P., 1991. 'The Roman fighting technique deduced from armour and weaponry', in V.A. Maxfield and B. Dobson (eds.), *Roman Frontier Studies 1989 (Proceedings of the Fifteenth International Congress of Roman Frontier Studies)*. Exeter: Exeter University Press, 358–63.

Connolly, P., 1997. '*Pilum, gladius* and *pugio* in the late Republic'. *Journal of Roman Military Equipment Studies* 8: 41–57.

Connolly, P., 1998. *Greece and Rome at War*. London: Macdonald.

Collingridge, V., 2006. *Boudica: the Life of Britain's Warrior Queen*. Woodstock, NY: Overlook Press.

Coulston, J.C.N., 1985. 'Roman archery equipment', in M.C. Bishop (ed.) *The Production and Distribution of Roman Military Equipment (Proceedings of the Second Roman Military Equipment Conference)*. Oxford: British Archaeological Reports International Series 275, 220–346.

Cronin, V., 2010. *Nero*. London: Stacey International.

Cruse, A., 2004. *Roman Medicine*. Stroud: Tempus.

Cumont, F., 1911 (repr. 1956). *Oriental Religions in Roman Paganism*. New York.

Curle, J. 1911. *A Roman Frontier Post and its People: the Fort of Newstead in the Parish of Melrose*. Glasgow: James Maclehose & Sons.

Dalby, A., 2000. *Empire of Pleasure: a Geography of Roman Luxury*. London.

Dalby, A., 2001. 'Dining with the Caesars', in H. Walker (ed.) *Food and the Memory (Proceedings of the Oxford Symposium on Food and Cookery 2000)*. Totnes: Prospect Books, 62–88.

Daly, L.J., 1975. 'Verginius at Vesontio: The incongruity of *Bellum Neronis*'. *Historia* 24: 75–100.

Daszewski, W.A., 1973. 'A legionary gem from Nea Paphos'. *Report of the Department of Antiquities, Cyprus* 202–11.

Davies, R.W., 1989 (eds. D.J. Breeze and V.A. Maxfield). *Service in the Roman Army.* Edinburgh: Edinburgh University Press.

Dawson, D., 1996. *The Origins of Western Warfare: Militarism and Morality in the Ancient World.* Boulder, CO: Westview Press.

Dean, L.R., 1916. *A Study of the Cognomina of Soldiers in the Roman Legions.* Princeton dissertation: Princeton University.

Demmin, A.F, 1877 (repr. 1893). *Die Kriegswaffen im ihren Geschichtlichen Entwickelungen von den Ältesten Zeiten bis auf den Gegenwart.* Leipzig: P. Friesenhahn.

Dixon, K. and Southern, P., 1992. *The Roman Cavalry.* London: Routledge.

Dobson, B., 1972. 'Legionary centurion or equestrian officer? A comparison of pay and prospects'. *Ancient Society* 3: 193–207.

Dobson, B., 1974. 'The daily life of the soldier under the Principate'. *Aufstieg und Niedergang der Römischen Welt* 2.1: 299–338.

Dobson, B., 1978. *Die Primipilares.* Köln: Rheinland-Verlag.

Dudley, D.R. and Webster, G.A., 1962. *The Rebellion of Boudica.* London: Routledge & Kegan Paul.

Durry, M.,1938 (repr. 1968). *Les cohortes prétoriennes.* Paris: de Boccard.

Elsner J. and Masters, J. (eds.), 1994. *Reflections on Nero: Culture, History, and Representation.* Chapel Hill, NC: University of North Carolina Press.

Fabbricotti, E., 1976. *Galba.* Roma L'erma di Bretschneider (Studia Archaeologica 16).

Faas, P., 1994 (trans. S. Whiteside 2003). *Around the Roman Table.* London: Macmillan.

Ferrill, A., 1965. 'Otho, Vitellius, and the propaganda of Vespasian'. *Classical Journal* 60: 267–9.

Ferrill, A., 1985. *The Origins of War.* London: Thames & Hudson.

Feugère, M., 1993 (trans. D.G. Smith 2002). *Weapons of the Romans.* Stroud: Tempus.

Fields, N., 1995. 'A soldier's diet'. *Ad familiares* 8: 13–14.

Fields, N., 2006. *Roman Auxiliary Cavalryman, AD 14–193.* Oxford: Osprey (Warrior 101).

Fields, N., 2008A. *The Roman Army of the Civil Wars, 90–30 BC.* Oxford: Osprey (Battle Orders 34).

Fields, N., 2008B. *Warlords of Republican Rome: Caesar versus Pompey.* Barnsley: Pen & Sword.

Fields, N., 2009. *The Roman Army of the Principate, 27 BC–AD 117.* Oxford: Osprey (Battle Orders 37).

Fields, N., 2011A. *Boudicca's Rebellion AD 60–61.* Oxford: Osprey (Campaign 233).

Fields, N., 2011B. *Early Roman Warrior, 753–321 BC.* Oxford: Osprey (Warrior 156).

Fitzgerald, W., 2007. *Martial: The World of the Epigram.* Chicago: Chicago University Press.

Forni, G., 1953. *Il reclutamento delle legioni da Augusto a Diocleziano.* Milano & Roma: Università di Pavia.

Frangoulidis, S., 1991. 'Tacitus (*Histories* 1.40–43), Plutarch (*Galba* 26–27) and Suetonius (*Galba* 18–20) on the death of Galba'. *Favonius* 3: 1–10.

Gagé, J., 1952. 'Vespasien et la mémoire de Galba'. *Revue des études anciennes* 54: 290–315.

Gallivan, P.A., 1973. 'The false Neros: A re-evaluation'. *Historia* 22: 364–5.

Garnsey, P.D.A. and Saller, R.P., 1987. *The Roman Empire: Economy, Society and Culture.* London: Duckworth.

Gilliver, C.M., 2000. *The Roman Art of War.* Stroud: Suttton.

Goldsworthy, A.K., 1996 (repr. 1998). *The Roman Army at War, 100 BC–AD 200*. Oxford: Clarendon Press.

Goldsworthy, A.K., 2000. *Roman Warfare*. London: Cassell.

Goldsworthy, A.K., 2003. *The Complete Roman Army*. London: Thames & Hudson.

Goldsworthy, A.K., 2003 (repr. 2004). *In the Name of Rome: the Men who won the Roman Empire*. London: Phoenix.

Grant, M., 1958 (repr. 1968). *Roman History from Coins: Some uses of the Imperial Coinage to the Historian*. Cambridge: Cambridge University Press.

Grant, M., 1970 (repr. 1989). *Nero: Emperor in Revolt*. New York: Dorset Press.

Greenhalgh, P.A.L., 1975. *The Year of the Four Emperors*. London: Weidenfeld & Nicolson.

Griffin, M.T., 1976. *Seneca, A Philosopher in Politics*. Oxford: Oxford University Press.

Griffin, M.T., 1984 (repr. 1987). *Nero: the End of a Dynasty*. London: Routledge.

Griffiths, W.B., 1989. 'The sling and its place in the Roman imperial army', in C. van Driel-Murray (ed.) *Roman Military Equipment: The Sources of Evidence (Proceedings of the Fifth Roman Military Equipment Conference)*. Oxford: British Archaeological Reports International Series 476, 255–79.

Griffiths, W.B. and Carrick, P., 1994. 'Reconstructing Roman slings'. *Arbeia Journal* 3: 1–11.

Gunn, J.C., 1973. *Violence: in Human Society*. Newton Abbot: David & Charles.

Hainsworth, J.B., 1962. 'Verginius and Vindex'. *Historia* 11: 86–96.

Hammond, M., 1956. 'The transmission of the powers of the Roman emperor'. *Memoirs of the American Academy in Rome* 24: 61–33.

Hansen, M.H., 1993. 'The battle-exhortation in ancient historiography: fact or fiction?' *Historia* 42: 161–80.

Hardy, E.G., 1890. *Plutarch's Lives of Galba and Otho*. London: Macmillan.

Hardy, E.G., 1910. 'Tacitus as a military historian in the *Histories*'. *Journal of Philology* 31: 123–52.

Haynes, H., 2003. *The History of Make-Believe: Tacitus on Imperial Rome*. Berkeley & Los Angeles: University of California Press.

Haywood, C., 2001. *Wine-drinking Habits in Antiquity: from the Minoans to the Romans*. Dublin: University College Dublin.

Heath, E.G., 1980. *Archery: A Military History*. Oxford: Osprey.

Helgeland, J., 1978. 'Roman army religion'. *Aufstieg und Niedergang der römischen Welt* II.16.2: 1470–505.

Henderson, B.W., 1908. *Civil War and Rebellion in the Roman Empire, AD 69–70*. London: Macmillan.

Hingley, R. and Unwin, C., 2005 (repr. 2006). *Boudica: Iron Age Warrior Queen*. London: Hambleton Continuum.

Hopkins, K., 1978. *Conquerors and Slaves*. Cambridge: Cambridge University Press.

Holder, P.A., 1980. *Studies in the Auxilia of the Roman Army from Augustus to Trajan*. Oxford: British Archaeological Reports International Series 70.

Holder, P.A., 1982. *The Roman Army in Britain*. London: Batsford.

Holland, R., 2000. *Nero: the Man Behind the Myth*. Stroud: Sutton.

Homo, L., 1949. *Vespasien, l' Empereur du bon sens (69–79 ap. J-C)*. Paris: Éditions Albin Michel.

Houston, G.W., 1972. 'M. Plancius Varus and the events of AD 69–70'. *Transactions of the American Philological Association* 103: 167–80.

Hunt, R., 2003. *Queen Boudica's Battle of Britain*. Staplehurst: Spellmount.

Hyland, A., 1990. *Equus: The Horse in the Roman World*. London: Batsford.

Ignatieff, M.G., 1998. *Warrior's Honor: Ethnic War and the Modern Conscience*. New York: Metropolitan Books.

Jal, P., 1963. *La guerre civile à Rome: étude littéraire et morale*. Paris: PUF (Publications de la Faculté des Lettres et Sciences Humaines de Paris, série «Recherches», tome VI).

Janowicz, M., 1959, 2012. *Sociology and the Military Establishment*. Whitefish, MT: Literary Licensing, Llc.

Jones, B.W., 1971. 'Some thoughts on the propaganda of Vespasian and Domitian'. *The Classical Journal* 66: 251.

Jones, B.W., 1983. 'C. Vettulenus Civica Cerialis and the 'false Nero' of AD 88'. *Athenaeum* 61: 516–21.

Junkelmann, M., 1991. *Die Legionen des Augustus: Der romische Soldat im archaologischen Experiment*. Mainz-am-Rhein: Philipp von Zabern.

Kalyvas, S.N., 2006. *The Logic of Violence in Civil War*. Cambridge: Cambridge University Press.

Keegan, J., 1976 (repr. 1988). *Face of Battle*. London: Barrie & Jenkins.

Keegan, J., 1987. *The Mask of Command*. London: Jonathan Cape.

Kennedy, D.L., 1978. 'Some observations on the Praetorian Guard'. *Ancient Society* 9: 275–301.

Keppie, L.J.F., 1984 (repr. 1998). *The Making of the Roman Army: From Republic to Empire*. London: Routledge.

Korfmann, M., 1973. 'The sling as a weapon'. *Scientific America* 299.4: 34–42.

Knights, B.A., Dickson, C.A., Dickson, J.H. and Breeze, D.J., 1983. 'Evidence concerning the Roman military diet at Bearsden, Scotland, in the second century AD'. *Journal of Archaeological Science* 10: 139–52.

Knörzer, K-H., 1970. *Novaesium IV: Römerzeitliche Pflänzenfunde aus Neuss*. Berlin (Limes-forschungen 10)

Knörzer, K-H., 1981. 'Römerzeitliche Pflänzenfunde aus Xanten'. *Archeo Physica* 11: 3–176.

Kraay, C.M., 1949. 'The coinage of Vindex and Galba, AD 68, and the continuity of the Augustan Principate'. *Numismatic Chronicle* (series vi) 9: 129–49.

Kromayer, J. and Veith, G., 1928. *Heerwesen und Kriegführung der Griechen und Römer*. München: C.H. Beck.

Kyle, D.G., 1998 (repr. 2001). *Spectacles of Death in Ancient Rome*. London: Routledge.

Lepper, F.J., 1957. 'Some reflections on the "Quinquennium Neronis"'. *Journal of Roman Studies* 47: 95–103.

Lepper, F.J. and Frere, S.S., 1988. *Trajan's Army on Trajan' Column*. Stroud: Sutton.

Levick, B.M., 1985. 'L. Verginius Rufus and the Four Emperors'. *Rheinische Museum* 128: 318–46.

Levick, B.M., 1999. *Vespasian*. London: Routledge.

Liebeschuetz, J.H.W.G., 1991. *Barbarians and Bishops*. Oxford: Clarendon Press.

Lind, L.R., 1979. 'The tradition of Roman moral conservatism', in C. Deroux (ed.) *Studies in Latin Literature and Roman History*. Brussels: Latomus, 7–58.

López Sánchez, F. and Hollard, D., 2010. 'Les troupes germaniques des Julio-Claudiens: un témoignage numismatique sur l' accession Claude', in D. Hollard (ed.) *L' Armée et La Monnaie II*. Paris: Séna, 43–66 (Recherches et Travaux de la Société d' Études Numismatiques et Archéologiques no 3).

McEwen, E., 1978. 'Nomadic archery: some observations on composite bow design and construction', in P. Denwood (ed.) *Arts of the Eurasian Steppelands*. London: School of Oriental and African Studies, 188–202.

McLeod, W.E., 1965. 'The range of the ancient bow'. *Phoenix* 19: 1–14.

MacMullen, R., 1984. 'The legion as society'. *Historia* 33: 440–56.

Manning, W.H., 1976. 'Blacksmithing', in D. Strong and D. Brown (eds.), *Roman Crafts*. New York: Duckworth, 143–53.

Martin, R.H., 1981. *Tacitus*. Berkeley & Los Angeles: University of California Press.

Massey, D., 1994. 'Roman archery tested'. *Military Illustrated* 74: 36–9.

Matyszak, P., 2011. *Imperial General: the Remarkable Career of Petilius Cerealis*. Barnsley: Pen & Sword.

Maxfield, V.A., 1981. *The Military Decorations of the Roman Army*. Berkeley & Los Angeles: University of California Press.

Meijer, F., 2001 (trans. S.J. Leinbach 2004). *Emperors Don't Die in Bed*. London: Routledge.

Mellor, R., 1993. *Tacitus*. London: Routledge.

Millar, F.G.B., 1964. *A Study of Cassius Dio*. Oxford: Oxford University Press.

Millar, F.G.B., 1973. 'Triumvirate and principate'. *Journal of Roman Studies* 63: 50–67.

Millar, F.G.B., 1977 (repr. 1992). *The Emperor in the Roman World*. London: Duckworth.

Millar, F.G.B., 1993 (repr. 1995). *The Roman Near East, 31 BC–AD 337*. Harvard: Harvard University Press.

Miller, N.P., 1987 (repr. 1992). *Tacitus* Annals *14: a Companion to the Penguin Translation*. Bristol: Bristol Classical Press.

Miller, R., McEwen, E., and Bergman, C.A., 1986. 'Experimental approaches to ancient Near Eastern archery'. *World Archaeology* 18: 178–95.

Milner, N.P., 1996 (2nd edn.). *Vegetius: Epitome of Military Science*. Liverpool: Liverpool University Press.

Moltke, FM Graf Helmuth Karl Bernhard, von, 1911 (trans. H. Bell 1916). *Military Works, Volume IV, Operative Preparations for Battle*. The Great General Staff, Military History-Historical Section Berlin.

Momigliano, A., 1931. 'Vitellio'. *Studi italiani di filologia classica* 9: 117–87.

Mommsen, T., 1881. *Provinces of the Roman Empire*. London: Macmillan.

Morgan, M.G., 1992. 'The smell of victory: Vitellius at Bedriacum, Tacitus *Histories* 2.70'. *Classical Philology* 87: 14–29.

Morgan, M.G., 1994. '"Rogues" march: Caecina and Valens in Tacitus *Histories* 1.61–70'. *Museum Helveticum* 51: 103–25 .

Morgan, M.G., 2000. 'Clodius Macer and Calvia Crispinilla'. *Historia* 49: 467–87.

Morgan, M.G., 2005. 'The opening stages in the battle for Cremona, or the devil in the details (Tacitus *Histories* 3.15–18)'. *Historia* 54: 189–209.

Morgan, M.G., 2006. *AD 69: The Year of Four Emperors*. Oxford: Oxford University Press.

Murison, C.L., 1992. *Suetonius: Galba, Otho, Vitellius*. Bristol: Bristol Classical Press.

Murison, C.L., 1993. *Galba, Otho, and Vitellius: Careers and Controversies*. Hildesheim/Zurich/ New York: Georg Holms.

Nicols, J., 1978. *Vespasian and the* Partes Flavianae. Wisebaden (Historia Einzelschriften, Heft 28).

Nischer, E., 1926. 'Die Schlacht bei Cremona'. *Klio* 20: 187–201.

Nock, A.D., 1952. 'The Roman army and the Religious Year'. *Harvard Theological Review* 45: 187–252.

Noy, D., 2000. *Foreigners at Rome: Citizens and Strangers*. London: Duckworth.

Osgood, J., 2006. *Caesar's Legacy*. Cambridge: Cambridge University Press.

Passerini, A., 1939 (repr. 1969). *Le coorti pretorie*. Roma: Centro editoriale internazionale.

Parker, H.M.D., 1928 (repr. 1958). *The Roman Legions.* Cambridge: Heffer & Sons.

Parker, H.M.D., 1932. 'The *antiqua legio* of Vegetius'. *Classical Quarterly* 26: 137–49.

Paterson, W.F., 1966. 'The archers of Islam'. *Journal of the Economic and Social History of the Orient* ix.1–2: 83–4.

Perkins, C.A., 1993. 'Tacitus on Otho'. *Latomus* 52: 848–55.

Peterson, D., 1992 (repr. 2003). *The Roman Legions Recreated in Colour Photographs.* Marlborough: Crowood Press.

Plass, P. 1995. *The Game of Death in Ancient Rome: Arena Sport and Political Suicide.* Madison, WI: University of Wisconsin Press.

Pollard, N., 2000. *Soldiers, Cities and Civilians in Roman Syria.* Ann Arbor: University of Michigan Press.

Rainbird, J.S., 1976. *The Vigiles of Rome.* Durham thesis: Durham University.

Rajak, T., 1983. *Josephus, the Historian and his Society.* London: Duckworth.

Rankov, N.B., 1994 (repr. 1995, 1997, 1999). *Guardians of the Roman Empire.* Oxford: Osprey (Osprey Military).

Richardson, T., 1998. 'The ballistics of the sling'. *Royal Armouries Yearbook* 3: 44.

Robinson, J. (ed.), 2006 (3rd edn.). *The Oxford Companion of Wine.* Oxford: Oxford University Press.

Roth, J., 1994. 'The size and organisation of the Roman imperial legion'. *Historia* 43: 346–62.

Roth, J., 1999. *The Logistics of the Roman Army at War, 264 BC–AD 235.* Leiden: E.J. Brill.

de Ste. Croix, G.E.M., 1963. 'Why were the early Christians persecuted?' *Past & Present* 26: 6–38.

Saddington, D.B., 1982. *The Development of the Roman Auxiliary Forces from Caesar to Vespasian (49 BC–AD 79)* . Harare: Zimbabwe University Press.

Sancery, R., 1983. *Galba ou l' armée face au pouvoir.* Paris: Les Belles Lettres.

Santosuosso, A., 2001 (repr. 2004). *Storming the Heavens: Soldiers, Emperors and Civilians in the Roman Empire.* London: Pimlico.

Schwartz, S., 1997. *Josephus and Judean Politics.* Leiden: E.J. Brill.

Sealey, P.R., 1997 (repr. 2000). *The Boudican Revolt Against Rome.* Oxford: Shire (Shire Archaeology 74).

Shatzman, I., 1972. 'The Roman general's authority over booty'. *Historia* 21: 177–205.

Sherwin-White, A.N., 1970. *Racial Prejudice in Imperial Rome.* Cambridge: Cambridge University Press.

Shochat, Y., 1981. 'Tacitus' attitude to Galba'. *Athenaeum* 59: 199–204.

Shochat, Y. 1981. 'Tacitus' attitude to Otho'. *Latomus* 40: 365–77.

Shotter, D.C.A., 1967. 'Verginius Rufus and Tacitus'. *Classical Quarterly* 17: 370–81.

Shotter, D.C.A., 1977. 'Tacitus and Antonius Primus'. *Liverpool Classical Monthly* 2: 23–7.

Shotter, D.C.A., 1993. *Suetonius, Lives of Galba, Otho and Vitellius.* Warminster: Aris & Phillips.

Shotter, D.C.A., 2005 (2nd edn.). *Nero.* London: Routledge.

Shotter, D.C.A., 2008. *Nero Caesar Augustus, Emperor of Rome.* Harlow: Pearson Education.

Spaul, J.E.H., 1992. ALA²; *The Auxiliary Cavalry Units of the pre-Diocletianic Imperial Army.* Andover: Nectoreca Press.

Spaul, J.E.H., 2000. COHORS²: *The Evidence for and a Short History of the Auxiliary Infantry Units of the Imperial Roman Army.* Oxford: British Archaeological Reports International Series 841.

Speidel, M.P., 1978. *The Religion of Iuppiter Dolichenus in the Roman Army.* Leiden: E. J. Brill.

Speidel, M.P., 1978. *Guards of the Roman Army.* Bonn: Habelt.

Speidel, M.P., 1992. 'Roman army pay scales'. *Journal of Roman Studies.* 82: 87–106.

Speidel, M.P., 1994. *Riding for Caesar: the Roman Emperor's Horseguard.* London: Batsford.

Spence, L., 1937. *Boadicea, Warrior Queen of the Britons.* London: R. Hale.

Smith, L.V., 1994. *Between Mutiny and Obedience.* Princeton, NJ: Princeton University Press.

Smith, R.E., 1958. *Service in the Post-Marian Army.* Manchester: Manchester University Press.

Staccioli, R.A., 2009. *Legiones: Le legioni di Roma.* Roma: Archeoroma (Archeoroma 5).

Starr, C.G., 1960 (2nd edn.). *Roman Imperial Navy 31 BC–AD 324.* Cambridge: Cambridge University Press.

Stolte, B.H., 1973. 'Tacitus on Nero and Otho'. *Ancient Society* 4: 177–90.

Summerly, J.R., 1992. *Studies in the Legionary Centurionate.* Durham thesis: Durham University.

Sumner, G., 2002. *Roman Military Clothing (1), 100 BC–AD 200.* Oxford: Osprey (Men-at-Arms 374).

Syme, R., 1934. 'Some notes on the legions under Augustus'. *Journal of Roman Studies* 23: 14–33.

Syme, R., 1939 (repr. 1952, 1956). *The Roman Revolution.* Oxford: Clarendon Press.

Syme, R., 1958 (repr. 1985). *Tacitus,* 2 vols. Oxford: Oxford University Press.

Syme, R., 1970. *Ten Studies in Tacitus.* Oxford: Oxford University Press.

Syme, R., 1971. *Emperors and Biography: Studies in the Historia Augusta.* Oxford: Oxford University Press.

Syme, R., 1977. 'The march of Mucianus'. *Antichthon* 11: 78–92.

Syme, R., 1978. *History in Ovid.* Oxford: Oxford University Press.

Taylor, L.R., 1931. *The Divinity of the Roman Emperor.* Middletown: American Philological Association (Philological Monographs 1).

Thackery, H., 1968. *Josephus, the Man and the Historian.* Hoboken, NJ: Ktav Publishing.

Tomlin, R.S.O., 1998. 'Roman manuscripts from Carlisle'. *Britannia* 29: 31–84.

Toynbee, J.M.C., 1944. 'Dictators and Philosophers in the first century AD'. *Greece & Rome* 13: 43–58.

Toynbee, J.M.C., 1971. *Death and Burial in the Ancient World.* Ithaca, NY: Cornell University Press.

Treu, M., 1948. 'M. Antonius Primus'. *Würzburger Jahrbücher fur die Altertumswissenschaft* 3: 241–62.

Trow, M.J., 2003. *Boudicca: the Warrior Queen.* Sutton: Stroud.

Truschel, M., 2010. 'La *Guerre des Juifs* de Flavius Josèphe'. *Histoire Antique et Medievale* 52: 64–71.

Turcan, R., 1996. *Cults of the Roman Empire.* Oxford: Blackwell.

Turner, E.G., 1954. 'Tiberius Ivlivs Alexander'. *Journal of Roman Studies* 44: 54–64.

Venini, P., 1977. *Vite di Galba, Otone, Vitellio.* Turin: Paravia.

Wallace-Hadrill, A., 1982. *Suetonius.* London: Duckworth.

Warmington, B.H., 1969 (repr. 1981). *Nero: Reality and Legend.* London: Chatto & Windus.

Warry, J., 1980. *Warfare in the Classical World.* London: Salamander Books.

Watson, G.R., 1969 (repr. 1983, 1985). *The Roman Soldier.* London: Thames & Hudson.

Webb, A., 1991. *Archaeology of Archery.* Tolworth: Dean Archaeological Group.

Webster, G.A., 1979 (2nd edn.). *The Roman Imperial Army.* London: A. & C. Black.

Webster, G.A., 1993 (rev. edn. 1999). *Boudica: the British Revolt Against Rome AD 60.* London: Routledge.

Wellesley, K. (ed.), 1972. *Cornelius Tacitus: the* Histories *Book III.* Sydney: Sydney University Press.

Wellesley, K., 2000 (3rd edn.). *The Year of the Four Emperors*. London: Routledge (originally published as *The Long Year AD 69* in 1975 by Paul Elek).

Wells, C.M., 1992 (2nd edn.). *The Roman Empire*. London: Fontana.

Wilken, R.L., 1984. *The Christians as the Romans Saw Them*. New Haven: Yale University Press.

Wilkens, A., 2003. *Roman Artillery*. Oxford: Shire Publishing (Shire Archaeology 86).

Willems, W.J.M., 1986 (2nd ed). *Romans and Batavians: a Regional Study in the Dutch Eastern River Area*. Amsterdam: Universiteit van Amsterdam.

Wiseman, T.P., 1978. 'Flavians on the Capitol'. *American Journal of Ancient History* 3: 163–78.

Wiseman, T.P. (ed.), 1985. *Roman Political Life 90 BC–AD 69*. Exeter: University of Exeter (Exeter Studies in History 7).

Wiseman, T.P., 1995. *Remus: a Roman Myth*. Cambridge: Cambridge University Press.

Woodman, A.J., 1983. 'From Hannibal to Hitler: the literature of war'. *University of Leeds Review* 26: 107–24.

Woodman, A.J., 1998. *Tacitus Revisited*. Oxford: Oxford University Press.

Woods, D., 2009. 'Nero and Sporus'. *Latomus Revue d'etudes latines* 68: 73–82.

Woolf, G.D., 1998. *Becoming Roman: the Origins of Provincial Civilization in Gaul*. Cambridge: Cambridge University Press.

Woolf, G.D., 2006. *Et tu Brute? A Short History of Political Murder*. London: Profile Books.

Ulbert, G., 1969. '*Gladii* aus Pompeji. Vorarbeiten zu einem Corpus römischer *Gladii*'. *Germania* 47: 97–128.

Zancan, P., 1939. *La cris del Principato*. Padova (R. Università di Padova Pubblicazioni della Facaltà di Lettere e Filosofia. Vol. XVI).

Index